THE **COMPLETE** **IDIOTIC** **GUIDE**

D0764882

Music History

by Michael Miller

ALPHA

A member of Penguin Group (USA) Inc.

To Sherry: It's good to have someone to share the music with.

ALPHA BOOKS

Published by the Penguin Group

Penguin Group (USA) Inc., 375 Hudson Street, New York, New York 10014, USA

Penguin Group (Canada), 90 Eglinton Avenue East, Suite 700, Toronto, Ontario M4P 2Y3, Canada (a division of Pearson Penguin Canada Inc.)

Penguin Books Ltd., 80 Strand, London WC2R 0RL, England

Penguin Ireland, 25 St. Stephen's Green, Dublin 2, Ireland (a division of Penguin Books Ltd.)

Penguin Group (Australia), 250 Camberwell Road, Camberwell, Victoria 3124, Australia (a division of Pearson Australia Group Pty. Ltd.)

Penguin Books India Pvt. Ltd., 11 Community Centre, Panchsheel Park, New Delhi—110 017, India

Penguin Group (NZ), 67 Apollo Drive, Rosedale, North Shore, Auckland 1311, New Zealand (a division of Pearson New Zealand Ltd.)

Penguin Books (South Africa) (Pty.) Ltd., 24 Sturdee Avenue, Rosebank, Johannesburg 2196, South Africa

Penguin Books Ltd., Registered Offices: 80 Strand, London WC2R 0RL, England

Copyright © 2008 by Michael Miller

International Standard Book Number: 978-1-59257-751-4
Library of Congress Catalog Card Number: 2008920881

13   12   11   8   7   6   5   4

Interpretation of the printing code: The rightmost number of the first series of numbers is the year of the book's printing; the rightmost number of the second series of numbers is the number of the book's printing. For example, a printing code of 08-1 shows that the first printing occurred in 2008.

Printed in the United States of America

Note: This publication contains the opinions and ideas of its author. It is intended to provide helpful and informative material on the subject matter covered. It is sold with the understanding that the author and publisher are not engaged in rendering professional services in the book. If the reader requires personal assistance or advice, a competent professional should be consulted.

The author and publisher specifically disclaim any responsibility for any liability, loss, or risk, personal or otherwise, which is incurred as a consequence, directly or indirectly, of the use and application of any of the contents of this book.

Most Alpha books are available at special quantity discounts for bulk purchases for sales promotions, premiums, fund-raising, or educational use. Special books, or book excerpts, can also be created to fit specific needs.

For details, write: Special Markets, Alpha Books, 375 Hudson Street, New York, NY 10014.

Publisher: *Marie Butler-Knight*
Editorial Director: *Mike Sanders*
Senior Managing Editor: *Billy Fields*
Acquisitions Editor: *Tom Stevens*
Senior Development Editor: *Phil Kitchel*
Senior Production Editor: *Janette Lynn*
Copy Editor: *Michael Dietsch*

Cartoonist: *Shannon Wheeler*
Book Designer: *Trina Wurst*
Cover Designer: *Kurt Owens*
Indexer: *Brad Herriman*
Layout: *Brian Massey*
Proofreader: *John Etchison*

Contents at a Glance

Contents

Introduction

If you've ever sat through a typical high school or college music history class, you might think that music history is one boring subject. I know that I used to think that. The classes I took in college were all about memorization (when Bach was born, when Beethoven died, and other such dates), regurgitation (Mozart's most important works were ...), and repetition (listening to bits and pieces of those important works, over and over). And all presented in a dry, academic fashion. It's no wonder that so many students hate even the mention of music history.

But music history doesn't have to be boring. In fact, music history *isn't* boring—it's all a matter of how it's presented. There's actually a lot of interesting stuff to learn; not the names and dates, but the personalities and the trends and, of course, the music itself. We're talking about the most memorable music in history; this is fun stuff.

What fascinates me about the history of music is how one thing always leads to another, and why. It's the through line that matters, the connection from one composer or style to another. Throughout history, music has always evolved; it's that evolution that's interesting.

Music history isn't (just) about facts and names and dates; it's about trends and influences and brilliant developments. It's about musical inspiration and cultural influences. It's about people of above-average talent and how they used that talent. It's about great music, then and now.

Music history is also about more than just so-called "classical" music. That's always been one of my pet peeves about traditional music history courses and books, the assumption that serious music only existed in the concert halls of Western Europe, and that nothing important has happened since Stravinsky. That's simply not the case; I believe that twentieth-century popular music is every bit as important as the music of Bach and Beethoven, and that other regions around the world have also produced much music of note. If you only listen to Western "classical" music, you're only getting half the story.

All of which is to explain why I wrote the book you hold in your hands. *The Complete Idiot's Guide to Music History* is the book that tells the *rest* of the story, and in a way that I hope is interesting and entertaining. It's not dull and dry and academic, because music isn't dull and dry and academic. I try to bring alive the music, by telling you about how and why it came to be.

I also try to put all of history's musical developments in the proper historical context. After all, Bach and Beethoven didn't write and perform in a vacuum; they lived in the real world of their time, just as we live in ours. It's interesting to know that the same time Mozart was writing his great works, America was winning its war of independence, the Russo-Turkish War and the French Revolution were getting underway, the hot air balloon was being perfected, and Benjamin Franklin had just invented bifocals. All of this is important.

In addition, I cover more than just the music of Bach, Mozart, and Beethoven. This book also covers American popular music of the twentieth century, from Irving Berlin to the Sugarhill Gang, from the Great American Songbook to rock and rap and rhythm and blues. And there's coverage of world music, too, from Asia, India, the Middle East, Africa, Latin America, and the Caribbean. All of this is important, too.

My hope is that by the time you finish this book, you'll not only know about the important musical styles and works and composers, but also about the trends behind all of this history—why Baroque music sounds the way it does, how the Classical period influenced the Romantic era, how blues led to jazz and rock and R&B, and so forth. To me, the story behind the history is the most important of all the important things.

I also hope that, by reading *The Complete Idiot's Guide to Music History*, you'll gain a better appreciation for all different types of music. I guarantee you'll be exposed to music you haven't heard before; maybe you'll like some of it. (You probably won't like all of it, but that's okay; I don't, either.) The thing is to keep an open mind and open ears, and see where the history takes you. It's a fascinating journey.

Finally, I hope that after you read this book you'll agree with me when I repeat:

Music history doesn't have to be boring!

Who This Book Is For

When I wrote one of my first music books, *The Complete Idiot's Guide to Music Theory*, I learned that the audience for such a book was a lot broader than what I originally thought. That book appealed to current music students, to past music students, and to the general public—people who weren't necessarily musicians but were interested in the music all around them. Well, that's the same audience for this book.

If you're a music student, this book will cover much the same material you find in an entry-level music history class—but with the added coverage of popular and world music. And, I hope, cover that material in a more interesting and less academic fashion than what you might get otherwise.

If you used to be a music student or musician, this book will provide a nice refresher course for those important events and trends throughout music history. Sure, you remember Wagner and Debussy, but do you remember why they're important? This book will help you remember, and probably expose you to some things you didn't learn back then.

If you're just a music lover … well, there's no "just" about it. Your love of music has inspired you to learn more about that music, and this is the perfect book for you. You'll get an overview of all different types of music, but not be so overwhelmed by details that you lose interest.

What You Need to Know Before You Start

You don't have to know anything about music before you read this book. Yes, I've included a handful of musical examples throughout the book, which you can sing or play on any instrument. But you don't need to work through these examples to get the most from the book; they're there for those who can benefit from them, but if you can't read music, there's no major loss.

What you do need is a love for music and an open mind. You should have a CD or MP3 player handy, because I've recommended a lot of recordings to listen to throughout the book. Words alone can only go so far in describing a piece of music; it's far better to listen to that music performed, when you can.

What You'll Find in This Book

In the study of music history, everyone jumps in at a different place. My own study of music history started with Dvořák's New World Symphony and went both backward and forward from there. You might already have an interest in Haydn or Debussy or Ives; that's great, you can use that as an entry point to the rest of music history.

That said, a book like this has to start somewhere, and the best place to start is the beginning. So the very first chapter starts with the very first ancient music, and proceeds from there.

Of course, the path from ancient music to today isn't straight, and it isn't singular. To that end, I've divided the book into three major sections, each corresponding to a slightly different musical path.

Part 1, "Western Classical Music," presents the music you find in traditional music history courses and books—the "serious" music of Bach and Beethoven and the rest. We go chronologically by musical era, from the music of the ancient era through the Medieval, Renaissance, Classical, and Romantic periods, through and including the serious music of the twentieth century.

Part 2, "American Popular Music," recognizes that the popular music of today is the classical music of tomorrow. We start by examining the popular music of the seventeenth, eighteenth, and nineteenth centuries, move on to blues and jazz, examine the standards of the Great American Songbook, and finish up with the popular music of the past 50 years—rock, country, soul, hip hop, and such.

Part 3, "World Music," examines what was happening in the rest of the world while Bach, Beethoven, and Bacharach were doing their thing. Individual chapters look at the music of different cultures—China and India, the Middle East, Africa, and Latin America and the Caribbean.

The Complete Idiot's Guide to Music History concludes with a glossary of musical terms and a list of great composers. And this list, by the way, doesn't stop with Stravinsky—it also includes the likes of John Philip Sousa, Cole Porter, and Paul McCartney!

How to Get the Most Out of This Book

To get the most out of this book, you should know how it is designed. I've tried to put things together to make reading the book both rewarding and fun.

In addition to the main text, you'll find a number of little text boxes (what we in publishing call *margin notes*) that present additional advice and information. These elements enhance your knowledge or point out important pitfalls to avoid, and they look like this:

Note

These boxes contain additional information about the topic at hand.

Each chapter also includes three distinct sections that you should find informative. These include …

- Special *sidebars* that provide interesting information or commentary about the main topic of the chapter.

- A *listening list* of recommended recordings for the music of that chapter. These should be readily available on CD or for download from various online music sites.

- A *timeline* of important events—both musical and historical.

By the way, the recordings I recommend in each chapter aren't the only recordings you might find interesting. While my recommendations are always good bets, they're not exclusive; you might find equally valid recordings of the same works by other performers. That's okay; consider each listening list as a place to start, rather than the final word on such recordings.

My Other Books

I'd be remiss if I didn't mention the other music books I've written for Alpha Books over the years. While you don't need to read any of these to learn about music history, you might find them useful if you want to continue your musical studies:

- *The Complete Idiot's Guide to Music Theory, Second Edition* (2005), the perfect introduction to how music works—even if you can't read music yourself

- *The Complete Idiot's Guide to Music Composition* (2005), which shows you how to create your own songs and compositions

- *The Complete Idiot's Guide to Solos and Improvisations* (2004), a great guide for jazz musicians and rock guitarists

- ◆ *The Complete Idiot's Guide to Arranging and Orchestration* (2007), written for anyone creating arrangements for choirs, bands, or orchestras

- ◆ *The Complete Idiot's Guide to Playing Drums, Second Edition* (2004), for budding drummers and percussionists everywhere

- ◆ *The Complete Idiot's Guide to Singing* (2003; co-written with Phyllis Fulford), the perfect guide for aspiring singers and *American Idol* contestants

Of these, I recommend *The Complete Idiot's Guide to Music Theory* as the best companion to the book you're currently reading. In fact, that book was the inspiration for this one; music theory, after all, is thought of as just as boring as music history—even if it really isn't boring at all!

Let Me Know What You Think

I always love to hear from my readers. Feel free to e-mail me at musichistory@molehillgroup.com. I can't promise that I'll answer every e-mail, but I will promise that I'll read each one!

And, just in case a few mistakes happen to creep into the printed book, you can find a list of any corrections or clarifications on my website (www.molehillgroup.com/musichistory.htm). That's also where you can find a list of my other books, so feel free to look around—and maybe do a little online shopping!

Acknowledgments

Thanks to the usual suspects at Alpha, including Tom Stevens, Phil Kitchel, Janette Lynn, Billy Fields, Michael Dietsch, and Marie Butler-Knight, for helping to turn my manuscript into a printed book. Additional thanks to Frank Felice of Butler University's Jordan College of Fine Arts, for suggesting the technical reviewer for this book.

Special Thanks to the Technical Reviewer

Speaking of that technical reviewer, *The Complete Idiot's Guide to Music History* was reviewed by an expert who double-checked the accuracy of what you'll learn here, to help us ensure that this book gives you everything you need to know about composing music. Special thanks are extended to Emily Kausalik, for her review and comments in this regard.

Emily hails from Sandwich, Illinois, is a graduate of Butler University in Indianapolis, and is currently pursuing her Master's in music history at Bowling Green State University in Bowling Green, Ohio. I knew Emily was right for this book when I saw the title of her Master's thesis (currently in progress): "Musical Function and Thematic Autonomy in the 'Man With No Name' Trilogy." Anyone who can speak equally as well on stylistic traits of the Renaissance and Ennio Morricone's music for *The Good, the Bad and the Ugly* gets my approval!

My heartfelt thanks to Emily for her assistance and advice—and for helping to make this a better book.

Trademarks

All terms mentioned in this book that are known to be or are suspected of being trademarks or service marks have been appropriately capitalized. Alpha Books and Penguin Group (USA) Inc. cannot attest to the accuracy of this information. Use of a term in this book should not be regarded as affecting the validity of any trademark or service mark.

Part  **Western Classical Music**

Here's the "serious" part of the book, covering everything from Gregorian chant through Bach and Beethoven to the atonal music of the twentieth century. This is where you'll learn about the music played by your local symphonic orchestra or chamber ensemble—and that you hear on classical radio stations.

Chapter 1

From the Beginning: Ancient Music

In This Chapter

- ◆ Learn how prehistoric people made music
- ◆ Trace the evolution of music from ancient Egypt to the Roman Empire
- ◆ Discover how ancient Greek philosophers defined modern music theory

Music is as common as language—and likely almost as old. Music is part of every culture on Earth, from the least sophisticated to the most; it's found on every continent and in every country, and has been with us from ancient times to the present.

But just how did music develop? Although it's impossible to know the specifics (the ability to perform music existed long before humans developed the ability to write it down), it was likely a long evolutionary process that started somewhere on the plains of Africa.

Mimicking Nature: Prehistoric Music

Let's be up-front about it: no one knows who or where the first music was made. It may have been a caveman pounding out a beat on a hollow log; it may have been a cavewoman mimicking a nearby bird whistle while cooking dinner over the communal fire. Wherever or whatever it was, it was probably something very simple, at least compared to our modern notion of music.

The Sincerest Form of Flattery

The earliest music likely developed in response to the natural sounds that early humans heard all around them. Imagine a prehistoric man standing on the African veldt, listening to the sounds of insects and animals all around him, communicating with one another via a variety of sounds. Have you ever heard a noise and tried to mimic it? It's easy, then, to imagine our prehistoric man hearing a locust clicking its welcome and answering by making a clicking sound with his own mouth. He hears a lion growl in the distance, and echoes with his own growl. And when he hears a bird singing to its flock, our ancient friend does his best to imitate that bird call, by whistling the notes of *its song*.

It's a short step from imitating bird songs to creating uniquely human music, no matter how simple that music may be. But it's clear that the earliest music was an imitation of natural sounds, and thus shared similar tonality, patterns, and repetition to those sounds. In other words, our prehistoric musicians weren't whistling anything too complex; it's likely that the first snippets of music were short and simple and repeated over and over. This simple music may even have been used for the same purposes that other animals vocalized their sounds—to establish territory, to warn of danger, and to attract mates.

This earliest music, produced by humans in preliterate cultures, is called *primitive* or *prehistoric music*. The prehistoric era of music runs from at least 50,000 B.C.E. to about 4000 B.C.E.—when humans began to record their history in writing.

Rock Music

One thing is for sure, prehistoric humans had to create their own music; they hadn't yet developed musical instruments to play. Prehistoric music was primarily vocal music, either hummed or whistled—or even clicked or grunted. Again, simple sounds produced by simple humans.

At some point, it's likely that these vocal sounds were supplemented by some sort of beat or rhythm, created by pounding one object with the hands or with another object. That's right, the first instrument was some sort of drum—perhaps a hollowed-out log, an animal skin stretched over a frame made of bones, or even two rocks hit together.

The nature of rhythm probably evolved from the sounds made by primitive tools. Crude stone tools were first used by humans in the Paleolithic age, starting around 100,000 years ago. The noise produced by these tools led to the discovery of rhythm; duplicating these rhythmic sounds outside of work was a kind of music.

This development of musical rhythm is easy to understand. Think of the repetitive rhythm you hear when you pound nails into a board, or when you saw a piece of wood. When you get into a groove, the noises you make become more and more rhythmic. Keep it up, and you create a primitive drum track to your work; no doubt the same thing happened eons ago on the plains of Africa.

Put Your Lips Together and Blow

When archeologists find a group of oblong stone or bone objects dating back to the Paleolithic era, it's unclear whether these objects are tools or musical instruments; it's possible that they were used for both purposes. More clear, however, are those archeological finds of bone flutes, pipes, and whistles—objects fashioned from animal bone and meant to be blown into. These objects are true musical instruments, among the first of their kind.

A typical bone flute, like the one shown here, is a hollowed out piece of animal bone. Our prehistoric musicians would blow into one end of the bone and a musical tone would come out of the other. More sophisticated bone flutes had holes punched into the sides; by covering one or more of these holes, the musical pitch could be raised and lowered. The physics are similar to our modern flute, although few flutes today are made out of water buffalo bones.

> **Note**
>
> The oldest such bone flute on record is the so-called "Neanderthal flute" found in a Slovenian cave in 1995. This flute is estimated to be about 45,000 years old, and was made from the hollow femur of a juvenile cave bear.

A prehistoric bone flute—one of the first pitched musical instruments.

(Photograph by Flickr user asgitner, used by permission under the Creative Commons Attribution ShareAlike 2.0 license.)

Ancient Music in the Ancient World

Early humans became human somewhere on the African continent, and there they stayed until about 50,000 years ago. At that point they began to migrate northward and populate the other continents.

Prehistoric humans were so called because they had yet to write down their history; *prehistory* literally means a time before history was documented. That all changed around 4000 B.C.E., when humans developed written language. Now, all of a sudden, there was a history that future generations could read about.

At about the same time that humans learned to write, their music started to become more standardized—not just random sounds and pitches, but rather conscious patterns and repetitions that formed rhythms and melody. Music made in this literate, post-prehistoric era (from 4000 B.C.E. to just after the fall of the Roman Empire in 476 C.E.) is called *ancient music.*

> **Note**
>
> Music in different parts of the world—Africa, China, India, et al.—developed in subtly different ways. Our focus throughout these first chapters is on the development of Western music; to learn how music developed in other cultures, see Part 3.

Ancient music did not develop in the same way or at the same pace everywhere in the ancient world. Unlike today's society, where we're instantly connected to one another via Internet and satellite, different cultures and civilizations were almost totally isolated from one another. So an ancient musician who discovered a new series of pitches in Mesopotamia wasn't able to share that development with a pan-flute player in China. This made for a slow learning curve, but eventually music began to assimilate aspects of each native culture and evolve accordingly.

Unfortunately, we don't know how this ancient music sounded; it was made before the development of a standardized music notation. (That is, nobody knew how to write it down yet.) That said, it's clear that Western music, as we know it, evolved from ancient Near Eastern culture—so that's where we'll start.

Egypt: New Instruments

Ancient Egypt unified the many disparate cultures of the Nile Valley under a single pharaoh. It was an advanced culture for the time, known for its architecture (the pyramids), technology (the controlled irrigation of the Nile Valley), and art (a writing system and literature). Like many ancient societies, ancient Egyptians regarded music as a gift from the gods. The appearance and the sound of early musical instruments had symbolic significance in Egyptian culture, where music played an important role in religious practice.

Note

How do music historians determine what kind of music was played in ancient Egypt? Simple: by observing the position of the holes found on flutes used in that era.

While no examples of notated ancient Egyptian music exist, some music historians believe that ancient Egyptian music was based on a simple scale consisting of five tones. Both male and female voices were used in this music that was played in Egyptian temples.

Some of the earliest known musical instruments (beyond the simple bone flute) were developed in ancient Egypt. These included the stringed harps and lutes, known to be played as early as 4000 B.C.E., as well as lyres and double clarinets, played as early as 3500 B.C.E. Percussion instruments were added to Egyptian orchestral music circa 2000 B.C.E., while the tambourine was known to be used by the Hittites circa 1500 B.C.E.—along with the guitar, lyre, and trumpet.

A musician playing a lyre—a handheld harp.

By the way, harps, lutes, and lyres were the first stringed instruments; previously, all pitched instruments were flutes or whistles. The photograph on the previous page of ancient pottery shows a typical lyre—kind of a handheld harp. Sounds are produced on these instruments by plucking or strumming the individual strings.

Mesopotamia: The First Written Music

Mesopotamia is known as the cradle of civilization; it's a fertile crescent of land located near the convergence of the Tigris and Euphrates rivers, pretty much where the country of Iraq is located today. It was home to some of the world's first highly developed societies, including the kingdoms of Akkad, Assyria, Babylonia, Chaldea, and Sumer; the Mesopotamian people helped to launch the Bronze Age and developed many related technologies, including metalworking, glassmaking, and textile weaving. It's not surprising that this area was host to some of the earliest forms of ancient music—including the first documented song.

Note

Which came first—music or hunting? Many music historians believe that the development of the musical bow and the hunting bow occurred simultaneously.

Music has long been associated with religion; most ancient peoples used music to praise their deities (as do many modern ones). This was certainly true in ancient Mesopotamia, where all known societies made music central to their religious rites and festivals. Starting around 1800 B.C.E., Babylonian liturgical services were known to comprise a variety of psalms and hymns. The musical style consisted of two different voices alternating in chant; this type of music, with two or more voices, is called *antiphonal*. Typical Mesopotamian instruments were flutes, drums, harps, and lyres.

The earliest known written music was found in Sumer in southern Mesopotamia, at the site of the ancient city of Ur. This music was in the form of a cuneiform tablet, created about 2000 B.C.E. The so-called Ur tablet, sometimes referred to as the "oldest known song," was actually a set of instructions for performing that era's music. From this tablet, we've learned that the music of the time was composed in harmonics of parallel thirds, written in a diatonic scale. The notation on the tablet indicates the names of strings on a lyre.

Around 800 B.C.E., the first known musical scales, incorporating five and seven tones per octave, began to appear in Babylonian music. These scales preceded the seven-note modes later standardized in Greek culture.

Greece: Music and Mathematics

As time went on, northern Mediterranean culture became dominant in the ancient world—in particular, the culture of Greece. This was an advanced society: think of Homer's *The Iliad* and *The Odyssey*; the philosophy of Aristotle, Socrates, and Plato; the mathematics of Pythagoras and Euclid. Under the Greeks, civilization was advancing by leaps and bounds; it's not surprising, then, that the first truly European music evolved in Greece, in the period from 500 B.C.E. to 300 C.E.

The Greeks were concerned with explaining and defining the natural world. Greek scientists and mathematicians were known for discovering patterns and then creating formulae to define those patterns. (Think of Pythagoras's theorem to explain the three sides of a right triangle, or the definition of *pi* to describe a circle's circumference and diameter in Euclidian geometry.) That's how the Greeks approached music, as well—from a very mathematical perspective, but with religious overtones.

The religious aspect came from the fact that ancient Greek philosophers believed that music originated from the god Apollo, as well as from the mythological musician Orpheus and other divinities. They also believed that music reflected in microcosm the laws of harmony that rule the universe, and that music influenced human thought and actions.

As to the mathematical aspect, we need only turn to the Greek philosopher/mathematician Pythagoras (580 B.C.E.–500 B.C.E.), who apparently dabbled in music on the side. (Can you imagine a garage band made up of Greek philosophers?) Pythagoras not only dealt with triangles, he also discovered the mathematical relationships between specific frequencies and musical intervals, using a single-string instrument (called a monochord) to produce the various intervals. The way it worked is that Pythagoras divided the string into smaller and smaller lengths, kind of like how you shorten a guitar string by pressing your finger on a fret. For example, you effectively cut a string in half (making it half as long) by pressing down at the midpoint of the string.

Here's what Pythagoras discovered: when you have two notes whose frequencies form a ratio of 2:1, they sound one perfect octave apart; a ratio of 3:2 forms an interval of a fifth; a ratio of 4:3 forms a fourth; and so on. These basic intervals combine to create the modes and scales on which all Western melodies and harmony are based.

In 340 B.C.E., expanding on the findings of Pythagoras, fellow philosopher Aristotle (384 B.C.E.–322 B.C.E.) laid the foundations of modern music theory. In his treatise *The Politics*, Aristotle noted that different musical melodies, modes, and rhythms have different effects on the listener. He argued that since music has the power of forming character, it should be an important part of the education of the young. Those arguments are still sound today, which is why most Western schools include some sort of music program for their students.

Speaking of students, Aristotle's student, Aristoxenus of Tarentum (364 B.C.E.–304 B.C.E.), in his *Elements of Harmony*, formalized the Greek scheme of *modes*, which utilize a limited series of pitches defined by set intervals. These modes, such as the Dorian, Ionian, Lydian, and Phrygian, predated the modern major and minor scales that came to prominence in the sixteenth and seventeenth centuries C.E., and that we still use today. Prior to the ancient Greeks, there was no set linear relationship between pitches; the modal concept set one pitch after another in a defined manner.

As to ancient Greek music itself, it was primarily monophonic. In songs, the music duplicated the rhythms of the text; in instrumental pieces, the melody followed the rhythmic patterns of poems on which they were based. Common instruments included pipes, flutes, lyres, and the like—as well as numerous percussion instruments.

Note

When you sing the "do re mi" of the major scale, you're also singing the first three notes of the Greek Ionian mode. Interestingly, the words "ut re mi fa sol la" are taken from the first syllables of each stanza of text in the Latin hymn *Ut queant laxis*. These syllables correlate with the modern pitches C D E F G A.

The Roman Empire: Integrating Other Musical Cultures

The cultural dominance of the northern Mediterranean area was eventually passed on to the Romans, who, under Julius Caesar, began to make much of Europe their own. The Roman Empire eventually came to encompass a range of territories from England to Spain to Turkey to Egypt to Greece.

Fortunately, the musical principles and ideas developed by the Greeks were preserved by the Romans throughout their history. More important, Roman music was also influenced by the music of the many kingdoms conquered by the Roman Empire. From 27 B.C.E. to 192 C.E., slave musicians and dancers were recruited from throughout the Empire, musical theater flourished, and both Greek and Roman musicians had their own professional organizations. This blending of musical cultures helped to bring some small amount of diversity to the existing music, while still maintaining its Greek underpinnings.

Roman culture continued to preserve the musical ideas of Greek civilization until the fall of the Roman Empire (in 476 C.E.). As European society moved into the Middle Ages, however, the cultural center moved northward—and big changes were afoot, which we'll examine in the next chapter.

Why Western Music Sounds Western

In the first section of this book, we focus primarily on what we call Western music—the music of Europe and, at least initially, the Middle East. Know, however, that Western music is just one of several separate musical cultures (including those from China, India, Indonesia, and Japan), each of which has its own specific tunings, scales, and tonalities that define the cultures' unique musical sounds.

Western music uses a 12-tone scale, in which an octave is divided into 12 pitches, spaced at equal intervals. The relationships between these 12 pitches describe a set number of major and minor scales, which in turn provide the basis for chords and harmony. This may sound a bit academic to a nonmusician, but it's important, because other cultures divide the octave into more or fewer pitches than the Western 12. This results in different tonalities and a different musical sound in each culture; Indian music, for example, divides the octave into 22 closely spaced pitches.

The pitches of each musical scale reflect specific vibrational frequencies. For example, modern Western scales are standardized around a frequency of 440Hz, which represents the pitch identified as the A above middle C; all the other notes of the scale are pitched in relation to this tone. In earlier times and cultures, this central pitch had other values—as low as 376Hz in early eighteenth-century France, and as high as 560Hz in early seventeenth-century Germany (referred to as North German church pitch).

The history of Western music is the history of both standardization and increasing sophistication. Over the centuries, composers have learned to combine the 12 pitches of the Western tonal system in increasingly complex ways. Where music from earlier eras was limited to the naturally occurring (*diatonic*) notes of the major or minor scales, modern music is free to incorporate notes and harmonies from outside the natural scale. This approach, known as *chromaticism*, has extended the boundaries of traditional Western tonality—and resulted in new musical forms that challenge musicians and listeners alike.

Listening List

This brings us to the end of music's ancient era and to the end of this chapter. It also brings us to the first of many listening lists—recommended recordings that best represent the music discussed in that chapter.

This listening list is the shortest of all in the book, if only because so little ancient music survives to this time. The three recordings listed here do a good job of re-creating the music of ancient Egypt, Mesopotamia, and Greece; be prepared, though, because it sounds quite a bit different from the music of today.

Ankh: The Sound of Ancient Egypt (Michael Atherton)

Melpomen: Ancient Greek Music (Ensemble Melpomen; Conrad Steinmann, conductor)

Music of the Ancient Sumerians, Egyptians, and Greeks (Ensemble de Organographia)

Timeline: Prehistoric and Ancient Eras

100,000 B.C.E.	First use of stone tools
50,000 B.C.E.	Humans migrate from Africa
43,000 B.C.E.	First known bone flute
4000 B.C.E.	End of prehistory; ancient era begins; first stringed harps and lutes
3500 B.C.E.	First lyres and clarinets
2000 B.C.E.	Earliest documented written music
1500 B.C.E.	Hittites use guitars, lyres, trumpets, and tambourines
800 B.C.E.	Five- and seven-tone scales appear in Babylonia
700 B.C.E.	Homer writes *The Iliad* and *The Odyssey*
550 B.C.E.	Pythagoras determines musical intervals
340 B.C.E.	Aristotle lays foundations of music theory
320 B.C.E.	Aristoxenus defines musical modes
44 B.C.E.	Julius Caesar ascends to throne; start of the Roman Empire
8 B.C.E.	Jesus of Nazareth born
476 C.E.	Fall of the Roman Empire

Of Monks and Troubadours: The Medieval Period

In This Chapter

♦ Learn how the Greek modes influenced Gregorian chant

♦ Discover the emerging secular song of the troubadours

♦ Find out how polyphony developed in both secular and sacred music

♦ Learn all about organum, conductus, motets, and composer Guillaume de Machaut

Here's something interesting about the way history unfolds. Although succeeding generations often build on the previous culture, more often than not, there is some sort of rebellion against what came before. In fact, some new cultures go out of their way to ignore or even obliterate what has come before, often when the new culture has forcibly conquered the older one.

This sort of generational rebellion is often reflected in the music and art of the new era. If the previous music was simple, the new music would likely be more complex; if the previous music was ornate, the new music would likely be simpler.

This is what happened in the medieval period, after the barbarian forces of Europe brought about the fall of the Roman Empire. The resulting European society, strongly influenced by the newly powerful Christian church, did its best to replace the pagan culture of Greece and Rome with its own Christian religious culture. As far as music was concerned, it was a whole new ballgame; while medieval music built upon the musical modes developed by the Greeks, the music itself was now in service to the Christian church—and began to get a lot more sophisticated.

Welcome to the Middle Ages

On September 4, 476 C.E., the Roman Empire fell. On that date, Romulus Augustus, the last emperor of Rome, was deposed but not replaced; the empire had spread too far and too thin to defend itself against the hordes of Vandals, Visigoths, and Huns who invaded the empire's European territories.

After the fall of the empire, Europe splintered into numerous regional kingdoms and fiefdoms, isolated from one another and ruled by kings who enjoyed the support of the barbarian armies. This led to a cultural Balkanization, as it were; it was difficult, if not impossible, for culture to travel from one isolated country to another.

The lack of a single European ruling entity created a power vacuum that was filled by the newly emerged Christian church. The Christian religion, which began as an underground sect following the death of Jesus in the first century C.E., eventually went mainstream and was ultimately accepted as the official religion of the Roman Empire. After the fall of the empire, Christianity emerged as the central unifying force in Europe, controlling governments and dictating the destiny of art, literature, and music. This church-dominated era, which dated from the fifth century C.E. to the beginning of the Renaissance in the fourteenth century, was known as the Middle Ages or medieval era.

The Christian church's control over the arts resulted in most professional musicians being employed by the church; the majority of medieval music was created in monasteries. Because the church was opposed to the paganism associated with ancient Greece and Rome, this led to the dying out of Greek and Roman music (which tended to be in service to those cultures' pagan religions) and to the rise of new sacred musical forms.

The medieval period was a long one, lasting a full millennia. Over the course of a thousand years, one would expect significant musical development. But that isn't what happened—at least initially. While some evolution occurred, especially in the later years of the period, it was perhaps the lack of change that was surprising. This musical stability (or stagnation, if you prefer) was a direct result of the isolation of the various European cultures, as well as the heavy-handed influence of the Catholic Church, which wasn't a big fan of change in any way, shape, or form. So once the prominent medieval musical forms were established, they tended to stay as they were for long periods of time.

Music and the Mass: Gregorian Chant

Note

Monophonic music consists of a single melodic line with no accompaniment—perfect for singing by a single voice, or by multiple people singing in unison.

The earliest music of the medieval period was performed by the monks of the early Christian church. This music was an unaccompanied monophonic chant, called *plainsong* or *plainchant*. Such chants consisted of Latin words derived from the Roman Catholic Mass, set to simple modal melodies—that is, melodies derived from the seven church modes.

There are two primary types of plainsong: *responsorial* (developed from the recitation of psalms) and *antiphonal* (developed as pure melody). These vocal melodies were typically unaccompanied and performed in a free rhythm; that is, the rhythm of plainsong is the free rhythm of the spoken word.

This figure shows a typical medieval chant, in its original notation. As you can see, plainsong has its own system of notation, using a four-line staff (in contrast to the modern five-line staff) and no bar lines.

A typical medieval chant in the original notation.

Due to the isolation of the European countries during the Middle Ages (there were no highways or rail lines, remember), localized versions of chant developed in different regional centers. This localization of chant also served to support the regional liturgies used to celebrate Mass in each country. For example, the Mozarabic chant that developed in Spain showed the influence of North African music; Ambrosian chant, named after St. Ambrose, was the standard in Milan; Gallican chant was used in Gaul; and Celtic chant was the rule of the day in Great Britain and Ireland.

Localized chant became a bit more universal around 600 C.E., when Pope Gregory I moved to standardize the Mass and encourage a ritualized use of music by the church. By this time Rome was the religious center of Western Europe, so a new Mass was created by combining the Roman and Gallican regional liturgies. The resulting chant eventually became known as Gregorian chant, after Pope Gregory. Over the next several hundred years, Gregorian chant superseded all the preceding localized chants, with only a few exceptions.

Gregorian chant was typically sung in churches by choirs of men and boys, as part of the Roman rite of the Catholic Mass. It was also sung by the monks and nuns of religious orders in their chapels. In fact, Gregorian chant continues to be sung today; the modern Roman Catholic Church still officially considers it the music most suitable for worship.

Music and Modes: Understanding the Church Modes

At this point in our examination of the music of the Middle Ages, we need to take a quick time out and discuss the concept of *modes*. All medieval music was based on a specific set of modes, which were often called *church modes* (because the modal plainsong was the music of the church). But modes weren't new to this period; they were originally developed by the ancient Greeks prior to the fall of the Roman Empire. As you recall from Chapter 1, a musical mode is a series of pitches in a defined order, with specific intervals between each pitch. Modes predate modern major and minor scales, but serve much the same function in defining melody and harmony.

Even if you're not a musician, you're familiar with scales. The major scale, for example, consists of the pitches associated with "do re mi fa sol la ti do," where the second "do" is a repeat of the first one, one octave higher. That series of seven notes (with the eighth a repeat of the first) is the scale, and the notes of the scale are used to create melodies and chords.

Well, before there were scales, there were modes. A mode is just like a scale, except with different sequences of intervals between each tone.

There are seven essential modes, each of which can be thought of as starting on a different degree of the modern major scale. To play the mode, you use the same notes of the relative major scale; you just start on a different tone.

For example, the Dorian mode starts on the second degree of the major scale. In relation to the C major scale, for example, the D Dorian mode starts on D and continues upward (D, E, F, G, A, B, C, D). The same holds true for the Phrygian mode, which starts on the third degree of the related major scale—in C major (E Phrygian): E, F, G, A, B, C, D, E. And so on for the other modes, as shown in the following table:

Note

The Ionian mode is identical to the modern major scale; the Aeolian mode is identical to the natural minor scale.

Modes

Mode	Starts on This Relative Major Scale Tone	Example (based on the C major scale)
Ionian	1	
Dorian	2	
Phrygian	3	
Lydian	4	
Mixolydian	5	

Modes

Mode	Starts on This Relative Major Scale Tone	Example (based on the C major scale)
Aeolian	6	
Locrian	7	

If you want to write your own Gregorian chant, just pick a mode and use the notes of that mode to create a simple melody. Remember to start and end on the home note of the mode; for example, if you're writing in D Dorian, start and end your melody on D. And try your best to stay within the modal octave. That's because most modal melodies stay within the octave or to one pitch outside the octave.

Music for the Masses: Troubadours and Secular Song

Not all music of the Middle Ages was sacred in nature. Toward the latter half of the period, around the turn of the new millennium, sacred musical forms were supplemented by a developing folk music tradition. These secular works typically took the form of poetry set to music, performed on simple string instruments by traveling troubadours.

Troubadour, Troubadour, Sing a Song for Me

Sometime prior to the eleventh century, a form of secular music sprang forth in southern France. This music was played and sung by roving poet-minstrels, called *troubadours*, who went from castle to castle singing songs, telling stories, and otherwise entertaining the lords and ladies of the upper class. Think of a troubadour, such as the gentleman pictured on the next page, as the medieval equivalent of today's folksinger or singer-songwriter, but without the big recording contract—and, instead of singing in coffeehouses and concert halls, performing for the very wealthiest people in town.

The music of the troubadours was monophonic, just like plainsong, which meant there were no backup singers or duets or anything like that. The troubadour typically accompanied himself on a string or percussion instrument, such as the lyre, lute, fiddle, and drums.

Note

Both sacred and secular music of the Middle Ages incorporated voices and a wide variety of instruments, including the lyre, medieval fiddle (viele), organ, small drums, and bells.

A typical French troubadour, complete with lute, entertaining a local crowd during the Middle Ages.

Note _____

One of the most famous troubadours was Adam de la Halle, whose best-known work is "Jeu de Robin et Marion."

The melodies of the troubadours' songs tended to be simpler in design than those produced in the church of the time, although they also were based on the existing church modes. These secular songs were often faster in tempo than sacred songs, and used the common language of the people instead of the Latin text of Gregorian chant.

On a cultural level, the troubadours often sang of war, chivalry, and courtly love (*fin amours*). Of these, courtly love was a very popular topic, much as love songs still dominate the Top 40 today. Under the notion of courtly love, the lover, who relentlessly pursued his often illicit love, was ennobled by the experience; it was a love at once passionate and morally elevating. Note, however, that courtly love typically took place outside the boundaries of marriage, which tended to raise the ire of the Medieval church.

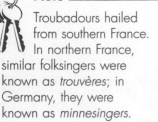

Note _____

Troubadours hailed from southern France. In northern France, similar folksingers were known as *trouvères*; in Germany, they were known as *minnesingers*.

Unfortunately, this ire was given force by the Albigensian or Cathar Crusade (1209–1229), which was Pope Innocent III's attempt to eliminate what he viewed as the heresy of the Cathars, a Gnostic sect that flourished in France in the twelfth and thirteenth centuries. While it was purely a side effect of the campaign, this crusade forcibly dispersed the troubadours from southern France to Spain, northern Italy, and northern France. And thus the troubadours spread their secular music across the whole of Europe.

By the dawn of the fourteenth century a greater range of secular song forms began to emerge. Many of these forms, such as the *ballade*, *rondeau*, and *virelai*, were based on existing poetic forms or peasant dances. Several of these forms were polyphonic in nature—which we'll get into in just a few paragraphs.

Machaut, the Medieval Master

Since the late Middle Ages also saw the rise of music notation (which we'll also get into in short order), individual songwriters began to be recognized. Before notation, songs were passed along via live performance only, and the composers were often forgotten; with notated music, the songwriter's name tended to be attached to the written music. ASCAP and BMI would have been happy, if they had been around at the time.

One of the most celebrated composers of the late Middle Ages—and the first individual musician you need to take notice of in this survey of music history—was Guillaume de Machaut (1300–1377). Machaut was a poet and a composer, prolific in his time and a strong influence on those who immediately followed him. He played an important role in the development of various musical forms of secular song, including the motet.

Music wasn't Machaut's only gig. From 1323 to 1346 he was employed as secretary to John I, Count of Luxemburg and King of Bohemia; he later became a priest and accompanied King John on various trips around Europe. After the death of King John in 1346, Machaut entered the service of other European aristocrats and rulers, including Charles II of Navarre, Jean de Berry, and Charles, Duke of Normandy (who later became King Charles V).

When he wasn't gallivanting about on his church and diplomatic duties, Machaut found time to compose over a hundred known songs (most on the familiar topic of courtly love) and write several motets and Masses. He was also one of the first known composers to explore polyphonic forms. We'll catch up with Machaut later in this chapter, when we examine his music for the Catholic Mass.

Two Parts Are Better Than One: The Rise of Polyphony

Music in the early Medieval period was almost exclusively *monophonic*, meaning that it contained a single melody line with no harmonic accompaniment. In the middle part of the Medieval period, these monophonic melodies began to be accompanied by other instruments in the form of strummed chords, especially in the secular forms of the troubadours.

But in general, Western music remained monophonic through approximately 900 C.E. At that time, for whatever reason, many musicians felt the need for music more elaborate than an unadorned melody. Thus it was that *polyphony* developed, in the form of additional melodic lines sung simultaneously with the original melody.

Note

Polyphony is the mixing together of several simultaneous and independent melodic lines. This is in contrast to **monophony**, which has only a single melodic line.

Chant + One: Organum

The first polyphonic musical form was known as *organum*, which added an extra vocal part sung in tandem with sections of preexisting Gregorian chant. This daring (for the time) innovation was born in various monasteries, most notably the Abbey of St. Gall in Switzerland; the first document detailing organum is attributed to the Benedictine monk Hucbald of St. Amand.

The added voice part in early organum was quite simple. As you can see in the following figure, the second voice was sung a fourth or a fifth interval above and parallel to the chant melody.

Later variations were more complex, featuring the second voice singing an independent countermelody. In fact, by the early twelfth century, organum incorporated three and four separate voices. This ultimately lead to the development of harmony and counterpoint—two hallmarks of the following Renaissance era.

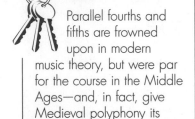

> **Note**
>
> Parallel fourths and fifths are frowned upon in modern music theory, but were par for the course in the Middle Ages—and, in fact, give Medieval polyphony its unique sound.

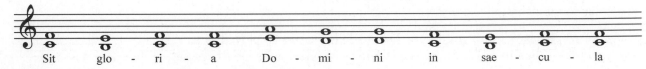

Sit   glo - ri - a   Do - mi - ni   in   sae - cu - la

Polyphony in organum—parallel fourths throughout.

Speeding It Up: Conductus

To the southwest, in the south of France, another type of polyphonic composition was born. This new form, called *conductus*, was musically similar to organum but used newly composed texts, often secular in nature.

What truly set conductus apart from organum, however, was speed; in conductus, the words were declaimed at a rapid rate, compared to organum's slower pace. Conductus eventually evolved into the later *motet*.

The New Music of Ars Nova

As the Middle Ages neared their natural end, musical evolution began to speed up. The world was changing, and changing fast.

The fourteenth century saw a major stylistic development dubbed *ars nova* (Latin for "new art"); this was a more sophisticated music, incorporating a new rhythmic complexity. Composers of ars nova used rhythmic patterns of a dozen or more notes, repeated over and over in multiple voices. By layering other melodies over these isorhythmic voice parts, composers created intricate polyphonic designs.

As groundbreaking as ars nova was, it was still based on existing Medieval forms—in particular plainsong. In the music of ars nova, the foundation voice, known as the *cantus firmus*, was typically borrowed from Gregorian chant. Thus we see the evolutionary chain, from Greek modes to Medieval chant to ars nova polyphony—and on to the motet and the Mass.

Music in Two Voices: The Motet

The concepts of ars nova and isorhythm led to the development of the *motet*, a short unaccompanied choral work for two voices. In a motet, the ornate upper voice (called the *tenor*) is given a different text from the chant melody or *cantus firmus*. In this respect a motet is like a song accompanied by a tenor, as shown in this example by Machaut.

Riches d'amour et mandians d'amie

Music by: Guillaume Machaut

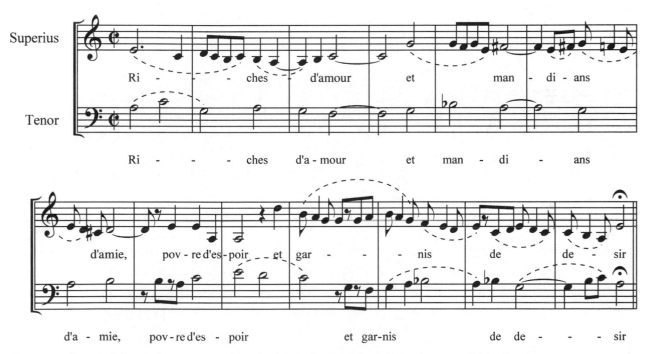

A motet with two independent voices—in this instance, Machaut's Riches d'amour et mandians d'amie.

The early motet was exclusively a sacred form, based on preexisting melodies; other words and melodies were added in counterpoint. It stayed secular through the fifteenth century, when Guillaume Dufay introduced secular melodies as part of the motet's cantus firmus. But that gets us into the Renaissance, which is the topic of Chapter 3, where you'll read about the further development of the motet form by composers such as Josquin and Palestrina.

Note

The motet form was expanded late in the thirteenth century, when three- and four-voice motets were introduced.

The Polyphonic Mass

Polyphony also found its way into the Roman Mass, which had incorporated music—in the form of plainchant—since at least the fourth century. During the early Middle Ages, however, ceremonial music was limited to the Proper of the Mass. (The Proper is just one section of the longer Mass.)

The first known setting of the Ordinary of the Mass was *Le Messe de Nostre Dame*, written in the early 1360s by our friend Machaut. (I told you he was an influential composer!) This piece was the first to set all movements of the Mass in four-part scoring; the following figure shows an excerpt from Machaut's Mass, in all its four-part glory.

Le Messe de Nostre Dame

Guillaume de Machaut

An excerpt from Machaut's Le Messe de Nostre Dame—*four-part polyphony.*

During the late fourteenth century, composers began to create Mass settings in which the movements were musically related to each other. In England, Lionel Power (1375–1445) and John Dunstable (1390–1453) unified the Mass by basing all the movements on the same plainchant cantus firmus. By the end of the Medieval period these English Masses had migrated to northern Italy; their impact helped to launch the fully unified Mass cycle that reigned through the end of the seventeenth century, and to establish the polyphonic Mass as the most serious musical form of the Renaissance period to come.

The Development of Music Notation

The rise of polyphony contributed to the development of the modern system of music notation; musicians had to be able to read and perform several different parts simultaneously, hence the need for a precise system of pitch and rhythmic notation. The eleventh-century Benedictine monk Guido d'Arezzo (995–1033) thus conceived of a five-line staff, with each line and space representing a specific pitch; individual notes were represented as square symbols called *neumes*.

A system of rhythmic notation was similarly introduced in the late thirteenth century by German theorist Franco of Cologne (1240–1280). Previously, rhythm was indicated by a series of longs and breves (shorts); a note could either be long or short, but there was no indication as to how long or short. Franco devised a system of notation where different rhythmic values were indicated by differently shaped notes. That system evolved into the series of whole, half, quarter, and eighth notes we use today.

Listening List

So the medieval period, all 1,000 years of it, started out by using simple monophonic melodies based on Greek modes to express Christian beliefs, and ended with very ornate two- and more-part polyphonic melodies in both sacred and secular musical forms. To that end, this chapter's listening list represents both the simplicity of the early Middle Ages and the quite complex nature of the later period.

Listen to these recordings and you'll hear a variety of both sacred and secular medieval forms, including two very popular samplings of that old staple, Gregorian chant, a healthy serving of Machaut, and a bit of troubadour music.

An English Ladymass: Medieval Chant and Polyphony (Anonymous 4)

Chant (The Benedictine Monks of Santo Domingo de Silos)

Guillaume de Machaut: Le Messe de Nostre Dame; Songs from Le Voir Dit (Oxford Camerata; Jeremy Summerly, director)

Guillaume de Machaut: Motets (the Hilliard Ensemble)

Troubadours, Trouvères, Minstrels (Studio der frühen Musik; Thomas Binkley, conductor)

Timeline: The Middle Ages

476	Fall of the Roman Empire; beginning of the Middle Ages
600	Pope Gregory I standardizes the Catholic Mass
750	*Beowulf* written
768	Charlemagne begins rule in Europe
900	First use of polyphony
1000	Rise of the troubadours in southern France
1020	D'Arezzo invents music notation
1050	First agricultural revolution begins
1066	William the Conqueror invades England
1095	First Crusade begins
1099	Crusaders capture Jerusalem
1100	Beginnings of secular music
1189	Richard the Lionhearted assumes English crown
1209	Cathar Crusade; troubadours flee southern France
1225	Thomas Aquinas teaches at the University of Paris
1247	Robin Hood dies (according to legend) at Kirklees priory
1270	Franco of Cologne invents modern rhythmic notation
1272	Edward I establishes English Parliament
1300	Machaut born
1310	Rise of ars nova
1337	Start of Hundred Years' War between France and England
1347	The Black Death begins to plague Europe
1350	Lute playing becomes popular across Europe
1360	Machaut writes *Le Messe de Nostre Dame*
1377	Machaut dies
1390	First Mass settings with all movements related to each other

Chapter 3

Masses, Motets, and Madrigals: The Renaissance Period

In This Chapter

- ◆ Understanding the art, science, and exploration of the Renaissance
- ◆ Discovering Renaissance polyphony
- ◆ Following the evolution of the Catholic Mass
- ◆ Introducing the madrigal
- ◆ Presenting the masters of Renaissance music: Dufay, Josquin, and Palestrina

The long, relatively dark era of the Middle Ages eventually led to a great cultural awakening. This Renaissance era, which spanned the late fourteenth through the mid-seventeenth centuries, is considered by most historians to be the true beginning of modern history.

The Renaissance saw the explorations of Christopher Columbus and Sir Francis Drake, the scientific advancements of Galileo and Copernicus, the realistic art of Michelangelo and Leonardo da Vinci, and the groundbreaking plays of Christopher Marlowe and William Shakespeare. It also saw the dawn of a new musical era full of sprightly polyphony, experimentation in the Mass and motet forms, the spread of secular song, and the introduction of a new polyphonic vocal form called the madrigal.

Out of the Dark Ages, into the Renaissance

The word "renaissance" is French for "rebirth," and that's exactly what the Renaissance period represented—a rebirth of Western culture. Beginning around 1350 in Florence, Italy, and later spreading to the rest of Europe, the Renaissance represented a revival of classical learning (based on ancient Greek and Latin texts), the development of perspective and realism in painting, advancements in science and mathematics, and a refinement of the polyphonic musical styles first explored in the medieval period.

Defining the Renaissance Man

The Renaissance was a cultural movement that profoundly affected all aspects of European intellectual life. The advancements made during the Renaissance encompassed practically all disciplines—literature, philosophy, politics, science, religion, art, and music.

Consider some of the great lights of the period, individuals expert in multiple fields, such as Leonardo da Vinci and Michelangelo. Leonardo was a scientist, mathematician, inventor, anatomist, architect, painter, writer, and musician; Michelangelo excelled at painting, sculpting, poetry, and engineering. These so-called polymaths defined the term "Renaissance man;" it's difficult to imagine any individual in modern society mastering so many disparate disciplines, but that was more the norm than the exception in the Renaissance era. Intellectuals didn't specialize during the Renaissance, they let one discipline influence the others.

Exploring New Worlds

Imagine Europe of the late 1400s. Leonardo da Vinci had just published his first detailed sketches of the human body, England's Henry VII defeated Richard III in the War of the Roses, Spain pushed the Moors out of Europe (and expelled its Jewish population, as well), and syphilis began to spread throughout the continent—an unintended consequence of the Renaissance expansion, to be sure. In the following decades, Copernicus would posit that the Earth circles the sun (instead of the other way around), and Martin Luther would launch the Protestant Reformation. There was a lot going on.

Note

The Americas were named in 1507 by cartographer Martin Waldseemüller, in honor of post-Columbus explorer Amerigo Vespucci.

Just as travel across Europe became more widespread, so did travel outside of Europe. It was during this period that seafaring explorers from many nations began to venture further and further from home, most in search of trade and commerce. Perhaps the most noteworthy of these explorers was Christopher Columbus, an Italian in the employ of the court of Spain. In 1492, Columbus's three ships set sail in search of a new trade route west to India, instead of the standard eastern route. It was a bit of a gamble, as many cartographers of the day still held to the belief that the Earth was flat; if common wisdom was true, Columbus would eventually sail off the edge of the Earth.

It turns out that the common wisdom wasn't true and Columbus didn't sail off the edge of the flat Earth. Neither, however, did he find a direct route to India, because there were two continents in his way. Those continents, of course, were North and South America, as they were to be named. Columbus's discovery of this new world led to rampant expansion and colonization, of course—and, a few centuries later, several new and exciting musical styles. But those are stories for later chapters; for now, let's keep our focus on Europe.

The Rise of the Middle Class

While Columbus was discovering new continents half a world away, back home a new middle class population was emerging. Instead of just rulers and serfs, which was the norm during the Middle Ages, the Renaissance saw a flourishing class between the two extremes—a middle class of merchants, tradespeople, and bankers.

This growing middle class population had more than enough money to meet their basic needs for food, clothing, and shelter; they used their modest wealth to purchase large homes, fine art, and other luxuries. They also had more leisure time, which they spent on education and entertainment—which encouraged the expansion of the arts.

Art and Literature in the Renaissance

Art of all sorts flourished during the Renaissance period. In the late 1400s, artists across Europe began to embrace a distinctly Renaissance style. Painters developed the use of a linear perspective, and in fact trended towards much more realistic portrayals of all types of subjects—the human body included. Here is where Leonardo da Vinci was important, with his famous studies of human anatomy. Other artists followed suit, building on Leonardo's work to create highly realistic portrayals of human subjects. And whereas most art prior to this period was in service to religious subjects, later Renaissance artists created an increasing number of purely secular works.

> **Note**
>
> Literature became better disseminated in the Renaissance, thanks to Johann Gutenberg's invention of the printing press in 1430. Now the written word—and written music—could be mass-produced and mass-distributed. Hence the first book of sheet music printed from movable type, Ottaviano Petrucci's *Harmonice Musices Odhecaton*, a 1501 collection of chansons from Josquin des Préz and others.

Fast forward a hundred years, and we come to the preeminent Renaissance man of letters, William Shakespeare. A popular poet and playwright, Shakespeare's plays transformed the worlds of literature and theater. Few artists of any era have created such a body of work that remains vital to this day: *The Tempest*, *The Two Gentlemen of Verona*, *A Midsummer Night's Dream*, *As You Like It*, *Richard II*, *Henry VIII*, *Romeo and Juliet*, *Macbeth*, *Hamlet*, *Othello*, and dozens more.

Shakespeare produced his main works between the years 1590 and 1613. His plays and sonnets influenced latter-day novelists such as Thomas Hardy, Charles Dickens, and William Faulkner; his texts have been the basis of numerous operas, musicals, and movies. Not bad for a few decade's output!

Changes in the Church

Even though the Roman Catholic Church remained dominant during the Renaissance, its influence began to be supplemented by other sacred and secular influences. As is obvious from the changing art and literature of the day, individuals were subtly moving away from the church to better study and more accurately represent the secular world.

In addition to this gradual secularization of the culture, the Catholic Church relinquished its monopoly in Europe when the Protestants broke away from the church. The Protestant Reformation began in 1517 when Martin Luther published his 95 Theses, thus setting the stage for the formal severing of ties. That break would eventually lead to an alternate forum for religious music, apart from the traditional Catholic Mass.

The Music of the Renaissance

It's not surprising that music, like all the arts, flourished during the Renaissance. With the rise of the middle class, more people moved to cities and spent their leisure time attending plays, concerts, and other types of performances. Music became part of the common education, and—thanks to the invention of the printing press—sheet music and method books (for lute, recorder, and guitar) were made available to the populace.

Simplifying the Complex

And what kind of music did people of that era listen to? The music of the Renaissance, while building on the polyphonic developments of the late Middle Ages, reflected a reaction against the complexities of ars nova. (As we learned in Chapter 2, it's common for one era to rebel slightly against the excesses of the previous era.)

Where the music of the late Middle Ages was often overly ornate, Renaissance music incorporated simpler, smoother-flowing melodies and harmonies, with less emphasis on highly structured counterpoint. This made for music that is, perhaps, more pleasing to the modern ear, thanks to its stronger focus on the melodic line.

In addition, many new instruments came to prominence during the Renaissance. These included the viol (predecessor to the modern violin), lute, guitar, harp, recorder, and sackbut (predecessor to the trombone), as well as the first keyboard instruments, the harpsichord and clavichord. Many of these instruments—the stringed instruments, in particular—were accessible to both the upper and middle classes, for their own private instruction and performance.

Renaissance Polyphony: Counterpoint and Canon

Polyphony in the Renaissance period evolved from the independent counterpoint of the early 1400s into a more harmonious form of melody and accompaniment. As such, Renaissance polyphony is characterized by the equal participation of voices in an exchange of motifs and phrases.

The contrapuntal music of the Renaissance grew to rely heavily on statement and imitation, where the additional voices successfully restate parts of the original melodic idea. That is, one voice states a melodic line and a second line echoes that line, either exactly or with variations.

When one part imitates another consistently for a relatively long time span, the two voices form what is called a *canon*. Think of a canon as a type of "call and response;" as you can see in the following figure, the first voice is the call or statement, while the second voice is the response or imitation.

Note _____
Counterpoint is the use of two or more simultaneous, independent lines or voices. This is a general definition, of course; music theorists apply strict rules to the creation of contrapuntal lines.

Qui habitat
(excerpt)

Josquin des Prez

Contrapuntal imitation in the form of a canon: an excerpt from "Qui habitat," by Josquin des Préz.

Renaissance Church Music—Masses for the Masses

Church music in the Renaissance reflected the growing influence of secular music—despite the attempts of Catholic authorities in Italy and Spain to curb what they viewed as that music's seductive and profane excesses. Beyond this secular influence, sacred music in the Renaissance was also impacted by the Protestant Reformation. Martin Luther's desire to break with tradition and utilize songs that could be sung by the whole congregation, not just the choir, had significant impact on the music of the day.

Note _____
It's interesting that even back in the 1400s and 1500s, traditional church leaders thought of the popular music of the day as the work of the devil. This type of prejudice didn't start with rock and roll!

The Evolution of the Mass

Perhaps the most important musical form of the Renaissance was the Latin Mass, which inspired many great vocal works. The five passages of the Mass that are frequently set for choir or for choir and vocal soloists include the *Kyrie eleison* ("Lord have mercy"), *Gloria in excelsis Deo* ("Glory be to God on high"), *Credo* ("I believe"), *Sanctus* ("Holy, holy"), and *Agnus Dei* ("O Lamb of God").

As you recall, polyphony first came to the Mass in the fourteenth century, thanks to Machaut. Those early Masses used a cantus firmus based on Gregorian chant. In the fifteenth century, however, secular tunes were introduced into the Mass; the cantus firmus was frequently based on chansons or other secular melodies, and used to unify all five sections.

By the end of the sixteenth century, the Mass had evolved into an unaccompanied contrapuntal style, as practiced by Giovanni Pierluigi da Palestrina, William Byrd (1542–1623) and others. The Renaissance-era Mass was also more elaborate than that of the medieval period; composers became more ambitious, using more voices and instruments and adding more and more elaborate ornamentation to the music. It was during the Renaissance that the Mass became a monumental genre, comparable in scope to the symphonies of the nineteenth century.

Making More of the Motet

At the beginning of the Renaissance, the motet was a relatively small-scale sacred form. But as the Mass form peaked in the fifteenth and sixteenth centuries, composers turned to the motet as a vehicle of experimentation. These later motets were full of contrasts, with passages for all voices paired with passages for just two or three voices, or sections in duple time followed by sections in triple time.

This more sophisticated motet form is best represented by the works of Orlande de Lassus (1532–1594), who also emphasized the depiction of individual words in the text, incorporating techniques developed earlier in the madrigal form. Other notable motet composers were Palestrina, who composed 180 motets, and Guillaume Dufay, who introduced secular melodies into the cantus firmus.

Introducing the Protestant Chorale

The rise of the Protestant church in the 1500s created a new musical tradition, less rigid than that of the Catholic Church. Martin Luther commissioned a new catalog of songs with easy-to-sing melodies, based on familiar folk songs, for unison singing by the entire congregation; this reflected Luther's desire to restore the congregation's role in church services. This new style of sacred song—dubbed the *chorale* —was the basis for many of the Lutheran hymns that are still sung today, and presaged the more elaborate chorales of J. S. Bach and his contemporaries in the Baroque era.

Publication of various hymnbooks during and after Luther's lifetime helped to establish the chorale as a central item in the Protestant service. The earliest chorales utilized existing melodies; after 1600 or so, newly composed melodies were added to the repertoire, by Johann Walter (1496–1570), Johann Crüger (1598–1662), and others.

Most chorales feature simple devotional words set to familiar tunes—either folk songs or the traditional ecclesiastical melodies known as plainsong—intended for singing by the entire congregation. This is in contrast to the more formal Catholic Mass, which is sung by a separate choir.

Early Lutheran chorales had much of the free rhythm of plainsong, often mixing duple and triple time. Later chorales employed a more rigid metric scheme. The melody of early chorales was often placed in the tenor voice; during the seventeenth century the melody moved to the soprano voice. As you can see in the following figure, the soprano melody was typically accompanied by simple harmony and canonical responsive lines.

Gelobet seist du Jesu Christ

Johann Walter

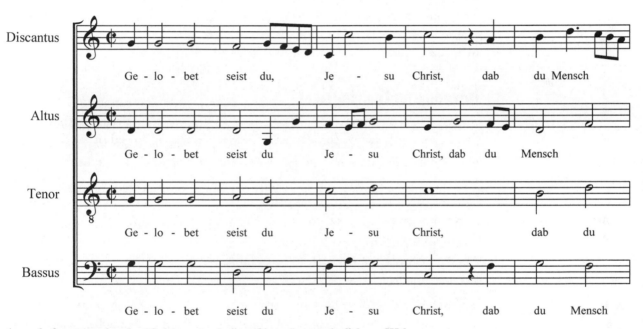

An early four-part chorale: "Gelobet seist du Jesu Christ," music by Johann Walter.

Secular Music in the Renaissance

As with other forms of art and literature, secular music began to grow in importance throughout the Renaissance period, thanks to both solo troubadours and larger vocal groups. Music was increasingly enjoyed in settings outside the church; both men and women of the upper classes were expected to understand and perform music, while those of the middle class became an eager audience for these performances.

Secular music in the Renaissance took the form of various types of song. Early Renaissance song forms were monophonic; later song forms incorporated various degree of polyphony and counterpoint.

From Troubadours to Chanson

Remember the ars nova movement of the late Middle Ages? While initially embraced by sacred composers, ars nova was also incorporated into the secular music of the early Renaissance period.

In particular, the unharmonized melodies sung by thirteenth-century troubadours evolved during the early fourteenth century into two- and three-voice pieces called *chanson* (French for "song"). The type of line repetition used determined the overall form of the music; the most commonly used schemes were the *rondeau*, the *virelai*, the *ballade*, the *caccia*, and the *ballata*. Notable early chanson composers included Dufay and Gilles de Bins dit Binchois (1400–1460).

By the sixteenth century, chanson grew from its simple beginnings to include elaborate contrapuntal melodies and vocal effects that emulated birdcalls, the cries of street vendors, and the like. Masters of this later form of chanson included Claude de Sermisy (1490–1562) and Clément Janequin (1485–1558).

Introducing the Madrigal

A further song form inspired by the ars nova movement was the *madrigal*, which survives in Christmas celebrations to this day. It was the most important secular music of its time, coming into its own in the latter half of the sixteenth century.

The first madrigals were sung in Italy at the end of the thirteenth century, but by the sixteenth century, the form had become more complex in its polyphony and had spread across all of Europe. The typical madrigal is a polyphonic composition for four to six voices (usually five), typically unaccompanied, based on a poem or other secular text. (The example on the next page shows a typical five-part madrigal.)

The madrigal was introduced to England in the late sixteenth century, most notably by the 1588 publication of *Musica Transalpina* by Nicholas Yonge (1560–1619). Yonge's work was a collection of Italian madrigals with English words. English madrigals evolved a style that was reflective of the Elizabethan age, with a blend of simplistic lyrics and musical word-painting techniques.

The most important English madrigal composers include William Byrd (1543–1623), Thomas Morley (1557–1602), and Thomas Weelkes (1576–1623). In Italy, Lassus and Palestrina were prolific madrigal composers; also notable are the madrigals of Claudio Monteverdi (1567–1643), who bridged the Renaissance and Baroque eras.

Note

The migration of the madrigal to England was also influenced by Italian madrigalist Alfonso Ferrabosco (1543–1588), who held a position in Queen Elizabeth I's court during the 1560s and 1570s.

If women could be fair

William Byrd

A five-part madrigal: "If Women Could Be Fair," by William Byrd.

The Madrigal Tradition

Almost every American high school student is familiar with the tradition of the Madrigal Dinner or Madrigal Feast. These celebrations are typically held during the Christmas season, and involve a simulated Renaissance feast (complete with wassail and fake boar's head), madrigal music performed by the high school choir, and some sort of short play. The choir dresses in Renaissance garb complete with big hats and puffy shirts.

While most madrigal dinners are not strictly authentic, at least in terms of the food served, they do preserve the tradition of the madrigal form. The music sung at these feasts typically ranges from the late medieval period through the Renaissance and into the early Baroque, capturing the full range of the French, Italian, and English madrigal. Several songs are traditional in these settings, including "The Wassail Song" and "The Boar's Head Carol."

If you have the opportunity to attend a madrigal dinner, by all means do so. It's a good opportunity to immerse yourself in madrigal music—and have a merry good time, besides.

Important Composers of the Renaissance

When examining the Renaissance period, three key composers stand out among the rest. These composers—Dufay, Josquin des Préz, and Palestrina—all helped to develop the art of polyphony in various musical forms.

Dufay, Master of All Trades

The first major musical figure of the Renaissance, chronologically, was Guillaume Dufay (1397–1474). Born in Brussels, Dufay was both a music theorist and a very prolific composer.

Dufay composed in almost every available musical form of the time. He wrote sacred music (Masses, motets, hymns, and chants) and secular chansons, of which more than 150 separate pieces survive to this day. His work was copied, distributed, and sung throughout all of Europe; almost all his successors absorbed some elements of his style.

Despite his influence and impressive output, however, Dufay was not really an innovator; his importance is more for his control of the forms in which he worked than for any great innovations to those forms. He was both one of the last composers to use medieval techniques and one of the first to incorporate the expressive melodies and harmonies of the early Renaissance. During the fifteenth century he was universally regarded as the greatest composer of his time.

Josquin des Préz, Master of Polyphony

Following Dufay, and focusing more on the development of polyphonic music, was Josquin des Préz (1450–1521). Like many of his contemporaries, Josquin's music was mostly in the service of the ruling classes; he served at the court of King René of Anjou, for the Duke of Ferrara, as a provost of Notre Dame, and in the papal choir of both Pope Innocent VIII and Pope Alexander VI.

Josquin was one of the first to use repetition or imitation of melodies within a composition. While his most famous Mass, *Missa Pange Lingua,* is based on a stable cantus firmus, his later Masses incorporated fully contrapuntal passages.

Outside of his embrace of polyphony, probably the most important facet of Josquin's music is the melody. He had a supreme melodic gift, and was capable of writing both unadorned and complex melodic lines. He distinguished himself by writing 18 Masses, nearly 100 motets, and more than 70 chansons and other secular works.

Note
Josquin's last name is alternately spelled des Préz, des Prés, and Després—which may be why he is more commonly known by his first name. He was born in either France or the area now known as Belgium. Such are the vagaries of historical details of that time period.

Palestrina, Master of the Mass

Where both Dufay and Josquin wrote in a variety of musical forms, our third Renaissance master concentrated on writing for the Catholic Mass. Giovanni Pierluigi da Palestrina (1525–1594), was the most famous representative of the Roman School of composition in the sixteenth century.

Palestrina, Renaissance master of the Roman School.

Like many composers of his time, Palestrina was closely associated with Catholic Church music throughout his entire career. He spent most of his life in Rome, where he served as maestro di cappella of the papal choir at St. Peter's Basilica, musical director of the Julian Chapel, and official composer to the Sistine Chapel. His first published book of Masses was personally praised by Pope Julius III.

Palestrina's 104 Masses are considered the epitome of the Renaissance Mass style; his most famous work is the renowned *Missa Papae Marcelli,* or the Pope Marcellis Mass. He also wrote a variety of other church music, as well as more than a hundred secular madrigals.

The "Palestrina style" is synonymous with the Renaissance polyphony still taught in music schools today. His compositions feature well-balanced vocal parts and beautiful harmonizations. In fact, his harmony takes precedence over

independent polyphonic lines, which represents the most distinct break to date from the complex polyphony of the Middle Ages—and the perfect bridge to the even more sophisticated music of the coming Baroque era.

Listening List

I'll admit, listening to the recommended pieces for the previous two chapters requires a bit of work; ancient and medieval music are both far enough removed from our current sensibilities as to be almost unlistenable for some. Not so the music of the Renaissance. Here you'll find more palatable use of polyphony, more modern harmonies, and a refinement of the melodic style.

Any overview of Renaissance music has to include work by the three masters, Dufay, Josquin, and Palestrina. You'll also find some fun madrigals and a nice selection of Protestant chorales, so put on your pointy hats and frilly blouses and get ready to enjoy!

Des Prés: Missa Pange Lingua/Missa La Sol Fa Re Mi (The Tallis Scholars)

Dufay: Chansons (Ensemble Unicorn; Michael Posch, conductor)

Dufay: Missa L'homme armé / Supremum est mortalibus (Oxford Camerata; Jeremy Summerly, conductor)

English and Italian Renaissance Madrigals (The Hilliard Ensemble)

Musik der Reformation: Ein feste Burg is unser Gott (Music of the Reformation: A Strong Fortress is Our God; Dresdden Kreuzchor, Fidicinia Capella; Hans Gruss, conductor)

Palestrina: Missa Papae Marcelli/Missa Aeterna (Oxford Camerata; Jeremy Summerly, conductor)

Timeline: The Renaissance Period

1350	Birth of the Renaissance in Florence, Italy
1397	Dufay born
1430	Gutenberg invents the printing press; Joan of Arc burned at the stake
1450	Josquin des Préz born
1465	First printed music
1474	Dufay dies
1485	Henry VII defeats Richard III, ending the War of the Roses
1498	Leonardo da Vinci paints *The Last Supper*
1492	Columbus discovers the New World; Spain pushes Moors out of Europe and expels the Jews
1500	First Caesarian section performed
1502	Josquin des Préz publishes *First Book of Masses*
1503	Leonardo da Vinci paints *The Mona Lisa*
1509	Europe launches African slave trade with the New World

1511   Michelangelo completes painting the ceiling of the Sistine Chapel

1514   Josquin des Préz composes *Missa Pange Lingua*

1515   Copernicus develops heliocentric theory

1517   Martin Luther leads the Protestant Reformation

1519   Magellan launches first round-the-world voyage

1521   Josquin des Préz dies

1525   Palestrina born

1530   Secular tunes introduced into the Mass

1551   Palestrina named director of music at St. Peter's

1553   First modern violin

1562   Palestrina composes *Missa Papae Marcelli*

1567   Monteverdi born

1595   Shakespeare writes *Richard II* and *Romeo and Juliet*

1588   Nicholas Yonge publishes *Musica Transalpina*, introduces the madrigal to England

1594   Palestrina dies

1600   Mass evolves into an unaccompanied contrapuntal style

Ornate Patterns: The Baroque Period

In This Chapter

◆ Meet the masters of Baroque music: Monteverdi, Handel, Vivaldi, and Bach

◆ Find out how the changing religious environment affected the music of the times

◆ Discover the secrets to Baroque composition

◆ Learn about the era's newest musical form, the opera

The music of the Renaissance was good in its own way, but the period that followed really ramped it up a notch. The Baroque period is full of invention and experimentation, with plenty of great melody and harmony along the way.

The Baroque is the first era of truly legendary composers and of music that is familiar to even the masses of today. We're talking music like Pachelbel's *Canon in D*, Handel's *Messiah*, and Vivaldi's *The Four Seasons*. And, even more notable, the Baroque was the era of Johann Sebastian Bach —perhaps the greatest composer in all of music history.

The Baroque era covers the period between the rise of Monteverdi and the deaths of Bach and Handel, from roughly 1600 to 1750. While half a century shorter than the Renaissance and hundreds of years shorter than the medieval period, there was more happening musically than in any previous period—by several orders of magnitude.

God Is in the Details: Welcome to the Baroque

The Baroque period was all about drama and ornamentation. Buildings of the Baroque featured great curving forms with undulating facades; both men and women's fashions favored elaborate patterns and fancy lace trimming. Baroque art—as exemplified by the paintings of Rembrandt and Rubens—was similarly dramatic, using strong contrasts of light and shadow to enhance the sense of movement and tension.

The Baroque in History

The Baroque period began as an artistic movement dictated by the Roman Catholic Church. It all started at the Council of Trent (1545–63), when the church, in response to the Protestant Reformation, launched the Counter-Reformation. Attempting to become more populist (and popular), it demanded that paintings and sculptures speak directly to the masses instead of just to the elite. This led to the more representational and dramatic art that kicked off the start of the Baroque around 1600.

At the same time, awareness of nature and the scientific world was continuously expanding. New and important scientific discoveries were happening on a regular basis. The turn of the seventeenth century saw Galileo invent the telescope and observe the planets of our solar system; just 60 years after that, Newton devised his Theory of Gravitation.

Unfortunately, these early scientists weren't always well received by religious leaders. In particular, the Copernican notion that the Earth wasn't at the center of the universe was seen as heresy by many in the Catholic Church. Galileo suffered much abuse by the church when he published his books, *The Starry Messenger* and *Dialogue on the Two Great World Systems*, which upheld and advanced Copernicus's theories. Galileo's second book was banned by the church, and Galileo himself was called in 1633 to Rome to stand trial before the Inquisition. He was eventually forced to publicly repudiate the Copernican doctrine, sentenced to indefinite imprisonment, and forbidden to publish any new works.

That's right, the Baroque was the period of those tribunals officially called the "Supreme Sacred Congregation of the Universal Inquisition." Initiated by Pope Paul III in 1542 and lasting through the late 1700s, the so-called Roman Inquisition was a system of tribunals staffed by cardinals and other church officials. The goal was to prosecute individuals accused of heretical crimes; the notion that the Sun didn't revolve around the Earth was one such heresy.

Note

The Roman Inquisition of the Baroque era is related to but distinct from the Spanish Inquisition that lasted from 1478 to the mid-1600s.

Note

This sort of church-sponsored terror was not limited to Europe. North America, for example, had the Salem witchcraft trials of 1692. Those trials—which occurred in Essex, Suffolk, and Middlesex counties of colonial Massachusetts—resulted in more than 150 people (both men and women) being accused of practicing witchcraft; 29 were convicted and 19 of them were hanged.

The Inquisition aside, the culture of the Baroque era was slowly and steadily becoming more secular. The growing realization that the Earth was not at the center of the universe led to the Enlightenment of the eighteenth century, an intellectual movement in which ideas concerning man, God, reason, and nature were synthesized into a single worldview. One of the key figures of the Enlightenment was John Locke, a physician and philosopher whose writings influenced later philosophers such as Hume and Kant, not to mention the American revolutionaries who wrote the Declaration of Independence.

Meanwhile, Across the Atlantic ...

Speaking of America, all of this scientific and philosophical advancement coincided with an increasing amount of trade and colonization within and outside of the European continent. In 1606, King James I of England granted a charter to the Virginia Company, a group of entrepreneurs intent on settling the New World discovered by Christopher Columbus 100 years earlier. The following year, 104 settlers from the Virginia Company, led by Captain John Smith landed on Jamestown Island in Virginia. The Jamestown Colony was the first English settlement in the Americas.

Other settlers soon followed, most notably a group subsequently known as the pilgrims, who fled religious persecution in England. A group of 102 pilgrims sailed on the ship *Mayflower* in 1620, landing on Cape Cod in late November of that year. This new colony became the second successful English settlement in America.

The English colonization of America had begun; the population would grow rapidly throughout the rest of the 1600s and into the 1700s. By the end of the Baroque era, the American colonists would grow weary of their perceived second-class status at the hands of their British rulers and foment the seeds of rebellion—but that's a story for the next chapter. (And, besides, we all know how that worked out.)

Baroque Architecture

The Baroque era is easily identified by its architecture. Baroque architects manipulated interior spaces to be more plastic and flowing than ordered Renaissance spaces. Using stucco, an inexpensive and infinitely malleable material, they created free-flowing surfaces and elaborate decorations that would have been too expensive to carve in marble and other fine stonework.

This type of Baroque architecture is dominant in the churches of the day, as well as many secular structures. Recall how the Baroque got started, when the Catholic Church reasserted its primacy among the faithful following the Protestant Reformation. To this end, many great Baroque churches were designed and built after the Counter-Reformation to meet the continuing need to both attract and impress the masses. Giovanni Lorenzo Bernini, one of the great Baroque architects, asserted that churches should "reach out to Catholics in order to reaffirm their faith, to heretics to reunite them with the church, and to agnostics to enlighten them with the true faith."

Outside the church, the aristocracy of the Baroque saw this dramatic style of architecture as a means of both expressing their power and impressing visitors.

For example, French architects developed grand designs of buildings and their surroundings, among which were the king's palaces—including both the Louvre in Paris (the king's official residence until 1674) and the Palace of Versailles. Baroque palaces were typically built around an entrance sequence of courts, anterooms, grand staircases, and reception rooms of increasing magnificence.

The Palace of Versailles—a grand example of Baroque architecture.

(Photograph by Eric Pouhier, used by permission under the Creative Commons Attribution ShareAlike 2.5 license.)

Beginning in the 1720s, Baroque architecture began to be superseded by the Rococo style, especially in building interiors. This was a more decorative style than that of the earlier Baroque, full of ornate and often "fussy" details. In fact, Rococo is more decoration than true style, using multiple curves to elaborate the underlying Baroque constructions.

Baroque Art

Art in the Baroque era was both more realistic and more dramatic than the art of the Renaissance. The details were everywhere; cloth and skin textures were realistically rendered, anatomy was physically precise, and faces reflected individual personalities.

Baroque art often exhibited a sense of movement and energy. Strong contrasts of light and shadow were used to enhance dramatic effects, and many paintings suggested an infinite space, rather than the confined spaces common during the Renaissance. When the subject was sacred, scenes of ecstasies and miraculous apparitions were common.

Famous Baroque artists include Rembrandt, Johannes Vermeer, Peter Paul Rubens, and Anthony van Dyck—and, at the beginning of the period, the Italian cousins Agostino and Ludovico Carracci.

Understanding the Music of the Baroque

Baroque music represented a significant advancement over the music of the Renaissance. Think of the Renaissance as the practice rounds to the Baroque's final forms; the experimentation of the Renaissance took on definite shape during the Baroque era.

Evolving Styles, New Forms

In many ways, the music of the Baroque echoed the extravagant styles of the period's fashions and architecture. Simple melodies evolved into flamboyant airs, full of trills and turns and other ornamentation. Elaborate melodies were layered on top of one another, and the concept of chordal accompaniment gained favor. New musical forms came into prominence, incorporating more and different combinations of instruments—and, in the case of opera, encouraging the interplay of voices and instruments. Harmony and counterpoint ousted simple polyphony, and orchestral color made its first appearance on the musical scene.

Instead of employing all polyphonic voices equally, as was normal during the Renaissance, Baroque composers often concentrated on the "outside" parts—the soprano and bass lines—filling in the middle parts with harmonizing chords. Many composers left the exact composition of these parts to the performers; keyboard players often improvised their own accompaniment.

At the end of the day, Baroque music is lively and melodious yet quite precise in its nature, constructed to reflect the so-called "perfect order" of the universe. The best of the Baroque is almost mathematical in its approach; it's a music that is both logical and tuneful.

> **Note**
>
> Many Baroque compositions, such as Bach's *Inventions* and *Sinfonias*, sound almost like musical exercises—which, in fact, they were. Both Bach and Vivaldi wrote numerous pieces for the education of their students, exercises that were strong enough to stand on their own as performance pieces.

Baroque Instruments

It was during the Baroque period that many of the "modern" orchestral instruments still in use today were first developed. Wind instruments that came to prominence during the Baroque period included the flute, clarinet, oboe, bassoon, trumpet, and French horn. In addition, the entire string family that we know today was developed during the Baroque period—including the violin, viola, cello, and double bass.

The Baroque era also saw the development of the modern keyboard family, most notably the introduction of the pianoforte (predecessor to the modern piano). Early Baroque music tended to favor the harpsichord, a keyboard instrument with internal strings that are plucked when keys on the keyboard are pressed. Unfortunately, this setup allows for little variation in loudness; you can hit a harpsichord's keys as hard as you like, but the volume level remains the same. Not so with the piano, which uses touch-sensitive keys to move tiny hammers that strike its internal strings. For this reason, the piano replaced the harpsichord as the keyboard instrument of choice in the later Baroque.

> **Note**
>
> Some of the finest violins ever made came out of the Baroque, thanks to master craftsman Antonio Stradivari. The Latinized form of his surname, *Stradivarius*, is commonly used to refer to the instruments he built during his lifetime.

The harpsichord—instrument of choice during the early Baroque period.

Music for Money: Baroque-Era Composers

The composers of the Baroque era were even more popular and influential than their counterparts of the Renaissance. Even nonmusicians today know who Bach is, while few if any recognize the names Dufay or Palestrina. And the music of the Baroque, especially from these top composers, remains well-known to this day.

It's interesting the way things worked back then. Instead of being in the service of the church, as was common during the Renaissance, composers of the Baroque were often employed by the wealthy ruling class as part of what was called the patronage system. As such, the patron paid the composer for each work, and usually decided what kind of piece the composer should write. Even the major composers partook of this patronage; Bach spent several years as *Kapellmeister* (music director) to Prince Leopold of Anhalt-Cöthen; Handel wrote various works for the Duke of Chandos, and D. Scarlatti was in the employ of Princess Maria Barbara of Portugal for most of his career.

Just who were these in-demand and well-paid composers? You start with Claudio Monteverdi, who bridged the Renaissance and Baroque eras. (Palestrina, who we discussed in Chapter 3, also served as something of a bridge figure.) But the most influential Baroque composers were those of the later period—notably Johann Sebastian Bach and George Frideric Handel, both of whom created music that was virtuosic in its mastery of harmony and tonality. Other outstanding composers of the Baroque period included the Brit Henry Purcell (1659–1695), Italians Alessandro Scarlatti (1660–1725) and his son Domenico (1685–1757), and fellow Italian Antonio Vivaldi.

Another Baroque composer many nonmusicians recognize is Johann Pachelbel (1653–1706), composer of the famous *Canon in D Major* (1680), which is a must-play at weddings and ubiquitous on popular classical music compilation recordings. You've heard it; it's a basic canon form, with the melody from the first violin repeated four bars later in the second violin, and then four bars after that in the third violin. The following figure shows how it looks on paper.

Canon in D Major

Johann Pachelbel

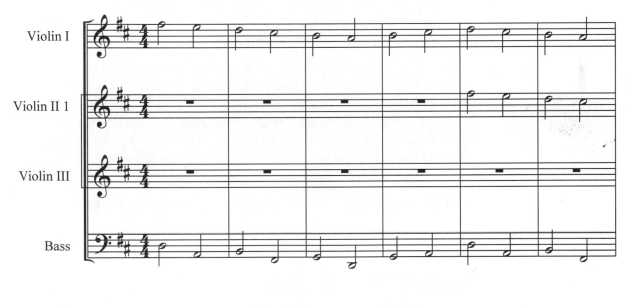

The beginning of Pachelbel's Canon—a soothing repetition known to all.

But for all the great talent of the Baroque, it pays to focus on the "big four" composers of the era: Monteverdi, Handel, Vivaldi, and Bach. We'll look at each of them in more detail.

Bridging the Eras: Monteverdi

Claudio Monteverdi (1567–1643) was an Italian composer who got started during the Renaissance and completed his career during the Baroque. His work successfully bridged the two eras, and both reflected and influenced the transition in musical styles.

Monteverdi was regarded as somewhat of a revolutionary, as he helped to bring about the change in styles that marked the beginning of the Baroque era. He was also a pioneer of sorts, composing some of the earliest operas.

Monteverdi created his first music, motets and madrigals, starting in 1582. He published his first book of madrigals in 1587, and in 1590 found work at the court of Vincenzo I of Gonzaga in Mantua as a vocalist and viol player. He worked for the court of Mantua for 21 years, eventually as court conductor.

Up until age 40 or so, Monteverdi specialized in writing madrigals, composing a total of nine books of madrigal song. The break between the Renaissance and Baroque forms was delineated in his *Fifth Book of Madrigals*, published in 1605, which described two different styles. *Prima practica* followed the polyphonic contrapuntal approach of the sixteenth century; *seconda practica* used the much freer counterpoint and hierarchy of voices common in the seventeenth century, along with a continuo instrumental accompaniment.

Later in his career, Monteverdi composed several notable operas. His first opera, *L'Orfeo* ("Orpheus"), premiered in 1607; he wrote at least 17 more, only three of which survive to this day.

Operas and Oratorios: Handel

George Frideric Handel (1685–1759) was a German-born composer and organist, although he spent most of his life in England. (He became a British citizen in 1727.) Handel, along with Bach, was acknowledged as one of the greatest composers of his age. It is reported that Bach said of Handel, "He is the only person I would wish to see before I die, and the only person I would wish to be, were I not Bach." Beethoven called him "the master of us all." High praise indeed.

Music wasn't Handel's first career choice. Young Handel started out studying law, per his father's wishes, but abandoned law for music on his father's death in 1703. He accepted a position as violinist and harpsichordist at the Hamburg opera house in 1704, and wrote his first two operas the following year, when he was just 19.

Handel contributed to every musical genre of his time, with operas dominating his early career. He spent his later years focusing on large-scale vocal works, such as the English oratorio, which he invented. His most famous composition was the *Messiah* (1741), an oratorio set to texts from the King James Bible; it is today considered the greatest oratorio ever written. The following figure shows the beginning of the oratorio's famous Hallelujah chorus, which is a traditional part of many Christmas and Easter programs.

Hallelujah

From Messiah

George Frideric Handel

The opening notes of the Hallelujah chorus from Handel's Messiah.

Handel wrote more than 20 oratorios, along with nearly 50 operas and hundreds of concerti grossi and orchestral pieces. His other notable works include *Water Music* (1717), the *Coronation Anthems* (1727), Trio Sonatas Op. 2 (1722-1733) and Op. 5 (1739), Concerto Grosso Op. 6 (1739), and *Music for Royal Fireworks* (1749).

In analyzing Handel's work, one finds an efficiency in composition, to the point of him sometimes reusing common themes from one piece to another. (And, say some, "borrowing" themes from other composers.) Aside from his creation of the oratorio, which itself is an evolution of that era's operatic form, he wasn't really an innovator; instead, he was a master of existing musical ideas. And what a master; his themes are expertly developed and dramatically expressed. One need only listen to the *Messiah* to recognize the power of Handel's music. He had a near-perfect sense of style and expression.

Note _____

Amazingly, Handel wrote the *Messiah* in just 18 days!

A Man for Four Seasons: Vivaldi

It's amazing how much musical talent existed in Europe around the turn of the eighteenth century. You had Handel in England, Bach in Germany, and Vivaldi in Italy, all writing at the peak of their powers. What a wonderful time it must have been for music lovers!

Initially a violin teacher and a priest, Antonio Vivaldi (1678–1741) published his first sonatas in 1705; he was 27 years old at the time. Early on, Vivaldi was employed by the Ospedale della Pieta, an orphanage in Venice. He composed for the children there, primarily the young girls that formed the renowned orchestra and choir of the orphanage.

Vivaldi very quickly became known and admired throughout Europe as both a virtuoso violinist and a talented composer, especially for the violin as a solo instrument. Not surprisingly, he is known primarily for his string concertos, especially the four concertos known as *The Four Seasons*.

Vivaldi's compositions displayed an extraordinary variety and invention, and embraced instrumentation unusual for the time. His notable works include Op. 3, *L'estro armonico*, 12 concertos for various instruments (1711); Op. 4, *La stravaganza*, 12 violin concertos (1714); Op. 10, 6 flute concertos (1728); *Gloria* in D; and Op. 8, *Il cimento dell'armonia e dell'inventione*, 12 violin concertos—the first four (E, G minor, F, and F minor) known as *The Four Seasons* (1725).

In contrast with the seriousness of Handel, Vivaldi's music was playful and exuberant. This lightness in composition made Vivaldi's work particularly accessible to the wide public, not just to an intellectual minority—which explains why his music remains popular to this day.

The Greatest Composer of All Time: J. S. Bach

When it comes to Baroque-era composers, I've saved the best till last. The music of the late Baroque era is best represented by the numerous works of Johann Sebastian Bach (1685–1750). Bach was a true musical genius; he produced an astounding variety of chamber and orchestral works, as well as a large number of organ and keyboard works. His choral works include a variety of sacred and secular cantatas, motets and other large choral pieces, and chorales and sacred songs. The only musical form in which he didn't work was opera.

J. S. Bach, Baroque master.

What makes Bach unique is his absolute mastery of the strict compositional techniques of his day. His innate talent enabled him to combine expressive melodies with the rigorous intricacy of counterpoint and the fugal form—most notably in his suites for solo violin and solo cello, as well as in much of his harpsichord music.

The result is a huge body of work, all of it of exceptional quality. Bach was not only one of the top musicians of his day, but also one of the most influential composers of all time—if not arguably the greatest.

Note _____

As famous as he is, J. S. isn't the only Bach in music history. The Bach family included more than 50 known musicians and several other notable composers, including Sebastian's sons Carl Philipp Emanuel (C. P. E.), Wilhelm Friedemann, and Johann Christian.

Born to Make Music: The Life and Times of J. S. Bach

Johann Sebastian Bach was born in Eisenach, Germany, into a family of notable musicians. He first gained fame as a keyboard virtuoso; believe it or not, Bach's accomplishments as a composer were not fully recognized until almost 200 years after his death, when later composer Felix Mendelssohn led a Bach revival. (Handel was the acknowledged master composer to audiences of the Baroque.)

Young Sebastian (as he was called; they went by their middle names back then) was the youngest of eight children born to musical parents. As a child he mastered both the organ and the violin, and was said to be an excellent singer. His parents died when Sebastian was 10; the child was taken in by his older brother, Johann Christoph, who continued his musical training.

In 1703, the 18-year-old J. S. Bach took the position of organist at the St. Boniface Church in Arnstadt. Similar posts at other churches followed, and in 1708 Bach and his wife moved 40 miles north to Weimar, where he became "court organist" and later *Konzertmeister* (concertmaster) to Duke Wilheim. Bach stayed there until 1717, when he was named Kapellmeister to Prince Leopold of Anhalt-Cöthen.

Serving as head musician to the ruling elite provided ample opportunity for Bach to hone his composing skills; the position dictated a constant flow of new music. During these years, Bach composed a huge volume of instrumental music, including pieces for solo keyboard, dance suites, sonatas for various instruments, and concertos for solo instruments with orchestra. Emblematic of these compositions were the six concertos he composed for the Duke of Brandenburg in 1721—the now-famous Brandenburg Concertos. It's fascinating to note that these were essentially works for hire, pieces composed as part of his "day job" as Kapellmeister to fill the unending need for fresh music.

In 1723, after the death of his first wife and his marriage to his second, Bach took the position of organist and *Kantor* (teacher) at St. Thomas Church in Leipzig. This led to a switch to more religious compositions, again in service to his employer. St. Thomas was a Lutheran church and Bach a devout Lutheran, so his religious work was Protestant in nature—although a few Masses did slip out, as well as the famous *St. Matthew Passion*.

Bach's eyesight began to fail him in 1749, which led him to undergo corrective surgery by a traveling English oculist named John Taylor. The results, unfortunately, were tragic; following the surgery, Bach was completely blind. He continued to compose, however, dictating his work to a pupil. He died the following year, aged 65—a good long life in that era.

In summary, Bach's musical career can best be divided into three main creative periods:

◆ Early (1708–1717), when he composed most of his organ works

◆ Middle (1717–1723), when he composed most of his instrumental works

◆ Late (1723–1750), when he composed most of his sacred choral music

Note

To put things in perspective, the year Bach died was 2 years before Ben Franklin discovered electricity by flying a kite, 4 years before the French and Indian War, and 15 years before the Boston Massacre helped to launch the American Revolution. It's quite likely that future revolutionaries such as Franklin, Adams, and Jefferson listened to performances of Bach's works in drawing rooms and concert halls throughout the American colonies.

Bach's Musical Legacy

Bach's music can best be described as a perfect combination of intellectual logic, technical precision, and artistic splendor. His melodies have a unique beauty that is then expanded upon with almost mathematical precision. He was a master of counterpoint and the development of melodic motifs. The technical complexity of his work probably grew out of his own improvisational mastery of keyboard and string instruments; it's not unlikely that some of his ornate elaborations were simply transcriptions of what he may have improvised during performances. In any case, his work is musically complex yet uniquely accessible; he never sacrificed technique for melody.

Note

The mathematical aspect of Bach's music is explored in the Pulitzer Prize-winning book *Gödel, Escher, Bach: An Eternal Golden Braid* (Douglas Hofstadter, Basic Books, 1979). I recommend this wonderful book for all scientifically minded music lovers.

A good example of Bach's style, and a good starting piece for anyone interested in Bach, is the *Air* from his Orchestral Suite No. 3 in D Major. As you can see in the following figure, the melody is easily recognizable; it starts with a simple two-measure statement but is then elaborated on in the subsequent measures. It's mathematically precise yet easily melodic.

Note

The most popular version of the *Air* is called *Air on the G String*, was arranged by August Wilhelmj in the late 19th century for solo violin and piano. Wilhelmj transposed the piece from its original D major down to C major, which enabled him to play the entire piece on a single string (the G string) of his violin.

Air
From Orchestral Suite No. 3

J.S. Bach

The initial phrase from Bach's Air—*melodic in a methodical type of way.*

Also representative is Bach's *Minuet in G Major*, shown next. You may remember this piece as the tune of "A Lover's Concerto," a 1965 pop hit by the Toys. The melody has a very logical, mathematical construction, repeating (with logical alterations) the basic motif throughout.

Minuet in G Major

J.S. Bach

Another perfectly logical Bach melody, from Minuet in G Major.

Bach produced solo works for harpsichord and organ, chamber music for small ensembles, and more elaborate works for larger orchestras. Personally, I find Bach's keyboard works most compelling, especially those anthologies that functioned almost as musical textbooks on how to build and expand upon a theme. For example, the two books of *The Well-Tempered Clavier* methodically present a pairing of prelude and fugue in each of the 24 major and minor keys—48 related pieces in all. Similar in approach are the *Goldberg Variations*, essentially an aria with 30 variations.

Bach wrote for a variety of solo instruments—violin, cello, flute, lute, organ, you name it. In addition, he composed solo sonatas, which paired a solo instrument with a larger ensemble. He was also a master of the early orchestral form, in both suites and concertos.

Note

Bach's works are cataloged via a unique numbering system, compiled by historian Wolfgang Schmieder in 1950. In this system, each work is assigned a BMV (for Bach-Werke-Verzeichnis, or Bach Works Catalogue) number. All pieces are organized thematically: BMV 1-224 are cantatas; BMV 225-240 are large-scale choral works; BMV 250-524 are chorales and sacred songs; BMV 525-748 are organ works; BMV 772-994 are other keyboard works; BMV 995-1000 consist of lute music; BMV 1001-1040 are chamber music; BMV 1041-1071 are orchestral music; and BMV 1072-1112 are canons and fugues.

In terms of vocal music, Bach wrote a number of chorales during his career, many containing only a melody line and a figured bass part to be played on an organ or other keyboard instrument. His choral works included a variety of sacred and secular cantatas (one for each Sunday and holiday of the church year), motets and other large choral pieces (including *St. Matthew Passion* and the *Christmas Oratorio*), and sacred songs.

Bach's most notable works, out of a large and impressive catalog, include *Toccata and Fugue in D Minor* (1707); the *Brandenburg Concertos* (1721); *Die Wohltemperierte Klavier* (*The Well-Tempered Clavier*; Book I: 1722, Book II: 1744); *Orchestral Suite No. 3 in D Major* (1723); *St. John Passion* (1723); *St. Matthew Passion* (1727); *Concerto in D Minor for Two Violins* (1731); Cantata No. 140 (*Wachet auf*; 1731); *Goldberg Variations* (1741); *Die Kunst der Fuge* (*The Art of Fugue*; 1745); and *Mass in B Minor* (1749).

Drama + Music = Opera

The general populace today tends to think of music from the Baroque (and later eras) as a kind of highbrow music, not something the average Joe listens to. But at the time, this wasn't music for highbrows; it was the popular music of the day.

As you've learned, wealthy patrons commissioned much of the music of the Baroque. The musical forms favored by these patrons included dances, suites, and preludes. While writing within these genres could be creatively limiting, the best of the Baroque composers were able to thoroughly explore, and in some cases expand, these and other Baroque-era forms.

Europe in the seventeenth century was host to a great rise in dramatic theater. In England this dramatic revival was led by the works of William Shakespeare and Christopher Marlowe; in France, by Pierre Corneille and Jean Racine. In Italy, however, this movement was not in the spoken word, but rather in a new form that combined drama with music: *opera*.

Opera (short for *opera in musica*) is a drama set to music. In practice, opera consists of vocals with instrumental accompaniment, with the singers typically in costume in an elaborate theatrical production; while musical passages may be separated by spoken dialogue, the music is an integral part of the opera. (This is in contrast to the later musical theater, where the plot can often exist separate from the music.)

Early Operas

The operatic form originated in Florence, Italy, in the Renaissance, near the end of the sixteenth century; it grew out of attempts to recreate the affect of ancient Greek and Roman dramas. The opera's immediate predecessors were the madrigal, madrigal cycle (a type of madrigal comedy), masque, and intermedio.

The earliest known opera was *Daphne*, written in 1597 by Jacopo Peri (1561–1633). Other notable early operas include Peri's *Euridice* (1600); Stefano Landi's (1586–1639) *Sant'Alessio* (1631), which formalized the various sections of the opera; and Monteverdi's *L'Orfeo* (1607), one of the first works to combine choruses, dances, madrigals, and duets.

Many of these formative works were only half-sung, with vocal passages separated by orchestral interludes. Peri, along with Giulio Caccini (1545–1618) and Emilio de' Cavalieri (1550–1602), pioneered a new style of solo singing that

Note

These early operas were referred to as *drama per musica* (drama through music), and their plots were typically based on myth, much like their inspiration, the classic dramas of ancient Greece and Rome. Later operas most often concerned themselves with historical figures.

could be used for dramatic purposes, a blend of spoken recitation and singing. Half-sung passages, called *recitatives*, alternated with orchestral interludes and choruses that commented on the dramatic events. Improvisation was discouraged; all ornamentation and other expressive details were carefully written out, and the continuo accompaniment was carefully paced to match the rhythms of the singer's words. Also contributing to the development of the recitative style was A. Scarlatti, who composed 115 operas and introduced instrumental accompaniment for recitative sections.

It was Monteverdi who most contributed to the development to the opera form in the early seventeenth century. Monteverdi was responsible for establishing the fully sung *aria* (in place of the earlier recitative); for utilizing a larger and richer-sounding orchestra; and for developing the *bel canto* style. He was also the first to reflect the emotions of the libretto in his music. Monteverdi's work became a model for the operatic composers who followed and helped to bring opera to the masses, first in Venice and then throughout Europe.

> **Note**
>
> In contrast to the recitative, the aria was more expressive and melodious, with the music more important than the words. The aria was used prominently in the later operas of Monteverdi, especially *Il ritorno d'Ulisse in patria* ("The Return of Ulysses to His Country"; 1640) and *L'incoronazione di Poppea* ("The Coronation of Poppea"; 1642). Over time, the aria became a showcase for virtuoso singing.

Late-Baroque Operas

While opera was born in Venice and Rome, it quickly spread throughout all of Europe. By 1700, Vienna, Paris, Hamburg, and London were all major operatic centers.

In France, Jean-Baptiste Lully (1632–1687) developed the *tragédie lyrique* style, with its greater emphasis on the recitative, its prominent roles for choir and orchestra (and, often, dancers), and its use of shorter *airs* in place of the more elaborate Italian *arias*. Heinrich Schütz (1585–1672) and Reinhard Keiser (1674–1739) established the operatic form in Germany, and in London, Handel was composing a series of powerful operas, including *Radamisto*, *Orlando*, *Ariodante*, *Alcina*, *Rinaldo*, and *Giulio Cesare* ("Julius Caesar").

By the dawn of the eighteenth century, opera had become the most widely cultivated musical form, with most major composers contributing to the repertory. The late Baroque saw the rise of several different operatic styles, including *opera seria* (serious opera), *opera buffa* (comic opera), and the French *opera ballet*, which merged opera with narrative dance.

Sacred and Secular: Baroque Vocal Works

In addition to the new form of opera, other genres of vocal music developed during the Baroque era. Most of these vocal forms were sacred in nature.

Motet and Grand Motet

The motet continued to be an integral part of the Roman Catholic tradition throughout the Baroque era. In France, however, the motet evolved into the *grand motet*, which contrasted solo voices (accompanied by continuo instruments, such as bass viol or harpsichord) with a larger chorus. In Germany, the grand motet was characterized by *antiphonal* exchanges between choirs and instruments.

The grand motet is a motet for large ensembles of voices and instruments, contrasting solo voices with the larger chorus. The grand motet was originally performed in the liturgies of the court Chapel of Louis XIV, and later performed as concert pieces throughout eighteenth-century France and Germany.

Note

Antiphony involves the alternative singing of two different parts in response to one another.

Anthem and Chorale

The English church separated from Rome in 1534, giving rise to the Anglican Church of England. The main feature of the Anglican choral service became the *anthem*, in which verses for solo voices (with organ accompaniment) alternated with verses sung by the full choir. In contrast to the Roman Catholic Mass, anthems were sung in English, not Latin.

In essence, the anthem is the Anglican Church's version of the Latin motet. In most instances the choir is accompanied by organ; many anthems include passages for vocal soloists, either individually or in combination. Major composers of this form include Henry Purcell and John Blow (1649–1708).

In the Lutheran church, reformists did away with grand choir works, developing instead the *chorale*, a hymn sung in German (rather than Latin) by the congregation. You remember the chorale from Chapter 3; it's essentially a hymn with an easy-to-remember tune. Not unexpectedly, one of the most prolific composers for the chorale was J. S. Bach, himself a Lutheran. Bach composed some 30 chorales and reharmonized 400 others; he also used several chorale melodies in his *St. John Passion* and *St. Matthew Passion*.

Oratorio

An *oratorio* is a dramatic musical setting of a sacred libretto, for solo singers, choir, and orchestra. An oratorio is like a religious opera, but without the scenery or costumes. Vocal soloists are accompanied by orchestra or instrumental ensemble; singing can be in either recitative or aria style.

Note _____
Some secular works, such as Handel's *Semele*, are also considered oratorios—or, in some cases, *opera-oratorios*. Certain biblical oratorios, such as Schütz's *The Christmas History*, are called *historia*.

Note _____
While he was Kantor in Leipzig, Bach provided a new cantata every single Sunday—close to 300 in all!

The oratorio originated in plays given in the Oratory of Saint Philip Neri in sixteenth-century Rome. Emilio de' Cavalieri's (1550–1602) *La rappresentazione di anima e di corpo* ("The Representation of Soul and Body"), first performed in 1600 is generally recognized as the first oratorio. Later oratorios were written by A. Scarlatti, Schütz, Handel, and Bach, as well as Georg Philipp Telemann (1681–1767), Giacomo Carissimi (1605–1674), and numerous composers of later periods.

Cantata

The term *cantata* has described different musical forms over the centuries. The earliest form, as practiced during the Baroque period, refers to a dramatic madrigal sung by a solo vocalist or vocalists, accompanied by lute or basso continuo. There were two variations of this cantata form, the secular *cantata da camera* ("chamber cantata") and non-secular *cantata da chiesa* ("church cantata").

A. Scarlatti was one of the chief proponents of the cantata form, writing more than 600 pieces, primarily for solo voice. Scarlatti bridged recitatives and arias with passages sung midway between the two styles, called *arioso*. Also notable are the cantatas of Handel, Schütz, Telemann, and Bach.

During the eighteenth century the cantata became longer and more complex, typically containing recitatives and arias—much like a short, unstaged opera. This type of cantata typically was written for soloist with organ or orchestral accompaniment. Representative cantatas of this period include Bach's *Coffee Cantata* and *Peasant Cantata*.

Soloists to the Front: Baroque Instrumental Works

Instrumental music also became more prominent during the seventeenth century. Composers began to write music for a specific instrument, rather than music that could be sung or played by any combination of voices or instruments, as had been the case in previous eras.

Ricercare

One of the earliest Baroque instrumental forms was the *ricercare*, which was first developed as a literal transcription of an existing vocal work for keyboard or other instruments. By the mid-Baroque period the ricercare had evolved into an independent instrumental form with newly composed music, primarily contrapuntal in nature. The mature ricercare was a single-movement form, with no clear-cut division of sections.

There are two types of ricercare: homophonic (with a single melody line) and contrapuntal (with two or more contrasting melody lines). The last style is more common, typically with elaborate fugal or canonic stylings, as witnessed in Bach's *Das musikalische Opfer*.

Sonata

Even more notable was the development of a competing type of instrumental piece, composed of contrasting sections, called the *sonata*. During the early Baroque era, the sonata took the form of a piece for two melody instruments and continuo—typically two violins with cello or harpsichord—called the *trio sonata*. By the late Baroque, this had evolved into the *solo sonata*, for solo instrument and continuo. The Baroque-era sonata was typically in four movements (slow-fast-slow-fast), with the third and fourth movements based on popular dances, such as the sarabande and gigue.

During the Baroque period the violin was the most popular sonata instrument, although sonatas were written for all variety of instruments, including the oboe, flute, and cello—as well as for solo keyboard. D. Scarlatti, for example, wrote more than 500 sonatas for harpsichord, all in single-movement form.

Note _____
Before 1600 the church had been the center of music, with vocal music dominating; after 1600, violin became the main instrument, and the influence of church music began to wane.

Note _____
Baroque-era sonatas designed for performance in secular venues are called *sonata da camera* or chamber sonata. Sonatas from the same era designed for performance in church are called *sonata da chiesa* or church sonata. The *sonatina* ("little sonata") is a short sonata, typically lighter and easier to perform than a regular sonata.

Suite

Contrast was important in the Baroque era, which led to the development of longer instrumental forms that incorporated multiple contrasting sections. Most notable was the *suite*, which was constructed from individual dance movements, often in the same key. In the early Baroque the suite consisted of four core movements (allemande, courante, sarabande, and gigue); by the late Baroque, composers had gained the freedom to supplement these four movements with additional dances.

Examples of Baroque-era suites include Handel's *Water Music* and *Music for the Royal Fireworks* and Bach's six cello and four orchestral suites. Also notable are the suites by Jean-Philippe Rameau (1683–1764).

Concerto

During the late Baroque period, orchestral music gained popular status in the public concerts that proliferated in many European cities. The late-Baroque orchestra typically included strings, woodwinds (flute, recorder, oboe, bassoon), trumpets and other horns, and timpani.

The focus now was on solo virtuosity, and the early eighteenth century saw the rise of the *concerto* form. As developed by Vivaldi, Handel, Bach, and their counterparts, the concerto focused on one or more solo instruments supported by the larger orchestra. Vivaldi alone wrote close to 350 concertos, mainly for violin, but also for flute, oboe, and other instruments.

There were many different types of concertos during the Baroque era. A concerto designed for performance in a secular venue was called *concerto da camera*, or chamber concerto. A concerto designed for performance in church was called *concerto da chiesa*, or church concerto. A concerto with a small group of soloists (called a *concertino*), in addition to the traditional orchestra or string ensemble, was called *concerto grosso*, or great concerto.

Improvisation in the Baroque _____

In addition to strictly composed instrumental works, the Baroque era also saw various types of improvisatory pieces, such as the *prelude, toccata,* and *fantasia.* These works enabled musicians of the day to display their virtuosic keyboard skills.

Interestingly, many famous composers were also noted instrumentalists; Bach, for example, was a highly accomplished keyboardist, and Vivaldi was a virtuoso violinist. In fact, it's likely that this improvisational background played an important role in Baroque-era compositions. For example, much of the era's instrumental music featured ample room for improvisation by the accompanist, who embellished the basic harmony with all manner of fancy finger work; even when the accompaniment was written out (as Bach tended to do in elaborate detail), it often had an improvisational feel about it.

Even some of the era's solo music felt improvisational. For example, Bach's well-known *Toccata and Fugue in D Minor* starts with an improvisatory toccata section, followed by an independent fugue movement. The work is dazzling in its complexity; it's hard to imagine anyone other than a brilliant improviser concocting its dense runs and cascading passages. In that aspect, the music of the Baroque is somewhat like jazz music in the second half of the twentieth century, where improvisation informs the written composition.

Listening List

Now that we're in the Baroque era, where the music is a tad more familiar to most casual listeners, our listening list is getting longer. Heck, I could do a full page of recommended Bach recordings alone; there was just a ton of memorable music written during this period.

Anyway, I've included a half-dozen essential Bach works, the expected Handel pieces, necessary works by Monteverdi, Scarlatti, and Vivaldi, and the requisite recording of Pachelbel's *Canon in D*. All in all, enough great listening to keep your ears busy for a week or two—and to provide pleasure for a lifetime.

Bach: The Art of the Fugue (Emerson String Quartet)

Bach: The Complete Brandenburg Concertos (Boston Baroque; Martin Pearlman, director)

Bach: Complete Sonatas and Partitas for Solo Violin (Arthur Grumiaux)

Bach: The Goldberg Variations (Glenn Gould)

Bach: Mass in B Minor (New Philharmonia Orchestra; Otto Klemperer, conductor)

Bach: Matthaus-Passion (St. Matthew Passion; Collegium Vocale Orchestra; Phillippe Herreweghe, conductor)

Bach: Violin Concertos/Double Concerto/Air on the G String (Capella Istropolitana; Oliver von Dohnanyi, conductor)

Handel: The Messiah (London Philharmonic Orchestra; London Philharmonic Choir; John Alldis, conductor)

Handel: Orlando (Les Arts Florissants; William Christie, conductor)

Handel: Music for the Royal Fireworks/Water Music (Academy of St. Martin-in-the-Fields; Neville Marriner, conductor)

Monteverdi: L'Orfeo (Le Concert d'Astree; Emmanuelle Haïm, conductor)

Monteverdi: Madrigals (The Consort of Musicke; Anthony Rooley, conductor)

Pachelbel Canon and Other Baroque Hits (Baroque Chamber Orchestra, other artists)

Scarlatti: Sonatas for Harpsichord (Ewald Demeyere)

Vivaldi: The Four Seasons (Boston Symphony Orchestra; Seiji Ozawa, conductor)

Timeline: The Baroque Period

1600	Peri writes *Euridice* opera
1605	Monteverdi publishes *Fifth Book of Madrigals;* Guy Fawkes leads the Gunpowder Plot in England
1607	Monteverdi writes *L'Orfeo* opera; Jamestown Colony founded
1609	Galileo invents telescope
1618	Beginning of Thirty Years War
1620	Pilgrims arrive in America on the *Mayflower*
1632	Galileo publishes *Dialogue on the Two Great World Systems*
1642	Rembrandt paints *The Night Watch;* English Civil War begins
1643	Monteverdi dies
1648	Aria and recitative become two distinct parts of opera
1652	The minuet comes into fashion at the French court; first Viennese opera house opens
1666	Isaac Newton develops Theory of Gravitation; Great Fire of London
1675	Vivaldi born
1677	King Louis XIV of France moves to the Palace of Versailles
1680	Stradivari makes his first instrument (a cello)
1685	Bach and Handel born
1692	Salem witchcraft trials
1693	Scarlatti writes *Teodora* opera

1703	Bach becomes organist at St. Boniface Church
1704	Handel writes *St. John Passion*
1708	Bach moves to Weimar
1709	Invention of the pianoforte
1717	Handel's *Water Music* first performed; Bach moves to Anhalt-Cöthen
1720	Beginning of Rococo style
1721	Bach writes *The Brandenburg Concertos*
1722	Bach publishes the first book of *The Well-Tempered Clavier*
1723	Bach moves to Leipzig
1725	Catherine I becomes Empress of Russia
1727	Bach writes *St. Matthew Passion*
1732	London's Covent Garden Opera House opens; Haydn born
1733	Benjamin Franklin publishes first *Poor Richard's Almanack*
1741	Handel writes *The Messiah*
1743	Benjamin Franklin invents the Franklin stove
1749	Bach finishes *Mass in B Minor*
1750	Bach dies

Chapter 5

A Lyrical Revolution: The Classical Period

In This Chapter

◆ Understanding the societal revolutions behind the Classical period's musical revolution

◆ Mastering the music of the Classical period—and understanding how it's different from the Baroque

◆ Introducing the three great masters of the Classical period—Haydn, Mozart, and Beethoven

◆ Learning the dominant musical form of the Classical period: the symphony

The general populace tends to refer to all serious music prior to the dawn of the twentieth century generically as "classical" music, whether that music be from the Renaissance, Baroque, or other eras. It might surprise the uneducated masses, then, to learn that there actually was a distinct Classical period that ran from 1750 (the death of Bach) to about 1820.

The Classical period was host to some of the most celebrated composers of all time, including Haydn, Mozart, and Beethoven, who created some of the most well-known musical works in history. It was also the era in which the orchestral symphony rose to prominence—and other musical forms reached their mature states.

Revolutionary Times: Living in the Classical Era

As you've seen throughout this book, each new period in Western music is marked by a revolt against the conventions of the previous period. This was especially so for the Classical period, where younger musicians rebelled against the heavy ornamentation and perceived restrictions of Baroque-era counter-point, as well as the emotionally constrained constructions of Bach and Handel.

The musical revolution of the Classical period mirrored the cultural and political revolutions taking place in the last half of the eighteenth century. This period was host to the American Revolution, the French Revolution, and the Napoleonic Wars; writers such as Voltaire, Rousseau, and Paine challenged conventional political thought; and the Enlightenment helped to diminish the dominance of the church on Western society.

Enlightenment and Revolution in Europe

There was an enormous amount of societal change in the second half of the eighteenth century, some of it quite literally revolutionary. The Europe of the early 1800s barely resembled the Europe of the early 1700s; countries and cultures alike were turned upside down.

To begin with, the eighteenth century was host to the European Enlightenment, which, as you recall from Chapter 4, was an intellectual movement that advocated reason as the primary basis of authority. These ideas led to a decrease in the power of the church and other nobility, an increase in religious tolerance, greater rights for the common people, a consolidation of governments, and the creation of new nations (not least of which was the United States of America).

These changes didn't always come easily. The eighteenth century was a time of war and revolution, as numerous monarchies fell to populist movements; the English monarchy ceded power to the Parliament, while the French Revolution (1789–1799) changed that country from a monarchy to a people's republic. In country after country, governmental power shifted from the hands of the elite to a civil bureaucracy, and the working class (serfs, peasants, and merchants alike) saw the expansion of their civil and economic liberties.

Many of these revolutions were violent, but the violence in the Classical era wasn't limited to wars of liberation. During the second half of the eighteenth century, the various European nations were almost constantly at war with each other. This period saw the Seven Years War (1755–1763) between England, Prussia, and Portugal on one hand and France, Austria, Russia, and Spain on the other; the French Revolutionary Wars (1792–1802), between France and a variety of other countries, including England, Austria, Russia, Spain, and the Ottoman Empire; the Napoleonic Wars (1803–1815), between Napoleon's France and a similar cast of adversaries; and, a continent away, the American Revolutionary War (1775–1783), between England and its American colonies.

Amidst this turmoil, yet another revolution was going on, this one bloodless. The Industrial Revolution saw the European economy change from agricultural to industrial, which permanently altered the face of both industry and society. This revolution was accompanied by profound social changes, not least of which was the move from a primarily rural populace to a predominantly urban one. One side effect of this societal change was the rise of the great European cities—which in turn helped to concentrate and incubate the era's musical talent.

American Independence and Expansion

Of all the revolutions of the eighteenth century, the most important one was undoubtedly the American Revolution. When the American colonies declared their independence from England in 1776, a new European nation was established on the North American continent. The United States of America was the first nation built from scratch on Enlightenment ideals, secular values, and the notions of individual liberty and equality.

The seeds of the American Revolution were planted in 1763, when the military threat to the English colonies from France ended. (Prior to this, England and France were embroiled in the Seven Years War—known in North America as the French and Indian War.) At that point, Britain thought that the colonies should shoulder some of the costs of defending themselves, and imposed a series of taxes (including the famed tea and stamp taxes) that were wildly unpopular among the colonists. At the same time, the middle and upper classes were embracing the republican ideals of the enlightenment and questioning their lack of representation in the British Parliament. These factors, combined with the increasingly heavy-handed British rule, led the colonists to rally around the cry for independence from the mother country.

Protests broke out across the colonies, but particularly in New England. This led to an increased presence of British troops; numerous skirmishes ensued, including the so-called Boston Massacre of 1770, when five Boston citizens died at the hands of British soldiers. Formal hostilities commenced in 1775, with the Continental army led by General George Washington. The colonies officially declared their break with England in 1776, with the famed Declaration of Independence. The Revolutionary War continued through 1783, when the colonists received their independence via the Treaty of Paris, and the United States of America came into being.

From there, things just kept on happening. America quickly grew beyond the first 13 colonies, to the Mississippi and beyond. The Louisiana Purchase from France expanded the borders of the country to the Pacific Ocean, and many Americans thought it was their manifest destiny to occupy all the lands between here and there. People were on the move.

As all this was happening, serious European music began to make its way across the pond. The first American performance of Handel's *Messiah* took place at Trinity Church in New York, in 1770, the same year as the Boston Massacre; performances of classical oratorios and opera were popular in both New York and Boston in the early 1800s.

While Americans obviously had a keen appreciation of the European music of the time, no serious American classical music tradition ensued. Perhaps Americans were too busy revolting and pioneering to create music of the European school; perhaps there was simply too much distance between continents for the roots of the culture to effectively spread. In any case, there were no notable composers of serious music in the United States until the dawn of the twentieth century. (There was, however, an important tradition of American folk music—which we'll cover in Chapter 8.)

Note _____

I find it fascinating that when Mozart was composing his three great symphonies in 1788 (E-flat, G Minor, and "Jupiter"), America was busy ratifying its Constitution, 11 ships from Botany Bay had just landed in Australia, and C. P. E. Bach passed away in Hamburg. And here's an even better one: while Beethoven was composing his "Eroica" Symphony No. 3 in 1804, Aaron Burr and Alexander Hamilton had their famous duel, American president Thomas Jefferson made the Louisiana Purchase, Lewis and Clark embarked on their great exploratory expedition, and, back across the ocean, Napoleon Bonaparte was crowned Emperor of France. It was, even then, a small and interestingly interconnected world.

Neoclassicism in Arts and Architecture

The Classical period got its name from the European style of arts and architecture known as neoclassicism. This style reflected a desire to return to the perceived purity of classic Greek and Roman art and philosophy, as filtered through a more modern sensibility.

Compared to the previous Baroque style, the neoclassical style was cleaner and clearer, with brighter contrasts and colors, favoring simplicity over Rococo complexity. This structural clarity was evident in the architecture of the era, which stripped excess ornament from the older Baroque forms to reveal their basic geometric power. The result, when applied to architecture, grafted classic Greek elements onto familiar European forms; many new American government buildings of the era featured the arches and columns of this style.

Note _____

The era of neoclassic architecture in America is sometimes referred to as the Greek Revival.

In the arts, neoclassicism dictated simple compositions, especially compared to the visually busy paintings of the Baroque. Neoclassic paintings, for example, tended to include only a few figures in stoic poses derived from ancient Greek statues; themes were inspired by classic Greek literature. In fact, many neoclassic paintings look like sculpture, with their static poses and anatomically correct renderings. It was all about heroic themes and poses.

This trend towards simple lines and heroic themes was reflected in the music of the period. While Classical music didn't revert all the way back to Greek modes and monophonic forms, it did simplify the complexity of the Baroque.

The Speed of Change

It's interesting how each successive musical era gets shorter yet includes more rapid musical development. The ancient era ran for almost 5,000 years; the Middle Ages spanned 1,000 years; the Renaissance lasted for about 250 years; the Baroque era ran 150 years; and the Classical period lasted for just 70 years. What one sees is that the speed of musical development increases significantly over time; Classical composers accomplished more in 70 years than Baroque composers did in 150.

This increasing rate of musical development is due in part to the increased travel and communication between cultural centers in more recent eras. The more musicians could talk and listen to each other, the more they fed off each other's ideas. In ancient times, there was no communication because there was no travel; in the Classical period, in contrast, travel between European cities was easily accomplished via horse and carriage or (for coastal cities) by ship.

Classical period musicians also benefited from a larger, better-educated population centered in a handful of big cities. The Viennese School is a prime example of this; with so many musicians working so closely together, Vienna served as a kind of cultural incubator to new ideas. It's the same as how jazz musicians in New York City fed off each other in the 1940s and 1950s, or how the Motown sound percolated from a concentration of talented soul musicians in 1960s Detroit. Talented musicians working closely together make each other better, and help to advance the art form.

A Quieter Revolution: Music of the Classical Period

Equally significant to the populist revolutions in Europe and America was the musical revolution of the Classical period. By the mid-1700s, the patronage system of the Baroque era had died out and was replaced by public concerts; this offered composers a newfound freedom of choice in terms of compositional inspiration and form. Polyphony gave way to pleasing harmony, counterpoint gave way to straightforward melody, and ornamentation gave way to simplicity—and emotional detachment gave way to a more spontaneous and emotional musical expression.

Lyricism Abundant: The Classical Style

This new musical expression took different form in different countries during the early Classical period. In France, the new style was called *gallant* (courtly), and bridged the Baroque and the Classical eras by blending a gracefully ornamented melody with chordal accompaniment. In Germany the new style was known as *Empfindsamer Stil* (sensitive style), and resulted in longer compositions and the development of large orchestral forms, such as the concerto, sonata, and symphony. Italians did not have a name for their new style, although they were also important contributors to the development of the symphony and other new genres.

The later Classical period saw the development of a more definitive lyrical style, and a focus on structural clarity rather than textural intricacy. Composers began to exploit the web of harmonic relationships among separate tones and chords within a key, and among several keys. The dominant approach was that of obbligato harmony rather than structured polyphony, with each voice playing an essential role in the texture and harmony of the music; graceful melodies with a light accompaniment replaced the heavy counterpoint of the Baroque period.

 Note

To distinguish music of the Classical period from generic "classical" music, I'm capitalizing the word "Classical" throughout this book. That may or may not be grammatically correct, but it helps to keep things clear.

Exploiting the Talent Pool

The population shift concurrent with the Industrial Revolution served to dramatically increase the population of major urban centers. This had the interesting effect of increasing the number and quality of musicians in Europe's largest cities—which then enabled Classical composers to take advantage of this higher level of musicianship.

Think about it. In the Baroque era, when the patronage system was in effect, a composer was limited to having the local musicians in his town or church perform his works; this was typically not a large pool of talent. This forced the composer to "dumb down" his music for the locals to play, resulting in less-demanding individual parts and simpler compositions. (Except, that is, on the occasion of having a virtuoso musician in the neighborhood, which then inspired the composer to write spectacular and somewhat idiomatic parts for a single instrument.)

That all changed in the Classical period, when large numbers of musicians moved to large urban areas. With so many musicians concentrated in such a small area, there was much more talent for a composer to choose from and write for. Composers could write more consistently challenging parts and expect them to be reliably performed by available performers. The result was music of much greater complexity, as evidenced in the instrumental music of the day.

A Hotbed of Creativity: The Viennese School

As important as Germany and Italy and England were in the scheme of things, much of the great music of the Classical period came from a single city. By the mid-1700s, Vienna, Austria, had become a magnet to musicians from throughout all of Europe, thanks in part to an abundance of wealthy patrons. This confluence of talent resulted in convergence of musical styles and a melting-pot of ideas, even after the end of the patronage system, out of which emerged the full-blown Classical style.

These Vienna-based musicians included Haydn, Mozart, and Beethoven—the biggest names of their day, and the most innovative composers of the era. Collectively, they were known as the Viennese School, and they were responsible for practically all the major musical developments of the Classical period.

The Sound of Classical Music

So what does Classical music sound like? Compared to Baroque music, it is lighter, clearer, and less complicated. Classical music is primarily homophonic, meaning that there is a single melody above chordal accompaniment. The melodies themselves are more graceful and lyrical; they're not overly embellished or ornamented, as was the case in the Baroque. They're also shorter, with clear-cut phrases.

In listening to longer Classical pieces, you'll hear a more noticeable variety and contrast between sections. When a piece moves from one section to another, the transition is readily apparent via the use of different keys, tempos, rhythms, and dynamics.

And these longer pieces were likely performed by larger ensembles. That's because the orchestra increased in size and range during this period; the Classical orchestra was the first to include full string, brass, and woodwind sections.

The music itself, due in part to these bigger instrumental ensembles, was also bigger—majestic and powerful. Composers were inspired by the heroic ideal, as was typical in most neoclassical art of the period, and in some instances by the democratic and republican revolutions taking place across Europe and around the world.

Finally, Classical music was primarily instrumental music. Not that vocal forms went away (the opera reached new heights during this era), but the emphasis was clearly on the instrumental, in the form of sonatas, concertos, and symphonies.

And that is the sound of Classical music.

Note _____

In simpler works, Classical composers favored the piano over the harpsichord, which was more common during the Baroque.

The Big Three: Haydn, Mozart, and Beethoven

The new Classical style was primarily forged by the three most influential composers living in Vienna during that era: Haydn, Mozart, and Beethoven. These three musical geniuses created a body of work—consisting of majestic sonatas, string quartets, symphonies, and operas—that has for generations defined the term "classical music."

Master of the Early Classical Period: Haydn

The first Classical-era genius, chronologically, was Franz Joseph Haydn (1732–1809). Haydn was born in Austria and made Vienna his home during his entire career—outside of a few important trips across the English Channel.

Franz Joseph Haydn, the father of the symphony.

The most celebrated composer of the early Classical period, Haydn was known as the "father of the symphony," having composed 104 symphonic works. Think about that—more than a hundred full-blown symphonies; that's quite a body of sophisticated work. And that's not all he did; Haydn also helped to develop the string quartet and contributed to the development of the sonata and the sonata form.

> **Note**
>
> Johann Joseph Fux (1660–1741) was an Austrian composer of the late Baroque era. He is best known, however, as a music theorist; his book, *Gradus ad Parnassum* (*Ascent to Mount Parnassus*), was essentially the Bible for Baroque-era counterpoint and polyphonic composition.

The early part of Haydn's career was spent scraping away at various musical odd jobs. At one time or another he was a chorister at St. Stephan's Cathedral, a music teacher, a street serenader, and even a valet-accompanist for the Italian composer Nicola Porpora. Knowing that he didn't have adequate training in music theory and composition, Haydn studied the counterpoint exercises of Fux and the published works of C. P. E. Bach. This helped him improve his skills to the point where he began to establish a public reputation as a freelance composer. His first public work was an opera, *Der krumme Teufel* ("The Limping Devil"), written in 1753.

In 1761, Haydn was hired as Kapellmeister for the wealthy House of Esterházy, a noble Hungarian family, where he served Prince Nikolaus for almost two decades. In this position, Haydn had a variety of responsibilities that included playing chamber music for and with his patrons, managing the orchestra, mounting operatic productions, and creating new compositions. This was an ideal environment for the prolific Haydn; the Esterházy princes were musical connoisseurs who appreciated his work and provided ample resources to realize his musical ideas.

During his years serving the House of Esterházy, Haydn produced a multitude of musical works that helped to increase his popularity in the world outside the court. He eventually began to write for outside publication as well as for his employer; some of his most important works, including the Paris symphonies and *The Seven Last Words of Christ* (1787), were commissioned by others.

In 1790, when Prince Nikolaus was succeeded by Prince Anton, the Esterházy family decided it no longer had a use for court musicians; this was coincident with the decline of the patronage system overall. Due to his long years of service, however, Haydn was retained on a nominal appointment—although he spent most of his time on trips to England, which proved particularly fruitful.

Unlike many of his Classical contemporaries, Haydn lived to the ripe old age of 77. He died in Vienna, shortly after an attack on that city by Napoleon's French army during the Napoleonic Wars. Among Haydn's last words was his attempt to calm his servants after cannon shot fell in their neighborhood.

Haydn's most famous compositions were written during his two long visits to London (1791–1792 and 1794–1795). These trips were at the behest of German impresario Johann Peter Salomon, who offered Haydn the opportunity to write and conduct new symphonies with a large orchestra. The resulting works were the 12 so-called "London" symphonies (Nos. 93–104), which included the notable *The Surprise* (No. 94), *The Military* (No. 100), *The Clock* (No. 101), *The Drum Roll* (No. 103), and *The London* (No. 104). The first of these, *The Surprise*, is among the most popular symphonies of the Classical period; it is so named because of a sudden loud chord appearing after the tranquil beginning of the second movement, as shown in the following figure. (This is also a good demonstration of Haydn's sense of musical humor!)

Excerpt

Symphony No. 94
"Surprise"

Franz Joseph Haydn

The surprise in Haydn's Surprise *symphony—it's the big chord at the end of the last measure.*

Haydn's music is known for its perfection of form, along with its clarity, earnestness, and depth of feeling. He excelled in almost every musical genre; few composers, then or now, matched his levels of productivity and musical quality. One common characteristic of his music is the development of short, simple motifs into larger musical structures.

Haydn's most notable works include Symphony No. 22 in E flat Major (*The Philosopher*; 1764), Symphony No. 45 in F-sharp Minor (*The Farewell*; 1772), Sun Quartets Op. 20 (1772), the opera *Orfeo ed Euridice* (1791), Symphony No. 94 in G Major (*The Surprise*; 1791), Symphony No. 100 in G Major (*The Military*; 1794), Symphony No. 101 in D Major (*The Clock*; 1794), Symphony No. 103 in E flat Major (*The Drum Roll*; 1795), Symphony No. 104 in D Major (*The London*; 1795), Concerto in E flat for Trumpet and Orchestra (1796), Mass No. 7 in C (*In tempore belli—Paukenmesse*; 1796), String Quartet Op. 76 (1797), *Die Schöpfung* (*The Creation*; 1797–1798), *Missa in Angustiis* (*Nelson Mass*; 1798), and *Die Jahreszeiten* (*The Seasons*; 1798–1801).

Master of the Middle Classical Period: Mozart

Our second Classical master is one most people are familiar with. Wolfgang Amadeus Mozart (1756–1791) was a composer, keyboard player, violinist, violist, and conductor. He produced a huge volume of nearly flawless work in a relatively short time span, and is regarded by many as the world's greatest natural musical genius. Mozart was kind of a rock star of his time; he lived hard, burned out fast, and died young.

Wolfgang Amadeus Mozart, rock star of the Classical period.

Little Amadeus was born in Salzburg, Austria; his father was deputy Kapellmeister to the court orchestra of the Archbishop of Salzburg. Baby Mozart had music in his blood, which was apparent from an early age. He started picking out notes on the family clavier at age three, began formal lessons at age four, and composed his first pieces when he was just five years old. This wasn't just childish noodling; Mozart was a true child prodigy.

As a child, Mozart's parents took him on several trips throughout Europe, where his musical skills were exhibited. By the age of eight he had performed (on violin) before the courts of Louis XV and George III. A three-and-half-year concert tour followed, taking Amadeus and his family to the courts of Munich, Mannheim, Paris, London, The Hague, and Zurich. By this time Mozart was also a fertile composer; he composed his first symphony at age 12, and his first opera at age 14.

In 1773, the 17-year-old Mozart was employed as a court musician by Prince-Archbishop Hieronymus Colloredo, the ruler of Salzburg. He stayed there on and off for eight years, composing a number of symphonies, sonatas, string quartets, and serenades.

Mozart moved to Vienna in 1781, and spent the rest of his life there. Vienna was a hotbed of musical activity, and Mozart was much in demand as a performing pianist. Here Mozart became acquainted with the works of Bach and Handel, which led to a string of compositions that imitated the Baroque style, including the fugal passages in *The Magic Flute* and Symphony No. 41.

Note _____

Sometime after his move to Vienna, Mozart met and became friends with Haydn. In fact, the two musical geniuses often played together in a local string quartet, and Mozart dedicated six of his own quartets to his friend.

While in Vienna, Mozart composed a variety of different pieces. He wrote three or four piano concertos each concert season, as well as a number of famous operas. He was active as a performer through about 1786, when his career began to decline. Even though he opted to play fewer public concerts, however, Mozart continued to compose (symphonies and operas, mainly) up until his death in 1791 at the young age of 35; he had fallen ill earlier that year at the premier of his opera *La clemenza di Tito* in Prague, and died on December 5 of what was probably rheumatic fever.

Note _____

Mozart's life was fictionalized in the film *Amadeus* (1984), which played up a (mostly) fictional feud with fellow composer Antonio Salieri (1750–1825). In the film, it is suggested that Mozart's death was due to poisoning at the hands of his rival; there is no evidence to suggest that anything remotely like that actually happened. In fact, most evidence points to a cooperative relationship between the two composers.

Mozart's writing style represents a synthesis of many different elements that coalesced into what is now seen as a peak of Viennese Classicism. While his early work incorporated various Baroque elements, including counterpoint, Mozart's mature compositions are distinguished by their melodic beauty, formal elegance, and richness of harmony and texture. He had a real gift for memorable melodies, which many consider the hallmark of his style. As an example, see the opening melody from his String Quartet in D Minor (K. 421), with an octave leap followed by a series of more stable repeating notes. It's an interesting technique that makes for a melody that sticks in your head.

String Quartet KV. 421

W.A. Mozart

The opening of Mozart's String Quartet in D Minor (K. 421); the melody is in the top violin part.

Over the course of his career, Mozart was as prolific as he was prodigious, with more than 600 compositions to his name; he excelled in every musical form current in his time. He composed 41 symphonies, 26 string quartets, 10 instrumental quintets, 42 violin sonatas, 17 piano sonatas, 27 piano concertos, 40 divertimenti and serenades, 19 Masses, 42 arias, and 20 operas. Of these genres, the one that he almost single-handedly pioneered was the piano concerto; the others he simply mastered.

Notable works include String Quartet in D Minor (K. 421, 1783), Mass No. 17 in C minor (*Great Mass*; K. 427, 1783), Violin Piano Sonata in B flat (K. 454, 1784), Piano Concerto No. 21 in C (K. 467, 1785), Piano Concerto No. 24 in C minor (K. 491, 1786), Serenade No. 13 in G for Strings (*Eine kleine Nachtmusik*; K. 525, 1787), Symphony No. 39 in E flat Major (K. 543, 1788), Symphony No. 40 in G Minor (K. 550, 1788), Symphony No. 41 in C (*Jupiter*; K. 551, 1788), Requiem in D minor (K. 626, 1791), and the operas *Le nozze di Figaro* (*The Marriage of Figaro*; K. 492, 1786), *Don Giovanni* (K. 527, 1787), and *Die Zauberflöte* (*The Magic Flute*; K. 620, 1791).

Note

Mozart's works were cataloged by music historian Ludwig Ritter von Köchel in *Chronologisch-thematisches Verzeichnis sämlicher Tonwerke Wolfgang Amadé Mozarts* (1862), which assigned each piece a unique number (the so-called "K number").

Master of the Late Classical Period: Beethoven

Ludwig van Beethoven (1770–1827) is another composer with whom most folks are familiar. Beethoven was a composer and pianist of the late Classical period; in fact, his work bridges the Classical and Romantic eras. Beethoven's early accomplishments as a composer built on the Viennese Classical tradition of Haydn and Mozart, while his later works inspired the burgeoning Romantic Movement. His later career, unfortunately, was marked by increasing deafness which, along with a history of unsuccessful personal relationships, informed some of his most personal and profound works.

Ludwig van Beethoven, musical giant of the Classical and Romantic eras.

Beethoven was born in Bonn, Germany; his father, himself a tenor in the service of the Electoral court of Bonn, was his first music teacher. Although not quite the child prodigy that Mozart was, young Ludwig's talent was visible at an early age, and by the time he turned eight years old he was already studying piano, organ, and viol.

In 1787, when Beethoven was 17, he moved to Vienna in hopes of studying with Mozart. While there is no indication that the two masters ever met, Beethoven did eventually study with both Haydn and Salieri. By 1793, Beethoven had established a reputation as a piano virtuoso, and the piano would be dominant in most of his compositions, the first of which (a set of three piano trios) appeared in 1795.

Rather than working for a church or noble court, as was common earlier in the period, Beethoven instead supported himself through a combination of individual gifts and annual stipends from members of the aristocracy, income from subscription concerts and private lessons, and proceeds from the sale of his works. This gave him considerable freedom as to what and how he composed.

One well-known but unfortunate aspect of Beethoven's life was his growing deafness. He began to lose his hearing around 1796, at the age of 26, suffering a severe form of tinnitus that caused a ringing in his ears that made it difficult for him to hear his own music. By 1814 he had gone completely deaf; the fact that he composed such magnificent works without being able to actually hear them is a testament to his innate musical ability.

Beethoven's deafness probably didn't do much to improve his disposition, which was decidedly irritable. He had a strong personality and treated most other people badly; in spite of this, he had a close and devoted circle of friends. Outside of that circle, however, he had a disdain for authority and for people who outranked him socially. This disdain even evidenced itself at his many performances; Beethoven would reportedly stop playing the piano if the audience failed to give him their full attention. Eccentric and egotistic, yes, but perhaps justified by the sheer magnitude of his talent.

Like many of his generation, Beethoven was attracted to the ideals of the Enlightenment and, later in life, to the growing Romanticism in Europe. This is reflected in his music; for example, the fourth movement of his Ninth Symphony features an elaborate choral setting of Schiller's "Ode to Joy," an optimistic hymn championing the brotherhood of humanity. It's one of Beethoven's best-known works.

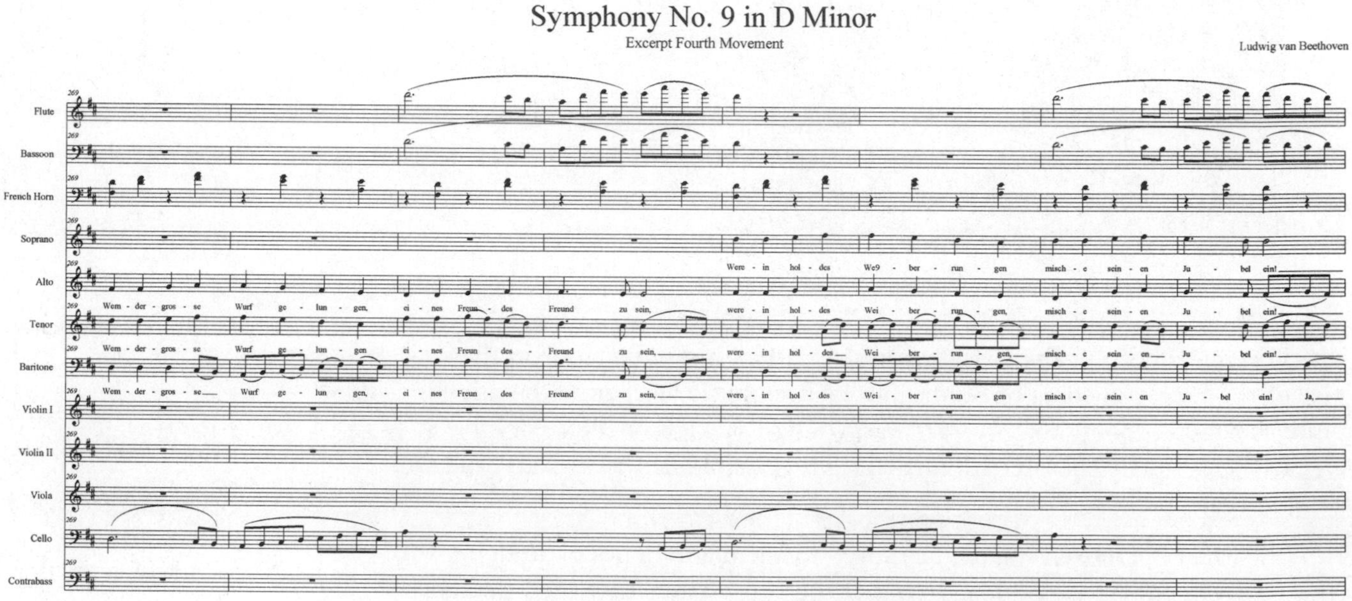

Note

Johann Christoph Friedrich von Schiller was a German poet, philosopher, dramatist, and historian.

Symphony No. 9 in D Minor
Excerpt Fourth Movement
Ludwig van Beethoven

From the fourth movement of Beethoven's ninth symphony, the famous "Ode to Joy" passage. (The vocals are in the middle.)

Beethoven eventually developed complications from lead poisoning, which led to his death in 1827. He was 57 years old.

As a composer, Beethoven was uniquely innovative and influential. He radically transformed every musical form in which he worked; his mastery of structure and key relationships established him as the dominant musical figure of the nineteenth century.

Beethoven was one of the first composers to use interlocking melodic themes to achieve inter-movement unity in his longer works. His compositions—including 9 symphonies, 5 piano concertos, 32 piano sonatas, and 2 Masses—shattered the musical rules of length, intensity, and originality. In Beethoven's hands, all musical genres—especially and including the symphony—reached majestic heights, with longer and more ambitious movements within each piece.

His career can be divided into three major periods:

◆ Early (1779–1802), where his work emulated that of his predecessors Haydn and Mozart. Important pieces from this period include his first and second symphonies, the first six string quartets, the first three piano concertos, and the first three piano sonatas—including the famous *Moonlight* sonata.

◆ Middle (1803–1814), which is known for large-scale works expressing heroism and struggle. Important works from this period include symphonies 3 through 8, the fourth and fifth piano concertos, five string quartets, seven piano concertos, the triple concerto and violin concerto, and Beethoven's only opera, *Fidelio*.

◆ Late (1815–1827), was a period of intense and deeply personal compositions that led from the Classical to the Romantic period. These innovative works include his last five string quartets, five piano sonatas, the massive Ninth Symphony, and the *Missa Solemnis*.

In general, Beethoven's music was majestic and musically complex. The typical Beethoven piece is a powerful piece of music, full of emotional depth and lasting resonance. Take, for example, the famous opening theme to his Symphony No. 5 in C Minor, shown in the following figure. Beethoven works this simple four-note theme into a cascading wall of sound, building large blocks of chords with massive power. It's no wonder this theme is so easily recognizable almost 200 years later.

Symphony No. 5 in C Minor
Op. 67

Ludwig van Beethoven

The well-known opening theme from Beethoven's fifth symphony.

Note _____

Many musical works, including those of Beethoven, are classified via opus numbers. (For example, Opus 1— abbreviated Op. 1.) Opus numbers typically run in order of original publication for that composer.

Any desert island list of Beethoven's works would include Piano Sonatas No. 14, Op. 27, in C# Minor (*Moonlight*; 1800–1801); Symphony No. 3 in E flat (*Eroica*), Op. 55 (1803–1804); Piano Sonata No. 23, Op. 57, in F Minor (*Appassionata*; 1804–1805); Symphony No. 5 in C Minor, Op. 67 (1804–1808); the opera *Fidelio* (1805, revised 1806 and 1814); Violin Concerto in D, Op. 61 (1806); Symphony No. 6 in F (*Pastorale*), Op. 68 (1807–1808); Piano Concerto No. 5 in E flat (*Emperor*), Op. 73 (1809); Symphony No. 9 in D Minor, Op. 125 (1817–1823); Mass in D Major (*Missa Solemnis*), Op. 123, (1819–1822); String Quartet No. 13, Op. 130, in B flat (1825–1826); and String Quartet No. 14 in C Sharp Minor, Op. 131 (1825–1826).

Instrumental Music in the Classical Period

During the Classical period, instrumental music finally became more important than vocal music. This was due in part to the improved technical quality of instruments achieved during this period, the development of several new and more expressive instruments, and the increasing technical ability of musicians in the large city centers.

The Piano and the Classical Orchestra

Chief among these new instruments was the pianoforte (Italian for "soft-loud"), known simply as the piano. The first piano was created around 1700, but during the late 1700s the instrument developed into the form we know today. The piano supplanted previous keyboard instruments such as the harpsichord and clavichord, and was capable of a wider range of dynamics than those earlier instruments.

The Classical period also saw the development of the modern orchestra. During the Baroque period the orchestra was dominated by the string section, with wind instruments used only for doubling, reinforcing, and filling in harmonies. By the late eighteenth century, however, wind instruments were being used for more important and more independent material. The wind instruments were now regarded as equal to the strings in terms of playing the melody, as well as supplying harmony.

Haydn and Mozart helped to standardize the instrumental makeup of the modern orchestra—pairs of flutes, oboes, clarinets, bassoons, horns, and trumpets, along with the standard first and second violins, violas, cellos, double basses, and timpani. In the Classical orchestra, strings and winds were self-contained, melodically and harmonically independent of each other.

The String Quartet

Chamber music gained popularity in the Classical period, with works for small instrumental ensembles designed to be played in private residences. The most popular form of chamber music was the string quartet, with its extremely versatile grouping of two violins, viola, and cello.

The string quartet as we know it today was primarily the invention of Haydn. Haydn's quartets consisted of four movements: fast, slow, minuet, and fast, with the first, second, and final movements in sonata form. Later, Mozart built on Haydn's themes, adding a more sophisticated four-part texture and chromatic effects.

During the later Classical period, the string quartet moved from the private salon to the concert hall, firmly establishing the form in musical history.

On a Smaller Scale: Chamber Music _____

Chamber music is music for a small group of solo instruments, originally designed for performance in houses and small halls—not intended for the church, theater, or large concert hall.

Chamber music is easiest understood as what it is not. It is not music for a vocal or instrumental soloist, nor is it music for an orchestra or chorus. Instead, most chamber music is written for two (duet), three (trio), four (quartet), five (quintet), six (sextet), seven (septet), or eight (octet) instruments, with all the parts being relatively equal in importance—that is, the music is not for a soloist with accompaniment.

Chamber music can be written for string or wind instruments. Perhaps the most popular form is the *string quartet*, composed of two violins, one viola, and one cello.

Haydn could be considered the father of modern chamber music. Before Haydn, most music of this type was supplied with a figured bass, improvised on harpsichord. Haydn introduced the concept of four (or more) equal parts, precisely arranged without room for extemporization. Subsequently, most major composers have contributed in some way to the modern chamber music repertory.

Sonata

In the Baroque period, sonatas were characterized by a light, dance-music style. In the Classical era, the Viennese composers injected drama and complexity into the sonata, creating a substantially new form with richer textures, more varied accompaniments, and a broader harmonic vocabulary. Notable in this regard is Haydn's Sonata in C Minor No. 36, which is rightly said to mark the introduction of the Viennese Classical style.

Many Classical composers embraced the newest instrument of the period, the piano, with its capacity for dynamic contrast and dramatic effects. This resulted in many notable piano sonatas, including Beethoven's *Pathètique* and *Moonlight* sonatas.

Note _____

Key to the development of the Classical sonata was the *sonata form*, with its three-part structure of *exposition*, *development*, and *recapitulation*. This form was used not only in sonata pieces, but pervades nearly all the music of the Classical era, especially in regards to its treatment of tonality and theme.

Concerto

The concerto form continued forward from the Baroque period. Haydn's early concertos were heavily influenced by the earlier work of J. S. Bach and his son C. P. E. Bach (1714–1788), while Mozart tended to write more in the Italian style. Mozart later wrote many concertos for piano and orchestra, with the orchestra sharing some of the melodic themes in addition to providing accompaniment. Mozart also introduced the *cadenza*, a virtuoso solo passage designed to display the technical skills of the soloist.

Symphony

Arguably the most important instrumental form of the Classical period, however, was the symphony. The symphony has its roots in the Italian *overture* of late seventeenth-century operas, but came to maturity in the Classical era.

To the early symphony, the Viennese composers introduced a richer, more developed orchestral style, and standardized the individual movements with well-defined contrasts of theme and color. The modern symphony is a large-scale instrumental composition, much like a sonata for orchestra, usually in four movements (although this varies). In the Classical and Romantic periods, the typical symphony opens with an allegro movement, followed by a slow movement, then a minuet or scherzo, ending with an allegro or rondo movement; in some instances the slow movement is moved to the third or fourth position.

The symphonic orchestra of the eighteenth century typically included strings, woodwinds, horns, and a harpsichord or other continuo instrument. Symphonic composers of this era included C. P. E. Bach, Giovanni Battista Sammartini (1700–1775), François Gossec (1734–1829), William Boyce (1711–1779), and Johann Wenzel Stamitz (1717–1757).

As you've read previously, it was Haydn who most completely defined the symphonic form. Haydn's 104 symphonic works helped to expand the form, and to break it from its rigid four-movement structure. His symphonies drew on a broad variety of source material, including folk songs and music originally written for plays, and he employed all manner of forms and variations.

Haydn thus influenced his friend Mozart, who made his own impressive contributions to the repertory, most notably No. 38 in D (*Prague*) and No. 41 in C (*Jupiter*). Mozart's later symphonies further influenced Haydn's last twelve "London" symphonies, especially No. 94 in G (*Surprise*) and No. 102 in B flat (*London*).

The dawn of the nineteenth century saw a new artistic peak for the symphonic form. Building on Haydn's example, Beethoven confirmed the symphony as a grand, unified structure, the apex of instrumental composition and arrangement. He introduced a heightened level of emotional expression to the form, accompanied by a boldness of harmony and tonal relationships, beginning with No. 3 in E flat (*Eroica*). Beethoven's other defining symphonies included No. 6 in F (*Pastoral*) and No. 9 in D Minor (*Choral*), which was one of the first symphonies to incorporate vocals along with the instrumental passages.

Vocal Music in the Classical Period

Even though the emphasis of the Classical period was on new and longer instrumental works, the great composers continued to create both secular and sacred vocal works—in particular, Masses and oratorios.

Mass

The Mass, as a musical style, continued to flourish in the Classical period, even as it took on more modern stylings. The Viennese composers introduced a more integrated structure to the Mass, often merging the *Gloria* and *Credo* into a single section. Hayden employed symphonic techniques alongside more traditional practices, as did Mozart; Mozart's *Coronation Mass* contains many symphonic devices, as well as an almost operatic intensity in the solo voices.

Oratorio and Cantata

Sacred and secular cantatas declined in importance during the Classical period. The oratorio, however, increased in popularity.

In Italy, the most popular type of oratorio was the *oratorio volgare*, a two-part form with Italian (rather than Latin) lyrics. In Germany, there were two primary types of oratorio: a dramatic form with Biblical themes, and a contemplative form that emphasized sentimental expression.

The most notable oratorios of the late Classical period were composed by Haydn. His oratorios—in particular, *Die Schöpfung* (*The Creation*) and *Die Jahreszeiten* (*The Seasons*)—are poetic celebrations of faith and nature, in a mature symphonic style.

Opera

Opera underwent many important changes in the Classical era. By the late Baroque period, Italian opera had become a series of overly wrought arias designed to display the talents of superstar singers. As a reaction to this perceived vocal excess, Classical composers cut back on the ornamentation, reintroduced instrumental interludes and accompaniments between arias, and made greater use of choral singing. They also sought to combine groups of recitatives, arias, duets, choruses, and instrumental sections into unified scenes.

The Classical period also saw the decline of serious Italian opera (*opera seria*) and the rise of lighter forms, such as *opera buffa* and *opéra comique*. These new forms utilized more realistic spoken dialogue interspersed with songs; the music was also of a simpler style.

In England, the *ballad opera* was the most popular form during the Classical era. A good example is *The Beggar's Opera*, written by John Gay (1685–1732) and Johann Christoph Pepusch (1667–1752) in 1728. This popular piece satirizes London society and the conventions of *opera seria*.

Perhaps the most important of opera's reformers during the Classical era was Christoph Willibald von Gluck (1714–1787). In his works—including *Orfeo ed Euridice* (1762), *Alceste* (1767), and *Iphigénie en Tauride* (1779)—the music served the drama, without interruption by unnecessary orchestral passages or florid singing. He was notable for shortening the aria and emphasizing vocal ensembles and the operatic choir.

The reformation movement climaxed in the stage works of Mozart, in which every aspect of the vocal and instrumental portions contributed to the overall plot development and characterization. Mozart brought the orchestra to the forefront of the opera; in his operas, such as *Le nozze di Figaro* (*The Marriage of Figaro*, 1786) and *Don Giovanni* (1787), the music for each character is distinct in tone and style from the other characters, and the action is reflected in the structure of the work.

The beginning of the nineteenth century saw the comic operas of Gioachino Antonio Rossini (1792–1868), including *Il barbiere di Siviglia* (*The Barber of Seville*, 1816) and *Guillaume Tell* (*William Tell*, 1829), as well as the romantic operas of Carl Maria von Weber (1786–1826), such as *Der Freischütz* (1821) and *Euryanthe* (1823).

Moving Forward: Classical Romanticism

As the early nineteenth century progressed, the Classical period gradually gave way to its successor, the Romantic period. Unlike previous transitions, this was a soft one; it's almost impossible to tell where the Classical ends and the Romantic begins, especially when examining works by composers, such as Beethoven, who bridged the two periods. (Much of Beethoven's music—such as the famous *Moonlight Sonata*—was distinctly Romantic in nature.)

In fact, an entire school of these transitional composers are sometimes referred to as "Classical Romantics." These artists include Rossini, Weber, Franz Schubert, and Felix Mendelssohn, whom we'll discuss in Chapter 6. These composers were strongly influenced by the Classical style, even though they later developed a Romantic sensibility, especially when it came to harmony.

So the break between this chapter and the next is somewhat artificial. We discussed Beethoven in this chapter as a Classicist, because that's where the majority of his work lay, even though he created many works in the Romantic style; we'll discuss Schubert, Mendelssohn, and others in the next chapter, because they spent the majority of their careers as Romanticists. Just know that the line between the periods is a fuzzy one.

Listening List

A Classical-period listening list is almost exclusively a Haydn/Mozart/Beethoven listening list—and there's nothing wrong with that. This is great music and includes everything from solo piano works to majestic symphonies to full-scale operas. Enjoy!

Beethoven: Piano Sonatas (Complete; Friedrich Gulda)

Beethoven: The Complete String Quartets (Alban Berg Quartet)

Beethoven: Symphony No. 3 (*Eroica*; New York Philharmonic; Leonard Bernstein, conductor)

Beethoven: Symphonien Nos. 5 & 7 (Wiener Philharmoniker; Carlos Kleiber, conductor)

Gluck: Orfeo ed Euridice (La Petite Bande; Collegium Vocale; Sigiswald Kuijken, conductor)

Haydn: Symphonies Nos. 93-104, The London Symphonies (Austro-Hungarian Haydn Orchestra; Adam Fischer, conductor)

Haydn: String Quartets Op. 76 (The Lindsay String Quartet)

Mozart: Die Zauberflöte (*The Magic Flute*; Agnes Giebel; Christa Ludwig; Philharmonia Chorus & Orchestra; Otto Klemperer, conductor)

Mozart: Don Giovanni (Anton Dermota; Cesare Siepi; Vienna Philharmonic Orchestra; Wilhelm Furtwängler, conductor)

Mozart: Piano Concertos Nos. 6, 17 & 21 (Géza Anda)

Mozart: Requiem (The Monteverdi Choir; English Baroque Soloists; John Eliot Gardiner, conductor)

Mozart: Symphonies Nos. 35-41 (Berliner Philharmoniker; Karl Böhm, conductor)

Mozart: The Violin Sonatas (Itzhak Perlman; Daniel Barenboim)

Rossini: Il Barbiere di Siviglia (Teresa Berganza; Hermann Prey; London Symphony Orchestra; Claudio Abbado, conductor)

Timeline: The Classical Period

1750	Bach dies
1751	The minuet becomes fashionable dance in Europe
1752	Benjamin Franklin flies a kite to discover electricity
1755	Seven Years War begins
1756	Mozart born
1759	Handel dies; Haydn writes *Symphony No. 1 in D Major*
1763	Seven Years War ends
1764	Eight year-old Mozart writes first symphony
1769	Napoleon born
1770	Beethoven born; first American performance of Handel's *Messiah*; Boston Massacre occurs
1773	The waltz becomes fashionable in Vienna
1774	First Continental Congress
1775	American Revolution begins

1776	Thomas Jefferson writes the Declaration of Independence
1780	Haydn writes the *Toy Symphony*
1783	United States of America becomes independent nation via Treaty of Paris
1786	Mozart writes *The Marriage of Figaro*
1788	Mozart writes the three great symphonies: E flat, G Major, and *Jupiter*; United States Constitution ratified
1789	George Washington elected first president of United States; Montgolfier brothers fly first hot air balloon; French Revolution begins
1790	Benjamin Franklin dies
1792	Beethoven becomes pupil of Haydn in Vienna; French Revolutionary Wars begin
1794	"Auld Lang Syne" first published
1795	Beethoven writes three piano trios, Op. 1; Hayden completes the 12 London symphonies
1797	Schubert born; John Adams elected second president of United States
1799	George Washington dies
1800	Thomas Jefferson elected third president of United States
1803	The U.S. expands via the Louisiana Purchase; Napoleonic Wars begin
1804	Beethoven writes *Symphony No. 3 in E-flat Major* (*Eroica*); Napoleon coronated Emperor of France; Lewis and Clark begin their exploration
1807	Robert Fulton launches first commercial steamboat on the Hudson River
1808	Beethoven writes *Symphony No. 5* and *Symphony No. 6 (Pastoral)*
1809	James Madison elected fourth president of United States; Abraham Lincoln born; Haydn dies
1810	Chopin and Schumann born
1812	Beethoven writes *Symphony No. 7* and *Symphony No. 8*; War of 1812 between Britain and America
1813	Verdi born
1814	Schubert writes first lieder; Francis Scott Key writes poem, "Defense of Fort McHenry" (later set to music to become "The Star Spangled Banner")
1814	Beethoven goes deaf
1815	Napoleon meets his Waterloo
1816	Rossini writes *The Barber of Seville*

Chapter 6

Classical Music Matures: The Romantic Period

In This Chapter

◆ Understanding the roots of Romanticism and nationalism

◆ Learning the major composers of the Romantic era

◆ Discovering the expanded musical forms of the period

The period from 1820 to 1900 or so—almost to the start of the first world war—is known as the Romantic period. Unlike previous periods, this was not an era of revolution, but was rather one of evolution. Think of the Romantic era as the Classical period, part two.

This was a very rich period in all aspects—art, science, politics, and music. These years saw the establishment of travel by railroad, the invention of artificial light, photography, the telegraph, and the wireless radio, the discovery of radioactivity, the development of communism, and the abolition of slavery in Europe and the Americas. Modern literature flourished under the pens of Charles Dickens, Victor Hugo, Herman Melville, and Mark Twain. It was the era of the Wild West, the American Civil War, the Crimean War, the Franco-Prussian War, and the buildup to World War I.

And, in music, the Romantic period gave birth to lush, melodic works by Liszt, Mendelssohn, Schubert, Schumann, Tchaikovsky, Wagner, and dozens of other well-known composers. It was the era of waltzes and lieder, symphonies and ballets, operas and operettas. In short, the Romantic period had a little bit for everyone—which you'll read about in short order.

Progress and Reaction: Getting to Know Nineteenth-Century Romanticism

The Romantic period spans, for all intents and purposes, the bulk of the nineteenth century. And, more than any century prior, the nineteenth century was one of almost unimaginable change.

The Romantic movement of the nineteenth century started, as all movements do, as a revolt against what came before—in this instance, against the aristocratic and political norms of the Enlightenment, as well as the scientific rationalization of nature in art and literature. It took the power and majesty of the Classical period to new heights, stressing strong emotion as a source of aesthetic experience. In fact, Romanticism is all about emotion, often manipulated; if the Classical period represented pure drama, the Romantic period took it to the level of melodrama. It's more about feeling than thinking.

Note

The word "romantic" comes from the term "romance," which is a style of heroic prose or verse popular in Europe from the Middle Ages to the Renaissance. In the terms of the Romantic period, this indicates a throwback of sorts to that earlier era and its emphasis on heroic and romantic figures.

A Growing Nationalism

During the last half of the nineteenth century, the Romantic Movement was accompanied by the concept of *nationalism*, an often excessive pride in one's country or culture. Nationalism became a central theme of Romantic art and political philosophy, emphasizing local customs and traditions. This was evident in the politics of the day, where nationalistic movements fueled opposition to foreign occupation and the notion of imperial rule. It also informed the period's art and literature, drawing attention to ethnic and regional folklore and local folk music.

The mid-1800s saw a rare period of stability in Europe. This stability arose, to a large extent, from the formation of new states in Germany and Italy, as well as the populist reformations and revolutions in other European countries, such as England and France. Things stayed relatively calm until 1871, when a growing nationalistic fervor inspired the major European powers to renew their imperialistic ambitions. Thus came the rise of the British Empire as well as increased colonization from the other players. Conflict between nations was not far behind; the Crimean War (1854–1856) saw Britain and France on one hand and Russia on the other fighting over the Ottoman Empire, while the Franco-Prussian War (1870–1871) resulted in the unification of Germany and Italy and the collapse of the second French Empire.

In the United States, a different kind of war was being fought, only tangentially related to nationalism. The American Civil War pitted the northern states against the rebellious southern ones, in a fight over slavery and states' rights. This could, one supposes, be interpreted as a type of regional nationalism, but the result was unlike the nationalistic battles in Europe. At the end of the conflict, with more than 600,000 dead, the republic held together; American culture was solidified in a single nation, not split into separate, smaller nation-states.

Note

The Civil War and the years following it was a fertile period for American folk music. Learn more in Chapter 8.

The Science of the Nineteenth Century

The nineteenth century was also a period of significant scientific advancement. It wasn't all about the theory; rather, this era saw the practical application of scientific discovery.

Think of how the era started and then how it ended. At the beginning of the century, surgery was accomplished without anesthesia, travel was strictly by horseback, and the fastest communication was a letter delivered via pony express. By the end of the century patients were being vaccinated to prevent disease, cross-country travel was via speedy train, and instant communication was possible by telegraph and telephone.

The number of practical scientific advancements during the nineteenth century was mind-boggling. The year 1820 saw the first study of electromagnetism by Hans Christian Ørsted; that was followed by related experiments by André-Marie Ampère and Georg Simon Ohm. These experiments eventually led to the practical use of electricity, Thomas Edison's invention of the incandescent light bulb (1879), and the founding of the first electric utility (1882). Other practical inventions of the era include the telegraph (Samuel Morse, 1832), the telephone (Alexander Graham Bell, 1876), the internal combustion automobile (Karl Benz, 1885), and the wireless radio (Guglielmo Marconi, 1895).

Note

Busy man that he was, Edison also invented the phonograph, in 1877; this invention had enormous impact on both classical and popular music in the century following.

In geological science, Richard Owen first used the term "dinosaur" (literally, "terrible lizard") in 1841, to describe the fossil reptiles that were being discovered at the time. And Charles Darwin, in 1859, established the theory of evolution with his groundbreaking work, *On the Origin of Species by Means of Natural Selection.*

Medical science was also changing by leaps and bounds. Dr. Horace Wells, an American dentist, first used nitrous oxide as an anesthetic in 1846; before that, all surgeries were conducted on fully conscious patients. In 1881, Louis Pasteur (who had previously developed the process of Pasteurization) developed both the germ theory of disease and his first vaccine (against anthrax). Wilhelm Roentgen discovered x-rays in 1895, Pierre and Marie Curie discovered radium in 1898, and Dr. Felix Hoffman first concocted aspirin in 1899.

This era even saw the origins of the modern computer. Charles Babbage, in 1837, conceived his Analytical Engine, a machine capable of performing mathematical calculations, using punch cards as a form of memory. This was, for all intents and purposes, the predecessor to today's computer.

Equally important were developments in transportation. At the start of the nineteenth century, practically all land travel was still by horse or carriage. The first steam locomotive was built in 1804 by Richard Trevithick and Andrew Vivian in Great Britain, with the first passenger train following in 1807. By the late 1820s, passenger and freight railroads were being built all across Europe and North America, revolutionizing travel. East-West travel across the United States became a reality in 1869, when the Central Pacific and Union Pacific railroads met in Promontory Summit, Utah. The age of fast, affordable travel had arrived—which helped to spread East Coast culture across the entire continent.

Romanticism in Art and Literature

Romanticism is, technically, an artistic and intellectual movement that stressed strong emotion, imagination, and rebellion against social conventions—including the "classical" correctness in various art forms. By embracing emotionality, it can be seen as a rejection of the precepts of calm, order, harmony, and rationality that typified Classicism in the late eighteenth century.

Romanticism first rose to prominence as early as the 1770s in England and Germany, and had spread throughout Europe by the 1820s—the formal start of the Romantic period. Unlike the Enlightenment movement, which started among a small elite and slowly spread throughout the rest of society, Romanticism was more widespread in both its origins and its influence. It transformed the stage, the novel, poetry, painting, sculpture, ballet, and all forms of serious music.

Note

A good example of Romanticism in literature is Victor Hugo's epic *Les Misérables*—later turned into a very Romantic stage musical.

Romantic art and literature are characterized by a deep appreciation of the beauty of nature, a preoccupation with the heroic ideal, an embrace of emotion over reason and of the senses over intellect, and an obsessive interest in folk culture and national and ethnic origins (nationalism). In the world of art, the Romantic era was represented by the works of John Constable, Eugène Delacroix, and J. M. W. Turner; in the world of literature, Romantic authors and poets included William Blake, Lord Byron, Samuel Taylor Coleridge, Johann Wolfgang von Goethe, Victor Hugo, John Keats, Mary Shelley, Percy Bysshe Shelley, William Wordsworth, and William Butler Yeats.

In the United States, Romanticism was represented in a type of romantic gothic literature exemplified by the works of James Fenimore Cooper (*Last of the Mohicans*), Nathaniel Hawthorne (*The Scarlet Letter*), Washington Irving (*Legend of Sleepy Hollow*), Herman Melville (*Moby Dick*), and Edgar Allen Poe (*The Masque of the Red Death*), as well as the poetry of Emily Dickinson and Walt Whitman. A later American nationalist movement was led by Mark Twain (Samuel Clemens) and his uniquely homegrown works, including *The Adventures of Tom Sawyer* and *The Adventures of Huckleberry Finn*.

Listening to the Music of the Romantic Period

In the world of music, Romanticism began as a natural progression of the existing Classical movement. Beginning in the early nineteenth century, composers began to extend the Classical style in new and unique ways. Instead of adhering to the formal guidelines set forth in the Classical period, Romantic composers followed the inspiration of literary, historical, pictorial, and other nonmusical sources with the Romantic emphasis on emotion and the heroic ideal.

Music of the Romantic period, then, was typified by a personal expression of emotion and imagination. For want of a better word, it was *sensitive* music, birthing memorable melodies that remain ingrained in the popular culture of today.

The Romantic era also saw a newfound freedom from the rules of the Classical period. Unlike previous periods, there were no restrictions on the length of a piece, the number of movements, or the types of instruments or voices used. This expansion of form led to many variants of the Romantic style. In fact, there is no one set Romantic style; thanks to the growing influence of nationalism, different styles developed in different countries and regions.

That said, how can one determine the sound of the Romantic period? Despite the many variations, certain key elements are common, as compared to the music of the previous Classical period:

Note _____
Musically, Romanticism is still with us today, specifically in motion picture scores. One can find no better example of Romantic music than John Williams's soundtracks for the *Star Wars* movies.

- There is a wider dynamic range—softer softs and louder louds.

- The range of sound is also wider, with a greater variety of instruments used and different combinations of those instruments employed for different musical colors.

- Melodies are longer, more lyrical, more dramatic (some would say melodramatic), and more emotional.

- Extreme tempos are often employed—from very fast passages to extremely slow passages.

- Harmonies are fuller and often employ striking dissonances.

- Chromatic tones are more common in both melodies and harmony.

- In longer pieces, formal structures are expanded.

- There is greater technical virtuosity—especially from pianists and violinists.

- Greater use of native or folk melodies, in line with the trend towards nationalism.

There was, however, a significant difference between music of the early Romantic era and later Romantic music. We'll look at each period in turn.

Bigger and with More Emotion: Music of the Early Romantic Era

The music of the early nineteenth century is distinguished by one figure—Beethoven. As you learned in Chapter 5, Beethoven was a transitional figure, bridging the Classical and Romantic periods. His use of the larger orchestra, longer instrumental forms, and more lyrical melodies helped drive the early Romantic Movement. (His Symphony No. 9 is the perfect example of the early Romantic symphony.)

Other composers picked up on what Beethoven was doing and adapted it to their personal styles. Many music historians regard the years 1820 to 1848 as the true age of Romanticism in music, full of sweeping, lyrical melodies in a variety of musical forms.

Composers of this early Romantic era include Beethoven, of course, and also Hector Berlioz, Frederic Chopin, Franz Liszt, Felix Mendelssohn, Franz Schubert, Robert Schumann, and Carl Maria von Weber. Their works range from the intimate song cycles and lieder of Schubert and Schumann and the lyrical piano works of Chopin to the powerful symphonies of Berlioz and the majestic operas of Weber.

> **Note**
>
> The early Romantic period saw the rise of virtuoso concerts or recitals, pioneered by Niccolò Paganini, the famous violin virtuoso. The increase in cross-country travel, facilitated by the rise of the railroads, created international audiences for touring piano virtuosi such as Chopin, Liszt, and Clara Wieck (later the wife of composer Schumann). This period also saw the rise of performing institutions, such as the Philharmonic Society of London (founded in 1813), which promoted regular concert seasons to the public.

The Rise of Nationalism: Music of the Late Romantic Era

The early Romantic era—and the era of literary Romanticism—ended in 1848, with the revolutions in Italy, France, Germany, Poland, and other European states. Realism and nationalism rose to take the place of the early lyric Romanticism, while maintaining the overly emotional nature of the era.

During the late Romantic period, many composers created styles and forms associated with their national folk cultures. To that end, one found a distinctly German style (Wagner), Italian style (Verdi), Russian style (Mussorgsky, Tchaikovsky), and so forth. Nationalism was even an influence on less overtly political works, such as the Czech and American folk songs incorporated into the music of Dvořák.

One factor common to all these different nationalistic styles was the continued expansion of the harmonic vocabulary. Composers pushed the edges of the tonality envelope, using extended harmonies, chromaticism, and dissonance. Pieces didn't stay in the same key from beginning to end; frequent modulation to increasingly remote keys became common. Innovative chord progressions became common. All of these factors were leading music away from the expected harmonies of the Classical and early Romantic eras and into the near-abandonment of traditional tonality that would become common in twentieth-century music.

Great Composers of the Romantic Period

With so many uniquely national and personal variations of the Romantic style, perhaps the easiest way to examine the music of the Romantic period is by focusing on the composers themselves. While this era had no single composer with the overriding genius or influence of a Bach or Mozart (excepting, of course, Beethoven as a transitional figure), there was a profusion of musical talent—as evidenced by the large number of composers who remain important to this day. We'll look at each composer separately, in chronological order of their births.

> **Note**
>
> The sheer amount of music produced during the Romantic period dwarfed that of prior periods. There were several reasons for this: instruments became more standardized and easier to play, and the rise of the middle class fostered a boom in music education and a larger, more sophisticated listening audience. Together with the establishment of performing institutions in cities large and small, more new music was required to satisfy the needs of the larger audience.

Ludwig van Beethoven

We'll start our survey of Romantic composers with Ludwig van Beethoven (1770–1827), who bridged the Classical and the Romantic periods and was technically the first Romantic composer. For proof of this, examine the programmatic elements and extended form, along with emotionally charged melodies, of his Sixth Symphony ("Pastoral"), which he composed in 1808. To further prove the point, Beethoven also dabbled in the uniquely Romantic era song cycle, with his *An die ferne Geliebte* (*To the Distant Beloved*), composed in 1806.

We discussed Beethoven in much depth in Chapter 5, so there's no need to repeat that information here. Just remember that Beethoven is one of the half-dozen greatest composers in all of music history, no matter which musical period you put him in.

Gioachino Rossini

Gioachino Antonio Rossini (1792–1868) was a popular Italian composer. He wrote a variety of chamber music and sacred music, although he's best known for his 39 operas.

Like Beethoven, Rossini is a bit of a transitional figure; his early operas could be deemed Classical in nature, while his later ones are more definitively Romantic. He composed his first opera, *La Cambiale di Matrimonio* (*The Marriage Contract*), in 1810, although his first real success came with the 1813 production of *Tancredi*. His most famous opera, *Il Barbiere di Siviglia* (*The Barber of Seville*), which was written during a single two-week period in 1816. You probably know this opera from the *Largo al factotum* aria, with its later cry of "Figaro! Figaro! Figaro!"

> **Note**
>
> You've probably heard the "Figaro" aria parodied in the Bugs Bunny cartoons *Rabbit of Seville* and *Long-Haired Hare.*

Rossini's other famous opera is *Guillaume Tell* (*William Tell*), composed in 1829. This one is known for its memorable overture, the finale of which is popularized as the theme music for the radio and television series *The Lone Ranger.*

The Largo al factotum *aria from Rossini's* The Barber of Seville.

Franz Schubert

> **Note**
>
> Lieder (plural of *lied*, or "song") is music based on eighteenth- and nineteenth-century poetry, where composers attempted to portray with music the imagery and moods of the texts.

Franz Schubert (1797–1828) is a Viennese composer best known for his contributions in the areas of chamber music, piano music, and (especially) German *lieder*. Schubert's compositions incorporated a rich and subtle melodic and harmonic language; the piano accompaniments to his art songs were highly original and stood on their own alongside the vocal melodies.

Schubert's premature death (at age 31, of syphilis) cut short an extremely prolific career; between 1821 and 1828, he published more than 100 pieces, a rate of production unequalled by any of his Viennese contemporaries. His most notable works include Quintet in A Major ("Trout") for Piano and Strings (1819), *Fantasia* in C ("Wanderer"; 1822), Symphony No. 8 in B Minor ("Unfinished"; 1822), the song cycle *Die schöne Müllerin* (1823), String Quartet No. 14 in D Minor ("Death and the Maiden"; 1824), Symphony No. 9 in C Major ("Great"; 1825), Piano Trio No. 1 in B flat (1827), and more than 500 individual songs, including "Gretchen am Spinnrade" (1814), "Erlkönig" (1815), and "Ave Maria" (1825).

Hector Berlioz

Hector Berlioz (1803–1869) represented the French school of Romanticism. His forte was writing for the orchestra, and he's best known for his symphonies and other orchestral works. He contributed to the growth of the modern orchestra, sometimes to the extreme (one piece called for 1,000 performers!); his book *Grand Traité d'Instrumentation et d'Orchestration Modernes* (*Treatise on Instrumentation*) was a technical study of Western musical instruments, still used to this day.

Berlioz's best-known works include *Symphonie fantastique* (1830), *Grande Messe des morts* (*Requiem*; 1837), *Roméo et Juliette* (1839), and *La damnation de Faust* (1846). He also dabbled in songs for voice and piano, including most notably with the song cycle "Les nuits d'été" ("Summer Nights"; 1841).

Johann Strauss (I)

There are two Johann Strausses. The first Johann Strauss (1804–1849), also known as Strauss the Elder, was an Austrian composer known primarily for his waltzes. He's also known as the father of the slightly more famous Johann Strauss the Younger, whom we'll discuss later in this chapter.

One might consider this first Strauss the Duke Ellington or Count Basie of his day, a popular bandleader and composer. He gained fame in the 1820s as the conductor of various dance bands—the dance bands of that day being small string orchestras that played Viennese waltzes and German dances. In 1825, he decided to form his own band (the Strauss Orchestra) and write his own music. The result was a series of very popular waltzes, polkas, and marches, including the lovely waltz "Loreley-Rhein-Klänge" (1843) and the "Radetzky-Marsch" (1848). That said, his fame was eclipsed by his son Johann, who wrote even more popular waltzes.

Felix Mendelssohn

Felix Mendelssohn (1809–1847) was a German composer, pianist, organist, and conductor. The son of a rich German Jewish banker and the grandson of philosopher Moses Mendelssohn, Felix was a versatile and prolific prodigy who performed his first public piano concert at the age of nine and exhibited his fully developed musical style while still in his teens.

During his short career, Mendelssohn served as musical director of the prestigious Gewandhaus Orchestra in Leipzig and Kappelmeister to the King of Prussia. He was also one of the founders (in 1843) of the Leipzig Conservatory, the first major conservatory of music in Germany.

Like Beethoven, Mendelssohn's music bridged the Classical and Romantic periods, serving as what Nietzsche called a "lovely interlude" between Beethoven and Wagner in German music. His works exhibit a musical conservatism and lightheartedness, as well as a somewhat conventional sentimentality.

Mendelssohn wrote in all dominant musical styles, including symphonies, concertos, oratorios, piano music, chamber music, and the like. His most notable works include *A Midsummer Night's Dream*, Op. 21 (1826); Octet in E flat for Strings Op. 20 (1825); *Hebrides Overture (Fingal's Cave)*, Op. 26 (1830); Symphony No. 3 in A Minor, Op. 56 (*Scotch*; 1830–1842); Symphony No. 5 in D Minor, Op. 107 (*Reformation*; 1830–1832); Concerto No. 1 in G Minor for Piano and Orchestra, Op. 25 (1832); Symphony No. 4 in A, Op. 90 (*Italian*; 1833); Violin Concerto in E Minor, Op. 64 (1844); and the oratorio *Elijah*, Op. 70 (1846).

Frédéric Chopin

If you're a lover of piano music, I don't have to tell you about Frédéric Chopin (1810–1849). Born in Poland, Chopin was a noted pianist himself, and one of the greatest composers for the piano.

Chopin's piano music is technically demanding; it requires a skilled pianist to pull it off, and a virtuoso to make it sing. That's because despite the complexity, Chopin's music emphasizes nuance and expressive depth; it is distinctly Romantic in the way it conveys emotion through its lyrical melodies.

Chopin wrote in a variety of existing forms, including the piano sonata, waltz, nocturne, and étude. He also pioneered new forms, such as the ballade. His most notable works include Piano Concerto No. 1 in E Minor, Op. 11 (1830); Étude Op. 10, No. 12 (*Revolutionary*; 1831); Nocturnes Op. 9 (1831), *Fantaisie-Impromptu*, Op. 66 (1834); Ballade No. 1 in G Minor, Op. 23 (1836); Piano

Note

The third movement of Chopin's Piano Sonata No. 2 contains the well-known funeral march, recognizable for its slow and somber minor-key melody.

Sonata No. 2 in B flat Minor, Op. 35 (1839); Fantasy in F Minor, Op. 49 (1841); Polonaise Piano in A flat Major, Op. 53 (*Heroic*; 1842); and Waltz in D flat Major Op. 64, No. 1 (*Minute*; 1847).

Robert Schumann

German-born Robert Schumann (1810–1856) was, like many of his Romantic-era contemporaries, a master of many skills. He was a pianist, conductor, critic, and composer; he was also known as the husband of composer and pianist Clara Wieck Schumann (1819–1896). Despite his musical and literary productivity, Schumann's life was filled with melancholy; he suffered a nervous breakdown, attempted suicide, and died in an asylum at age 46.

Schumann's dual interest in literature and music led him to develop historically informed music criticism as well as a musical style deeply indebted to literary models. During his early career, Schumann was known primarily as a critic, as well as for his publication *Die neue Zeitschrift für Musik*, one of the first music journals. Later, as a composer, he made significant contributions to all the musical genres of his day.

Schumann is best known for his chamber music, piano music, and lieder. He tended to concentrate on one musical form at a time, in serial fashion: piano music from 1833–1839, art song in 1840, symphonic music in 1841, chamber music in 1842, oratorio in 1843, contrapuntal forms in 1845, dramatic music from 1847–1848, and church music in 1852.

Notable works include *Carnaval: Scènes mignonnes sur 4 notes*, Op. 9 (1834); *Fantasy* in C, Op. 17 (1836); *Kinderscenen*, Op. 15 (1838); the song cycle *Dichterliebe*, Op. 48 (1840); Symphony No. 4 in D Minor, Op. 120 (1841); Piano Concerto in A Minor, Op. 54 (1841–1845); and Quintet in E flat for Piano and Strings, Op. 44 (1842) .

Franz Liszt

Hungarian Franz Liszt (1811–1886), in addition to being a composer, was also a virtuoso pianist, noted at the time for his showmanship at the keyboard. Even today, historians consider Liszt to be one of the greatest pianists of all time.

Something of a rock star in his day, Liszt pioneered the modern solo piano recital and was also known for his piano arrangements of existing orchestral works and opera overtures. As a composer, he developed the musical form known as the symphonic poem—a single-movement orchestral work based on a literary work or character sketch. His most popular compositions include Symphonic Poem No. 3 (*Les Préludes*; 1848, revised 1854), Symphonic Poem No. 2 (*Tasso, Lamento e Trionfo*; 1849, revised 1854); Piano Concerto No. 1 in E flat Major (1849); Piano Sonata in B Minor (1853); Hungarian Rhapsodies for Piano (1853–1885); and Faust Symphony (1857).

Giuseppe Verdi

Giuseppe Verdi (1813–1909) was perhaps the greatest Italian musical dramatist, composer of some of history's most popular and critically acclaimed operas. Verdi's work continues to be performed to this day.

Verdi eschewed the symphonic leanings of Wagner and other contemporaries, preferring to concentrate on the more traditional operatic form. He eschewed modern chromaticism and hewed to diatonic harmonies; this inspired some to criticize his work as catering to the tastes of the masses.

Dramatically, Verdi exhibited a technical mastery of the operatic form and unsurpassed powers of characterization; the characters in his thirty-some operas are as real as the characters in Shakespeare and other traditional theater. That said, Verdi's work often veered close to melodrama, reinforcing his reputation as a populist rather than an intellectual innovator.

Verdi's most popular works include the operas *Macbeth* (1846–1847), *Rigoletto* (1850–1851), *Il trovatore* (1851–1852), *La traviata* (1852–1853), *Aida* (1870), *Otello* (1884–1846), *Falstaff* (1889–1892), and the *Requiem* Mass (1874).

Note

Verdi's popularity in Italy was unparalleled, and he became a national hero. On the occasion of his death, hundreds of thousands lined the streets of Milan, the schools were closed, and the Italian senate was called into special session.

Richard Wagner

We move into the late Romantic era with arguably the period's greatest composer. Richard Wagner (1813–1883) is a controversial figure, a composer, conductor, poet, and author with highly nationalist tendencies. He is primarily known for his grand operas; unlike other opera composers, Wagner always wrote the scenario and libretto for his works himself.

Wagner is one of the key figures in the history of opera, responsible for elevating the form to epic proportions through the use of larger orchestras, more prominent instrumental passages, and organically conceived, *through-composed* structures. Wagner's program of artistic reform built on the earlier grand opera to create a more grandiose style known as *music drama*.

Note

In a **through-composed** work, each act of the opera is a continuous piece of music with no breaks whatsoever. You find this style used today in some modern, all-singing, no-talking stage musicals, such as *Les Misérables*.

One can easily recognize Wagner's music for its power and size. He used huge orchestras augmented with vocal choruses, and his works often ran hours longer than comparable pieces from his contemporaries. (At the extreme, Wagner's complete Ring Cycle of four operas takes more than 15 hours to perform!) Wagner's music is also harmonically challenging, especially for the time; his use of extreme chromaticism and shifting tonal centers contributed to the atonal music of the twentieth century.

While Wagner's music dominated the late nineteenth century, it also split the music world into opposing camps—on one side the Classically influenced music of Brahms and Schumann, on the other the larger-than-life compositions of Liszt and other Wagnerites. In addition, Wagner's personal life alienated a good number of his contemporaries; he was anti-Catholic, anti-Semitic, a serial adulterer, and a supreme egotist. His incredible musical genius, however, produced works of incomparable scope—and forever changed the course of opera and orchestral music.

Richard Wagner, influential composer of the late Romantic era.

Note

A leitmotif is a theme assigned to a character. Think of the heavy music that plays whenever Darth Vader appears in *Star Wars,* for example.

Whatever one thinks of Wagner personally or professionally, there is no denying his influence on other composers. Not only did his work directly influence the school of twentieth-century composition (which we'll discuss in Chapter 7), his concept of leitmotif and integrated musical expression has become a stock in trade for motion picture scores. And Wagner's music has made it into the popular culture, from the use of the main theme for *Ride of the Valkyries* in the movie *Apocalypse Now* to the send-up of the Ring Cycle in the award-winning Bugs Bunny cartoon, *What's Opera, Doc?*

Wagner's Ride of the Valkyries—*"Kill the wabbit!"*

Wagner's notable works include Symphony in C (1832); *Der fliegende Holländer* (*The Flying Dutchman;* 1841); *Tristan und Isolde* (1857–1859); *Die Meistersinger von Nürnberg* (*The Mastersingers of Nuremberg;* 1862–1867); *Siegfried Idyll* (1870); *Parsifal* (1878–1882); and the opera cycle *Der Ring des Nibelungen* (*The Nibelung's Ring*): *Das Rheingold* (*The Rhine Gold;* 1853–1854), *Die Walküre* (*The Valkyrie;* 1854–1856), *Siegfried* (1856–1857), and *Götterdämmerung* (*Twilight of the Gods;* 1869–1874).

Jacques Offenbach

Jacques Offenbach (1819–1880) was a French composer and cellist. His main claim to fame is being one of the originators of the operetta form. (As we'll discuss later in this chapter, an operetta is a lighter, shorter, often comic opera.)

Offenbach's operettas were popular in both the French- and English-speaking worlds in the 1850s and 1860s, combining cultural and political satire with witty parodies of the then-popular grand opera.

Offenbach's most remembered works include the operettas *Orpheus in the Underworld* (1858), *La belle Helene* (1864), and *The Grand Duchess of Gerolstein* (1868), as well as the full-scale opera *Les contes d'Hoffman* (*The Tales of Hoffman*; 1880).

Anton Bruckner

Anton Bruckner (1824–1896) was an Austrian organist and composer known for his symphonies, Masses, and motets. His work is representative of the late Romantic period, full of rich harmonies and melodramatic melodies while also embracing dissonance and unexpected modulations.

Most of Bruckner's pieces are quite lengthy—although not nearly as long as a typical Wagner work. He was also prone to use overly large symphonic orchestras, again in keeping with the expansion in size of the day. His most notable works include Mass No. 1 in D Minor (1864), Symphony No. 4 in E flat Major (1874, revised 1878), String Quintet in F (1879), Symphony No. 7 in E Major (1883, revised 1885), Symphony No. 8 in C Minor (1887, revised 1890), Symphony No. 9 in D Minor (1896).

> **Note**
> Bruckner was prone to constantly revising his work—especially if a piece was panned by the critics. Thus it's difficult to accurately date his compositions; do you use the date of the original composition, or the date of the final revision?

Johann Strauss (II)

You remember Johann Strauss the Elder from earlier in the Romantic era. Now it's time to talk about his son, also named Johann Strauss (1825–1899) and often referred to as Johann Strauss the Younger or just Johann Strauss II. This Johann is the most famous member of the Strauss family, known during his lifetime as the "waltz king."

As you might suspect from that title, Strauss specialized in that dance form in triple time known as the waltz. Strauss revolutionized the waltz, elevating it from its origins a lowly peasant dance to entertainment fit for a royal court.

Strauss's most famous works include the waltzes "An der schönen blauen Donau" ("On the Beautiful Blue Danube"; 1867), "G'schichten aus dem Wienerwald" ("Tales from the Vienna Woods"; 1868), "Wein, Weib, und Gesang" ("Wine, Women, and Song"; 1869), and "Rosen aus dem Süden" ("Roses from the South"; 1880), as well as the operetta *Die Fledermaus* (*The Bat*; 1874).

> **Note**
> The waltz first became fashionable in Vienna in the 1780s, spreading throughout Europe in the following years. Waltzes are typically written in 3/4 or 6/8 time, the constant being the 1-2-3 count and generally slow tempo.

Johannes Brahms

Johannes Brahms (1833–1897), father of the self-named lullaby, was a German composer and pianist. Known for his chamber music, as well as the chamber-music qualities of his symphonic works, Brahms was able to spin themes, sections, and entire compositions from a few small motifs.

Brahms was regarded as the last of the true Romantics and the polar opposite of his more rebellious German contemporary, Wagner. A firm believer in conventional form and structure, Brahms in 1860 signed a manifesto opposing the "new music" methods adopted by Liszt and his followers. And Brahms's old-school nature is easily discerned in his music; there's no chromaticism or dissonance here, just very pretty, quite conventional melodies.

Brahms's best-received works were his piano pieces, lieder, and other art music; in these genres, he was regarded as the logical successor to Schubert and Schumann. Notable works include Piano Sonata No. 3 in F Minor, Op. 5 (1853); Symphony No. 1 in C Minor, Op. 68 (1855–1876); *Ein Deutsches Requiem* (*German Requiem*), Op. 45 (1857–1868); *Liebeslieder Waltzes*, Op. 52 (1868–1869); *Hungarian Dances* (1873); Violin Concerto in D Major, Op. 77 (1878); Piano Concerto No. 2 in B flat Major, Op. 83 (1878–1881); and Symphony No. 4 in E Minor, Op. 98 (1884–1885).

Note

Brahms's famous lullaby is actually the melody from a song titled "Wiegenlied: Guten Abend, gute Nacht" ("Good evening and good night") Op. 49, No. 4.

Johannes and Robert and Clara: A Romantic Soap Opera

We're used to the soap opera-like lives of modern music celebrities, but this sort of thing didn't originate with the rock era. In fact, one of the most famous celebrity soap operas occurred in the mid-1800s and involved Johannes Brahms, Robert Schumann, and Schumann's wife, Clara.

As you recall, Robert Schumann wasn't the only musician in his household; his wife, Clara Wieck Schumann, was a composer in her own right (66 pieces in all), and even better known as a talented concert pianist, playing works by Chopin, Brahms, and her husband. While Robert and Clara shared a passion for music, the problem of maintaining two active careers in the nineteenth century led to the expected friction between the two. Clara eventually gave up her musical career in deference to her husband's.

In 1849 the Schumanns fled a revolution in their home of Dresden and moved to Düsseldorf. It was there that Johannes Brahms entered their lives. Robert had often befriended and advised other composers, and in this fashion the younger Brahms came under his wing.

For several years the three of them—Robert, Clara, and Johannes—maintained a close friendship. But in 1854 Robert suffered a deep bout of depression, and committed himself to a mental institution. He died there two years later, leaving behind Clara, their eight children—and their friend Brahms.

During this trying period, music became Clara's solace. She eventually returned to the concert stage, resuming what became a 60-year performing career. She also turned to Brahms for consolation—which is where the soap opera part of the story begins.

Although Clara and Johannes's relationship was, by all accounts, strictly platonic, it did inspire much gossip in the music circles of the day. Brahms had moved into Clara's house, the better to help her and the children—although, to be fair, he had his own bedroom on a separate floor. And, while perhaps unconsummated, there was definitely a romantic component to their relationship, as evidenced by one letter Brahms wrote to Clara, where he expressed his yearning: "I can do nothing but think of you... What have you done to me? Can't you remove the spell you have cast over me?"

Clara became Brahms's muse, inspiring him to write music for her to perform. It is clear that she was the love of his life, and, perhaps, he of hers. While Brahms eventually moved out of Clara's house, he never married; the two of them remained connected to the end of their lives. When Clara died on May 20, 1896, Brahms was a pallbearer at her funeral. He died 11 months later.

Georges Bizet

Georges Bizet (1838–1875) was a minor French composer and pianist. He is best known for his symphonies and operas. Bizet's most popular work was the opera *Carmen*, first performed in 1875. Interestingly, *Carmen* was not initially well received; it took the attention and praise of contemporaries Debussy and Tchaikovsky (among others) for the opera to attain notice and enter the modern operatic repertoire.

Bizet died of a heart attack just a few months after *Carmen's* first performance. How many other great works might he have created had he not died so young?

Modest Mussorgsky

Modest Mussorgsky (1839–1881) represented the Russian Romantic school. He was one of a handful of innovative composers from St. Petersburg known as the Five (or the Mighty Handful); the others included Nikolai Rimsky-Korsakov, Mily Balakirev, César Gui, and Alexander Borodin. The Five had the nationalistic goal of producing a uniquely Russian kind of art music, rather than imitating older European forms.

Mussorgsky's major works were inspired by Russian history, folklore, and other nationalistic themes. His music is both powerful and sensitive, distinctly Romantic while using native Russian musical themes. His most notable works, many of which are staples of the today's orchestral repertoire, include the orchestral tone poem *St. John's Night on the Bald Mountain* (1867), the opera *Boris Godunov* (1869, revised 1874), and the piano suite *Pictures at an Exhibition* (1874)—famously orchestrated by Maurice Ravel in 1922.

> **Note**
> You probably remember *Night on Bald Mountain* from its use in the classic 1940 Walt Disney film *Fantasia*, and *Pictures at an Exhibition* from its 1971 interpretation by progressive rock band Emerson, Lake and Palmer.

Pyotr Illyich Tchaikovsky

When it comes to Russian Romantic composers, the most famous is arguably Pyotr Illyich Tchaikovsky (1840–1893). Tchaikovsky was both a composer and a conductor who achieved enormous popularity both in Russia and around the world.

While often criticized for his overt sentimentality and emotionalism (and fairly so, in my opinion), Tchaikovsky was an innate genius at creating melody. He was the first composer to assimilate the traditions of Western European symphonic music into the Russian national style, in the process creating a repertoire of richly lyrical works.

Tchaikovsky's melodies, while openly and often manipulatively emotional, are memorable—even to casual listeners. He was also not above riding the nationalistic wave, as evidenced in his famous *1812 Overture*, with its blaring horns and booming canons. You've heard it, probably performed at Independence Day concerts across the United States. (How's that for globalization—a Russian nationalistic piece written to commemorate France's unsuccessful invasion of Russia, used to celebrate American independence?)

> **Note**
> Tchaikovsky assembled eight of the more popular numbers from *The Nutcracker* ballet into a suite for concert performance. *The Nutcracker Suite*, Op. 71a, became perhaps more popular than the full ballet itself.

The famous theme from Tchaikovsky's booming 1812 Overture—*actually titled* Festival Overture "The Year 1812" in E flat Major, Op. 49.

Tchaikovsky's most famous compositions are his orchestral works and his ballets, which ushered in a new age of serious music composed specifically for dramatic dance. Notable works include *Romeo and Juliet* (1869); *Capriccio*, Op. 8 (1870); Piano Concerto No. 1 in B flat Minor, Op. 23 (1874–1875); *Swan Lake*, Op. 20 (1875–1876); Violin Concerto in D, Op. 35 (1878); *Festival Overture "The Year 1812"* in E flat Major, Op. 49 (1880); *The Sleeping Beauty*, Op. 66 (1888–1889); *The Nutcracker*, Op. 71 (1891–1892); and Symphony No. 6 in B Minor, Op. 74 (*Pathètique*; 1893).

Antonín Dvořák

By the late 1800s, nationalism had become an important influence on the music of the time. This is evidenced in the popular works of Antonín Leopold Dvořák (1841–1904), a Czech (Bohemian) composer of the late Romantic era.

One of the great nationalist European composers of the nineteenth century, Dvořák was a natural melodist with a flair for melodic invention and an innate ability to create complex melodic structures. Dvořák works emulated Bohemian folk songs, incorporating syncopated rhythms culled from native dances such as the polka and mazurka.

Dvořák most famous work, however, represented a completely different nationality. Following a trip to the United States in 1892, Dvořák was inspired by American Indian music, cowboy songs, and Negro spirituals; this is especially evident in his best-known work, the so-called *New World Symphony* (Symphony No. 9 in E Minor), which he wrote in New York City (and polished while summering in the Bohemian-settled town of Spillville, Iowa). This is a piece filled with memorable folk melodies, one of the most popular pieces in the modern "pops" orchestra repertoire. It is ironic, then, that the American nationalistic music movement was initiated by a Czech!

Note

Dvořák was so enthralled with America that he spent three years as director of Manhattan's National Conservatory of Music. He returned home to his native Prague in 1895, where he became director of the Prague Conservatory in 1901.

The American folk melody from the second movement (Largo) *of Dvořák's* New World Symphony.

Dvořák's works, tuneful as they are, are a particularly good way for the uninitiated to get into classical music; they're easy on the ear, and more modern sounding than works from earlier composers. His most notable compositions include *Romance* for Violin and Orchestra, Op. 11 (1873–1877); *Serenade* in E Major for Strings, Op. 22 (1875); *Slavonic Dances*, Op. 46 (1878); Symphony

No. 7 in D Minor (1884–1885) Op. 70; Symphony No. 8 in G Major (1889) Op. 88; *Carneval*, Op. 92 (1891–1892); Symphony No. 9 in E minor (*From the New World*; 1893) Op. 95; String Quartet No. 12 in F Major (*American*), Op. 96 (1893); and Cello Concerto in B Minor, Op. 104 (1894–1895).

Edvard Grieg

Nationalism in the late nineteenth century wasn't limited to the major European countries. This is evidenced by the works of Edvard Hagerup Grieg (1843–1907), a composer from Norway who was often called the "Chopin of the north."

Grieg's works drew inspiration from Norwegian folk music and dances. His best-known compositions include Piano Concerto in A Minor (1868), *Holberg Suite* (1884), and the incidental music to Henrik Ibsen's play *Peer Gynt* (1876)—which includes the suite *In the Hall of the Mountain King*. Grieg also composed 66 short piano miniatures, collectively known as the *Lyric Pieces*, from 1867 to 1901.

Nikolai Rimsky-Korsakov

Remember the Five, that group of Russian composers of which Mussorgsky was a member? Well, Nikolai Rimsky-Korsakov (1844–1908), another member of the Five, also makes our list of important Romantic-era composers.

Note
Rimsky-Korsakov is also known as a teacher of music harmony and orchestration. His book, *Principles of Orchestration*, is still read by music students today. (Me included!)

Rimsky-Korsakov was a prolific composer in the Russian nationalistic style, with 15 operas to his credit. His works incorporate lyrical Russian folk melodies and interesting modern orchestrations. His most notable compositions include the operas *The Tale of Tsar Saltan* (1900) and *Kashchey the Immortal* (1902), as well as the orchestral compositions *Capriccio espagnol* (1887), *Scheherazade* (1888), and *Russian Easter Festival Overture* (1888).

As skilled as he was at composition, Rimsky-Korsakov was perhaps an even more talented arranger and orchestrator of others' works. After Mussorgsky's death in 1881, Rimsky-Korsakov revised and completed several of his works (including *Night on Bald Mountain*) for publication and performance; in some instances, Rimsky-Korsakov's versions of these compositions achieved more success than Mussorgsky's originals.

Note
Rimsky-Korsakov's *The Tale of Tsar Saltan* includes the famous "The Flight of the Bumblebee" passage, which you might recognize as the theme song from the *Green Hornet* radio and television shows.

Gustav Mahler

The final Romantic-era composer that we'll discuss was one who, like Rimsky-Korsakov, bridged the nineteenth and twentieth centuries. Gustav Mahler (1860–1911) was an Austrian composer who initially gained fame as a conductor, including stints at the Budapest, Hamburg, and Vienna Court Operas. He later divided his time between conducting and composing, his works gaining popularity several decades after his premature death from a heart ailment.

Mahler was a disciple of Bruckner, a fellow Austrian. Mahler's music, especially his large symphonies, combined a romantic eloquence with subtle chromaticism and polyphony, which anticipated the coming avant-garde movement of the twentieth century. His most notable works include Symphonies No. 1 in D Major (1884–1888), No. 2 in C Minor (*Resurrection*; 1888–1894), No. 4 in G Major (1899–1900), No. 5 in C# Minor (1901–1902), No. 6 in A Minor (1903–1905), and No. 9 in D Major (1909–1910); *Das Lied von der Erde* (*The Song of the Earth*; 1907–1909); and the song cycles *Lieder eines fahrenden Gesellen* (*Songs of a Wayfarer*; 1884), *Des Knaben Wunderhorn* (*The Youth's Magic Horn*; 1888–1899) and *Kindertotenlieder* (*Songs on the Death of Children*; 1901–1904).

Bigger Than Ever: Romantic Instrumental Works

All those composers out of the way, let's take a quick look at the dominant musical forms of the Romantic period—starting with the period's instrumental music.

Note

As was the case throughout history, the music of the Romantic period was driven to some degree by the instruments that were available. To that end, the Romantic period saw the final evolution of most of the musical instruments used in symphonic orchestras today. Many of these developments—the use of valves on brass instruments, new key systems on woodwinds, and so on—made the instruments much easier to play, which encouraged their greater use in Romantic-era compositions.

The Romantic Symphony

The dawn of the nineteenth century saw a new artistic peak for the symphonic form. This is best seen in the later symphonies of Beethoven, which bridged the Classical and Romantic periods. Beethoven's Ninth Symphony, for example, is twice the length of his earlier symphonic works, and adds a large choir to the normal orchestral instrumentation.

In many ways the Romantic symphony is an expanded version of the Classical symphony. While symphonic music of the Romantic era remained faithful to the concept of the Classical symphony, it also responded to the grandeur suggested in Beethoven's later works. As the era developed, orchestras got bigger and symphonies got longer; Romantic-era symphonies tend to utilize larger orchestras than in the Classical period, and often incorporate more than four movements.

The Romantic period saw Mendelssohn and Schumann interject romantic feeling and pictorialism into the classic symphonic form, Liszt adapt the form into symphonic poems, Berlioz introduce programmatic elements (in his *Symphonie Fantastique*), and Brahms uphold the classical design. It is Bruckner's nine symphonies, however, that represent the epitome of the Romantic-era symphony, exploring classical principals on a grand architectural scale; his nine symphonies were on a monumental scale comparable to those of Beethoven, complete with soaring melodies and rich chromatic harmony.

Programme Music and the Symphonic Poem

The late Romantic period saw the development of *programme music*—an instrumental work that is associated with an extramusical image or narrative text. As originally described by Liszt, *programme music* is instrumental music that tells a story, illustrates a literary idea, or evokes a pictorial scene; programme music doesn't attempt a literal musical interpretation of the chosen text, but rather provides an impression that the listener can use as a starting point to grasp the poetic idea of the subject.

Primary contributors to the form included Liszt, Berlioz, Tchaikovsky, Strauss, and Mussorgsky. Notable works include Berlioz's *Symphonie fantastique*, Mussorgsky's *Pictures at an Exhibition*, and Richard Strauss's (1864–1949) *Also sprach Zarathustra* and *Don Quixote*.

The best-known type of programme music is the *symphonic poem*, a single-movement orchestral work on a symphonic scale. Liszt was the most visible proponent of this new genre; he composed 13 symphonic poems that dealt with subjects taken from classical mythology, Romantic literature, and imaginative fantasy, including *Prometheus* and *Les Préludes*. Other proponents of the form include Tchaikovsky, Bedřich Smetana (1824–1884), and Camille Saint-Saëns (1835–1921).

Concerto

The concerto also was expanded in the Romantic period. Starting with Beethoven, composers elevated the orchestra beyond mere accompaniment to more of an equal role to the soloist. In this respect, Romantic concertos began to take on symphonic qualities.

The Romantic period also saw an increase in popularity for the piano concerto. Mendelssohn, Schumann, and other composers created works that emphasized sustained dialogues between the piano and the orchestra, weaving both parts together into a dramatic whole.

Sonata

Just as Romantic-era concertos emphasized an equality between soloist and accompanying instruments, sonatas of the period increased the importance of the piano accompaniment in regards to the solo instrument. Romantic sonatas were as much piano works as solo vehicles, and often demanded a new level of technical dexterity of the keyboardist.

Later in the Romantic period, some composers began to expand the traditional three- or four-movement sonata form. Schumann, for example, created sonatas that more closely resembled fantasias; Liszt utilized a programmatic approach to unify the sonata's sections. Best representative of this newer approach is Liszt's Piano Sonata in B Minor, written in three thematically unified movements designed to be played without a break.

Singing a Simple Song: Romantic Vocal Works

Vocal music in the Romantic period explored the same boundaries as the instrumental music of the period—with both shorter, more intimate works and longer, more epic works joining the repertory.

Lieder

The most important new vocal form of the Romantic era was the simple song—in this case, the German art song, otherwise known as *lieder* (plural of *lied*, or "song"). Lieder are songs based on eighteenth- and nineteenth-century poetry, where composers attempted to portray with music the imagery and moods of the texts. The most popular lieder of the Romantic era were composed by Schumann, Strauss, Brahms, Schubert, and Hugo Wolf (1860–1903).

Most lieder consist of a single vocal line with piano accompaniment. This makes for a nice contrast with the massive orchestral and choral works that developed in Beethoven's wake.

Sacred Music

While the Romantic era was primarily secular, at least as far as music was concerned, one mustn't neglect the sacred music of the period—which, in terms of vocal music, means the Mass.

By the start of the nineteenth century, new Masses were being written largely to celebrate state occasions. These new works—such as Berlioz's *Grande messe des morts* —were typically conceived on a large scale, complete with orchestra and brass bands. In addition, the oratorio gained new prominence, along with similarly epic form, as typified by Mendelssohn's *Elijah* and Berlioz's *L'enfance du Christ.*

Opera, Operetta, and Ballet: Dramatic Music of the Romantic Period

Probably the most important form of vocal music in the Romantic era, however, was meant to accompany dramatic theatrical works. That's right, some of the most significant innovations in style and form were in musical drama—most notably the spectacular operas of France, Italy, and Germany.

Opera

Even with the introduction of new instrumental forms, opera remained the most popular music of the nineteenth century. During the Romantic period, the art of opera reached its zenith, producing grand spectacles and offering numerous showcases for spectacular singing. In every way, Romantic operas were longer, bigger, and more majestic than their Classical-era counterparts.

Characteristic of the new Romantic opera was the French *grand opéra*. This type of work—such as Berlioz's epic *Les Troyens*—was not only longer in duration than previous French opera, but also employed more musicians, more artists, more technicians, and more stagehands. This style was supplemented by *drame lyrique*, a more lyrical and sentimental style typified by Charles-François Gounod's (1818–1893) *Faust*.

In Italy, Rossini introduced a new style known as *bel canto* (literally, "beautiful singing"). This new style of opera featured complex and ornate melodic lines (which vocalists could ornament at will), simple harmonic structure, and musical numbers that combined to make composite scenes. Later in the nineteenth century, Rossini's fellow countryman Verdi introduced a new realism and intensity of expression to the form; his operas—such as *Rigoletto* and *La traviata*—combined rhythmic vitality with superbly crafted melodies to great popular acclaim.

In Germany, Wagner advanced the majestic *music drama*, which combined elements from Greek tragedy and the symphonies of Beethoven into a dramatic whole that was referred to as *Gesamtkunstwerk* ("Complete Artwork"). In this style, music and drama become one and indivisible.

Wagner's operas—most notably *Tristan und Isolde* and the four-opera cycle *Der Ring des Nibelungen*—pushed the boundaries of traditional tonality and impelled the art form to a larger scale. His groundbreaking work changed the nature of opera and influenced virtually all musical forms for decades to come.

Operetta

In stark contrast to Wagner's imposing dramatic operas, the Romantic period also saw the debut of a new, less-ponderous musical form called *operetta*. (Literally, a "little opera.") Rooted in the song and dance music of the late nineteenth century, the operetta was a form of light entertainment that—as practiced by Offenbach and Strauss—was a definite contrast the often self-consciously "heavy" music of the times. While this form was often dismissed as inconsequential and predictable, it proved phenomenally popular among audiences of the time.

A typical operetta is a play, often a musical comedy, with overture, songs, entr'actes, and dances. Examples include Offenbach's *La Belle Hélène* and Strauss's *Die Fledermaus*; also notable are the 14 operettas of Gilbert and Sullivan—Sir W. S. Gilbert (1836–1911) and Sir Arthur Sullivan (1842–1900). Their best-known works include *HMS Pinafore*, *The Pirates of Penzance*, and *The Mikado*.

Note

The ballet came into being in France and Italy during the sixteenth and seventeenth centuries, especially in the court of Louis XIV. The first ballet is generally acknowledged to be *Balet comique de la Royne,* given in Paris in 1581.

Ballet

A *ballet* is an entertainment in which dancers perform to music to tell a story or, in some cases, to express a mood. Over the years music for the ballet has proven as vital in the classical repertory as music for the symphony and the opera; most major composers—including Mozart, Beethoven, Verdi, Wagner, Tchaikovsky, Ravel, and Stravinsky—have composed for the ballet.

Prior to the Romantic period, music for the ballet was typically a mix of existing compositions and piecework by staff composers. Beginning with Beethoven's score for *Die Geschöpfe des Prometheus,* however, choreographers began to commission original music for their productions. This trend was particularly notable in Russia, where Tchaikovsky set new standards for the role of music in classical ballet. His most enduring works include *Swan Lake, The Sleeping Beauty,* and *The Nutcracker.*

Of these ballets, the average reader is probably most familiar with *The Nutcracker,* a favorite around Christmastime. The story involves a young girl named Clara, who is presented a toy nutcracker as a Christmas gift. Clara falls asleep and when the clock strikes midnight, the nutcracker and all the other toys come to life. The individual pieces within the ballet include the memorable *March* (of the toy soldiers), *Trepak* (Russian dance), *Waltz of the Flowers,* and *Dance of the Sugar-Plum Fairy.*

Listening List

A lot of well-known music was written during the Romantic period, which makes for a long and varied listening list. Here are some of the most popular pieces in history—in many cases, those that make up the repertoire of today's "pop" orchestras. This list includes piano music, vocal music, orchestral music, even waltzes, ballets, operas, and operettas. There should be something on this list for just about everyone!

Berlioz: Symphonie fantastique (New York Philharmonic; Leonard Bernstein, conductor)

Bizet: Carmen (Maria Callas; Nicolai Gedda; Paris Opera Orchestra; George Prêtre, conductor)

Brahms: Johannes Brahms Lieder (Anne Sofie von Otter)

Brahms: Hungarian Dances Nos. 1–21 (Budapest Symphony Orchestra; István Bogár, conductor)

Chopin: Favorite Piano Works (Vladimir Ashkenazy)

Dvořák: The Dvořák Album (Yo-Yo Ma; Boston Philharmonic Orchestra; New York Philharmonic)

Dvořák: Symphony No. 9 "From the New World" (Chicago Symphony Orchestra; Sir Georg Solti, conductor)

Gilbert and Sullivan: The Ultimate Gilbert and Sullivan Collection (New Symphony Orchestra of London; The D'Oyly Carte Opera Company and Chorus; Isidore Godfrey, conductor)

Grieg: Peer Gynt Suites Nos. 1 & 2/Lyric Suite/Sigurd Jorasalfar (Gothenburg Symphony Orchestra; Neeme Järvi, conductor)

Liszt: 10 Hungarian Rhapsodies (György Cziffra)

Liszt: Piano Concertos Nos. 1 & 2/Totentanz (Krystian Zimerman; Boston Symphony Orchestra; Seiji Ozawa, conductor)

Mendelssohn: A Midsummer Night's Dream (Boston Symphony Orchestra; Tanglewood Festival Chorus; Seiji Ozawa, conductor)

Mussorgsky: Pictures at an Exhibition/Night on Bald Mountain (New York Philharmonic; Leonard Bernstein, conductor)

Schubert: String Quintet in C, D (Emerson String Quartet; Mstislav Rostropovich)

Schubert: Symphonies 5, 6, 8, & 9/Rosamunde Overture (Berliner Philharmoniker; Herbert von Karajan, conductor)

Schumann: Kinderszenen/Kreisleriana (Martha Argerich)

Schumann: The Symphonies (Weiner Philharmoniker; Leonard Bernstein, conductor)

Strauss: Waltzes (Vienna Philharmonic Orchestra; Willi Boskovsky, conductor)

Tchaikovsky: Symphonies Nos. 4, 5 & 6 (Berliner Philharmoniker; Herbert von Karajan, conductor)

Tchaikovsky: The Nutcracker (St. Petersburg Kirov Orchestra; Valery Gergiev, conductor)

Verdi: Rigoletto (Joan Sutherland; Luciano Pavarotti; London Symphony Orchestra; Richard Bonynge, conductor)

Wagner: Die Walküre (Berit Lindholm; Birgit Nilsson; Vienna Philharmonic Orchestra; Sir Georg Solti, conductor)

Timeline: The Romantic Period

1820	The Missouri Compromise admits Missouri to the Union as a slave state
1822	Royal Academy of Music founded in London; Schubert writes Symphony No. 8 ("Unfinished")
1824	Beethoven writes Symphony No. 9 ("Choral")
1826	John Adams and Thomas Jefferson both die on July 4th (fiftieth anniversary of *Declaration of Independence*)
1827	Beethoven dies; Audubon publishes *Birds of America*
1829	Rossini's *William Tell* opera debuts
1830	Joseph Smith founds Church of Jesus Christ of the Latter-Day Saints

1831	Victor Hugo writes *Hunchback of Notre Dame*
1832	Samuel Morse invents the telegraph
1833	Brahms born; Chopin writes Twelve Etudes, Op. 10
1837	Charles Dickens writes *Oliver Twist*
1839	Daguerre invents photography
1840	Robert Schumann marries Clara Wieck; Tchaikovsky born
1841	Dvořák born
1846	United States declares war on Mexico
1848	Marx and Engels publish *Communist Manifesto;* gold discovered in California
1851	Verdi writes *Rigoletto*
1853	Wagner completes *Der Ring des Nibelungen;* Crimean War begins
1857	Supreme Court *Dred Scott* decision
1858	New York Symphony Orchestra gives first public concert; Puccini born
1861	American Civil War begins
1862	Debussy born
1863	Abraham Lincoln issues Emancipation Proclamation freeing slaves
1865	Wagner's *Tristan and Isolde* performed in Munich; Tolstoy writes *War and Peace;* Civil War ends; Lincoln assassinated
1867	Strauss (II) composes *The Blue Danube* waltz; Alfred Nobel patents dynamite
1870	Wagner's *Die Walküre* performed in Munich; beginning of Franco-Prussian War
1874	Strauss (II)'s *Die Fledermaus* performed in Vienna
1876	Alexander Graham Bell patents the telephone; baseball's National League founded
1878	Gilbert and Sullivan write *HMS Pinafore*
1879	Thomas Edison invents incandescent light
1882	Stravinsky born; Tchaikovsky writes *1812 Overture*
1882	Debussy writes *Le Printemps* orchestral suite
1884	Mark Twain publishes *The Adventures of Huckleberry Finn*
1887	Sir Arthur Conan Doyle publishes first Sherlock Holmes story (*A Study in Scarlet*)
1890	Massacre at Wounded Knee
1892	Tchaikovsky's *The Nutcracker* performed in St. Petersburg; Dvořák becomes director of New York National Conservatory of Music
1893	Tchaikovsky dies; Cole Porter born; Dvořák writes Symphony No. 9 ("From the New World")
1894	Debussy writes *L'Apres-midi d'un faune*
1895	Hindemith born; H. G. Wells writes *The Time Machine;* Marconi invents the wireless radio
1896	Richard Strauss writes *Also sprach Zarathustra;* Puccini writes *La Bohème*
1898	George Gershwin born

Chapter 7

The Death of Traditional Harmony: The Twentieth Century and Beyond

In This Chapter

- ◆ Discovering the multitude of twentieth-century musical styles, from Impressionism to atonality

- ◆ Learning the masters of twentieth-century music

- ◆ Understanding twentieth-century musical formats

If the Romantic period represented an evolution from the Classical period, composers in the twentieth century offered a revolution from their Romantic predecessors. The high value placed on individuality and personal expression in the late 1800s grew even more pronounced in the 1900s, with the very fabric of tonality being ripped apart in the search for new and unique musical forms.

The defining feature of twentieth-century music, then, is the lack of any central defining feature. Twentieth-century composers represent an enormous range of tastes, skills, and styles; what the general public continues to call "classical music" has splintered into a plethora of competing styles and genres.

Defining Moments of the Twentieth Century

Most readers of this book will be familiar with the major events of the twentieth century, having lived through many of them. It was a century of incredible change; it saw mankind move from trains to automobiles to airplanes to space-ships. The human race reached remarkable highs (landing on the moon) and unspeakable lows (the Holocaust). And, in the process, the world of serious music splintered into dozens of unrelated and sometimes unlistenable fragments.

Twentieth-Century History

The history of the twentieth century is one of both tremendous accomplishment and astonishing violence. On the plus side, a mastery of all things scientific changed daily life forever—we moved from a horse-and-buggy economy to a world full of automobiles, jet aircraft, personal computers, mobile telephones, the Internet, and iPods. The average household tossed out their iceboxes and replaced them with refrigerators and whole-house air-conditioning units. Medicine went from being barely sanitary to being able to prevent or manage even the most virulent diseases. And the rise of the middle class meant that millions of families could afford more than just basic clothing and shelter; even the masses were able to get a higher education.

But we also can't ignore the depths to which humankind sunk in the twentieth century. Two world wars devastated large swaths of the globe and killed millions of people, and numerous smaller wars killed millions more. Hitler's Holocaust introduced the notion of genocide into general society, but that wasn't the only instance of mass murder on that scale; consider Stalin's purges in Russia, Pol Pot's massacre of the masses in Cambodia, and various other "minor" incidents around the world that continue to this day. Add to that the horrors of the atomic bomb, and you get a picture that is less than shiny and bright.

Twentieth-Century Art and Literature

Earth in the twentieth century was a crazy, mixed-up place, and the art and literature of the time reflected this—often with disturbing results. In the world of art, the turn of the century started with the carryover of Impressionism, a late nineteenth-century style that emphasized the play of light on casual outdoors subjects. This style was succeeded by Fauvism, in which artists imaginatively used deep color and simplified shapes instead of the relatively representational approach of the Impressionists. By midcentury, Cubists were in the process of breaking subjects into basic geometric forms, while Surrealists were painting dreamlike images to suggest thoughts from the subconscious. Artists were doing everything except accurately representing the external world; it was as if the world itself was too dangerous to paint as is.

Modern literature also reflected this disintegration of the real world. Traditional narrative fell by the wayside in favor of linearly disjointed storytelling. A good example is the work of William Faulkner, in which the narrative is passed from character to character in different time frames; it is left to the reader to assemble the disjointed pieces of the narrative puzzle into a recognizable whole.

Variety Is the Spice of Life: Twentieth-Century Musical Styles

This disintegration of realism and abandonment of traditional narrative is reflected in the serious music of the twentieth century. Composers in the twentieth century experimented with all manner of musical styles, expanding on the sophisticated harmonies of the late Romantic period with increasingly radical explorations of chromaticism and non-traditional tonalities. The result was a multiplicity of musical styles and forms.

Unlike earlier eras where one or two styles ruled, the twentieth century saw no single dominant style. Bottom line, there is no such beast as "twentieth-century music," and no single sound that defines the era. Some twentieth-century music was lush and melodic, other music was harsh and chromatic; it was a century with a profusion and confusion of musical styles.

With so many different styles to choose from, many composers chose to work in multiple styles. That is, few composers were known for a single style; most wrote different pieces in different styles, or even combined styles within a single piece.

So the twentieth century was one of bold experimentation, dramatic rethinking of musical norms, and, at the end of the day, no single dominant style, form, or composer. To that end, the best way to examine the serious music of the twentieth century is to look at each musical style in turn—realizing, of course, that no single style represents the entirety of the period.

Note

All musical periods overlap to some degree, even those defined by a specific century. For our purposes, we'll say that twentieth-century music begins to develop during the 1880s, and continues into the first decade of the twenty-first century.

Impressionism

Twentieth-century music starts, to some degree, in the late nineteenth century, with the development of Impressionism. Starting around 1885 or so, French composer Claude Debussy became fascinated by Eastern music and the whole-tone and pentatonic scales. He helped create a style of music named after the impressionistic style of painting, where solo and orchestral music is created from subtle blends of sound similar to the blends of color in the paintings of Monet, Renoir, and Picasso.

Impressionism is all about suggesting a mood or subject using musical tones. It's a lulling kind of music that slowly surges forward and back; there are no distinct cadences or climaxes, as there are in earlier Romantic or Classical forms. Impressionist music uses more chromatic notes and dissonances, often to the point of abandoning traditional harmony. It's also a shorter form than the traditional symphony or concerto, whether in solo or ensemble form.

Note

Unlike traditional Western major and minor scales, which are composed of a defined series of half and whole note intervals, the whole note scale consists solely of a series of successive whole note intervals.

Take, for example, the opening flute theme from Debussy's *Prelude to the Afternoon of a Faun*, shown on the next page. The melody employs an easy chromaticism (the notes with accidentals—sharps and natural signs) that takes the line outside the traditional harmony and creates the appropriate atmosphere. Play the line for yourself on a piano or guitar, and you get a feel for how this Impressionism works.

The Impressionist movement lasted from the late nineteenth century into the mid-twentieth century. Besides Debussy, other composers working in the form include Maurice Ravel and Karol Szymanowski (1882–1937). Representative works include Debussy's *La mer* (*The Sea*) and *Prélude à l'aprés-midi d'un faune* (*Prelude to the Afternoon of a Faun*), and his opera *Pelléas et Mélisande*.

Debussy's Prelude to the Afternoon of a Faun—*an example of the Impressionistic approach.*

Note

Even though most Impressionistic musical works were composed in the twentieth century, some music historians define Impressionism as a Romantic musical style. This is understandable, given how pleasant Impressionist works sound compared to most other twentieth-century works. That said, the use of nontraditional harmonies and the whole tone scale firmly plants Impressionism in the style of the twentieth rather than the nineteenth century.

Chromaticism and Atonality

Impressionism is gentle, pleasant-sounding music; our next twentieth-century styles are not. And thus our introduction to chromaticism, which is, to many ears, an ugly-sounding music.

Throughout the Romantic era, chromatic notes became more and more common, typically augmenting the notes of the underlying musical scale. This Romantic concept of chromaticism continued to evolve in the modern era, to the point where the underlying scale was obliterated. Too many chromatic notes and there is no scale—and no underlying sense of tonality. This type of music with no underlying sense of tonal center or key is called *atonal*.

Note

Chromaticism is not unique to the twentieth century. Simply defined, chromaticism is the use of non-scale tones within a musical work. Normally, a composition uses the notes contained within a single major or minor scale. Any note not within that scale is a chromatic note, and such notes are common in earlier music forms—but, more often than not, used in passing.

You might think that by having no tonal center, atonal music would be extremely ugly or dissonant. Although atonal compositions can be dissonant, they don't have to be. It is possible for a composer to write chromatic melodies that are very smooth and lyrical, just as it is to write chromatic melodies that are ragged and dissonant. So don't think that atonally naturally equals ugly sounding; some atonal music is quite beautiful, if not wholly traditional sounding.

As an example, Arnold Schoenberg (1874–1951), Alban Berg (1885–1935), and Anton Webern (1883–1945) tend to write in a somewhat dissonant (or uglier) chromatic style. Béla Bartók (1881–1945) and Aaron Copland, on the other hand, tend to write more lyrical atonal music. There's a noticeable difference.

Representative atonal works include Schoenberg's *Pierrot lunaire* song cycle and Berg's opera *Wozzeck*.

The 12-Tone Method

In an attempt to more systematically distance this new atonal music from more traditional forms, Schoenberg introduced a rigid system of composition that became known as the *12-tone method*. In this system, the 12 tones of the chromatic scale are used once each in a predetermined order, called a *tone row*. This "melody"-like ordering can then be the basis for motifs, themes, and harmonies; just repeat the notes of the tone row in the predetermined order, and you have your "melodic" line. The result, however, sounds nothing like the melodies you're used to hearing in Classical and Romantic music; 12-tone music has an almost mechanical tonality with little or no relationship to the traditional tonalities of previous eras. It's as much math as it is music.

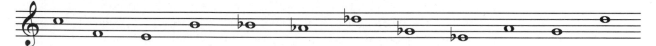

The 12 notes of the chromatic scale arranged in just one of the many possible tone rows.

If you want to hear what 12-tone music sounds like in practice, listen to Berg's *Lyric Suite* and Schoenberg's *Piano Concerto*. They're both representative of the style.

Serialism

The 12-tone method eventually evolved into another structured method called *serialism*. In this method, it's not just tones that are arranged in order; pitches, rhythms, and dynamics are all arranged in a predetermined fashion and then used (with accepted variations) to create the composition.

The most influential serial composers of the twentieth century include Karl-heinz Stockhausen (1928–2007), Milton Babbitt (b. 1916), and Pierre Boulez (b. 1925). Representative works include Babbitt's *Three Compositions for Piano*, Boulez's *Le marteau sans maitre*, and Schoenberg's serial opera, *Moses und Aron*.

Indeterminacy

While serialism is highly programmed, later composers believed that some aspects of their music should be left to chance. In practice, this means reducing the role of the composer as the controller of the music by letting the performer choose which notes to play, or basing some sound choices on the outcome of a random event, such as the rolling of dice. In some cases, proponents of *indeterminacy* use colors and symbols in place of traditional music notation.

Composers within this genre include John Cage (1912–1992) and Earle Brown (b. 1926). In theory, since no single work is played the same way twice, it's difficult to find representative works; in practice, indeterminism is a fad whose time has passed.

Polytonality

While some twentieth-century composers were working with highly programmatic serial compositions or highly random indeterminacy, both of which still used the 12 tones of the Western scale, other composers were looking for ways to expand the tonal alphabet. One such approach, known as *polytonality*, sought to use more than one tonality at the same time.

A polytonal composition is one that is written in two or more keys simultaneously. Although this sounds confusing, just imagine two separate ensembles, one playing in the key of F and the other playing in the key of G. The sound that results is polytonal.

There are two different ways to create a polytonal composition. One, as exemplified by the fanfare from Igor Stravinsky's ballet *Petrushka*, orchestrates a single melodic line as a duet between two different instruments, each playing the line in a different key. The second approach, often used by Charles Ives, involves the creation of two distinct compositions, in different keys, which are then played simultaneously. The end result is the same—a tonally unsettling experience for the listener.

A polytonal duet from Stravinsky's Petrushka.

Composers who worked with polytonality include Ives, Stravinsky, and Darius Milhaud (1892–1974). Representative polytonal works include Stravinsky's *Petrushka*; Ives's *Variations on a National Hymn, "America"*; and Milhaud's *Les Euménides* and *L'homme et son désir*.

Microtonality

The well-tempered system of tonality that we use today in Western music is by no means random, but neither is it absolute. Many other systems of intonation exist, though the exploration of them is fairly obscure in Western music. When playing such intonations on Western instruments, you end up using *microtones*—tones that fall in-between the well-tempered intervals, as represented by the keys on piano keyboard.

Another type of microtonality continues the evolution of tonality by dividing the octave into more and smaller harmonic intervals. So instead of having 12 chromatic notes in an octave, a microtonal scale might squeeze 24 pitches into the same space, thus creating quarter tones between the traditional half tones. The resulting sound is notably non-Western; some people might even think it sounds out of tune (at least, in relation to traditional Western tuning). Of course, a large quantity of world music would qualify as microtonal, at least to Western ears.

Western composers who pioneered the concept of microtonality include Bartók, Ives, Julián Carrillo (1875–1965), and Easley Blackwood (b. 1933). Representative pieces include Blackwood's *Twelve Microtonal Etudes for Electronic Music Media* and Carrillo's *Sonata casi fantasía*.

Minimalism

The style known as *minimalism* arose in response to the increasing complexity of both "classical" and popular music forms, including the highly sophisticated type of jazz known as bebop, which we'll learn more about in Chapter 9. Minimalism is hypnotic in its repetition, characterized by relatively simple melodies and rhythms employed with diatonic harmony and long pedal points.

A typical minimalist composition is based on a simple melodic motif, repeated numerous times with slowly evolving modifications. The same melody repeats over and over and over again, with only slight variation in instrumentation and harmonization.

Radical in the 1960s, minimalism has now become a completely normalized part of the compositional landscape. Consequently, it has evolved a much broader array of characteristics—and has achieved a great deal of popularity outside of classical music audiences, as well.

Chief among the minimalists of the late twentieth century are Philip Glass (b. 1937), Steve Reich (b. 1936), and John Adams (b. 1947). Representative works include Adams's minimalist opera *Nixon in China* (1987), and Glass's opera *Einstein on the Beach* (1975), as well as Glass's *Music in Twelve Parts* (1971–1974) and the score for the movie *Koyaanisqatsi* (1982).

Musique Concrète

Twentieth-century music doesn't have to be made on traditional musical instruments. In 1948, the French engineer and composer Pierre Schaeffer (1910–1995) began to use the newly developed magnetic tape recorder to record various everyday sounds, and then combine those sounds in various ways. The result was dubbed *musique concrète* ("concrete music"), as it consisted of real-world sounds, rather than the artificial sounds of musical instruments.

Other practitioners of what is admittedly an avant-garde style of music include Edgard Varèse (1883–1965), Ray Buttigieg (b. 1955), and rock composer Frank Zappa (1940–1993). Representative works include Varèse's *Poème électronique* and Buttigieg's *Earth Noise*.

> **Note**
>
> *Musique concrète* was also incorporated in several popular works by the Beatles and Pink Floyd, most notably in "Being for the Benefit of Mr. Kite" from the Beatles' *Sgt. Pepper's Lonely Hearts Club Band* album. All those swirly organ notes and crowd noises are part and parcel of the "found" sounds inherent in *musique concrète*.

Electronic Music

> **Note**
>
> Electronic music became more prevalent (and integrated into other musical forms) as newer types of electronic and digital instruments were developed in the later years of the twentieth century.

Musique concrète marked the beginning of what we now call electronic music. In this new and developing genre, electronic equipment—including but not limited to tape recorders, computers, and electronic synthesizers—is used to generate, modify, and combine all manner of sounds.

Notable composers of electronic music included Cage, Stockhausen, Varèse, Herbert Eimert (1897–1972), Iannis Xenakis (1922–2001), and Louis (1920–1989) and Bebe Barron (b. 1927). Representative works include Stockhausen's *Mixtur* and *Cosmic Pulses*, as well as the Barrons's all-electronic soundtrack for the science-fiction movie *Forbidden Planet*.

Neoclassicism and Neoromanticism

In a world of increasingly experimental and eclectic compositions, the styles known as *neoclassicism* and *neoromanticism* offered a welcome respite from oppressively progressive musical approaches. These styles marked a return to the classic concept that all elements of a composition should contribute to the overall structure of the piece; they blended formal schemes from the Baroque and Classical eras with a modified sense of tonality that embraced chromaticism and other elements of the Romantic and modern eras.

The foremost proponent of the neoclassical style was Igor Stravinsky. Retreating from the experimentation of his earlier works, Stravinsky began, in the early

1920s, to embrace the musical forms and instrumentation of earlier periods. He abandoned the dense chords and shifting meters characteristic of *The Rite of Spring* and other controversial works, substituting a more traditional tonality—although still filtered through modern harmonic sensibilities.

Other composers utilizing the neoclassical style included Europeans Sergei Prokofiev (1891–1953), Dmitri Shostakovich (1906–1975), and Paul Hindemith (1895–1963), along with American composers Virgil Thomson (1896–1989) and Elliott Carter (b. 1908). Representative works include Stravinsky's *The Symphony of Psalms* and *Oedipus Rex*.

The neoromantic style, distinct from neoclassicism, essentially continued the music of the Romantic era into the twentieth century. This style, like the original Romanticism, was freely chromatic over an overall traditional harmonic structure. Notable composers in this style include Ravel, Copland, Giacomo Puccini, and Sergei Rachmaninoff (1873–1943).

Nationalism and Folk Music

Throughout the centuries, music has been defined by various nationalistic movements. In the twentieth century, composers such as Copland and Ives introduced themes from American folk and religious music into classical forms, similar to the way Dvořák integrated folk melodies into his music of the late Romantic period, thus creating a new American nationalistic movement.

Other modern composers also worked with the folk music of their native countries; notable examples include Hungarian Béla Bartók, Czechoslovakian Leoš Jánaček, (1854–1928), and Englishman Ralph Vaughan Williams (1872–1958). Representative works in this style include Copland's *Appalachian Spring* and Vaughan Williams's *A London Symphony*.

American Music and Third Stream

While Copland helped to define distinctly American "classical" music in the twentieth century, other composers further wedded native musical forms (such as blues and jazz) to create an even more complete American musical language. Chief among these architects were George Gershwin (1898–1937) and Gunther Schuller (b. 1925), who coined the term *third stream* for the new musical styles that combined jazz and concert works. Representative of this third stream music are Gershwin's *Rhapsody in Blue* and *An American in Paris*, as well as the *Sketches of Spain* collaboration between jazz trumpeter Miles Davis and composer/arranger Gil Evans (1912–1988).

The Sounds of Silence—and Color

The musical forms discussed in this chapter are merely some of the best-known twentieth-century forms. There were even more unusual forms tossed around during the course of the period, some of them almost nonmusical in approach.

For example, some composers decided to forgo traditional compositional techniques to create *soundscapes* based on colors or shapes, which enable performers to interpret these symbols into pitches and rhythms. Others worked with *pitch-class sets*, which apply mathematical constructs to the compositional process. And still others embraced *biomusic*, in which sounds are created by animals or plants instead of human musicians. In these forms, the definition of music itself is being challenged; a piece can consist of any type of sound, not just traditional chords and melodies.

The most extreme of these extreme forms was the literal sound of silence created by John Cage in his famous work, *4'33"*. This was a piece for any instrument or combination of instruments; the score instructs the performer not to play the instrument during the entire duration of the piece. That's right, Cage's work was precisely 4 minutes and 33 seconds of silence! I'm not at all convinced that this type of thing is actual music; it seems more like a piece of conceptual art, to me. But whatever you call it, it's definitely avant-garde—and extremely controversial.

Notable Twentieth-Century Composers

I wrote earlier that there was no single dominant composer in the twentieth century. That is true; there was no Bach or Beethoven, Monteverdi or Mozart. That said, several composers stood above the pack and deserve individual mention. Their bios follow.

Giacomo Puccini

Giacomo Puccini (1858–1924) was a transitional composer, bridging the Romantic era and the twentieth century. Puccini's claim to fame was as a composer of popular operas, primarily in the Romantic or neoromantic style.

Puccini's first opera (*Edgar*) was a failure, but his second (*Manon Lescaut*) was a triumph, and led to further successes. His operas were marvels of characterization, sentiment, and craftsmanship; Puccini's mastery of melody and genius for orchestration made his works among the most popular and beloved in the repertoire. His later works included influences from contemporaries such as Debussy and Schoenberg.

Puccini's most memorable operas include *Manon Lescaut* (1890–1892), *La Bohème* (1894–1895), *Tosca* (1898–1899), *Madama Butterfly* (1901–1903), *La rondine* (*The Swallow*; 1914–1916), and *Turandot* (1920–1926).

Claude Debussy

Achille-Claude Debussy (1862–1918) was also a transitional figure, creating his most celebrated works during the turn-of-the-century years between 1890 and

1915. His music defines the transition from Romanticism to Impressionism; Debussy himself was the first musical Impressionist (although he himself disliked the term).

Born and raised in France, Debussy was a talented pianist from an early age. He entered the Paris Conservatoire at age 11, where he studied composition, harmony, piano, and organ with the major figures of the day. He began writing around 1880, and by 1890 was employing the chromatic harmonies and whole tone and pentatonic scales that would characterize his mature work.

In fact, it was the whole tone scale that came to define Debussy's later work. If you're unfamiliar with this scale, it's a succession of notes with the interval of a whole step between each note. (The following figure shows the C whole tone scale.) This is unlike the traditional major or minor scale, which uses a mix of whole and half-step intervals between notes. The sound of the whole tone scale is somewhat open ended, with no distinct resolving or home tone; whole tone melodies have that same unresolved quality.

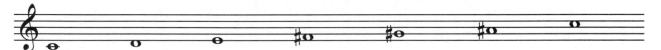

The C whole tone scale—the chromatic notes take it outside the traditional harmony of the C major scale.

Debussy's best music, for both solo piano and full orchestra, has a dreamy, lyrical nature, full of gently rolling piano figures and lush harmonies. His most famous works include *Arabesques* (1888, 1891); *Suite bergamasque: Prelude, Menuet, Clair de lune, Passepied* (1890); *Prélude à l'aprés-midi d'un faune* (*Prelude to the Afternoon of a Faun*; 1894); *Trois Nocturnes: Nuages, Fêtes, Sirènes* (1897–1899); *Le Mer* (*The Sea*; 1903–1905); *Children's Corner* (1906–1908); the opera *Pelléas et Mélisande* (1893–1902); and the song cycle *Chansons de Bilitis* (1897–1914).

Maurice Ravel

Joseph-Maurice Ravel (1875–1937) was a French composer and pianist. Like Debussy, Ravel was an Impressionist, known for the richness and poignancy of his music. He wrote for a variety of different instruments and ensembles, including solo piano, symphony orchestra, vocal choir, and chamber music; he was also known for his orchestrations and piano arrangements of existing works.

Ravel's best-known works include the piano compositions *Jeux d'eau* (1902), *Miroirs* (1904–1905), and *Gaspard de la Nuit* (1908–1909), as well as the orchestral works *Daphnis et Chloé* (1909–1912) and *Boléro* (1928). This last work is famous for taking a simple, unembellished theme and gradually building the orchestra around it. As Ravel purportedly remarked to a friend, "I'm going to try and repeat it a number of times without any development, gradually increasing the orchestra as best I can." And so he did.

Richard Strauss

Richard Strauss (1864–1949) was a German-born composer, conductor, and pianist. Equally adept at conducting and composing, Strauss was a master of several musical forms, most notably operas and orchestral tone poems. He wrote his first symphony at age 16, and assumed his first principle conductorship at 21.

> **Note**
>
> Don't confuse Richard Strauss with the two Johann Strausses from the Romantic era. (They're unrelated, in case you're curious.) As you remember from Chapter 6, both Johanns primarily composed waltzes; Richard composed tone poems and symphonies.

> **Note**
>
> You'll remember R. Strauss's *Also sprach Zarathustra*, of course, from the movie *2001: A Space Odyssey*—which also featured Johann Strauss's *Blue Danube* waltz. (How's that for a double dose of Strauss in a single movie?)

Strauss's richly melodic work, influenced by equal measures of Mozart, Mendelssohn, and Wagner, embraced a fading romanticism in stark contrast to the increasingly atonal musical environment of the early twentieth century. The success of his symphonic poem *Don Juan* established him as the natural successor to Wagner; subsequent works confirmed his stature in both the orchestral and operatic worlds.

His most notable works include the tone poems *Tod und Verklärung* (1888–1889), *Till Eulenspiegels lustige Streiche* (1894–1895), *Also sprach Zarathustra* (1896), *Don Quixote* (1897), *Ein Heldenleben* (1897–1898), and *Don Juan* (1898); the operas *Salome* (1903–1905), *Elektra* (1906–1908), and *Der Rosenkavalier* (1909–1910); and the symphonic works *Metamorphosen* (1945) and *Vier letzte Lieder (Four Last Songs;* 1947–1948).

Igor Stravinsky

Now we move to one of the most controversial figures of the twentieth-century music scene. Igor Stravinsky (1882–1971) was a Russian-born composer, conductor, pianist, and writer, the son of Fyodor Stravinsky, principal bassist of St. Petersburg's Imperial Opera. One of the most widely performed and influential composers of the twentieth century, Stravinsky explored a variety of musical styles over the course of his career; he had the uncanny ability to absorb other idioms without sacrificing his integrity and unique personal style.

Stravinsky's early ballets were somewhat traditional, reflecting a neonationalism typical of Russian composers of the time. During World War I, however, he broke with the Soviet Union and moved to Paris; his work in this period became increasingly progressive as he experimented with chromaticism and dissonance. Stravinsky's most notorious composition, the ballet *The Rite of Spring*, dates from this period; its initial performance shocked Parisian audiences with its abrasive harmonies and jagged rhythms, causing rioting in the theater. (That's right, folks—rowdy crowds at a classical music concert!)

In 1939, Stravinsky moved to the United States and embraced a more traditionally melodic neoclassical style. His final works, in the 1950s and 1960s, exhibited a return to experimentation, this time with twelve-tone serial music.

Stravinsky's most important works include *The Firebird* (1909–1910), *Petrushka* (1910–1911), *The Rite of Spring* (1911–1913), *Les Noces* (1914–1917), *L'histoire du soldat* (*The Soldier's Tale*; 1918), *Symphonies of Wind Instruments* (1918–1920), *Oedipus Rex* (1926–1927), *Symphony of Psalms* (1930), Symphony in C (1938–1940), Symphony in 3 Movements (1942–1945), and *Orpheus* (1947).

Arnold Schoenberg

Next up are two pioneers of atonal music. First in line is Arnold Schoenberg (1874–1951), an Austrian-born composer, conductor, and teacher who became an American citizen in 1941.

Schoenberg became famous for developing the revolutionary 12-tone system of composition, where each of the 12 notes in an octave are played in a set order, resulting in a rigid atonality. Himself self-taught, Schoenberg became a teacher to many notable twentieth-century composers, including Webern and Berg.

Schoenberg began exploring chromatic harmony in 1903, arriving at atonality in 1909 with *3 Pieces* for pianoforte and the song cycle *Das Buch der hängenden Gärten*; performances of these works were met with open hostility from audiences and critical acclaim from supporters. His "method of composition with 12 notes" was first expressed in 1923, with *5 Piano Pieces* and *Serenade*. In his later years, he alternated between 12-tone and traditional tonal compositions.

Notable works include *Pelleas und Melisande*, Op. 5 (1902–1903); *3 Pieces* for pianoforte, Op. 11 (1909); *Das Buch der hängenden Gärten*, Op. 15 (1908–1909); *5 Orchestral Pieces*, Op. 16 (1909); *Pierrot Lunaire*, Op. 21 (1912); *5 Piano Pieces*, Op. 23 (1920–1923), *Serenade*, Op. 24 (1920–1923); and *Suite* for piano, Op. 25 (1921).

Alban Berg

Our second atonalist is Alban Berg (1885–1935), another native Austrian. While embracing both atonality and the 12-tone method, Berg brought a welcome emotionality to what were often perceived as cold and calculating forms, making him one of the most influential composers of the early twentieth century.

His early studies with Schoenberg, along with a friendship with fellow composer Webern, influenced Berg's entry into the avant-garde. His first compositions were performed by other Schoenberg pupils in 1907; a 1913 concert of his works, conducted by Schoenberg, was continually interrupted by an outraged audience. (See a trend here?) Berg's later works, which applied atonality less formally than his mentor's strict 12-tone system, met with more popular success.

Notable works include *Altenberglieder* (1912); *Chamber Concerto* for pianoforte, violin, and 14 wind instruments (1923–1925); *Lyric Suite* for string quartet

(1925–1926); *Der Wein* (1929); Violin Concerto (1935); and the operas *Wozzeck* (1914–1922) and *Lulu* (1929–1935)

> **Note**
>
> As you might have noticed (and might have expected, actually), the move to atonality was not immediately embraced by concertgoers. Audiences reacted adversely to groundbreaking works by Stravinsky, Schoenberg, Berg, and others, sometimes jeering, occasionally rioting at performances. It was not what one would call "popular" music.

Charles Ives

Our final two twentieth-century composers are the first major American composers of so-called serious music. We'll start with Charles Ives (1874–1954), a native of Danbury, Connecticut.

Ives was one of the most individual figures in the history of Western music, his work foreshadowing the innovations of younger avant-garde composers. Ives's father, George, was a town bandleader who experimented with tone clusters, polytonality, and quartertones; Charles Ives inherited this fascination with clashing rhythms and tonalities, as exemplified by two bands playing different tunes at the same time or different sections of the orchestra playing in different keys.

As a teenager Ives was a church organist, and composed his *Variations on "America"* when he was 17. He composed his first symphony when he was a student at Yale; after graduation, he became a clerk at an insurance company, while continuing to play organ and compose. Throughout his life Ives balanced business and music, running his own successful insurance agency while composing a variety of complex vocal and instrumental works. In 1947, his Third Symphony won the Pulitzer Prize.

> **Note**
>
> I love Ives's music. He was somehow able to blend polytonality with lush, almost traditional melodies; of all the avant-garde twentieth-century composers, Ives is definitely the most listenable.

Ives's notable works include *Variations on a National Hymn, "America"* (1891); *Psalm 67* (1893); *Song for Harvest Season* (1893); Symphony No. 3 (*The Camp Meeting*; 1904–1911); *New England Holidays* (1904–1913); *The Unanswered Question* (1906, rev. 1932); *Orchestral Set No. 1 (Three Places in New England*; 1908–1914); Sonata No. 2 (*Concord, Mass. 1840–1860*; 1911–1915); and Symphony No. 3 (1913).

Aaron Copland

Aaron Copland (1900–1990) was known as the "dean of American composers," and he's arguably the most listenable of the bunch. This Brooklyn-born son of Jewish immigrants from Lithuania, Copland was instrumental in forging a distinctly American style of composition; his musical voice was the voice of rural America, incorporating simple harmonies and folk tunes.

Copland was, at heart, a neoromantic, although he did at times incorporate more modern techniques, such as tone rows, polytonality, and polyrhythms.

His work is richly melodic yet unsentimentally emotional; it is as American as a Norman Rockwell painting.

The dean of American composers, Aaron Copland.

Copland composed for both the concert hall and the screen; he scored numerous Hollywood movies, including *Of Mice and Men* (1939), *Our Town* (1940), *The Red Pony* (1948), and *The Heiress* (1949). His most memorable concert works include *El Salón México* (1934), *Fanfare for the Common Man* (1942), *A Lincoln Portrait* (1942), *Old American Songs* (1952), and the ballets *Billy the Kid* (1938) and *Appalachian Spring* (1944).

The main theme for Copland's memorable *Fanfare for the Common Man*, shown in the following figure, should be familiar to you. This piece was written at the request of conductor Eugène Goossens for the Cincinnati Symphony Orchestra; Goossens had commissioned similar fanfares from 17 other composers to open a series of concerts, but Copland's was the one that broke out from the pack. Copland considered titles for the piece along the lines of *Fanfare for Soldiers* and *Fanfare for Four Freedoms*, but decided to go with something a bit more egalitarian.

> **Note**
>
> If you love reading about and listening to music, you should check out Copland's book, *What to Listen for in Music* (Aaron Copland; Mentor; 1939—soft-cover revision 1999). It's eminently readable and thoroughly informing, a must-have for any serious music lover.

The theme from Copland's Fanfare for the Common Man.

Extending the Tradition: Twentieth-Century Musical Forms

We've looked at the myriad twentieth-century musical styles and the half-dozen or so most important twentieth-century composers. Now it's time to look at the musical forms used by these composers—from the traditional symphony to a new form: the movie score.

Symphony

Most major composers of the twentieth century utilized and expanded upon the traditional symphonic form. The modern symphony, however, was likely to incorporate extreme dissonances and jagged rhythms; many composers abandoned traditional tonality to embrace the various experimental styles typical of other twentieth-century music.

Representative of the modern symphonic form are the later works of Gustav Mahler and the symphonies of Jean Sibelius (1865–1957). As you remember from Chapter 6, Mahler composed lengthy works for large orchestras, some augmented by vocal soloists and massed choirs. Sibelius's compositions, in contrast, were shorter works for more traditional orchestras; he viewed the form as an abstract drama with a tight internal logic.

Opera

Opera in the first half of the twentieth century continued to be influenced by the works of the Romantic era—and, in fact, could be considered either Romantic or neoromantic in nature. For example, Richard Strauss, who bridged the Romantic and modern eras, composed intense works that reflected the tremendous influence of Wagner; Giacomo Puccini, with works such as *Turandot*, continued the Italian grand opera tradition of Verdi and Rossini.

World War II proved to be a turning point for twentieth-century opera, with post-war composers seeking to revitalize the form that had apparently come to a conclusion with the outbreak of hostilities in Europe. These newer composers, led by Benjamin Britten (1913–1976), breathed new life into opera by judiciously integrating other twentieth-century movements into the established art form.

Britten himself often worked outside opera's conventional boundaries, writing operas for children, for the church, and even for television. Later composers, such as Stockhausen and Krzysztof Penderecki (b. 1933), further pushed opera's musical boundaries, while Virgil Thomson and Douglas Moore (1893–1969) injected American musical styles into the form. At the dawn of the new millennium, composers such as Philip Glass and John Adams continued to change the face of opera, introducing multimedia elements, political commentary, rock music, and other unconventional elements into the operatic form.

Ballet

Ballet in the early twentieth century continued the recent practice of using specially written music by noted composers, such as Debussy, Ravel, Stravinsky, and R. Strauss. Perhaps the most notable—or notorious—of these new ballets was Stravinsky's *The Rite of Spring*. With music by and choreography by Vaclav Nijinsky, as you've already read, this 1913 work shocked audiences of the time with its jarring dissonances and equally revolutionary costumes and dance; its Parisian premiere resulted in a near-riot among concertgoers. Stravinsky's score was revolutionary, full of violent rhythms and harsh harmonies, its dissonant

Note

Other important symphonic composers of the twentieth century include Rachmaninoff, Prokofiev, and Shostakovich.

melodies masterful yet unsettling. While the original audiences were overwhelmed by the work's originality, critics recognized its genius, and *The Rite of Spring* has become one of the best-known and most influential pieces in the twentieth-century repertoire.

The second half of the century saw many ballet companies return to the historic practice of staging new ballets to existing compositions. There were several notable exceptions to this practice, however, including *Billy the Kid* and *Rodeo*, both by Aaron Copland; *Undine* by Hans Werner Henze (b. 1926); and Britten's *The Prince of the Pagodas*.

Musical Theater

The art form known as *musical theater* evolved from the operettas of the Romantic era and from the American vaudeville and European music hall traditions. During the last half of the twentieth century, many serious composers were drawn to the form, creating works that were very much in debt to the traditional opera. Most notable were Leonard Bernstein (1918–1990) and Stephen Sondheim (b. 1930); their operatic-like works, together and apart, include *Candide*, *West Side Story*, and *Sweeny Todd*.

> **Note**
> American musical theater is even more important in the context of twentieth-century popular music. Learn more in Chapter 10.

Film Music

The newly developed cinematic art form of the twentieth century presented another new venue for serious musical development, in the form of movie scores. That's right; one of the best places to hear "classical" music in the twentieth century was at the movie theater!

The most innovative film composers—including Erich Wolfgang Korngold (1886–1957), Max Steiner (1888–1971), Dmitri Tiomkin (1894–1979), Bernard Herrmann (1911–1975), Elmer Bernstein (1922–2004), Ennio Morricone (b. 1928), and John Williams (b. 1932)—utilized all manner of modern musical conventions in their film scores. In addition, many of the twentieth century's so-called "serious" composers (such as Copland and Glass) also made contributions to the genre or had their works adapted for the screen.

The best original film scores were neoclassical or neoromantic in nature; many composers utilized 12-tone and other chromatic/atonal techniques to establish specific moods and effects. The most notable scores of the century include *King Kong* (1933, Max Steiner), *The Adventures of Robin Hood* (1938, Erich Korngold), *Psycho* (1960, Bernard Herrmann), *The Magnificent Seven* (1960, Elmer Bernstein), *The Good, The Bad & The Ugly* (1966, Ennio Morricone), *Once Upon a Time in the West* (1968, Ennio Morricone), and *Star Wars* (1975, John Williams).

The Death of Serious Music

Let's be honest: while "classical" music was the "popular" music of centuries past, that was not the case during the twentieth century. The popularity of so-called serious music waned in the years after the first world war; in its place came wave after wave of popular song, from Tin Pan Alley tunesmiths, Brill Building songwriting teams, and Liverpudlian lads with shaggy haircuts.

Why did serious music fade from popularity during the twentieth century? I think it's because it became too complex, too intellectual. The average listener can hear a simple folk melody and identify with its traditional harmonies and common cadences; it's much more difficult to make any sort of connection with music that has no set tonal center, or that abandons traditional scales for excessive chromaticism. Let's face it, most people don't like to have to work at their entertainment—and most twentieth-century music requires a lot of work on the part of the listener. Whether you're talking Schoenberg's tone rows or Cage's 4 minutes and 33 seconds of silence, these are not tunes that you can walk away humming.

Thus did serious composers eventually abandon the concepts of melody and harmony that drove the music from the Baroque through the Romantic eras. I suppose one could argue that all that could be said using these traditional forms had been said; one could also argue that a talented composer can always find something new to say, no matter how old the form. In any case, serious composers eventually evolved themselves out of favor; newer music, particularly that of the second half of the twentieth century, has not found much of an audience.

That doesn't mean that there is no longer an audience for serious music. Evidence to the contrary is found in the schedule for any major metropolitan symphony orchestra, which is chock-full of music from the Baroque, Classical, and Romantic periods. It's not that audiences don't want to listen to serious music; it's just that they want to listen to serious music with memorable melodies. So don't worry; Bach, Beethoven, and Mozart (and, for that matter, Dvořák, Debussy, and Copland) will never go out of favor.

That said, the true popular music of the twentieth century was made by guys named Gershwin, Porter, and Berlin—as well as Lennon, McCartney, and Bacharach. These composers wrote shorter pieces, mere songs, but achieved a popularity that eclipsed that of the classical masters in their prime. This new popular music is every bit as important as the traditional "classical" music, and thus warrants its own section in this book. So turn to Part 2, "American Popular Music," to learn this new music history. It's a fascinating story.

Listening List

I'm going to be gentle with you and not pack this particular listening list with lots of odd-sounding atonal and 12-tone works. Oh, there's a little of that (I'd be remiss to exclude it completely), but the bulk of the recordings here are of a more listenable nature—works you've probably heard or heard of, in other contexts.

Bartók: Concerto for Orchestra; Music for Strings, Percussion and Celestra (Brussels BRTN Philharmonic Orchestra; Alexander Rahbari, conductor)

Berg: Chamber Concerto; Three Orchestral Pieces, Op. 6; Violin Concerto (BBC Symphony Orchestra; London Symphony Orchestra; Pierre Boulez, conductor)

Britten: War Requiem, Op. 66 (Atlanta Symphony Orchestra; Robert Shaw, conductor)

Copland: Orchestral Works (Academy of St. Martin-in-the-Fields; Detroit Symphony Orchestra; London Sinfonietta; Los Angeles Philharmonic Orchestra)

Debussy: La Mer (Montreal Symphony Orchestra; Charles Dutoit, conductor)

Debussy: Piano Works (Pascal Rogé)

Gershwin: Rhapsody in Blue; Piano Concerto in F; An American in Paris (Pittsburgh Symphony Orchestra; André Previn, conductor)

Glass: Koyaanisqatsi (Philip Glass Ensemble; Michael Riesman, conductor)

Ives: Concord Sonata; Songs (Pierre-Laurent Aimard; Susan Graham)

Ives: The Symphonies/Orchestral Sets 1 & 2 (Los Angeles Philharmonic Orchestra; The Cleveland Orchestra; Academy of St. Martin-in-the-Fields)

Morricone: The Good, The Bad & The Ugly (Original Motion Picture Soundtrack)

Morricone: Once Upon a Time in the West (Original Motion Picture Soundtrack)

Puccini: Madama Butterfly (Maria Callas; Lucia Danieli; La Scala Theater Orchestra; Herbert von Karajan, conductor)

Ravel: Bolero (Montreal Symphony Orchestra; Charles Dutoit, conductor)

Schoenberg: Gurrelieder (Berlin Philharmonic Orchestra; Ann Sofie von Otter, conductor)

Schoenberg: Verklärte Nacht; Pelleas und Melisande (Berlin Philharmonic Orchestra; Herbert von Karajan)

Strauss: Also sprach Zarathustra/Don Juan (Berliner Philharmoniker; Herbert von Karajan, conductor)

Stravinsky: Petrushka; Le Sacre de printemps (The Cleveland Orchestra; Pierre Boulez, conductor)

Stravinsky: The Rite of Spring; The Firebird Suite (New York Philharmonic; London Symphony Orchestra; Leonard Bernstein, conductor)

Timeline: The Twentieth Century

1900	Aaron Copland born; Puccini's opera *Tosca* premieres
1901	Queen Victoria dies
1902	Debussy's opera *Pelléas et Mélisande* debuts
1903	Wright Brothers' first flight
1904	London Symphony Orchestra founded; New York subway opens
1908	Schoenberg introduces the concept of dissonance; Debussy writes *Children's Corner Suite*; Henry Ford introduces the Model T
1910	Stravinsky finishes *The Firebird*
1912	Sinking of the *Titanic*

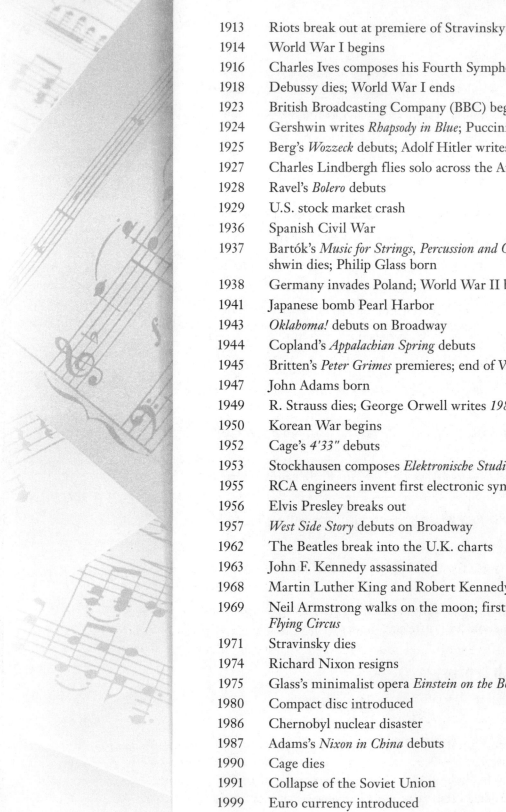

1913	Riots break out at premiere of Stravinsky's *The Rite of Spring*
1914	World War I begins
1916	Charles Ives composes his Fourth Symphony
1918	Debussy dies; World War I ends
1923	British Broadcasting Company (BBC) begins first broadcasts
1924	Gershwin writes *Rhapsody in Blue*; Puccini dies
1925	Berg's *Wozzeck* debuts; Adolf Hitler writes *Mein Kampf*
1927	Charles Lindbergh flies solo across the Atlantic
1928	Ravel's *Bolero* debuts
1929	U.S. stock market crash
1936	Spanish Civil War
1937	Bartók's *Music for Strings, Percussion and Celestra* debuts; George Gershwin dies; Philip Glass born
1938	Germany invades Poland; World War II begins
1941	Japanese bomb Pearl Harbor
1943	*Oklahoma!* debuts on Broadway
1944	Copland's *Appalachian Spring* debuts
1945	Britten's *Peter Grimes* premieres; end of World War II
1947	John Adams born
1949	R. Strauss dies; George Orwell writes *1984*
1950	Korean War begins
1952	Cage's *4'33"* debuts
1953	Stockhausen composes *Elektronische Studie I*; DNA discovered
1955	RCA engineers invent first electronic synthesizer
1956	Elvis Presley breaks out
1957	*West Side Story* debuts on Broadway
1962	The Beatles break into the U.K. charts
1963	John F. Kennedy assassinated
1968	Martin Luther King and Robert Kennedy assassinated
1969	Neil Armstrong walks on the moon; first broadcast of *Monty Python's Flying Circus*
1971	Stravinsky dies
1974	Richard Nixon resigns
1975	Glass's minimalist opera *Einstein on the Beach* premieres
1980	Compact disc introduced
1986	Chernobyl nuclear disaster
1987	Adams's *Nixon in China* debuts
1990	Cage dies
1991	Collapse of the Soviet Union
1999	Euro currency introduced

Chapter 8

This Led to That: The Evolution of Classical Music

In This Chapter

- ◆ Learn how classical music evolved from era to era
- ◆ Discover how music changed from sacred to secular
- ◆ Find out how a composer's employer determined what type of music he wrote
- ◆ Learn how the evolution of musical instruments affected musical styles
- ◆ Follow the evolution of melody and harmony through the ages

In the first seven chapters of this book, we've looked at each successive period in classical music history, from the prehistoric era to the twentieth century. That's all well and good, but it's kind of hard to see the big picture when you're focusing on the details of an individual era. And the big picture is important; how, after all, did we get from Bach to Stravinsky? There is a thread (more than one, actually) that connects the two, but you need to step back a few paces to see it.

That's what this chapter is about—stepping back from the details to help you see the big picture. To see that big picture, we'll look at classical music history from several different directions to tie all the disparate bits and pieces together over time.

Musical Evolution by Era

Let's start with the traditional way of looking at music history—by era. That's how we've looked at it throughout this book, so it doesn't hurt to use the same approach to recap musical evolution across the eras. Using this approach, one characterizes the evolution of classical music through six major stylistic periods.

Era	Years	Characteristics	Sacred or Secular?	Major Composers
Middle Ages	476–1400	Simple monophonic Gregorian chant, secular troubadour songs, harmony based on fifths and octaves	Primarily sacred	Machaut
Renaissance	1400–1600	Polyphonic sacred music with all parts of equal importance	Primarily sacred; some secular madrigals	Josquin des Préz, Palestrina, Dufay
Baroque	1600–1750	Ornate multiple-part sacred music	Mix of sacred and secular	Bach, Handel, Monteverdi, Vivaldi
Classical	1750–1820	Lyrical melodies with chordal accompaniment in both chamber music and larger ensembles	Primarily secular, with some sacred masses and oratorios	Haydn, Mozart, Beethoven
Romantic	1820–1900	Lush, overly emotional melodies overlaid with subtle use of chromatics, especially in large symphonic and choral ensembles	Primarily secular	Tchaikovsky, Verdi, Wagner, Chopin, Brahms, Mendelssohn, Dvořák
Twentieth Century	1900–2000	Chromaticism, atonality, Impressionism, serial music	Primarily secular	Debussy, Stravinsky, Copland, Schoenberg, Ives

Looking at the evolution of classical music in this fashion, we see where each period (save for the last) has its own unique musical characteristics. Medieval music is simple and mainly monophonic; Renaissance music becomes more complex with equally-weighted polyphony; Baroque music elaborates on that with heavily ornamented melodies; Classical music simplifies the ornamentation and focuses on lyrical melodies; Romantic music becomes even more emotional and introduces a degree of chromaticism over the traditional harmonies; and twentieth-century music abandons traditional harmony completely in favor of full chromaticism and atonality. It's a continuous evolution.

This approach also lets you easily place any individual composer or composition within a specific era. When you hear an ornate Bach piano piece, you know it's Baroque; when you hear a lush and melodramatic piece by Chopin, you know it's Romantic; when you hear Stravinsky's tapestry of tonal madness, you know it's a twentieth-century piece.

Of course, this approach isn't perfect; some composers bridge eras. Take Beethoven, for example; listening to a Beethoven symphony, it's difficult to say whether it's Classical or Romantic in nature. Same thing with Debussy—do his Impressionistic pieces fall into the Romantic or twentieth-century categories?

Still, this approach is perhaps the easiest way to categorize serious music over the years; it works both stylistically and chronologically. What it doesn't do, unfortunately, is answer the "why" behind the "what." When you want to know why music evolved from era to era, you have to examine other factors—which we'll do throughout the rest of this chapter.

> **Major Composers**
>
> Traditional music history looks at classical music by era and by major figures. It helps, of course, that most musical periods were defined by a handful of important composers, and that few composers bridged multiple eras.
>
> If you're short on time and memory, you can focus on the Big Three composers: Bach, Mozart, and Beethoven. Bach, of course, defined the Baroque era, which is the first era that contributes heavily to today's classical repertoire. (Not a lot of local symphonies play medieval or Renaissance music today.) Mozart is a pure Classical-era composer, and Beethoven, while technically a bridge figure, is used in this instance to define the late Classical and Romantic eras. Remember the Big Three, then, and you cover the three most important musical eras.
>
> Of course, a more thorough historian would include more than just three composers in his survey of important musical figures. I think we can comfortably expand the list to the Big 10 composers, in chronological order:
>
> Handel
> Bach
> Haydn
> Mozart
> Beethoven
> Tchaikovsky
> Wagner
> Debussy
> Stravinsky
> Copland
>
> Listen to the works of these composers and you'll cover most of what's important from the Baroque era through the twentieth century—Handel and Bach for the Baroque; Haydn, Mozart, and Beethoven for the Classical; Tchaikovsky and Wagner for the Romantic; and Debussy, Stravinsky, and Copland for the most important aspects of twentieth-century music.
>
> Why these ten composers? That's a good question; the contents of any such list can always be debated. Some historians, for example, might argue that Monteverdi is historically more important than Tchaikovsky, or that Schoenberg is more influential than Copland. Those are fair arguments, but this is my book and this is my list; it reflects my biases but also does a good job of representing the most important (and, to some extent, the most popular) music of the various eras. So remember these composers (and any others that you particularly like) and you'll cover most of your musical bases.

Musical Evolution: Sacred vs. Secular

When you're looking at what influenced the evolution of music through the eras, one important factor to consider is religion. This is because a huge amount of music (and art and literature, to be sure) over the years has been directly or indirectly inspired by or written for the church.

Consider the earliest music on record, back in the Middle East. The ancient Egyptians made music an important part of their religious ceremonies; ancient Babylonian liturgical services included antiphonal hymns; and the Hebrews played music in their religious festivals. Even the ancient Greeks equated music with religion; they believed that music originated from the god Apollo.

So early music was primarily sacred, in the honor of whichever god or gods a society worshipped. This continued into the Medieval period, with the only change being that the Christian god replaced the various pagan gods as the subject of the sacred music. This era was dominated by the plainchant and Gregorian chant used in the Roman Catholic Mass and other religious ceremonies; while roaming troubadours played some secular music, this was predominantly a period of sacred music.

Moving ahead into the Renaissance, we find sacred music still dominating. The Mass was the most important musical form; also important were the motet and chorale, two more sacred forms. But the late Renaissance period also saw a flowering of secular music, in the form of chanson and madrigals. In terms of the sacred/secular balance, change was in the air.

This balance tipped some more during the Baroque era. Composers like Haydn and Bach continued to write sacred works, to be sure, but also produced a great number of secular pieces. Bach, for example, wrote his share of Masses and chorales (as well as large-scale sacred choral works, such as *St. Matthew Passion*), but also produced a large number of purely secular instrumental pieces. In addition, the Baroque era saw the rise of the secular opera, as well as new secular instrumental forms such as the sonata and concerto.

By the start of the Classical period, sacred musical works were in the minority. Classical composers such as Mozart and Beethoven based their compositions on primarily secular topics; in this age of nationalism and revolution, the heroic ideal was in full force. Yes, most composers continued to produce some sacred works (Masses and oratorios, mainly), but the majority of compositions were secular in nature—and this trend continued into the Romantic and twentieth-century periods.

Why this shift from sacred to secular music? In part, it reflected the declining importance of the church in society; the Western world itself had become more secular over time. But this change also reflected who was commissioning the work. In earlier eras, most musicians were in the employ of the church, and thus were compelled to write music for church services. Palestrina, for example, served as musical director of the Julian Chapel and official composer to the Sistine Chapel; is it any surprise that he composed over a hundred sacred Masses?

As we progress to the Baroque and Classical periods, we find more and more composers embracing the patronage system, where they were employed by wealthy noblemen and the ruling elite. No longer working for the church, musicians were not as compelled to write church music. Instead, they wrote secular music for their secular employers.

Thus you can trace the evolution of classical music by examining the sacred or secular nature of the music. More sacred music was created during the earlier eras; music of the later eras was more likely to be secular in nature.

Musical Evolution by Employer

Let's elaborate on that last factor a bit. You may not have thought of this before, but how a composer paid his bills influenced the type of music he wrote.

In earlier eras, a composer was likely to be employed by a local church, either as choirmaster or musical director. The bigger the church, the more prestigious the job. And, as terms of employment, the composer was expected to produce work that would be sung or played at church services. Hence the profusion of Masses and other sacred works in the medieval and Renaissance eras.

Moving into the Baroque era, we see the start of the patronage system. In this system, a composer would be employed by a patron—typically a member of a royal court or a wealthy family. The composer was employed to provide music for the court or family; he typically performed himself, accompanied other musicians, and conducted both small and large ensembles. Of course, the composer was also expected to provide original works for his employer's various functions, which led to a profusion of secular compositions in this and succeeding eras.

A great example of the patronage system at work can be seen in the life of Haydn, who for most of his career was employed as Kapellmeister for the House of Esterházy. He provided all manner of chamber music and orchestral compositions that were played at various court functions, and was paid well for his efforts. He also gained such notoriety that he began to freelance outside of his day job; he was fortunate that his employers let him create works on commission for other wealthy music lovers in Vienna.

The patronage system continued through the beginning of the Classical period, but had died out by the end of that era. (Haydn was let go by the Esterházys in 1790, although they were kind enough to provide him with a ceremonial title and nominal stipend in consideration for his previous years of service.) Without wealthy employers paying the bills, composers had to pay their own way, essentially becoming self-employed freelancers.

This worked out well for some, less well for others. In reality, most composers paid the bills by performing, either their own works or works of others. Then as is today, there was big money to be made on the concert circuit, which favored those composers who were also popular and prolific performers. (It's telling that Mozart's fortunes hit the skids when he cut back on his concert work—even though he kept composing right up until his death.)

The most famous composers, of course, could make a living performing or conducting their own works. Beethoven, for example, made money by arranging subscription concerts—in essence, becoming his own concert promoter. He also was able to sell his works to music publishers, which supplemented his concert income.

Once composers freed themselves from the patronage system (and from the cushy incomes associated with it), they were free to write anything they wanted to. They were no longer writing on commission for a specific patron or for works to be played at specific events; they were creating for the sake of creation, composing the music they wanted to create as opposed to music that others wanted to hear. This enabled composers to break free from the bonds of tradition and familiarity and explore new creative ground. Starting from the late Classical period and into the Romantic era, then, we see increasing amounts of experimentation, in terms of form, instrumentation, and harmony.

This trend became even more extreme in the twentieth century. The culture had changed; no longer were composers "big names" among the general populace, as Mozart and Beethoven had been. Once we got past Stravinsky, the typical composer of serious music faded into the background, his work performed to smaller and smaller audiences over time. Ives, after all, had a day job as an insurance agent; other composers made their money teaching at music schools.

On the plus side, this freed twentieth-century composers to write virtually any type of music they wanted; they didn't have to cater one bit to popular opinion. On the minus side, it perhaps disconnected some composers from the tastes of the general public. Serious music became more theoretical and less popular, which is where it remains today.

Musical Evolution by Instrument

Another way to look at the evolution of serious music is to consider the available instruments in each era. To some extent, composers write for what instruments are available; the more and more versatile the available instruments, the more sophisticated the resulting compositions.

Consider the earliest music, in the prehistoric and ancient periods. Music in these years was limited by the primitive instruments available, simple flutes and drums and such. You can't play anything too complicated on instruments like these, which no doubt contributed to the simple monophonic melodies produced in those eras.

Moving into the Middle Ages, we see the adoption of multiple-stringed instruments, such as lutes and lyres. This was important for two reasons. First, a stringed instrument lets you play intervals of any size, as opposed to the limited intervals possible with simple flutes. Second, when you have multiple strings, you can play more than one note at the same time—that is, you can strum a chord. This led to the melody-plus-accompaniment style common in the music of the troubadours.

The Baroque era saw the development of more modern wind instruments— clarinet, trumpet, French horn, and so forth. These instruments were capable of reproducing a full range of scalar pitches, and combined to create a variety of different musical sounds and colors. For the first time, composers could write for reedy woodwinds and full-throated brass instruments; this, along with the development of modern bowed string instruments, led to the creation of the early orchestra.

Note

The best-paid classical composers today are film composers. These composers, in a sense, are part of a new patronage system; their patrons are the big movie studios that commission their work.

Note

Flute-like instruments can play only a limited number of notes, depending on how many holes are present in the instrument. The fewer the holes, the fewer the notes possible—typically with very large intervals between each pitch.

The other important development in this era was the evolution of the keyboard family. At the beginning of the Baroque era the primary keyboard instrument was the harpsichord, which was incapable of dynamics; everything came out at the same volume level. By the end of the Baroque, the harpsichord had pretty much been replaced by the piano, which had a large dynamic range (and a bigger keyboard, too—which meant lower low notes and higher high ones). The piano is an extremely versatile instrument, and inspired composers to create works of great technical challenge. This, in turn, led to the creation of the new piano sonata musical form, and of the use of the piano as a full-featured accompaniment instrument.

By the start of the Classical period, the modern orchestra as we know it was fully in place. And with all those instruments available, why not use them? That seemed to be what Beethoven was thinking as he expanded the size of the orchestra in his later symphonies; the same thinking informed the majestic works of Wagner and other Romantic-era composers. More instruments, larger orchestras, more powerful symphonies. That was the trend.

That was the trend, at least, until the advent of electronic instruments in the second half of the twentieth century. Why go to all the trouble (and expense!) of hiring and rehearsing a 100-piece orchestra when you could create similar sounds from an electronic synthesizer? Constantly in search of new sounds, twentieth-century composers embraced electronic synthesizers, sequencers, and other digital instruments to create fully electronic soundscapes—or, in some cases, integrated electronic sounds with traditional acoustic instruments. With all these options available, composers of the twenty-first century will be able to create virtually any sound they can imagine.

And there's the trend. Composers utilize whatever instruments are available. When the only instrument available was the bone flute, composers wrote for the limited range of that instrument. When the piano was invented, composers expanded their works to incorporate all 88 white and black notes. And with the advent of electronic instruments, they added all sorts of swirling bleeps and bloops to their compositions. Composers are like little kids; they like to play with all the toys in the toy box.

Musical Evolution in Melody and Harmony

Finally, we can look at music history in terms of the ongoing evolution of melody and harmony. Over the ages, Western harmony has progressed from simple to complex—and then, in the twentieth century, expanded beyond all existing boundaries.

The earliest music was the simplest. Ancient music was strictly monophonic, meaning only one melodic line was present, no accompaniment and no harmony. These early melodies, up to and including Gregorian chant, were based on seven-note modes, first defined by the ancient Greeks but later embraced by the medieval church. It was simple music with a very distinct modal sound.

In the late Middle Ages, music got geometrically more complex with the development of polyphony. If monophony incorporated a single melody line, then polyphony incorporated two or more melody lines at the same time. The initial polyphony was actually implied harmony—that is, the second line was always a constant interval distant from the first. (For example, the second line might be a constant fourth below the main melody.) Two voices at once—what a concept!

This early polyphony soon developed into something a bit more elaborate. Instead of simply mirroring the first voice, the second voice began to have a mind of its own. Renaissance polyphony featured an independent second voice, in the form of counterpoint. That is, the second voice moved independently from the first; if the first voice went up, the second might go down, and vice versa. Eventually the second voice evolved to create its own melody, weaving in and out of the melody of the first voice.

This led to the creation of the fugue and canon, where the second voice echoed the melody of the first, but starting a few beats or bars later, in a kind of round. Advanced examples of these forms featured three or four voices, each starting a bit after the previous, all echoing the same line but at a different point in development.

All these different voices playing at once got a bit complicated, which inspired composers to pull back a bit and simplify their work. As we move into the Classical era, we find this type of multi-voice polyphony decreasing in favor of what we now call traditional harmony—that is, a melodic line supported by simple chordal accompaniment. One voice plays the melody, while the other voices play the notes of the underlying chord. Sometimes a second voice might provide a subsidiary melodic line, sometimes a few voices might fill in the spaces with a call-and-response figure, but the basic thrust was melody with chords—and all in the same key.

That's right, through the Classical period all music tended to be diatonic, meaning few or no chromatic notes outside the underlying major or minor scale. If the piece was in C major, the melody included only the notes C-D-E-F-G-A-B, no A flats or D sharps. And the same thing with the harmony, which was based on chords created from the underlying scale notes.

Some composers found that limiting, however, and by the start of the Romantic era we saw an increasing use of chromaticism—notes outside the underlying major or minor scale. Now, instead of using only the notes of the C major scale, for example, a composer might throw in an occasional flat or sharp for color or effect, or toss in a D major chord instead of the expected D minor. This expanded the tonal boundaries of the composition, and opened up a whole new world of musical possibilities.

Throughout the Romantic period music continued to become more chromatic, until the chromatic notes started to overwhelm the diatonic ones. When this happened, late in the nineteenth century and moving into the twentieth, we saw the birth of atonality—music without a set tonal center. This type of music could be lush and dreamy (witness Debussy's use of the chromatic whole tone scale) or harsh and ugly (Stravinsky at his most forceful); what it wasn't was settling. By removing the tonal center, audiences had no sense of "home"; the music had progressed beyond the comfort level of most listeners.

And there you have the evolution of music, from modal monophony to chromatic atonality. Similar to the way composers took advantage of the development of instruments over time, they also utilized all the harmonic elements available to them in each era. When seven notes were all there were, that's what they used. As those seven notes expanded into the full chromatic scale (or beyond, as in various microtonal schemes), adventuresome composers utilized every note that was available to them.

The history of classical music, then, is the history of expansion and exploration in all forms. Music has become longer, bigger, wider, more complex. The simple modal melodies of the Renaissance sound too simple today, and the staid harmonies of the Baroque and Classical eras too traditional for modern ears. We have been exposed to the worlds inside and outside the Western scale, and those worlds inform the music we make today—including that not-so-serious music we call popular music.

With that, we end our survey of so-called classical music history, and get ready to explore the world of popular music. The two are related, as you'll see—the popular music of one era becomes the classical music of the next. Turn to the next part, "American Popular Music," to learn more.

Listening List

I've already provided, in previous chapters, essential recordings for each of the major musical periods. More of that isn't necessary here. Instead, I'll recommend a few compilation recordings that provide an overview of the major styles and eras of music—kind of a classical music starter set, as it were. So if you don't want to purchase all the individual recordings listed earlier, these compilations function as a quick and dirty substitute.

50 Classical Highlights (Various artists, St. Clair Entertainment)

Essential Baroque (Various artists, Decca Records)

Essential Choral Classics (Various artists, Decca Records)

The Essential Collection: Great Classical Highlights (Various artists, West End Records)

The Essential Hollywood (Various artists, Sony Records)

Essential Opera (Various artists, Decca Records)

Essential Piano: The Ultimate Piano Collection (Various artists, Decca Records)

Essential Violin (Various artists, Decca Records)

Timeline: Classical Music

4000 B.C.E.	Prehistory
4000 B.C.E.–476 C.E.	Ancient period
476–1400	Medieval period (Middle Ages)
1400–1600	Renaissance period
1600–1750	Baroque period
1750–1820	Classical period
1820–1900	Romantic period
1900–2000	Twentieth-century music

Part 2

American Popular Music

Music history is more than just classical music; that's why this part takes a look at all sorts of American popular music, from ragtime and brass band marches to jazz and blues to rock and hip hop. And don't forget the music of the Great American Songbook—the classic songs of Berlin, Gershwin, Kern, and more!

Chapter 9

Setting the Stage: American Popular Music Pre-1900

In This Chapter

- The European roots of American popular music
- New England choral music and Appalachian folk music
- Minstrel music, brass bands, and ragtime
- Sousa, Foster, Joplin, and other great early American composers

The music we've discussed so far in this book is alternately referred to as "classical," "serious," or even "art" music. This is distinct from "popular" music, or the music of the masses. While it's true that the music of Bach and Beethoven was enjoyed by the masses of their times, it's also true that this music was made by and for the elite—it wasn't what the common man was playing or singing in his home.

Popular music, then, is music that is accessible to the general public, as opposed to that music which is created for an elite class. This is typically simpler music, more easily grasped and more easily played or sung. It's also typically the music of song, rather than of longer, more complex musical works.

While many snooty music historians tend to focus solely on classical music, popular music is just as important—especially in recent times, when printed music, recorded music, and musical instruments are readily accessible to all levels of the citizenry. It's not like it was back in Bach's day, when only the well-heeled could afford a harpsichord or a concert ticket; today, even those with relatively low incomes can buy a guitar, obtain sheet music, or listen to music on the radio. This has led to a musical democratization, enhancing the importance of popular music.

All this is in the way of setting the stage for this second part of the book, which provides an overview of American popular music, from colonial times to today.

It's not enough just to know Bach, Mozart, and Beethoven; in the complete history of modern music, you also need to know Foster, Gershwin, and Bacharach.

Popular Music in Colonial Times

Our focus in this chapter is popular music in America, from the earliest settlements through the dawn of the twentieth century. Given that America is a nation of immigrants, it should go without saying that there is no such thing as "native" American music (save for that made by the native American Indians, of course); virtually every American musical form originated in another country.

You see, the settlers of what would become the United States brought their popular music with them from their native countries. Early American music consisted of imported English hymns and folk ballads, Irish reels, Scottish fiddle tunes, and so forth. That said, these imported musical forms quickly mutated to take on a uniquely American sound—and to deal with uniquely American topics.

Note

In addition to the popular music of the day, upper-class colonists listened to performances of the top classical music of their time, including works by Haydn, Bach, and Mozart. Chamber music was performed in individual homes; larger works were performed in local concert halls and theaters. Opera also became popular; the first opera performed in the United States was John Gay's *The Beggar's Opera*, in 1750.

Church Music

The first music of the early American colonists was religious music, in the form of traditional English hymns brought across the ocean. The Plymouth pilgrims originally sang directly from the *Ainsworth Psalter*, a book of psalms set to music, published in Amsterdam in 1612. They used this book until a local hymn book, the *Bay Psalm Book*, was published in 1640. This book became the standard used by New England churches for many years.

These traditional psalms were eventually supplemented by newly composed hymns. One of the foremost musical figures of the Colonial era was William Billings (1746–1800), a Boston-area composer with no formal musical training. Billings, a friend of Samuel Adams and Paul Revere, wrote hundreds of hymns and secular songs, including "When Jesus Wept," "David's Lamentation," and "Chester" (the unofficial national hymn of the American Revolution). In 1770, he published the first book of American music, *The New-England Psalm-Singer*. His hymns were all written for four-part *a cappella* chorus, reflecting that period's objection to playing instruments in churches.

> **Note**
>
> The Congregationalist churches of New England tended to frown on the use of musical instruments in churches. This helped to promote choral music, rather than instrumental music, in the northern churches. When churches did embrace instruments, the main and often only instrument was typically the organ. When a church couldn't afford an organ, it employed more portable instruments, such as the bass fiddle, cornet, flute, and violin.

Billings was the first of what became known as the First New England School. This was a group of composers, including Andrew Law (1749–1821), Supply Belcher (1751–1836), and Daniel Read (1757–1836), who composed and arranged hymns in a uniquely American fashion. Their chief innovation was doubling the male and female voices in an octave and then filling out the harmony with close-position chords; this texture was unknown in the European choral tradition.

Secular Folk Music

Church music wasn't the only music heard in the colonies. Many private citizens owned and played their own instruments—fifes, fiddles, violins, and flutes were common. The people used these instruments to play folk tunes and ballads, typically derived from British, Irish, and Scottish forms.

Folksingers of the day performed both traditional and newly composed songs; often the new songs were merely new lyrics over traditional folk tunes. Once the Revolution got underway, newly written songs such as "The Battle of the Kegs" and "Hail Columbia" expressed the patriotism of the day.

So the colonists were singing folk tunes that originally came from Europe. But where did those European folk tunes come from?

Indirectly, most Western European folk music evolved from the troubadours of the Middle Ages. Recall from Chapter 2 that the troubadours originated in southern France around the eleventh century; they were roving minstrels who sang their secular songs for lords and ladies of the upper classes. The troubadours spread throughout Europe during the thirteenth century, giving rise to similar minstrels in England, Germany, and other countries.

> **Note**
>
> Dance music was also popular during the 1700s, as dancing was a popular pastime of the colonists. Colonial dance tunes included reels, jigs, and minuets, typically accompanied by a single fiddle or violin—or whatever instruments were handy.

These singer-songwriters wrote and disseminated the folk songs native to each of their countries. In England, for example, the troubadour tradition led both to the madrigal and to traditional folk tunes such as "Barbara Allen," "Greensleeves," "Chevy Chase," and the like. As British pilgrims migrated to the new world, they brought their folk tunes with them—repeating many as-is, altering the lyrics of others, and using some of the tunes as the basis for new songs with completely new lyrics.

Barbara Allen

Traditional Scottish Ballad

"Barbara Allen"—a Scottish folk tune also popular in the American colonies.

The Story of "Yankee Doodle"

Perhaps the most famous folk song from the Revolutionary War era is "Yankee Doodle." You know how it goes, but do you know how the song came about? Perhaps, as Paul Harvey would say, it's time to learn the *rest* of the story...

The song "Yankee Doodle" actually originated as a tune sung by British military officers prior to the Revolutionary War. The lyrics mocked the disheveled and disorganized colonial "Yankees" with whom they served in the French and Indian War (1754–1763). At the time, the word "doodle" was a derogatory term for "fool."

The Brits' original lyrics for "Yankee Doodle" differed significantly from those known today. Take these verses, for example:

> *Brother Ephraim sold his Cow*
> *And bought him a Commission;*
> *And then he went to Canada*
> *To fight for the Nation;*

> *But when Ephraim he came home*
> *He proved an arrant Coward,*
> *He wouldn't fight the Frenchmen there*
> *For fear of being devour'd*

Not very complimentary, would you say? But the Yanks had the last laugh. During the Revolutionary War, the colonists embraced the song and made it their own. They made up new lyrics and used them to mock the Brits who had mocked them previously; the British army learned to hate the song.

By the way, the version sung by schoolchildren today, with the verse about sticking a feather in his hat and calling it macaroni, was apparently a British variant, not the American version. At the time, a "macaroni" was a dandyish young man who affected upper-class mannerisms; it was a joke that a Yank could stick a feather in his hat and think that was enough make him fashionable.

The result was a batch of folk tunes, sung either a cappella or accompanied by guitar or fiddle, performed by folksingers in taverns and pubs across the colonies. Popular songs of the colonial era include "The Devil's Curst Wife,"

"The Nightingale," and "The Willow Tree," as well as the English folk tunes mentioned previously. Most of these songs featured simple diatonic harmonies with just a handful of chords (I, IV, and V were common); some melodies, especially those based on older tunes, tended toward the modal.

Military Music

The final type of music heard in the colonies was military music, especially with the advent of the Revolutionary War. Musicians were employed to play contrapuntal music for officers during meals and at dances, as well as at parades; a typical ensemble consisted of clarinets, oboes, bassoons, and horns. Also popular was the field music of fifes and drums played during the march, for various camp duty calls, and during battle.

From the Revolution to the Civil War

After the United States won its independence, the population began to spread beyond the original 13 colonies. Various regional musical styles developed, as did a new strain of patriotic music to accompany the War of 1812 and the coming Civil War.

Appalachian Folk Music

The folk music from the colonial era seemed to find a permanent home in the Appalachian mountains of the central states. This area was settled from 1775 to 1850 or so, primarily by poor Europeans of Irish and Scottish descent. It's no surprise, then, that Appalachian music resembled native Irish and Scottish folk music.

Note

Contemporary audiences were exposed to "old time" Appalachian music in the soundtrack to the movie *O Brother, Where Art Thou?*, which featured traditional songs performed by contemporary bluegrass and country musicians.

Listen to Appalachian music of the day (or of today, for that matter; the music hasn't changed much), and you hear echoes of Celtic folk tunes, Scottish harps and bagpipes, and British broadside ballads. Melodic lines followed simple traditional harmonies, often with a distinctive "slide" between notes of the vocal line. Singers were typically accompanied by guitar(s), banjo, fiddle, harp, and other easy-to-play and easy-to-make instruments.

Note

A broadside ballad was a popular folk song whose lyrics were printed (typically by hand) on broadside sheets of paper, then sold by merchants or traveling peddlers. Broadside ballads were popular across Western Europe starting in the sixteenth century.

The lyrics of Appalachian folk tunes commonly addressed love and romance (often the failed kind), as well as more morbid topics such as murder, accidental death, and sensationalistic disasters. Livelier music was used to accompany various folk dances, including buck dancing, clogging, and square dancing.

As I noted, Appalachian folk music continues in much the same fashion today, in the form of what some call "old time" music. It is also a big influence on modern bluegrass and country music.

African American Work Songs and Spirituals

African slavery is a blight on the history of the United States, but it's a part of our history that can't be ignored. It was also a source of some uniquely American music, in the form of work songs and spirituals.

The first slaves were delivered to the colonies from West Africa as early as 1619. These slaves brought with them music from their native countries, including religious music and work songs—music sung as they toiled in the fields. Many slave owners encouraged their slaves to sing as they worked, believing that it improved morale. Thus the typical work song consisted of one or more unaccompanied vocal lines, often with a noticeable beat that matched the rhythm of the work being done.

The most notable characteristic of this music was its call-and-response vocal style, where one or more singers would echo or answer the vocal line of another. African music also differed from traditional western music in its use of rhythm. Whereas the sacred and folk music of the time employed relatively simple rhythms, African folk styles were much more rhythmically complex. This rhythmic complexity would find its way into the African-influenced music of later generations, especially jazz and rock and roll.

During the 1830s, the work song gained religion and morphed into the spiritual. This accompanied a religious revival (called the Second Great Awakening) that arose in the United States at the time. This period saw a profusion of outdoor worship gatherings, called camp meetings; during these meetings, hymns (called *camp songs*) were sung and traveling preachers (circuit riders) would preach.

While slaves were not generally allowed to participate in these camp meetings, they were allowed to watch. The camp songs of these meetings inspired the slaves to sing their own religious songs, Negro spirituals that applied African vocal styles and rhythms to the traditional hymns.

Many of these songs, such as "Swing Low, Sweet Chariot" and "Go Down Moses," directly or indirectly used religious imagery to symbolize their own plight. Here's a typical lyric, from "Let My People Go":

> *When Israel was in Egypt's land*
> *Let my people go*
> *Oppressed so hard they could not stand*
> *Let my people go*
> *Go down, Moses, way down in Egypt's land*
> *Tell ol' Pharaoh, Let my people go.*

As you can see, highly symbolic. In this sense, the Negro spiritual was both an expression of religious devotion and a (somewhat veiled) yearning for freedom from bondage.

Note

The Second Great Awakening also saw the rise of songs from the New England Shaker denomination. These were highly melodic hymns and anthems, and included such works as "Mount Zion" by Issachar Bates (1758–1837) and "Simple Gifts" by Joseph Brackett (1797–1882)—the latter made famous in Aaron Copland's *Appalachian Spring* ballet.

Spirituals were often sung a cappella, or with the choir accompanied by piano or organ. Musically, these songs typically adhered to a very simple harmonic structure, often using just the five notes of the pentatonic scale.

The five notes of the C pentatonic scale.

Note

Starting in the 1870s, spirituals began to be sung in concert performances, by groups such as the Fisk Jubilee Singers (from all-black Fisk University in Nashville, Tennessee).

The spiritual tradition became ingrained in the African American church, where it continues to this day. Spirituals also influenced the development of other musical forms, such as the blues and American soul music. (Aretha Franklin, after all, grew up singing spirituals in her father's church.)

Patriotic Music and the Civil War

The year was 1814. Beethoven's *Fidelio* had its final premiere in Vienna, and Schubert had already written the first of his many lieder. Napoleon was defeated at the Battle of Leon and exiled to Elba. And in America, the War of 1812 was in its third year.

On September 13, 1814, the British navy bombarded Baltimore's Fort McHenry. Francis Scott Key (1779–1843), a 35-year old amateur poet, was inspired to write a poem about the experience, titled "The Defense of Fort McHenry." This poem was set to music the following year. The resultant song, "The Star-Spangled Banner," was not the first or the last patriotic song written about the United States; it did, however, become the country's official national anthem.

The War of 1812 ended with the Battle of New Orleans in late 1814 and the signing of the Treaty of Ghent on February 16, 1815. That international conflict behind them, Americans turned inward as the country lurched toward the Civil War of 1861–1865.

The Civil War almost tore the country apart, resulted in the deaths of more than 600,000 Americans, and also served as a catalyst in the development of the American musical culture. The war, which brought together soldiers from across disparate areas of the country, helped to merge regional music traditions and create a more unified American musical style. Individuals from different army units traded instruments, tunes, and techniques; the result was the first truly American music.

The war also inspired numerous patriotic songs on both sides. Songs made popular during this period include "Dixie," "The Battle Hymn of the Republic," "The Bonnie Blue Flag," "John Brown's Body," "Oh Shenandoah," and "When Johnny Comes Marching Home." Like previous American songs, these tunes were harmonically simple, easy enough for even the uneducated patriot to sing. For example, the melody line of "When Johnny Comes Marching Home" has a diatonic (almost pentatonic) melody with a range of exactly an octave—a very easy song to sing.

When Johnny Comes Marching Home

Louis Lambert

The simple melody of "When Johnny Comes Marching Home," by Louis Lambert.

Note

The military culture of the Civil War also led to the popularization of brass band music, which would become even more popular in the later years of the nineteenth century. Also derived from the military tradition was the bugle call, including the well-known "Taps," still played at military funerals today.

From Reconstruction to the Turn of the Century

After the Confederacy was defeated and slavery abolished, the Reconstruction period addressed the issues that remained: how the Southern states would return to the Union, the legal status of the freed slaves, and so on. These years—from 1865 to 1877 or so—also saw the rise of the American brass band, as well as the growth of a new type of music found in the burgeoning minstrel shows of the era.

Brass Bands

The late nineteenth century was the heyday of the brass band movement and the instrumental march. Brass bands first came to prominence in America during the early 1850s, some accompanying military units and others sponsored by individual towns and companies. With the end of the Civil War, brass bands became common in towns large and small. Think of the fictional River City brass band of the musical *The Music Man*, and you get an idea of how brass band fever swept the nation.

Note _____

The brass band movement actually started in England during the early nineteenth century, as an offshoot of the Industrial Revolution. Employers urged factory workers to form bands, as a way of both increasing worker morale and discouraging nascent political activity. In other words, brass bands were initially formed to keep the working classes preoccupied during their leisure hours.

The typical brass band wasn't all brass, however. In addition to the "76 trombones" (never quite that many, of course) and accompanying cornets, the average brass band also included clarinets, saxophones, flutes, and various drums and cymbals. And instead of marching, most brass bands were what we today would call concert bands; they sat down and played.

Perhaps the best-known bandleader/composer of the era was John Philip Sousa (1854–1932). Known as the "March King," Sousa led the U.S. Marine Band from 1880–1892. He then formed his own famous brass band, touring throughout the United States and Europe for the next four decades.

John Philip Sousa, America's "March King."

The typical brass band composition was a march, most often in ²⁄₄ time, and Sousa wrote lots of them, including such well-known marches as "The Washington Post" (1889), "The Liberty Bell" (1893), and "The Stars and Stripes Forever" (1896). In total, Sousa wrote 136 marches as well as a handful of operettas and waltzes.

Ragtime

In the 1890s, the march form became the basis for a new piano instrumental style called ragtime. Ragtime took the "oom-pah" beat of the march and syncopated it—that is, placed its emphasis on the upbeat rather than the downbeat, creating a herky-jerky type of rhythm.

As the century turned, ragtime spread in popularity across the country. During the genre's heyday from 1900 to 1925, more than 1,000 rags were published; even the top composers of the Tin Pan Alley era, such as Irving Berlin and George Gershwin, dabbled in the ragtime oeuvre. (Witness Berlin's famous "Alexander's Ragtime Band"—a kind of sort of ragtime tune, at least in name.)

The foremost ragtime composer was Scott Joplin, who had composed marches himself before turning to the piano rag. Joplin influenced many other composers of the day, including Arthur Marshall (1881–1968), James Scott (1885–1938), and white composer/pianist Joseph Lamb (1887–1960), all of whom emulated his style.

Note

Ragtime music was introduced to modern audiences in the 1973 film *The Sting*—which used Joplin's "The Entertainer" as its theme song.

Minstrel Songs

Ragtime was black music for both black and white audiences. Another form of popular black music was so-called minstrel music—the music that accompanied the minstrel shows of the time.

The minstrel show was born in the period just prior to the Civil War. A minstrel was a white performer who performed in blackface, presenting sanitized versions of Negro songs and dance tunes in a vaudeville-like music and comedy revue.

The first American minstrels worked as solo acts, but by the 1840s minstrel troupes gained popularity. The typical minstrel group included four or more singers accompanied by banjo, violin, and tambourine. Some of the best-known groups included the Virginia Minstrels (featuring Dan Emmett), the Dan Bryant Minstrels, and the Christy Minstrels.

These minstrel shows toured the United States, helping to popularize the burgeoning genre of the minstrel song. These songs were written by professional songwriters such as Stephen Foster and Dan Emmett—whom we'll discuss next.

Note

Don't confuse the Christy Minstrels minstrel group with the New Christy Minstrels, a folk group popular in the 1960s. The original Christy Minstrels were led by Edwin P. Christy, a minstrel performer and budding entrepreneur, who also operated a chain of Christy's Opera Houses in several American cities.

Famous American Songwriters

Prior to the early 1800s, the creators of American popular songs remained largely unknown—save for Billings and his fellow hymn writers, of course. But starting around 1840, a group of professional songwriters came to the public forefront, benefiting both from the popularity of the minstrel show and the rise of the nascent music publishing industry.

Stephen Foster

The first great American popular songwriter was undoubtedly Stephen Foster (1826–1864). Foster wrote in a variety of styles, but first made his name with minstrel songs, many of which he sold to Edwin P. Christy, leader of the Christy Minstrels.

Stephen Foster, the first great American songwriter.

Foster was born near Pittsburgh, Pennsylvania, the youngest of 10 children. He had no formal music training, but nevertheless published his first song, "Open Thy Lattice Love" (1844), when he was just 18. When he was 20, Foster moved to Cincinnati, where we penned his first hit, "Oh! Susanna" (1848); this song would become the unofficial anthem of the following year's California Gold Rush.

He returned to Pennsylvania in 1850 and signed a contract to provide music to the Christy Minstrels. He wrote some of his most famous songs during this period, including "De Camptown Races" (1850), "Old Folks at Home" (1851; also known as "Swanee River"), "My Old Kentucky Home" (1853), and "Hard Times Come Again No More" (1854). Later in his career, Foster turned to writing sentimental ballads, most famously "Jeannie with the Light Brown Hair" (1854) and the posthumously published "Beautiful Dreamer" (1864).

While Foster was self-trained, he had a particular way with melody, even when simply harmonized. Some historians have compared his highly melodic work with that of Franz Schubert, although his melodies were far from European in nature.

Foster was notable for being one of America's first professional songwriters—that is, a composer who made his living from writing and publishing songs, rather than from performing live. That said, the copyright laws were primitive in those days, and Foster saw very little of the profits that his songs generated for the sheet music publishers. For example, Foster was paid a flat $100 for the rights to "Oh! Susanna"—a fraction of what the song actually earned. And Foster's name didn't even appear on some printings of his music. As a result, Foster died virtually penniless, at the age of 37, in a Bowery hotel in New York City.

An early printing of "Old Folks at Home"—credited to E. P. Christy, not Stephen Foster.

Dan Emmett

Another popular songwriter of the time, although lesser known today, was Daniel Decatur Emmett (1815–1904). Dan Emmett left home at age 17 to join the army, where he became an expert fifer and drummer. In 1835 he employed his percussion skills in the Spalding and Rogers circus as a drummer; there he learned the blackface technique. Shortly after, he joined the Thomas "Daddy" Rice minstrel troupe, where he sang and played banjo. In 1842 he formed his own Virginia Minstrels Troupe, where he made his mark as both a performer and a composer.

After growing up in Virginia and performing in blackface, Emmett was more attuned to the culture of the Southern states than Foster, and his music showed it. Emmett was the first composer to use the word "Dixie" to describe the South, in his song "Johnny Roach" (1859). His other popular tunes include "Old Dan Tucker" (1843), "De Boatman Dance" (1843) "Polly Wolly Doodle," (late 1840s), "The Blue-Tail Fly" (1846; also known as "Jimmy Crack Corn"), and "I Wish I Was in Dixie's Land" (1859; also known simply as "Dixie").

Scott Joplin

Not all American songwriters of that era were white men. Scott Joplin (1867–1917) was a black man born in eastern Texas who later moved to New York City. At the height of his popularity, Joplin worked in Tin Pan Alley alongside composers like Irving Berlin and George Gershwin.

Scott Joplin, the most famous African American composer of the nineteenth century.

Joplin was a formally trained musician who first heard Sousa's brass band music at the 1893 World's Fair in Chicago. His first compositions were marches and minstrel songs; he was even part of a minstrel troupe himself for a short period in the early 1890s. He sold his first songs in 1895, and had turned to the rag-time genre by 1898.

Joplin's ragtime work was a big hit, propelling him to the front of that era's professional songwriting ranks. His "Maple Leaf Rag" (1899) was the first instrumental sheet music publication to sell over a million copies, and became the classic model both for Joplin's later works and for rags by other prominent composers.

Joplin was able to create a multitude of different moods working within the constraints of the ragtime form. He was a master creator of memorable melodies, from the bouncing "The Entertainer" (1902) to the lyrical "Wall Street Rag" (1908) and "Heliotrope Bouquet" (1907), the latter co-written with Louis Chauvin (1881–1908). He also has two operas to his credit, including the award-winning *Treemonisha* (1910). Like Foster, he died relatively young, of syphilis at the age of 50.

Charles K. Harris

Toward the end of the nineteenth century, Charles K. Harris (1867–1930) became a prominent hit-maker. Known as the "king of the tear-jerkers," he published more than 300 songs, including "After the Ball" (1893) and "Break the News to Mother" (1897).

Harris was unique that, starting with "After the Ball," he published his own songs, rather than selling his tunes to an existing publishing house. Within a few months of the publication of "After the Ball," the song had sold over two million copies, and eventually sold over five million. Harris went on to become one of the founding members of New York's Tin Pan Alley publishing community.

African American Composers

Scott Joplin wasn't the only—or the first—African American composer who found success in the late nineteenth century. Most notable was James Bland (1854–1911), a minstrel performer (black man performing in blackface) and songwriter best remembered for his major hits, "Carry Me Back to Ole Virginny" (1873), "Oh, Dem Golden Slippers" (1879), and "In the Evening by the Moonlight" (1880). Other prominent African American composers of the turn-of-the-century era include Will Marion Cook (1869–1944) and Bert Williams (1875–1922), also a famous comic performer.

The Growth of the Music Publishing Industry

The American music industry showed remarkable growth in the final three decades of the nineteenth century, but it was a much different world than it is today. There was no radio to listen to or Internet to download from. Instead, just about every middle-class household had a piano; pianos were as ubiquitous then as personal computers are today. If you wanted to hear new music, you had to play it yourself on your own piano, from sheet music you purchased at your local music store.

Thus was the music industry of the late nineteenth and early twentieth century driven by the sales of printed sheet music. When sheet music first appeared in the middle of the century, it spurred the growth of regional publishing houses, which provided opportunities for individual composers to publish their songs to a broader market. Toward the end of the century, the smaller publishing houses essentially became "farm teams" for bigger companies, so that a local hit would eventually be purchased for republication by a larger house, gaining it national exposure.

Sheet music, then, was the primary way for music to be disseminated, and for songwriters to earn a living. Publishers would hire song demonstrators to play new tunes at department stores and music stores across the country; a customer would hear a tune she liked, purchase the sheet music, and go home to play it on piano. It took longer for a song to become a hit, but hits were made, nonetheless. In fact, the most popular sheet music sold millions of copies—not unlike what a hit song sells today.

Listening List

Our listening list for pre-1900 American music is a varied one. There are church hymns, folk songs, minstrel songs, rags, even marches and spirituals—and the requisite collection of Stephen Foster songs. This list should give you a good sense of how American music developed from colonial times to the eve of World War I; there's some good stuff here.

American Dreamer: Songs of Stephen Foster (Thomas Hampson)

Billings: Early American Choral Music Vol. 1 (His Majestie's Clerkes; Paul Hillier, conductor)

Classic Mountain Songs from Smithsonian Folkways (Various artists)

Early American Roots (Hesperus)

Sousa Marches: Stars and Stripes Forever (Philip Jones Brass Ensemble)

The Civil War: Traditional American Songs and Instrumental Music Featured in the Film by Ken Burns (Original Soundtrack Recording)

The Early Minstrel Show (Various artists)

The Greatest Ragtime of the Century (Various artists)

Wade in the Water, Vol. 1: African American Spirituals: The Concert Tradition (Various artists)

Timeline: Pre-1900 Popular Music

1619	Beginning of slave trade
1640	*The Bay Psalm Book*, first book printed in colonial America
1763	British soldiers sing "Yankee Doodle" to mock colonists
1770	Billings publishes *The New-England Psalm-Singer*
1776	Signing of Declaration of Independence
1812	War of 1812 begins
1815	Francis Scott Key publishes "The Star-Spangled Banner"
1830	First Negro spirituals
1840	Minstrel troupes become popular
1842	Philharmonic Society of New York founded
1848	Joseph Brackett writes "Simple Gifts"
1850	American Express Company founded; Stephen Foster writes music for the Christy Minstrels
1851	Harriett Beecher Stowe publishes *Uncle Tom's Cabin*
1854	Henry David Thoreau publishes *Walden, or Life in the Woods*
1858	Colorado Gold Rush
1859	Dan Emmett writes "Dixie"
1860	First baseball game
1861	Start of Civil War; Western Union completes transcontinental telegraph line
1864	Stephen Foster dies
1865	End of Civil War; Abraham Lincoln assassinated
1867	Johann Strauss writes *The Blue Danube* waltz
1868	QWERTY typewriter patented; Louisa May Alcott publishes *Little Women*
1870	Fifteenth amendment gives African Americans the right to vote; John D. Rockefeller incorporates Standard Oil Company
1871	Great Chicago fire; Jesse James robs his first passenger train
1876	Sitting Bull defeats General Custer at the Battle of Little Big Horn; Alexander Graham Bell invents the telephone; National Baseball League founded
1881	Billy the Kid killed; shoot-out at the O.K. Corral
1883	Metropolitan Opera House opens in New York
1884	Mark Twain publishes *The Adventures of Huckleberry Finn*
1885	Music publishers congregate in Tin Pan Alley
1886	Sears, Roebuck Company founded; Coca-Cola invented

1889	*The Wall Street Journal* begins publication
1891	James Naismith invents the game of basketball
1892	General Electric company founded
1893	Charles K. Harris self-publishes "After the Ball"
1896	John Philip Sousa composes "Stars and Stripes Forever"
1896	Jell-O created
1898	Spanish-American War
1899	Scott Joplin writes "Maple Leaf Rag"

Chapter 10

From the Bayou to Bourbon Street: Blues and Jazz

In This Chapter

- Discovering how rural blues evolved into urban and electric blues

- Uncovering the roots of New Orleans jazz

- Learning why swing music was the popular music of the 1930s and 1940s

- Discovering all the different types of jazz, from bebop to cool jazz to jazz/rock

- Learning about the three most important figures in blues and jazz music: W. C. Handy, Louis Armstrong, and Miles Davis

The African American culture contributed significantly to the American musical landscape of the twentieth century. Beginning with the rural blues, black music evolved into a variety of musical styles, from jazz to rhythm and blues to hip hop—and informed virtually all forms of popular music in the second half of the century.

With that in mind, let's delve into those two most uniquely African American musical styles—blues and jazz. One informs the other, and both helped to define American popular music throughout the twentieth century.

Deep in the American Soul: The Blues

The blues is a uniquely African American musical style. It originated in the rural African American communities of the southern United States, evolving from traditional work songs, field hollers, and spirituals. While the blues itself remains a viable musical genre in the twenty-first century, the blues style has also influenced virtually every type of popular music, from jazz and soul to rock and roll and hip hop.

Over the years many different types of blues have evolved, most often distinguished by instrumentation and type of beat. These different types of blues include rural blues, Delta blues, urban blues, electric blues, and the like. The basic blues chords and harmonies, however, stay relatively constant across all these forms.

Understanding the Blues Form

The blues is a distinct vocal and instrumental style, easily recognizable. What distinguishes the blues from other musical forms is the narrowly defined blues chord progression and blues scale, as well as the theme of the lyrics. In essence, the blues is a very strict musical form.

We'll start with the notes used to create blues melodies—the so-called *blues scale*. The key here is that several notes of the major scale—the third, the fifth, and the seventh—are flattened, to create so-called *blue notes* between the normal scale notes. The resulting blues scale is a six-note scale (not counting the octave) that looks like this, in relationship to a major scale:

1   ♭3   4   ♭5   5   ♭7.

This blues scale is unusual in that it doesn't have a second or sixth degree, but it does throw in a flatted fifth in addition to the regular perfect fifth. It's the flatted third, flatted fifth, and flatted seventh notes—the so-called blue notes—that define the color of the blues scale. The following figure shows how this looks in traditional music notation, in this instance the C blues scale.)

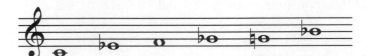

The C blues scale.

Also distinctive are the chords played behind the melody, the unique *blues progression*. Most blues tunes follow a classic twelve-bar chord progression. This twelve-bar form is composed of three phrases, each four bars long. Musically, the chords of the blues progression go like this:

I-I-I-I   IV-IV-I-I   V7-IV-I-I

In the key of C, the chords go like this:

C-C-C-C   F-F-C-C   G7-F-C-C

This blues progression is utilized in many forms of popular music, not just the blues. You'll find this progression used in many songs of the Great American Songbook, much rock and country music, and a whole lot of jazz. It's a uniquely versatile chord progression, with many popular variations.

Finally, we come to the lyrical themes of blues music. Early blues lyrics often took the form of a linear narrative, telling a story of personal woe, lost love,

Note

The final I chord of the blues progression is often substituted with a V7 chord.

hard times, and the like. This theme of loss and misery continues in most modern blues lyrics; the blues, after all, describes a human state as well as a musical form.

The Birth of the Rural Blues

When you think of the blues, you may think of an old black man singing with his acoustic guitar. Or you may think of a black man wailing on an electric guitar. Or you may think of a group of black singers singing a cappella. Or you may think of a bar band cooking along to a boogie-woogie beat.

The blues is all of this, and more. In fact, the style commonly called the blues is actually an entire family of musical styles, all sharing similar roots. And, while the exact origin of the blues is undetermined, it's likely that the first blues was performed in the rural South, in the style we now call the *rural blues* or *country blues*. This type of blues evolved in the post–Civil War period, when the guitar was first introduced to rural black culture.

Recall from Chapter 9 that poor rural African Americans of the mid-1800s had a rich musical heritage of work songs and spirituals. These vocal forms shared the use of "blue notes," or the flattened notes of the normal major scale. These flattened notes created the unique sound of the blues form, which was further defined by the use of call-and-response vocal lines.

In addition, black guitarists of the time created a unique style of accompaniment when playing behind these vocals. The guitarist echoed the voice of the singer by "bending" the guitar notes, pushing against the strings with the fingers of his fretting hand. This enabled the guitarist to play half tones and even quarter tones between the main notes of the scale, creating the unique sound of the blues.

This rural blues eventually moved to urban areas and evolved into other types of blues music. The rural blues also migrated into the white community, giving birth to early country music. In fact, through the 1930s or so, it was difficult to tell the difference between blues and country music, save for the race of the performer.

Note

Some guitarists further developed a "slide guitar" technique using a sliding bar (such as the neck of a bottle). By tuning the guitar to an open chord, the guitarist could slide the bar up and down the neck, the better to emphasis the blue notes between the scale tones.

The Hard Life of the Delta Blues

The rural blues style evolved geographically; every musician in every small town played a slightly different type of blues. By the end of the nineteenth century, there were many different blues styles being played throughout the South.

For example, the style of blues played in the Mississippi Delta area was known as the *Delta blues*. This style was characterized by an intense, highly charged performance style that evolved in the saloons, whorehouses, and the streets of the Delta region. Lyrically, the Delta blues described the dark underside of life among gamblers, pimps, and prostitutes. It was typically a slow blues with heavy use of solo guitar. Famous Delta bluesmen include guitarists Charley Patton (1891–1934), Robert Johnson (1911–1938), and Son House (Edgar James

Note

Robert Johnson was the mythic guitarist from the 1930s who supposedly sold his soul to the devil in return for his incredible musical skills.

House Jr., 1902–1988), whose slide guitar style was revolutionary in the 1930s and 1940s.

The Lighthearted Side of the Ragtime Blues

Around the turn of the century, a more lighthearted blues, known as *ragtime blues*, became popular in the middle South. This type of blues got its name from its syncopated, ragtime-like melodies. In this blues style, guitarists would pick the individual strings with their fingers, using the thumb to establish a bass line like that played in ragtime piano. The other picked notes would be syncopated against this steady bass line.

Most ragtime blues songs consisted of verses that expressed a more rosy outlook on life than did the Delta blues. Often, the lyrics were deliberately comical. Famous ragtime blues performers include Blind Boy Fuller (Fulton Allen, 1907–1941) and Blind Blake (Arthur Blake, 1893–1933).

W. C. Handy and the City Sound of Urban Blues

Probably the biggest evolution in the blues style came at the turn of the twentieth century, when rural blacks migrated from the country to the city. This led to a new urban blues style that was slightly more sophisticated than the earlier rural blues.

Unlike the rural blues, which was typically just a singer accompanied by a single guitar, the urban blues often employed a full backup band—piano, guitar, bass, drums, and such. It was also a blues that benefited from association with formally trained musicians.

One of the primary proponents of the new urban blues was composer W. C. Handy (1873–1958). Handy was a trained musician born in Alabama; his main instrument was the cornet. He played in various blues bands and minstrel shows before moving to Memphis in 1909, where he lived on famed Beale Street. It was there that he wrote the song "Memphis Blues" (1909, published in 1912); the song, originally a campaign song for a local politician, became a huge national hit.

W. C. Handy, the "Father of the Blues."

(Photograph courtesy of Library of Congress, Prints & Photographs Division, Carl Van Vechten Collection.)

What Handy did, in this and similar songs, was to smooth out the irregularities of the rural blues and merge it with the dance band format, thus making it more attractive to a city audience. Known as the "Father of the Blues," Handy composed dozens of best-selling works, including "St. Louis Blues" (1912) and "Beale Street Blues" (1916). When Handy died in 1958, more than 150,000 people took to the streets of Harlem to pay their respects.

Another new aspect of the urban blues was the introduction of female singers; the previous rural blues was primarily played by men. One of the great urban blues singers was Ma Rainey (Gertrude Malissa Nix Pridgett, 1886–1939), the first city blues singer to achieve a major hit recording. Known as the "Mother of the Blues," Rainey started singing professionally at age 14 with the Rabbit Foot Minstrels. She switched to the blues style in 1902, continuing to sing with the minstrel troupe. Later in her career, she performed with many famous jazz musicians, including Louis Armstrong and Fletcher Henderson.

Ma Rainey was followed by perhaps the best-known of all blues performers, Bessie Smith (1894–1937), known as "The Empress of the Blues." Smith was introduced to the business by Rainey herself, forming her own act in 1913. She began recording for Columbia Records in 1923, and often was accompanied by the great jazz players of the day, including Louis Armstrong. Smith's recordings, including one of Handy's "St. Louis Blues," were tremendously popular; her use of blue notes, syncopated delivery, and occasional gospel shouts all became standard jazz vocal techniques.

The Soulful Sound of Religious Blues

Another popular blues form of the early twentieth century joined words about religious experiences with a blues guitar accompaniment. These *religious blues* were related to the spirituals sung in African American churches; the difference was that the lyrics were now accompanied by blues guitar. Noted religious blues singers include Blind Willie Johnson (1897–1945) and Reverend Gary Davis (1896–1972).

The Modern Sound of Electric Blues

After World War II, the blues migrated northward (up the Mississippi River) to Chicago and Detroit, and became electrified. The invention of the electric guitar helped to bring the blues to an even wider audience; the amplification enabled blues guitarists to perform in noisy bars and helped in the recording of the music. It also ushered in a new type of blues guitar solo that emphasized single melodic lines over the previous melody-plus-accompaniment style.

Note

This new electric blues influenced the development of the rhythm and blues style in the 1940s and 1950s. In the 1960s, electric blues was integrated into the burgeoning rock movement, resulting in many blues-based rock bands, such as the Rolling Stones, the Paul Butterfield Blues Band, the Yardbirds, and John Mayall's Bluesbreakers.

Famous electric bluesmen, guitarists all, include Muddy Waters (McKinley Morganfield, 1913–1983), Howlin' Wolf (Chester Arthur Burnett, 1910–1976), and B. B. King (Riley B. King, b. 1925).

Hot and Cool: Jazz

The blues was America's first native music, but it was just a precursor for what followed—that music we call jazz.

Jazz is America's homegrown classical music. Derived from the blues, it is one of this country's truly indigenous musical styles. For a time, jazz was the country's popular music; audiences listened to and danced to jazz music just as they dance to rock or country or hip hop today.

While it's true that jazz isn't nearly as popular today as it was in the 1930s and 1940s, it remains a vital part of the American music scene. Most large cities still have a dedicated jazz radio station, and jazz artists still perform in clubs and concert halls across the country.

Read on, then, to learn more about this essential American musical genre— what it is, where it came from, and how it sounds today.

Jazz Is ...

What is jazz? Some people might define jazz as music with improvised solos. Of course, jazz isn't the only type of music to feature improvisation; there are plenty of rock and blues musicians who are fluent improvisers, but who don't play jazz.

Others might define jazz as music with a swing beat—a rolling, "spang spang-a-lang spang-a-lang" kind of rhythm. This is another bad definition; some swing music isn't really jazz, and a lot of jazz music has a rock or funk beat.

As you can see, jazz is a music that's hard to define. Jazz is different from rock or the blues, although it often incorporates elements from those two genres. It can be played over a swing beat, a rock beat, a funk beat, or a Latin beat. It can be played by any size group, from a solo pianist to a big band. And it's a complex music, often with very sophisticated chords and harmonies—and lots of improvisation.

Perhaps the best way to describe jazz is to look at its history—how it started and where it eventually ended up. For that, we need to take a trip down the Mississippi River, to that grand old city of New Orleans.

Birth of the Beat: New Orleans and Dixieland Jazz

The earliest form of jazz was born in New Orleans between 1885 and 1915. This type of jazz—call it *classic jazz*, *New Orleans jazz*, or *Dixieland jazz*—grew out of the existing blues, ragtime, and brass band traditions. What was unique about this music is that it allowed musicians to embellish traditional melodies, with the resulting arrangements varying considerably from performance to performance.

New Orleans bands of that era usually had five to seven pieces, led by cornet, clarinet, and trombone on melody, with tuba or string bass, piano, banjo or guitar, and drums on accompaniment. Initially, there were no soloists; rather, the group would play all at once, with the melody instruments improvising around each other's parts. The rhythmic accompaniment emphasized a regular, four-beat rhythm (referred to as "four on the floor"), leaving plenty of space for the melodic syncopation. These bands played for dances, parades, funeral processions, and the like. They also were hired as entertainers for the riverboats that worked the Mississippi River.

One of the first great jazz musicians was cornetist Buddy Bolden (Charles Joseph Bolden, 1877–1931). Today, little is known of his sound or style, although contemporaries reported that he played with a loud, piercing tone that could be heard over considerable distances. His band, circa 1905, was made up of cornet, trombone, clarinet, string bass, and piano; his repertoire was said to include folk and blues standards such as "Make Me a Pallet on the Floor" and dance numbers like "Funky Butt, Funky Butt, Take It Away."

Warming It Up with Hot Jazz

This original New Orleans jazz quickly evolved into what was called *hot jazz*. The big difference between classic and hot jazz is improvisation, which became prominent in hot jazz groups. With hot jazz, it's not unusual for there to be multiple improvisations going on simultaneously, with the various frontline instruments— most often trumpet or cornet, clarinet, saxophone, and trombone—playing off each other in a kind of improvisational counterpoint.

One of the first proponents of the hot jazz style was cornet player Joseph "King" Oliver (1885–1938). Oliver took Buddy Bolden's style to a new level, first in New Orleans but more importantly on the road in Chicago, where in 1919 he fronted King Oliver's Creole Jazz Band. Oliver specialized in playing slow blues, using a growling style that would influence the later "jungle" style of Duke Ellington, among others.

Oliver was also notable for promoting the career of another young trumpet player, one Louis Armstrong (1901–1971), who originally served as second cornetist in Oliver's band.

Note

Other important early jazz musicians included trumpeter Bix Beiderbecke (1903–1931); saxophonist Coleman Hawkins (1904–1969); guitarist Eddie Condon (1905–1973); and pianists Earl "Fatha" Hines (1903–1983) and Fats Waller (1904–1943).

The Ambassador of Jazz: Louis Armstrong

One name towers over all others in the history of early jazz: cornetist and vocalist Louis Armstrong. Armstrong was the leading proponent of hot jazz—and of jazz in general for several decades. Armstrong's small-ensemble recordings of the mid-1920s with his Hot Five and Hot Seven groups revolutionized jazz music and introduced the era of the virtuosic leader/soloist. His recordings are true classics that influenced every succeeding generation of jazz musicians.

The most important figure in early jazz: the great Louis Armstrong.

Note

Armstrong was also known by the nicknames "Satchmo" and "Pops."

Armstrong was born to a poor family in New Orleans. His father abandoned the family when Louis was an infant, and his mother left him and his sister in the care of his grandmother. He dropped out of school at the age of eleven, joining a group of boys who sang in the streets for handouts. Armstrong was given his first cornet by a Jewish Russian immigrant family that had hired him to do odd jobs; he learned to play at the hands of local trumpeters Bunk Johnson and King Oliver, later joining Oliver in his well-known band.

Unlike King Oliver, who functioned as a musical coequal of his other band members, Armstrong stood out from the rest of the group; he was the star, and his solo breaks, comic vocals, and overall musical personality dominated all of his recordings. His virtuoso trumpet style was brash and forceful, his solos daring and sophisticated while remaining highly melodic.

In addition to his influential trumpet playing, Armstrong also pioneered the vocal style of scat singing, improvising on nonsense syllables instead of actual lyrics. He was the first singer to scat sing on record ("Heebie Jeebies," 1926), when he purportedly dropped his lyric sheet while recording and was forced to improvise nonsense lyrics.

Armstrong's music was an important bridge between the earlier New Orleans jazz and the newer Chicago/New York/Los Angeles urban jazz that was quickly supplanting it. His classic recordings of this period include "Muskrat Ramble" (1926), "Potato Head Blues" (1927), "West End Blues" (1928), "Star Dust" (1931), "Lazy River" (1931), "Chinatown, My Chinatown" (1932), and "When the Saints Go Marching In" (1939).

From Armstrong's heyday in the 1920s and 1930s all the way to the end of his career in the 1960s, Louis Armstrong was a recognized and hugely popular figure among both jazz lovers and the general populace; he even had several hit vocal recordings in the rock era, including "What a Wonderful World" (1968) and "Hello, Dolly!" (1964), from the musical of the same name. (He also appeared in the movie version of the musical, as well as numerous other films—essentially playing himself onscreen.)

Louis Armstrong was a true musical ambassador for America in general and jazz in particular, appearing around the world with various ensembles. He may, in fact, be the most revered and possibly the most important musical figure of the twentieth century.

Tickling the Ivories: Jelly Roll Morton and Jazz Piano

In addition to being the home for early small-group jazz, New Orleans was also a center for the development of jazz piano. The city's notorious Storyville district—a legal center for bars and houses of prostitution—created a great demand for pianists to accompany the showgirls and entertain patrons between acts.

The New Orleans piano style evolved from the earlier ragtime style, keeping the "stride" bass in the left hand. Arguably the greatest of the New Orleans jazz pianists was Jelly Roll Morton (Ferdinand Joseph La Menthe, 1885–1941). Morton's flamboyant piano style melded blues, Spanish dance rhythms, ragtime, and folk and classical influences. He was also a notable composer of the jazz song; his works include "King Porter Stomp" (1923) and "Jelly Roll Blues" (1938).

Gone and Back Again: The Death and Rebirth of New Orleans Jazz

By the mid-1920s, the center of jazz development had moved from New Orleans to major urban centers, notably Chicago and New York. There, popular songs, new dance styles, and more virtuosic players quickly transformed the music. While the more versatile New Orleans musicians, such as Louis Armstrong, were able to adjust to this new style, many remained at home and continued to play in the earlier classic jazz or Dixieland style.

Note ___

The Dixieland revival continues to this day, thanks to performances by the Preservation Hall Jazz Band and other groups.

There was, however, a revival of interest in New Orleans jazz following World War II. This was partly a reaction to the more esoteric modern styles, such as bebop; many listeners were nostalgic for the simpler and easier-to-comprehend Dixieland style. Older musicians who had never abandoned the style enjoyed the resurgence, while many younger musicians also adopted the style. Even Louis Armstrong benefited from the revival, forming his successful "All Stars" band in the late 1940s, featuring New Orleans–styled arrangements.

Taking the Country by Storm: Swing

During the 1930s hot jazz evolved into *swing*, and most jazz groups grew into big bands. For not the first time, jazz became dance music; what was different was that this swing music appealed to both black and white audiences. Indeed, big band swing was the popular music of its day, featuring a combination of complex arrangements, innovative improvisation, and smooth vocals by the likes of Bing Crosby and Frank Sinatra. (That's right—Bing Crosby was once regarded as a jazz vocalist!) The best of the big bands were hard-driving jazz machines, advancing the art of jazz improvisation to new highs.

These bands embraced the swing style, which marked a basic change in approach to rhythm. The earlier New Orleans style inherited a kind of "oom-pah" beat from ragtime, with the emphasis on the first and third beats of the measure. Swing, on the other hand, evened out the rhythm, with all four beats lightly accented; then, on top of the basic beat, a "spang spang-a-lang" rhythm was superimposed. The result was a less-mechanical, swinging rhythm—perfect for both listening and dancing.

The Hit Parade: Big Band Jazz

Imagine America in the 1930s. A young couple going out on the town on a Friday night would head to the local ballroom, where a touring big band was set up on the bandstand. At the drop of the baton, the band would go into one of the hit swing tunes of the day, and the joint would be jumping, with couples doing the Lindy Hop or the jitterbug or one of the other popular swing dances.

Even couples that stayed at home got their fill of swing music. Radio ruled the day, with variety shows and musical extravaganzas on every half hour. As the big band would start to play, the vocalist would cozy up to the microphone and croon his or her current hit.

Note ___

Big bands of the swing era were often divided into two camps: "hot" versus "sweet" bands. The sweet bands, such as Whiteman's and Glenn Miller's, were thought inferior by jazz aficionados because they catered to a mass audience; hot bands, such as Benny Goodman's and Artie Shaw's, were considered the true jazz outfits, with more of an emphasis on improvised solos.

These bands, as popular then as any top-40 group is today, were playing jazz, pure and simple. These swing bands—sometimes called dance bands at the time—became popular in the late 1920s and remained so through the end of World War II.

One of the first of these larger dance bands was the Paul Whiteman Orchestra. Paul Whiteman (1890–1967) dubbed himself the King of Jazz, and his band ruled the dance floors and the airwaves of the 1920s. Whiteman was an innovator, even if his band didn't do a lot of improvising; in 1924, he commissioned George Gershwin to write *Rhapsody in Blue*, and Ferde Grofé's *Grand Canyon Suite* was also part of the band's repertoire.

Another popular band of the 1920s was the Fletcher Henderson Orchestra, led by Fletcher Henderson (1897–1952). Henderson pioneered what became the standard big band orchestration, divided between the reed section (saxophones and clarinets) and the brass section (trumpets and trombones)—supported by a rhythm section (piano, bass, and drums), of course. In this format, the two horn sections would trade riffs back and forth in a call-and-response format; individuals would improvise solos between orchestrated sections.

The Henderson style was emulated in all the primarily white big bands that followed in the 1930s and 1940s, who added one or more lead vocalists to the mix. These included the bands of clarinetist Benny Goodman (1909–1986), clarinetist Artie Shaw (1910–2004), trombonist Glenn Miller (1904–1944), and brothers Tommy (1905–1956) and Jimmy Dorsey (1904–1957). Hit songs of the era included Tommy Dorsey's "I'm Getting Sentimental Over You" (1935), Goodman's "Sing, Sing, Sing" (1936), Shaw's "Begin the Beguine" (1938), and Miller's "In the Mood" (1940) and "Chattanooga Choo Choo" (1941).

Note

Benny Goodman's big band and accompanying trio and quartet included some of the finest musicians of the day, including virtuoso drummer Gene Krupa (1909–1973). Goodman also was one of the first white bandleaders to break the color barrier with black pianist Teddy Wilson (1912–1986), vibraphone player Lionel Hampton (1908–2002), and electric guitarist Charlie Christian (1916–1942).

The Count and the Duke

There were also several notable black orchestras during the swing era, although they enjoyed somewhat less visibility and success among white audiences, due to the racial barriers of the time. These included the Count Basie Orchestra, led by William "Count" Basie (1904–1984), a heavily swinging outfit out of Kansas City. Basie's band was noted for its famous four-piece rhythm section— guitar, bass, drums, and Basie himself on piano.

Also notable was the big band of pianist/arranger/composer Duke Ellington (Edward Kennedy Ellington, 1899–1974). Ellington's band was formed in the late 1920s as the house band at New York's Cotton Club, and evolved into one of the most innovative ensembles of that or any time. Ellington was an unusually gifted composer and arranger, and he tended to craft his music to reflect the skills and personalities of the individual players in his band. Originally known for its "jungle" style, featuring growling trumpets and other campy effects, the later Ellington band matured into a virtual orchestra, complete with a multitude of musical colors.

Ellington's most famous compositions—many co-written with Billy Strayhorn (1915–1967)—include "East St. Louis Toodle-oo" (1926), the groundbreaking "Black and Tan Fantasy" (1929), "Mood Indigo" (1931), "It Don't Mean a Thing (If It Ain't Got That Swing)" (1932), "Sophisticated Lady" (1932), "In a Sentimental Mood" (1935), "Caravan" (1937), "Take the 'A' Train" (1941), "I Got It Bad (And That Ain't Good)" (1941), and "Don't Get Around Much Anymore" (1942).

Jazz's premiere composer, arranger, and band leader— Duke Ellington.

The End of the Big Band Era

Big bands became less fashionable after World War II, as jazz waned in popularity and evolved into more of a small group form. It didn't help when the American Federation of Musicians went on strike in 1942, halting all orchestral recordings through 1943; this single development led to the rise of the solo vocal recording, and contributed to the demise of the touring big band.

Big bands didn't die out entirely, however; in fact, they had a bit of a resurgence in the 1960s and early 1970s, incorporating more contemporary arrangements and modern rock rhythms. It's this type of big band music—from the Stan Kenton (1911–1979), Woody Herman (1913–1987), Buddy Rich (1917–1987), and Maynard Ferguson (1928–2006) bands—that is most often played by high school and college jazz ensembles today.

Jazz Vocalists of the 1930s and 1940s

The big band era was also the dawning era of the jazz vocalist. Most big bands had one or two vocalists (often a male and a female) to sing the hit songs of the day; instrumental solos typically followed the vocal verses.

Nearly every jazz singer of the era was associated with one of the leading bands, sometimes moving from band to band. Bing Crosby (1903–1977) sang with the Paul Whiteman Orchestra; Frank Sinatra (1915–1998) sang for both the Dorsey Brothers and for Henry James; and Ella Fitzgerald (1917–1996) sang with drummer Chick Webb's band (and became the band's de facto leader after Webb's death in 1939). Even Billie Holiday (1915–1959) was a band vocalist for a time, signing with both Count Basie and Artie Shaw.

Not until after World War II did singers like Sinatra achieve enough personal success to strike out on their own. This breaking from the big band was also facilitated by the musicians' strike of 1942–1943, which effectively killed big band recordings for those years; vocalists, however, could still record with small group backing. Thus Sinatra and Fitzgerald and others became solo artists—which we'll examine in more detail in Chapter 11.

Gypsy/Jazz Manouche

Swing wasn't the only jazz music of the 1930s and 1940s, nor was the jazz of the period confined to American musicians. These years also saw the development of a type of small group European jazz called *gypsy jazz* or *Jazz Manouche*, a mixture of American swing, French dance hall music, and Eastern European folk music.

Gypsy jazz was unique in that its main instruments were acoustic guitar and violin, often without full rhythm sections. (Many gypsy jazz recordings don't have drums, for example; the rhythm is kept by chords strummed on the guitar.) This was a very lyrical type of jazz, with lots of melodic improvisation; the most popular practitioners were guitarist Django Reinhardt (1910–1953) and violinist Stéphane Grappelli (1908–1997).

Beyond Traditional Jazz: Bebop

When swing started to decline in popularity in the late 1940s, jazz musicians began to develop a new musical approach, based on the exploitation of complex harmonic structures. This new music, called *bebop*, would become the dominant form of jazz for the next several decades.

Bebop is jazz played at a very fast tempo, with rapid chord changes—no more than two to four beats per chord, unlike the two to four *measures* per chord of swing music. Bebop chords are generally quite complex, heavy on the extensions and altered tones, and melodies are similarly harmonically complex and rhythmically quite busy.

The bebop style was developed primarily by saxophonist Charlie "Bird" Parker (1920–1955) and trumpeter Dizzy Gillespie (John Birks Gillespie, 1917–1993). Bird and Diz both came out of prominent Midwestern jazz bands, but did not start playing together until they were both living in New York City in the early 1940s. Along with a small group of like-minded young revolutionaries—including drummer Max Roach (1924–2007), pianists Thelonious Monk (1917–1982) and Bud Powell (1924–1966), and saxophonist Dexter Gordon (1923–1990)—the duo began jamming together and experimenting with new melodies, harmonies, and rhythms. The style demanded virtuoso performances, which is what this new group of young lions delivered.

This new style, however, was not universally embraced; it was a more intellectual form, depending on esoteric harmonies and advanced chord progressions. While jazz musicians had always improvised, boppers took improvisation to a new level. They would take a pop standard, such as "Cherokee," and purposefully avoid playing the melody, using the chord progression as a starting point for extended improvisation.

The typical bebop ensemble was much smaller than the preceding big bands, typically one or two lead instruments (trumpet or saxophone) accompanied by a small rhythm section (piano, bass, and drums). This was due partly to the demands of the music (it was difficult for larger groups to play such complex music together at breakneck speeds), partly to the space demands of small New York clubs (you couldn't fit many more musicians on the stage), and partly to economics (bop didn't attract large paying crowds).

For a taste of bebop, check out the compilation of Dizzy Gillespie tunes on *The Complete RCA Victor Recordings: 1937–1949*, as well as *Yardbird Suite: The Ultimate Charlie Parker*.

> **Note**
>
> In this fashion did the standard "(Back Home Again in) Indiana" become the bebop classic "Donna Lee." It may be difficult to hear the commonalities, but the melody of "Donna Lee" began as an improvisation on the chords of "(Back Home Again in) Indiana."

Chilling Out: Cool Jazz

During the 1950s, some players tired of the hard harmonics of bop music and offered a smoother, more melodic alternative. This so-called *cool jazz* mixed aspects of bebop and swing, smoothing out bebop's dissonances and adding more complex group arrangements.

Cool jazz was more of an intellectual form of jazz, wedding white classical music with black blues and soul. Cool jazzers also tended to disdain unnecessary showmanship, giving performances as cool as their music.

This type of cool jazz enjoyed remarkable popularity, especially among college students in the 1950s and early 1960s. One cool tune, the Dave Brubeck Quartet's "Take Five," even became a top 20 hit when it was released in 1959. ("Take

> **Note**
>
> Because so many cool jazz players were from Los Angeles, cool jazz is sometimes called *West Coast jazz*.

Five" was also remarkable for being in the odd time of ⁵⁄₄, unlike the traditional ⁴⁄₄ popular in music of that and later days.)

The top cool jazz players include trumpeters Miles Davis (1926–1991) and Chet Baker (1929–1988); saxophonists Paul Desmond (1924–1977), Stan Getz (1927–1991), Gerry Mulligan (1927–1996), and Art Pepper (1925–1982); and pianists Dave Brubeck (b. 1920) and Bill Evans (1929–1980). Popular cool jazz ensembles include the semi-classical Modern Jazz Quartet and the Dave Brubeck Quartet (with Brubeck on piano and Paul Desmond on saxophone). Representative albums of this style include Miles Davis's *Birth of the Cool* (1950), Chet Baker's *Chet Baker Sings* (1956), the Dave Brubeck Quartet's *Time Out* (1959), and the Bill Evans Trio's *Sunday at the Village Vanguard* (1961).

Blast from the Past: Modal Jazz

The late 1950s and early 1960s saw the birth of a cool jazz derivative called *modal jazz*. This style of jazz moved past traditional Western major and minor tonalities into more exotic modes—actually, the same modes pioneered by the ancient Greeks and used in Gregorian chant.

A typical modal composition consists of just a single chord, or one chord for each section of the song. That chord is usually a minor seventh chord, and the melody is based on a related mode—most commonly the Dorian mode.

The new breed of musicians who gravitated to modal music included trumpeters Miles Davis and Freddie Hubbard (b. 1938); pianists Bill Evans and Herbie Hancock (b. 1940); and saxophonist Wayne Shorter (b. 1933). Notable albums in this style include Davis's *Kind of Blue* (1959) and Hancock's *Maiden Voyage* (1965).

Back to Bop: Hard Bop

During the mid-1950s there came a new offshoot of bebop, known as *hard bop*. Hard bop was a reaction to both bebop and cool jazz; it featured more soulful melodies and rhythms than either the original bebop or cool styles, but with the carefully arranged compositions typical of cool jazz.

Many of the original bop players evolved into the hard bop style; newer players included saxophonists Sonny Rollins (b. 1930) and Julian "Cannonball" Adderley (1928–1975); trumpeters Clifford Brown (1930–1956) and Lee Morgan (1938–1972); trombonist J. J. Johnson (1924–2001); guitarist Wes Montgomery (1923–1968); pianist Horace Silver (b. 1928); and drummer Art Blakey (1919–1990). Representative recordings include Miles Davis's *Walkin'* (1954) and Art Blakey's *A Night at Birdland* (1954).

Going International: Brazilian and Latin Jazz

By the early 1960s, cool jazz had migrated south to Brazil, integrated with local samba rhythms, and made its way back to the states in the form of *Brazilian jazz*, sometimes called *bossa nova* music. This new musical mixture featured gentle melodies over hypnotic Latin beats; it was pioneered by Brazilians João Gilberto (b. 1931) and Antonio Carlos Jobim (1927–1994), and popularized in the United States by saxophonist Stan Getz and guitarist Charlie Byrd (1925–1999). The best-selling album of this genre was the 1964 crossover *Getz/Gilberto*, with its hit single "The Girl from Ipanema" (co-written by Jobim and sung by Gilberto's wife Astrud).

Of course, the jazz scene has always been influenced by south-of-the-border rhythms, in the form of what is now called *Latin jazz*. This intercontinental jazz, as played by Tito Puente (1923–2000) and others, is informed by a variety of Afro-Cuban and Latin rhythms. Representative of the style of Puente's 1958 album *Dance Mania*.

Getting Funky: Soul Jazz

Hard bop eventually mutated into a more R&B-oriented form called *soul jazz*, which became one of the most popular types of jazz in the 1960s. Soul jazz incorporates a more contemporary rock/soul beat, complete with a funky bass line, under hard bop and bebop-type chord progressions.

Popular soul jazz musicians include pianists Horace Silver and Ramsey Lewis (b. 1935); organist Jimmy Smith (1925–2005); and saxophonists Cannonball Adderley, Eddie Harris (1936–1996), and Stanley Turrentine (1934–2000). Representative recordings include Horace Silver's *Song for My Father* (1964), Ramsey Lewis's *The "In" Crowd* (1965), and Cannonball Adderley's *Mercy, Mercy, Mercy* (1966).

Further Out: Free Jazz

Cool jazz and hard bop weren't the end of jazz; in the 1960s, jazz musicians kept experimenting with new forms, harmonies, and rhythms. The result was *free jazz*, sometimes referred to as *avant-garde jazz*, which broke down any remaining barriers. In free jazz, musicians eschew all traditional arrangements and tonalities; it's free-form music that goes where the musicians take it.

Free jazz music is typically played at very fast tempo, with chords (when there are chords) lasting multiple measures; some pieces sit on a single chord for extended periods of time. This music employs complex tonalities and chord structures—when there's any structure at all. Harmonies are usually quite dissonant, and the rhythm is very free. In other words, it's a chaotic, somewhat random type of music, almost totally improvised.

The prime movers of the free jazz movement were saxophonists Ornette Coleman (b. 1930) and John Coltrane (1926–1967), as well as pianist/composer Cecil Taylor (b. 1929). Representative recordings include Coleman's *Free Jazz* (1962) and Coltrane's *Ascension* (1965).

Rocking the Beat: Jazz/Rock Fusion

The 1970s saw yet another evolution in jazz, this time combining hard bop harmonies and jazz improvisation with a driving rock beat. Alternately called *fusion* or *jazz/rock*, this new music was an electric, high-energy form that saw moderate mainstream acceptance.

Fusion music was inspired by the rise of rock and roll in the 1960s. With the dominance of the rock beat, traditional jazz with its swing beat was in danger of dying out. Melding jazz improvisation to the new rock beat—and adding electric instruments to the mix—was a shot in the arm to the jazz genre. It also helped to attract many younger musicians to the fold.

Chief practitioners of the fusion style were trumpeter Miles Davis, as well as keyboardists Herbie Hancock (b. 1940) and Chick Corea (b. 1941)—the latter with two completely different iterations of his group Return to Forever. Other popular fusion ensembles were the Mahavishnu Orchestra and Weather Report, the latter featuring saxophonist Wayne Shorter (b. 1933) and keyboardist Joe Zawinul (1932–2007).

Representative jazz/rock recordings include Miles Davis's *In a Silent Way* (1969), the Mahavishnu Orchestra's *Birds of Fire* (1973), Herbie Hancock's *Head Hunters* (1973), and Weather Report's *Heavy Weather* (1977).

Note

On the rock side of the jazz/rock fence, several early 1970s horn-oriented rock bands—including Chicago, Chase, and Blood, Sweat & Tears—featured extensive jazz improvisation.

Jazz's Premiere Innovator: Miles Davis

As you've perused the history of jazz from the 1950s through the 1970s, you've probably noticed one name crop up in the descriptions of almost every musical style. That name is Miles Davis, and he was perhaps jazz's most innovative musician.

Davis was at the forefront of almost every major development in jazz from World War II through the 1980s. He formed his first group in the late 1940s, and released the groundbreaking *Birth of the Cool* album in 1950. His next group, the Miles Davis Sextet, released the album *'Round Midnight* in 1955, which was one of the first recordings to explore the concept of modal jazz.

In 1957, Davis formed an ad hoc big band to record the album *Miles Ahead*. This album and several that followed utilized the Third Wave arrangements of Gil Evans (1912–1988), which blended elements from both jazz and classical music. The Davis/Evans collaboration was particularly notable on *Sketches of Spain* (1960), which added Latin music to the mix.

In 1959, Davis moved back into the cool jazz arena with the album *Kind of Blue*. This recording featured the work of pianist Bill Evans, and remains the best-selling jazz album of all time.

Davis continued to work in the cool jazz and modal styles throughout most of the 1960s. At the end of the decade, however, he embraced the burgeoning rock genre to create the new jazz/rock form, as represented by his albums *In a Silent*

Note

It's interesting that the three most important figures in blues and jazz—W. C. Handy, Louis Armstrong, and Miles Davis—were all trumpet players.

Note _____
John McLaughlin was the driving force behind the fusion powerhouse Mahavishnu Orchestra.

Way (1969) and *Bitches Brew* (1970). The first of these albums included seminal work by fusion pioneers Chick Corea, Herbie Hancock, and Joe Zawinul on keyboards, Wayne Shorter on saxophone, John McLaughlin (b. 1942) on guitar, and Jack DeJohnette (b. 1942) on drums.

By taking this final plunge into jazz/rock, Davis reasserted his role as a jazz innovator who was not just relying on the strength of his reputation. He also helped to introduce jazz music to an entire new generation who, once they heard the rock beat of his new albums, often returned to his classic recordings of the 1950s. In this way Davis attracted a wider audience for all jazz players—and solidified his reputation as one of history's most important jazz musicians.

Back to Basics: Post Bop

The jazz/rock experiment didn't last, at least not in its original incarnation. Instead, during the 1980s and 1990s, there was a resurgence of more traditional jazz music, incorporating hard bop harmonies with a variety of swing, rock, and funk beats.

This fresh approach to the jazz genre, which incorporates a variety of musical influences, is alternately known as *post bop*, *contemporary*, or *modern mainstream*—terms that describe pretty much all serious jazz being played today. The most popular of today's post bop young lions include saxophonists Kenny Garrett (b. 1960) and Joshua Redman (b. 1969); trumpeters Wynton Marsalis (b. 1961) and Terence Blanchard (b. 1962); guitarists Pat Metheny (b. 1954) and John Scofield (b. 1951); and pianist Keith Jarrett (b. 1945).

A More Commercial Sound: Smooth Jazz

Our final jazz style, *smooth jazz*, is one of those "is it or isn't it" musical forms. Jazz purists deride the slick arrangements and play-it-safe improvisations as a kind of modern elevator music; fans say that it's a particularly melodic and listenable form of jazz. Mood music or not, smooth jazz *does* feature a lot of improvised solos, and many of its adherents are veterans of the fusion scene. And even critics have to admit that smooth jazz has become the most commercially viable form of jazz since the 1940s.

Today's smooth jazz artists, many of whom are veterans of the 1970s/1980s fusion scene, include pianist David Benoit (b. 1953); guitarists George Benson (b. 1943), Larry Carlton (b. 1948), and Lee Ritenour (b. 1952); saxophonist David Sanborn (b. 1945); and the groups Fourplay, Spyro Gyra, and the Yellowjackets.

Parallel Developments: Comparing Blues and Jazz with Classical Music

Rural, Delta, and electric blues; swing, bebop, cool jazz, and fusion. How do you make sense out of all these different variations of the blues and jazz forms?

Interestingly, the evolution of blues and jazz parallels the evolution of European classical music. They both start very simple and grow more complex over time, eventually shattering into multiple competing styles. Don't believe me? Take a look at the following:

♦ **Simple melodies:** Blues music started as simple unaccompanied vocal lines, in the form of work songs and spirituals. Classical music started as similar unaccompanied vocal lines, in the form of plainsong and Gregorian chant.

♦ **Accompanied melodies:** The second stage of evolution came when the acoustic guitar was introduced to the blues form. This parallels the strummed accompaniment of the troubadours during late Middle Ages.

♦ **Multiple melodies:** When the blues morphed into New Orleans jazz, the typical performance involved multiple lead instruments playing at the same time. This is similar to the complex polyphony of the Renaissance period.

♦ **Popular melodies:** The next evolution of jazz came in the 1930s and 1940s, when a solo melodic line came to the fore and swing music gained mass popularity. This is exactly what happened during the Classical period, with its emphasis on melody and its attainment of popular status.

♦ **Sophisticated melodies:** When swing morphed into bebop, more sophisticated melodies and harmonies became common. This parallels the shift from the Classical to Romantic periods, where more chromatic melodies were played on top of traditional harmonies.

♦ **Stylistic explosion:** The final evolution in jazz was an explosion into multiple competing styles—cool jazz, modal jazz, hard bop, soul jazz, fusion, post bop, and the like—with no single style having prominence. This mirrors what happened to classical music in the twentieth century, with the dissolution into Impressionism, chromaticism, atonality, twelve-tone music, minimalism, and such.

As you can see, it's a parallel evolution. Both musical forms start simple, attain mass popularity as they mature, then become too complex and intellectual for their own good, eventually disintegrating into a chaotic collection of less-popular forms. This may be the way the universe works, from the Big Bang to expanded nothingness; it's certainly a good way to evaluate the evolution of musical forms.

Listening List

With so many variations on the blues and jazz genres, it's not surprising that this chapter has an especially long listening list. If you were to purchase all of these albums, you'd have the beginnings of a comprehensive blues and jazz library; these are the most essential recordings of these genres.

A Love Supreme (John Coltrane)

Ascension (John Coltrane)

Birds of Fire (Mahavishnu Orchestra)

Birth of the Cool (Miles Davis)

Breezin' (George Benson)

The Complete RCA Recordings (Tito Puente)

The Complete RCA Victor Recordings: 1937–1949 (Dizzy Gillespie)

The Duke at His Best (Duke Ellington)

The Essential Bessie Smith (Bessie Smith)

The Essential Count Basie, Volumes I & II (Count Basie)

Free Jazz (Ornette Coleman)

Getz/Gilberto (Stan Getz and Joao Gilberto)

Hard Again (Muddy Waters)

Head Hunters (Herbie Hancock)

Heavy Weather (Weather Report)

Hot Fives & Sevens (Louis Armstrong)

The "In" Crowd (Ramsey Lewis Trio)

In a Silent Way (Miles Davis)

Kind of Blue (Miles Davis)

King of the Delta Blues (Robert Johnson)

Live at Carnegie Hall: 1938 Complete (Benny Goodman)

Maiden Voyage (Herbie Hancock)

My Favorite Things (John Coltrane)

A Night at Birdland (Art Blakey)

The Original Delta Blues (Son House)

Sketches of Spain (Miles Davis)

Somethin' Else (Cannonball Adderley)

Song for My Father (Horace Silver)

Sunday at the Village Vanguard (Bill Evans Trio)

Time Out (Dave Brubeck Quartet)

The Ultimate Collection (B. B. King)

Vintage Grappelli (Stéphane Grappelli)

W. C. Handy's Beale Street: Where the Blues Began (W. C. Handy Preservation Band)

Yardbird Suite: The Ultimate Charlie Parker (Charlie Parker)

Timeline: Blues and Jazz

1885	New Orleans jazz evolves
1900	Urban blues evolves
1901	Louis Armstrong born
1905	Buddy Bolden forms his jazz band
1912	Handy writes "Memphis Blues"
1919	King Oliver forms his Creole Jazz Band
1923	Bessie Smith signs with Columbia Records
1924	Paul Whiteman Orchestra plays Gershwin's *Rhapsody in Blue*
1925	Louis Armstrong's first Hot Five recordings
1930	Swing music evolves
1936	Benny Goodman records "Sing, Sing, Sing"
1938	Billie Holiday sings with Artie Shaw band
1941	Duke Ellington records "Take the 'A' Train"
1942	American Federation of Musicians strike
1945	Electric blues evolves; Diz and Bird invent bebop
1950	Miles Davis releases *Birth of the Cool*
1954	Art Blakey releases *A Night at Birdland*
1959	Dave Brubeck Quartet's "Take Five" is a hit on the pop charts; Miles Davis releases *Kind of Blue*
1964	Brazilian jazz hits with "The Girl from Ipanema"; John Coltrane releases *A Love Supreme*
1965	Ramsey Lewis releases *The In Crowd*
1968	Louis Armstrong records pop hit "What a Wonderful World"
1969	Miles Davis releases *In a Silent Way*
1971	Louis Armstrong dies
1973	Herbie Hancock releases *Head Hunters*
1976	George Benson gives birth to smooth jazz with *Breezin'*
1977	Weather Report releases *Heavy Weather*
1991	Miles Davis dies

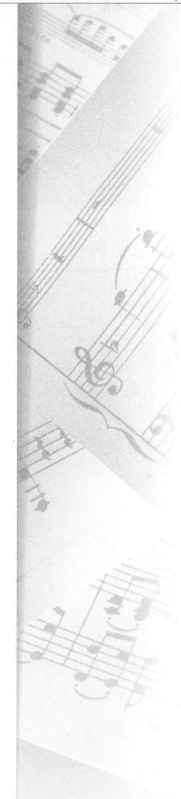

Chapter 11

Tin Pan Alley and Beyond: The Great American Songbook

In This Chapter

◆ Understanding the classic American popular song

◆ Discovering the composers of the Great American Songbook—Berlin, Gershwin, and more

◆ Remembering the singers of the classic popular song

◆ Learning about the evolution of the Broadway musical

The history of American popular music is the history of the popular song. And there is no greater era for the popular song than that period from 1900 to 1950, when giants like Berlin, Porter, and Gershwin strode the earth.

Some 300,000 compositions were copyrighted during this period, and the best of them comprise what aficionados call the "Great American Songbook"— perhaps the best-crafted works of music you'll ever listen to. We'll examine these songs (and their songwriters) in this chapter.

The Birth of the American Popular Song

Before the dawn of the twentieth century, American music was an amalgam of styles, derived from European parlor music, native folk music, and African American traditions. As best represented by the work of Stephen Foster, this music was meant to be performed in the parlors of middle-class people who owned and knew how to play pianos and other common musical instruments.

At the turn of the century, however, music began to move out of the parlors of private homes and into more public venues: vaudeville houses, musical theaters, and night clubs. Within a few decades, popular music gained an even wider audience, thanks to the technological advancements of records, radio, and movies.

Describing the American Popular Song

Before we discuss how the American popular song came about, we should take a few moments to describe this type of music. After all, the American popular song (pre–World War II, anyway), had a very distinct form, style, and sound.

First of all, the American popular song was short—typically clocking in at just under three minutes in length. There is a practical reason for this, having to do with the recording technology of the day. The early 78 RPM records could hold, at best, three minutes of recorded sound per side, so performers had to keep their recordings under three minutes in order to fit on a disc. Hence the three-minute popular song—a tradition that continues to this day, even though that recording limit has long since been breached.

Creating a three-minute recording dictated a particular form. Composers, producers, and performers quickly realized that if they started with a verse, repeated it, added a brief chorus, and then repeated the verse, they'd fill the three-minute slot almost exactly. Hence the development of the AABA song form—verse one (A), verse two (A), chorus (B), and verse three (A). Each of the verses typically have different lyrics, and sometimes the chorus is repeated at the end of the song, with the same lyrics. Each section is typically 8 measures in length, for a total of 32 measures.

Equally important to this structural consistency was the fact that the melodies of these songs were written so they could be sung by a person with no more than an average vocal range. This was accomplished by using easy step-wise melodies and avoiding large interval leaps. The reason for this limitation was also practical; these songs, at least early in the period, were designed to be sung by the average person in the comfort of their own living room, accompanied by the family's upright piano.

Speaking of that accompaniment, these songs typically employed traditional harmonies—no chords or notes outside the native scale. You found very little chromaticism and dissonance, and very few unexpected notes or harmonies.

Bottom line, the American popular song was designed to be sung by the average person without extensive musical training. More important, the songs could be listened to and appreciated by the musically untrained, which facilitated their acceptance by a mass audience.

By adhering to this common style and structure, the American popular songbook—as well as popular music from other countries that influenced the American genre—grew into an interconnected and evolving body of work, from the Tin Pan Alley tunes of the 1920s, to the Brill Building productions of the 1960s, to the slick commercial concoctions found on today's top-40 music charts.

Note

During the first half of the twentieth century, most popular music incorporated a light swing beat and jazz rhythms, with the emphasis on the first and third beats of the measure. In the second half of the century, popular music was more commonly built on straight eighth notes with a defined rhythmic structure, typified by an accented "backbeat" on the second and fourth beats of a measure of 4/4 time, as found in most rock and soul music.

Of Microphones and Vinyl: Technology and the Development of the Great American Songbook

The Great American Songbook might not exist if it weren't for two important technological developments. Oh, the songs would still have been written, we just wouldn't have remembered them.

The first such development was the invention of the microphone and other amplification technologies. Before the microphone, a singer needed a "big" voice to project over the backing orchestra, which favored operatic-type voices like Enrico Caruso or, in the popular vein, belters like Al Jolson. Subtlety—never mind intimacy—was lost.

With the invention of the microphone, however, singers could now get soft and intimate, wrapping their voices around a tune without relying on lung power to reach the back row of the theater. This new generation of singers, including Bing Crosby, Perry Como, and Frank Sinatra, tended to have light and intimate voices that would have been wholly out of place just 50 years earlier. This led to more personal styles of singing, and helped increase the importance of strong and meaningful lyrics—just the thing for the burgeoning Great American Songbook.

The second technological innovation was the long-playing 33⅓ RPM record. Before the 12" LP, recordings were made on 78 RPM discs that could only hold about three minutes of recording per side. The LP, thanks to its slower revolution and more densely packed grooves, could hold up to 25 minutes per side.

This longer playing time led to an interesting dilemma—how to fill all that time? The solution, fortunately for all of us today, was the classic songs of the Great American Songbook.

You see, in the first half of the twentieth century, the popular music business was based almost solely on the latest hit songs. A song would appear in a Broadway play or Hollywood movie, get recorded (on 78 RPM record) by Crosby or Sinatra or whomever, have a short life as a hit recording on the radio, and then fade from the public's consciousness. All those classic songs written by Berlin and Porter and Gershwin were pretty much heard once and then forgotten.

Forgotten, that is, until the advent of the long-playing record album. Singers still had current hit songs to record, of course, but then they had to fill another half hour or so to complete the album. Where to find songs to fill that space? From the Great American Songbook, of course. This need for LP filler rescued thousands of classic songs from obscurity, exposing them anew to succeeding generations of listeners.

If we have any one artist to thank for reviving the classic song catalog, it's probably Frank Sinatra. In 1955 he had the idea of creating a story around songs from the Great American Songbook, in the form of a concept album about lost love. That album was *In the Wee Small Hours,* and it included carefully selected songs such as Duke Ellington's "Mood Indigo," Hoagy Carmichael's "I Get Along Without You Very Well," Alec Wilder's "I'll Be Around," and the title song (by Bob Hilliard and David Mann), all with masterful arrangements by Nelson Riddle. The album was a huge hit, and led to a series of similar concept albums from Sinatra in the following years.

So thank Thomas Edison for inventing the microphone, which led to the vocal style that benefited the singing of popular song, and Columbia Records for developing the 12-inch long-playing record, which led to the rediscovery of the popular song catalog. Without those two developments, thousands of classic songs might never have been written—or would have been lost to history.

Writing the Great American Songbook

The story of American popular music in the first half of the twentieth century was written, in large part, by the professional songwriter. These skilled professionals applied their craft to the three-minute song, writing memorable words and melodies for other musicians to perform.

Welcome to Tin Pan Alley

The American music business first became a business in the late 1800s, with the creation of large music publishing companies. These companies typically purchased the rights to individual songs from songwriters, and then published printed versions of those songs as sheet music. This sheet music was then sold to consumers via music stores, department stores, and the like; people used the sheet music to play songs in their own homes, on their own pianos.

From approximately 1880 to 1940 or so, the American music publishing industry—and the songwriters who fed the publishing houses—were concentrated in that area of New York City on West 28th Street between Broadway and Sixth Avenue. This publishing center came to be known as *Tin Pan Alley;* writer Monroe Rosenfeld first coined the term, likening the cacophony of so many songwriters pounding on so many pianos to the sound of beating on tin pans. The name has since been applied to the Alley's product, its popular songs.

Note

Many of the Tin Pan Alley songwriters also wrote scores for Broadway shows and, after the movie musical burst on the scene in the late 1920s, had distinguished careers in Hollywood.

The lyricists and composers who worked in Tin Pan Alley during this period are remembered for creating some of the most memorable popular songs of the day. It was an interesting environment; songwriters, together and in teams, churned out their compositions in factory-like style. The best of these songs were sold to music publishing companies, and were then issued as sheet music (before the explosion of the record business) or picked up by one of the major singers of the day. Sometimes these Tin Pan Alley tunes ended up in vaudeville productions, Broadway plays, or Hollywood movies. The best of the best endured and became classics.

The most talented songwriters of a generation filtered through Tin Pan Alley. Irving Berlin, Cole Porter, George and Ira Gershwin, and their contemporaries were all professional songwriters for hire, writing songs for Broadway musicals and on commission by major performers. Their songs were sung by the top singers of the day—Fred Astaire, Bing Crosby, Frank Sinatra, Mel Tormé, Ella Fitzgerald, Tony Bennett, Nat "King" Cole, and the like. These songwriters contributed the bulk of the Great American Songbook—compositions filled with pretty melodies, sophisticated chord progressions, and mature, often witty, lyrics.

The Original Yankee Doodle Dandy: George M. Cohan

The century's first great popular songwriter was a legendary vaudeville and Broadway song-and-dance man, playwright, actor, and producer. George M. Cohan (1878–1942) is considered the father of American musical comedy; along with partner Sam H. Harris, Cohan produced more than three dozen Broadway shows between 1906 and 1926.

For these and other plays, Cohan wrote more than 1,500 original songs. Cohan's songs are noted for their hummable melodies, clever lyrics, and, during the World War I era, patriotic themes. While not as lyrically or harmonically sophisticated as songs from later composers, Cohan's songs were incredibly popular not only on the stage but also through sheet music sales of the day.

Cohan's best-remembered songs include "Give My Regards to Broadway" (1904), "The Yankee Doodle Boy" (1904; commonly known as "Yankee Doodle Dandy"), "Forty-Five Minutes from Broadway" (1905), "Mary's a Grand Old Name" (1906), "You're a Grand Old Flag" (1906), "Harrigan" (1907), and "Over There" (1917).

Note

George M. Cohan's life was memorialized in the highly fictional (but also highly entertaining) movie musical *Yankee Doodle Dandy*, starring actor James Cagney in a bravura performance as the loose-limbed Cohan.

The First Innovator: Jerome Kern

The American popular song became more sophisticated over time, and one of the first innovators in terms of style and sophistication was Jerome Kern (1885–1945). Kern was the first true master of twentieth-century musical theater, writing from the turn of the century through the 1940s. A composer, Kern wrote with various lyricists, including Dorothy Fields, Ira Gershwin, and Oscar Hammerstein II. During the course of his career, Kern wrote more than 700 songs and 100 scores for plays and films, including the groundbreaking 1927 musical *Show Boat* (with lyrics by Hammerstein).

Kern's songs were harmonically rich, which made them ideal for improvisation by jazz performers. His most notable songs include "Lovely to Look At" (1935), "A Fine Romance" (1936), "Never Gonna Dance" (1936), "Pick Yourself Up" (1936), and "The Way You Look Tonight" (1936), all with Fields; "Can't Help Lovin' Dat Man" (1927), "Ol' Man River" (1927), and "All the Things You Are" (1939), with Hammerstein; "Smoke Gets in Your Eyes" (1933) and "Yesterdays" (1933), with Otto Harbach; "Look for the Silver Lining" (1920), with Buddy G. DeSylva; and "Till the Clouds Roll By" (1946), with Guy Bolton and P. G. Wodehouse.

Note

Many classic songs from the Great American Songbook were first introduced in the series of movie musicals starring Fred Astaire (1899–1987) and Ginger Rogers (1911–1995). These movies, including *Top Hat* (1935) and *Swing Time* (1936), proved Astaire to be one of the best interpreters of the day's popular song.

The Father of American Song: Irving Berlin

Although many Tin Pan Alley songs were formulaic at best (Cohan's songs being prime examples), a number of composers rose above the crowd to create a distinct body of work. Perhaps the most prolific and successful of all was Irving Berlin (Israel Isidore Baline, 1888–1989), who had a long career creating some of America's best-loved songs.

Berlin was born in Russia but immigrated with his family to America when he was five years old. He was not musically trained and, unlike other families in the neighborhood, his family did not own a piano. Berlin's father died when he was 13; instead of being a burden to his mother, young Irving ran away from home. He sang for pennies outside of cabarets, became a chorus boy, a stooge in vaudeville, a singing waiter, and a song plugger. While all of these experiences

Note

A song plugger was a singer or piano player employed by music stores to promote the latest songs to customers.

introduced him to the world of music, none of it was formal training; perhaps it was this informal training that put him so in tune with the musical tastes of the average American public.

The father of American popular song—Irving Berlin.

Beginning in 1907 with the pseudo-Italian ditty "Marie from Sunny Italy," Berlin rode the crest of several fads in the musical world. He was responsible for popularizing ragtime music in his song "Alexander's Ragtime Band," a tremendous hit in 1911. In the 1920s and 1930s, Berlin created a jazzy swing in numbers like "Blue Skies" (1926) and his famous score for the Fred Astaire/Ginger Rogers film, *Top Hat* (1935; with several hits, including "The Continental," "Cheek to Cheek," and the title tune). Then, in 1938 Berlin captured perfectly a growing sense of patriotism by rereleasing his song "God Bless America" (which was actually written in 1918); two years later, in 1940, he penned the perennial holiday favorite "White Christmas."

Note

Interestingly, Berlin could not read or write music; he employed a secretary to notate the compositions he plunked out on the black keys of his piano.

Unlike other Tin Pan Alley songwriters who specialized in either words or music (and hence worked as part of a two-person team), Berlin wrote all his own music and lyrics. His output comprised more than 3,000 songs; he also composed the scores for 21 films and 17 Broadway shows. His songs are among America's best loved, and include "Puttin' on the Ritz" (1929), "Easter Parade" (1933), "Isn't This a Lovely Day (to Be Caught in the Rain)?" (1935), "Let's Face the Music and Dance" (1936), "Anything You Can Do" (1946), "A Pretty Girl Is Like a Melody" (1946), and "There's No Business Like Show Business" (1946).

The Genius and His Brother: George and Ira Gershwin

If Irving Berlin was the father of the American popular song, his favored son had to be George Gershwin (Jacob Gershwin, 1898–1937). Gershwin was an innovative composer whose work ranged from pop songs to classical pieces like *Rhapsody in Blue* (1924) and *An American in Paris* (1928).

George Gershwin—a true musical genius.

George and his older brother Ira were born in Brooklyn to Russian Jewish immigrant parents. His parents had purchased a piano for Ira, but it was the younger George, at around age 10, who took to the instrument. George studied with various music teachers, eventually getting a job as a song plugger for the Remick's music publishing company. This introduced him to the world of Tin Pan Alley; he wrote his first commercially successful song, "Rialto Ripples," in 1917. The national hit "Swanee" followed two years later.

Gershwin was arguably the most gifted composer of the twentieth century. Not only were his pop songs several notches above the competition in terms of melodic and harmonic structure, he also was one of the first composers to incorporate jazz-influenced rhythms and harmonies into his songs. And, when Gershwin did it, all his contemporaries followed—making his music highly influential.

More often than not, George's brother Ira collaborated on lyrics; Ira's clever rhymes perfectly matched his brother's sophisticated music. Together, the Gershwins composed music for more than a dozen Broadway shows, as well as the 1935 jazz opera *Porgy and Bess*.

The Gershwins' most famous songs include the ragtime-influenced "Swanee" (1919), "Fascinating Rhythm" (1924), "Someone to Watch Over Me" (1926), "I Got Rhythm" (1927), "But Not for Me" (1927), "Embraceable You" (1927), "'S Wonderful" (1927), "Bidin' My Time" (1930), "Summertime" (1935), "They Can't Take That Away from Me" (1937), "A Foggy Day" (1937), "Let's Call the Whole Thing Off" (1937), "Nice Work If You Can Get It" (1937), "Shall We Dance" (1937), "They All Laughed" (1937), and "Our Love Is Here to Stay" (1937).

Just look at that list of songs. Heck, just look at the songs composed in the single year of 1937—the year Gershwin passed away. It's a body of work that would be almost impossible to match today.

Tragically, George Gershwin died of a brain tumor at the age of 39. It's interesting to speculate how much more innovative and influential his music would have been had he lived a longer life. Still, we have a huge catalog of Gershwin's music to treasure, now and forever. It's terrific stuff, a large number of songs of a particularly high quality.

Wit Personified: Cole Porter

Cole Porter (1891–1964) was a contemporary of the Gershwins and Irving Berlin. Writing both words and music, Porter blended complex melodies and harmonies with witty, sophisticated lyrics and clever rhymes.

Note

Porter was often too witty for his own good. His lyrics often caught the attention of censors of the day; he tended to address the subject of romance with both cynicism and double entendres.

While he eventually became an East Coast sophisticate, Porter was born in Peru, Indiana, to a wealthy family that sent him to the best East Coast schools. At Yale University, as a member of both the Yale Glee Club and the Whiffenpoofs, Porter discovered his gift for song.

Porter composed music for numerous Broadway and Hollywood musicals, including *Gay Divorcee* (1932), *Anything Goes* (1934), *Red Hot and Blue* (1936), *Kiss Me, Kate* (1948), and *Silk Stockings* (1955). His vast songbook includes "Love for Sale" (1930), "Night and Day" (1932), "It's Bad for Me" (1933), "Anything Goes" (1934), "I Get a Kick Out of You" (1934), "You're the Top" (1934), "All Through the Night" (1934), "Begin the Beguine" (1935), "I've Got You Under My Skin" (1936), "It's De-Lovely" (1936), "In the Still of the Night" (1937), "Ev'ry Time We Say Goodbye" (1944), "I Love Paris" (1952), and "All of You" (1954).

The Wizard of Song: Harold Arlen

The next generation of Tin Pan Alley songwriters was represented by Harold Arlen (1905–1986). Arlen was a popular songwriter for both Broadway and Hollywood musicals, most notably *The Wizard of Oz;* he did his most notable work in the 1930s and 1940s. Arlen also wrote music for various dance bands of the era, working with a number of well-known lyricists.

Arlen wrote his first song in 1929, later forming successful partnerships with lyricists Ted Koehler, E. Y. "Yip" Harburg, and Johnny Mercer. Arlen's songs include "Blues in the Night" (1941), "That Old Black Magic" (1942), "One for My Baby (and One More for the Road)" (1943), "Accentuate the Positive" (1944), and "Come Rain or Come Shine" (1946), all with Mercer; "Last Night When We Were Young" (1935) and "Over the Rainbow" (1939), with Harburg; "It's Only a Paper Moon" (1932), with Harburg and Billy Rose; "I've Got the World on a String" (1932) and "Stormy Weather" (1933), with Koehler; and "The Man That Got Away" (1954), with Ira Gershwin.

The Jazz Composer: Hoagy Carmichael

Hoagy Carmichael (Hoagland Howard Carmichael, 1899–1981) was a talented songwriter in the Tin Pan Alley tradition, even if he didn't live or write in New York City. Like Porter, Carmichael was a native Hoosier; he hailed from Bloomington, Indiana, home of Indiana University, where he began his songwriting career.

Carmichael's easygoing compositions reflect his love of the jazz music of the 1920s; his best songs employ jazz-like harmonies and rhythms. Carmichael wrote with a number of the era's best lyricists, including Frank Loesser, Mitchell Parrish, and Johnny Mercer. His most famous songs include "Lazybones" (1933) and "In the Cool, Cool, Cool of the Evening" (1951), with Mercer; "Two Sleepy People" (1938) and "Heart and Soul" (1938), with Loesser; "Star Dust" (1927), with Parrish; "Georgia on My Mind" (1930), with Stuart Gorrell; "I Get Along Without You Very Well" (1939), with lyrics from a poem by Jane Brown Thompson; "Lazy River" (1930), with Sidney Arodin; "The Nearness of You" (1938), with Ned Washington; and "Ole Buttermilk Sky" (1946), with Jack Brooks.

The New Lion: Frank Loesser

In the later years of Tin Pan Alley, lyricist Frank Loesser (1910–1969) began composing his own songs. Loesser was an extremely versatile songwriter; each of his Broadway shows had its own unique flavor. The best known of these shows were *Guys and Dolls* (1950), with its Damon Runyonesque flavor; Danny Kaye's heartwarming movie musical *Hans Christian Andersen* (1952); and the sweetly satirical *How to Succeed in Business Without Really Trying* (1961).

Loesser's notable songs include "Once in Love with Amy" (1948), "Baby It's Cold Outside" (1949), "Luck Be a Lady Tonight" (1950), "Inch Worm" (1952), and "I Believe in You" (1961). He also wrote lyrics with Hoagy Carmichael ("Heart and Soul" and "Two Sleepy People").

The Dean of Musical Theater: Richard Rodgers

Richard Rodgers (1902–1979) was not technically a Tin Pan Alley writer (his office was located elsewhere), although his songs became staples of the Great American Songbook. Rodgers was the dean of twentieth-century musical theater; he created more than 40 Broadway musicals (many made into movies) and hundreds of popular songs.

Working originally with lyricist Lorenz Hart and later with Oscar Hammerstein II, Rodgers's compositions were known for their consistent inventiveness and sophistication. His later musicals redefined the form by using music to advance the plot, instead of as standalone vignettes.

Rodgers's songbook includes "Mountain Greenery" (1927), "Thou Swell" (1927), "Spring Is Here" (1928), "Isn't It Romantic?" (1932), "Blue Moon" (1934),

"My Romance" (1935), "The Lady Is a Tramp" (1937), "My Funny Valentine" (1937), and "Bewitched, Bothered and Bewildered" (1940), all with Hart; and "Oh What a Beautiful Mornin'" (1943), "People Will Say We're in Love" (1943), "You'll Never Walk Alone" (1945), "If I Loved You" (1945), "Some Enchanted Evening" (1949), "My Favorite Things" (1959), and "Climb Every Mountain" (1959), with Hammerstein.

The songwriting team of Rodgers (left) and Hart.

The Wordsmiths: Notable Tin Pan Alley Lyricists

Talking about Cohan, Kern, Berlin, Gershwin, Porter, Arlen, Carmichael, and Rodgers focuses on the music of the popular song at the exclusion of the words. Writing alongside these notable composers were a talented group of equally notable lyricists, all of whom deserve at least a brief mention here:

- **Irving Caesar** (1895–1996), who wrote with George Gershwin ("Swanee"), Vincent Youmans ("Tea for Two"), and Joseph Meyer and Roger Wolfe Kahn ("Crazy Rhythm").

- **Dorothy Fields** (1905–1974), who wrote with Jerome Kern ("The Way You Look Tonight" and "A Fine Romance"), Jimmy McHugh ("I Can't Give You Anything But Love, Baby" and "On the Sunny Side of the Street"), and Cy Coleman ("Big Spender" and "The Rhythm of Life").

- **Ira Gershwin** (1896–1983), who wrote with his brother George as well as with Harold Arlen ("The Man That Got Away") and Jerome Kern ("Long Ago (and Far Away)").

- **Oscar Hammerstein II** (1895–1960), who wrote with Jerome Kern ("Ol' Man River" and "All the Things You Are") and Richard Rodgers ("My Favorite Things" and "Climb Every Mountain").

- **E. Y. "Yip" Harburg** (1896–1981), who wrote with Harold Arlen ("Last Night When We Were Young" and "Over the Rainbow"), Jay Gorney ("Brother, Can You Spare a Dime?"), and Vernon Duke ("April in Paris").

- **Lorenz Hart** (1895–1943), who wrote primarily with Richard Rodgers ("The Lady Is a Tramp" and "My Funny Valentine").

- **Ted Koehler** (1894–1973), who wrote with Harold Arlen ("I've Got the World on a String" and "Stormy Weather") and Jimmy McHugh ("I've Got My Fingers Crossed").

- **Johnny Mercer** (1909–1976), who wrote with Harold Arlen ("That Old Black Magic" and "Come Rain or Come Shine"), Hoagy Carmichael ("Lazybones" and "In the Cool, Cool, Cool of the Evening"), Richard Whiting ("Hurray for Hollywood" and "Too Marvelous for Words"), Harry Warren ("You Must Have Been a Beautiful Baby" and "Jeepers Creepers"), Duke Ellington ("Satin Doll"), and Henry Mancini ("Moon River" and "Days of Wine and Roses").

- **Mitchell Parrish** (1900–1993), who wrote with Hoagy Carmichael ("Star Dust") and Duke Ellington ("Sophisticated Lady").

> **Note**
>
> In addition to being a prolific lyricist, Johnny Mercer was also a popular singer (of his own and others' songs) and the cofounder of Capitol Records.

Rock Intrudes: The End of an Era

The golden age of Tin Pan Alley ended after World War II, when the movie and stage musical began to go into decline, and when rock and roll and pop music for teenagers began to dominate the charts. That was when short-playing 45 RPM records ("singles") became the major means of selling songs and individual performers became more important than the songwriters.

During the late 1950s and particularly the 1960s, these factors contributed to a decline in sheet music sales, and it became less common for music publishers to hire their own stables of songwriters. Songwriters started to perform their own songs, and singers started to write their own music. The music publishing industry eventually dispersed from the Tin Pan Alley area, first taking up residence in the Brill Building further uptown and later moving west to California.

Despite the demise of Tin Pan Alley as a place, songwriting in the Tin Pan Alley tradition continues to this day. Music for hire is still common on Broadway, for Hollywood movie soundtracks, for the country music industry on Music Row in Nashville, and in some forms of commercial pop music. While there appear to be no new Berlins or Gershwins, there are still plenty of freelance songwriters who make a living writing music on spec.

Note

For further reading about the Great American Songbook, I recommend two books—one relatively new, one classic. The classic is Alec Wilder's *American Popular Song: The Great Innovators, 1900–1950* (Oxford University Press, 1972, new edition 1990), which provides a detailed, academic, yet thoroughly entertaining overview of the key songwriters and songs of the period. The newer book is Wilfrid Sheed's *The House That George Built: With a Little Help from Irving, Cole, and a Crew of About Fifty* (Random House, 2007); this book is more of a personal journey into the lives of the great American songwriters, and also quite entertaining.

Celebrating the Singers of the Popular Song

Any examination of the Great American Songbook would be incomplete without mention of the great singers who popularized these songs. These singers—on stage, screen, radio, and record—provided a voice to the songs of Berlin and Gershwin, bringing them into homes from East coast to West.

One of the earliest singers of the popular song was Bing Crosby (1903–1977). It may be hard for a modern audience to think of him this way, especially with still-vivid memories of an aging, sweater-clad pipe-smoker in his series of Christmas TV specials, but in his day Crosby was a jazzy innovator, one of the first singers to fully take advantage of modern microphone and recording technologies. His laid-back, crooning style influenced several generations of vocalists, including Perry Como and Dean Martin.

Singer Bing Crosby at a 1942 wartime scrap rubber drive.

In the movies and on the Broadway stage, Fred Astaire (1899–1987) was a sympathetic interpreter of the classic song. In addition to being one of the century's great dancers, Fred had an "everyman" kind of voice that was light and airy and perfectly suited to the songs of the day. As a result, his movie musicals with partner Ginger Rogers were used to introduce new tunes from the likes of Berlin, Porter, Kern, and the Gershwins—and Astaire's versions of these classic songs remain among the most definitive.

On the other side of the gender aisle, Ella Fitzgerald (1917–1996) was, perhaps, the premiere female interpreter of the popular song. Best known as a big band vocalist and jazz singer, Fitzgerald also released a series of critically acclaimed *Songbook* albums, each featuring songs from a specific great American songwriter. Her interpretation of these standards was hip and jazzy yet respectful of the original tunes; there may be no better representation of the songs of the Great American Songbook.

Note

I like *New York Times* columnist Frank Rich's observation on Ella's *Songbook* recordings: "Here was a black woman popularizing urban songs often written by immigrant Jews to a national audience of predominantly white Christians." That does a good job of demonstrating how the Great American Songbook—and Ella Fitzgerald, for that matter—cross cultural boundaries to create a truly American music.

When discussing the great popular vocalists of the twentieth century, one would be remiss not to discuss Frank Sinatra (1915–1998). Sinatra started out as a skinny kid singing vocals for the Harry James and Tommy Dorsey big bands, then came into his own with his solo recordings for Capitol Records in the 1950s. Sinatra practically invented the concept album, built around popular standards, with hit recordings like *In the Wee Small Hours* (1955), *Songs for Swingin' Lovers* (1956), *Come Fly with Me* (1958), and *Only the Lonely* (1958). In his later years he ruled Las Vegas with the Rat Pack and grew into the personality of the Chairman of the Board, but the middle-aged Sinatra almost single-handedly rescued the Great American Songbook from obscurity.

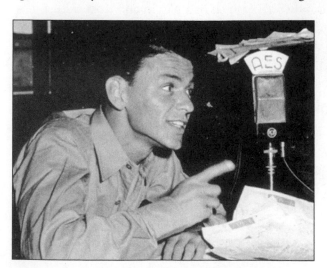

Crooner Frank Sinatra at the microphone for an Armed Forces Radio show during World War II.

Other classic singers of the American popular song include well-known singers such as Mel Tormé (1925–1999), Sarah Vaughn (1924–1990), Blossom Dearie (b. 1926), Nancy Wilson (b. 1937), and Tony Bennett (b. 1926). All have much to recommend in their interpretive styles.

In the modern era, the Great American Songbook has been kept alive by any number of Broadway, jazz, and cabaret singers, including Michael Feinstein (b. 1956), Diana Krall (b. 1964), and Harry Connick Jr. (b. 1967). There have also been several older rock singers who have tapped the classic catalog, to varying levels of success; the most successful of these contemporary ventures into classic territory include the albums "What's New" (1983) and "Lush Life" (1985) by Linda Ronstadt (b. 1946) and "My Romance" (1990) and "Moonlight Serenade" (2005) by Carly Simon (b. 1945)—both of whom have the vocal chops to pull off the more demanding classic material.

In Praise of the Broadway Musical

Most of the songs in the Great American Songbook were originally written for Broadway musicals. Songwriters of the Tin Pan Alley era found success by placing songs in Broadway plays, especially in the era before the music in musicals became integrated into the plot of the play.

The golden age of the Broadway musical stretches from the mid-1920s through the mid-1960s, and in turn fed a steady stream of film musicals over the same period. Hit songs from these shows often turned up on the pop charts of the day, forming a core repertoire for popular singers on radio and recordings.

1900–1927: The Musical Revue

The earliest American musicals were more like vaudeville reviews—a little song, a little dance, a little comedy, a little acting, with each bit only tangentially related to the rest. These early musicals, such as those by George M. Cohan and Florenz Ziegfeld, were showcases for the new music of the day, but didn't present the type of unified plot that we're used to today.

In fact, these early musicals didn't have much of a plot at all. Most were a disconnected series of unrelated song-and-dance numbers, some of which were quite elaborate. That said, these musicals were host to numerous classic songs, even if the songs were not tied together in any significant fashion.

1927–1943: The Birth of the Book Musical

In 1927, the revue-style musical was superseded by a new type of unified musical play. The so-called *book musical* is a musical play that tells a coherent story, with the songs tied to the plot. The first book musical was Jerome Kern's *Show Boat* (1927), with book and lyrics by Oscar Hammerstein II. For the first time, the songs followed the plot of the play, helping to advance the action.

The success of *Show Boat* influenced other Broadway composers, including the Gershwins and the team of Rodgers and Hart. The Gershwins' jazz opera *Porgy and Bess* (1935) shows the strong influence of *Show Boat* in its coherent story and theme of racial struggle. Rodgers and Hart's mid-1930s shows, including the classic *On Your Toes* (1936), also reflected a more mature approach to wedding story and music. Cole Porter was another innovator in the world of musical theater; his urbane wit helped his songs become instant classics in such well-loved shows as *Anything Goes* (1934), which made a star of a young Ethel Merman.

1943–1965: The Classic Era

In the early 1940s, Richard Rodgers dropped the increasingly erratic Hart and formed a new partnership with Oscar Hammerstein II, who had helped pioneer the book musical with Jerome Kern. The result was the landmark *Oklahoma!* (1943), which built on the innovations of *Show Boat* to fully integrate song and dance into the play's story. *Oklahoma!*, with its rich book, innovative staging, and classic songs, became the model for many other book musicals, including further Rodgers and Hammerstein musicals *Carousel* (1945), *South Pacific* (1949), *The King and I* (1951), *Flower Drum Song* (1958), and *The Sound of Music* (1959).

Alan J. Lerner (1918–1986) and Frederick Loewe (1901–1988) were notably influenced by Rodgers and Hammerstein. Their later musicals, including *Brigadoon* (1949), *My Fair Lady* (1956), and *Camelot* (1960), featured strong books with well-integrated songs.

Another prolific composer of the era was Jule Styne (1905–1994), initially working in collaboration with lyricist Sammy Cahn (1913–1993). After a successful career as a pop songwriter and some work in Hollywood, Styne had several major Broadway hits, starting with *High Button Shoes* (1947), and continuing through *Peter Pan* (1954), *Gypsy* (1959; with lyrics by Stephen Sondheim), and *Funny Girl* (1964; with lyrics by Bob Merrill).

The late 1950s and 1960s saw a further maturation of the classic musical form. Jerry Herman (b. 1933) composed the music for crowd-pleasing musicals *Hello, Dolly!* (1964) and *Mame* (1966); composer-lyricist-librettist Meredith Wilson (1902–1984) created the smash hit *The Music Man* (1957); and the team of lyricist Sheldon Harnick (b. 1924) and composer Jerry Bock (b. 1928) achieved success with the classic *Fiddler on the Roof* (1964).

1960s and Beyond: The Musical Matures

The musical form attained higher status when classical composer Leonard Bernstein (1918–1990) melded the traditional Broadway musical with serious twentieth-century music. Collaborating with young lyricist Stephen Sondheim (b. 1930) and choreographer Jerome Robbins (1918–1998), Bernstein created 1957's classic *West Side Story*. Based on Shakespeare's *Romeo and Juliet* but set among the street gangs of New York, it created a new standard for realism in musicals. It was also notable for blending twentieth-century compositional techniques with Tin Pan Alley songcraft.

More sophisticated musicals came from the pen of Stephen Sondheim, who took on both words and music for the musicals *Company* (1970), *Follies* (1971), *A Little Night Music* (1973), *Sweeny Todd* (1979), and *Sunday in the Park with George* (1984). Also notable were the operatic musicals from French composer Claude-Michel Schönberg (b. 1944), including *Les Misérables* (1980) and *Miss Saigon* (1989), and Englishman Andrew Lloyd Webber (b. 1948), including *Evita* (1976), *Cats* (1981), and *Phantom of the Opera* (1986).

While Broadway cast albums of the 1950s and 1960s were among the best-selling records of their time, the changing landscape of popular music led to a steady decline of Broadway's impact on the pop charts. Similarly, the aging of Broadway's most creative songwriters and the parallel graying of the Broadway audience led to fewer and fewer new musicals appearing on Broadway from the 1970s on.

While the musical is far from dead, the era of the hit Broadway song from the Tin Pan Alley songwriter is long over. Instead, American popular music is now driven by rock bands, hip-hop artists, and self-contained singer-songwriters—all of which we'll discuss in the next chapter.

Listening List

The Great American Songbook should be well represented in the libraries of all self-respecting music lovers. If your cupboard is unnecessarily bare, the following recordings should provide a basic listening list for the best of the classic American songwriters.

A Little Night Music (1973 original Broadway cast)

The Essential Collection (Hoagy Carmichael)

The Essential Collection: The Great American Songbook (Ella Fitzgerald)

The Essential George Gershwin (Various artists)

Fred Astaire & Ginger Rogers at RKO (Fred Astaire and Ginger Rogers)

Get Happy: The Harold Arlen Centennial Collection (Various artists)

My Huckleberry Friend: Johnny Mercer Sings the Songs of Johnny Mercer (Johnny Mercer)

In the Wee Small Hours (Frank Sinatra)

My Fair Lady (1956 original Broadway cast)

Oklahoma! (original motion picture soundtrack)

Phantom of the Opera (1986 original London cast)

Porgy and Bess (Willard White; Cynthia Haymon; London Philharmonic Orchestra; Simon Rattle, conductor)

Show Boat (original motion picture soundtrack)

The Sondheim Collection (Various artists)

The Songs of Irving Berlin (Various artists)

Till the Clouds Roll By: The Songs of Jerome Kern (Various artists)

The Very Best of Cole Porter (Various artists)

West Side Story (1957 original Broadway cast)

Timeline: Popular Song from 1900 to 1950

1904	George M. Cohan writes "Give My Regards to Broadway"
1911	Irving Berlin writes "Alexander's Ragtime Band"
1917	George M. Cohan writes "Over There"
1919	George Gershwin writes "Swanee"
1918	Irving Berlin writes "God Bless America"
1924	George Gershwin writes *Rhapsody in Blue*
1927	*Show Boat* debuts; George Gershwin writes "I Got Rhythm"; Hoagy Carmichael writes "Star Dust"
1932	Cole Porter writes "Night and Day"
1934	*Anything Goes* opens
1935	*Top Hat* released; *Porgy and Bess* premieres
1936	Jerome Kern writes "The Way You Look Tonight"
1937	George Gershwin dies of brain tumor; Rodgers and Hart write "My Funny Valentine"
1939	Harold Arlen writes "Somewhere Over the Rainbow"
1940	Irving Berlin writes "White Christmas"
1943	*Oklahoma!* debuts
1945	Jerome Kern dies
1948	Columbia Records releases first 12" 33⅓ RPM LP
1949	*Brigadoon* and *South Pacific* open
1950	*Guys and Dolls* premieres
1951	Hoagy Carmichael writes "In the Cool, Cool, Cool of the Evening"
1955	Frank Sinatra releases *In the Wee Small Hours* LP
1956	*My Fair Lady* premieres
1957	*West Side Story* and *The Music Man* debut
1959	*The Sound of Music* opens
1960	*Camelot* premieres; John F. Kennedy elected president
1961	*How to Succeed in Business Without Really Trying* opens
1964	*Fiddler on the Roof* and *Hello, Dolly!* debut
1970	*Company* premieres
1973	*A Little Night Music* opens
1976	*Evita* premieres
1979	*Sweeney Todd* debuts

1980	*Les Misérables* opens
1981	*Cats* debuts
1986	*Phantom of the Opera* premieres
1989	*Miss Saigon* debuts
1989	Irving Berlin dies

Rock, Rhythm, and Rap: Popular Music from 1950 to Today

In This Chapter

◆ Discovering folk and country music

◆ Learning about R&B and soul music

◆ Uncovering the roots of rock and roll

◆ Understanding rap and hip hop

After World War II, the world changed. Forget the Cold War; there was enough turmoil going on in the world of music to satisfy any fan of chaos and conflict.

Think of everything that happened in the course of a decade or so. The world of classical music splintered into dozens of strange-sounding variants; big bands faded from the limelight, to be replaced by bebop, cool jazz, and other niche styles; the blues gained rhythm to become R&B; and white people learned to sing black and invented rock and roll.

That's a lot of musical evolution, which means we have a lot of ground to cover in this chapter. So read on to learn about popular music in the second half of the twentieth century—from folk to R&B to rock and roll to hip hop and beyond.

The Popularization of American Folk Music

Since no musical evolution adheres to a strict, decades-based schedule, we have to start our look at post-1950s music earlier in the century. The first style we'll examine is American folk music—a simple, acoustic-based music that deals with everyday events and common people. Modern folk music stands alone as its own independent genre, yet also informs many other styles, including rock and country.

Woody Guthrie and the Weavers: Traditional Folk Music

As you remember from our discussion of Appalachian folk music in Chapter 9, most American folk music originated with English, Irish, and Scottish folk tunes brought over by the original settlers. Those folk tunes survive to this day in bluegrass and "old-time" music of the eastern mountain states, and informed the development of traditional folk music in the early part of the twentieth century.

One of the first documentations of traditional folk music was made in 1910, when Texas song collector John Lomax (1867–1948) published his *Cowboy Songs and Other Frontier Ballads*. The music was more completely documented in 1928, when the Library of Congress established its Archive of American Folk Song, to preserve and promote America's traditional music.

> **Note**
>
> Lead Belly got his nickname from his fellow prisoners, who marveled at his unusual strength and physical stamina.

John Lomax and his son Alan played a big role in documenting and popularizing what was then a regional music, passed on in the oral or performing tradition. In 1933, with the support of the Archive of American Folk Song, the Lomaxes began recording local folk and blues artists. During a trip to southern prisons, they discovered Lead Belly (Huddie William Ledbetter, 1885–1949), a black singer and virtuoso 12-string guitar player. Lead Belly sang of women, work, prison, drinking, and racism, in a style that defined the rural folk blues of the 1930s. The Lomaxes brought Lead Belly north to perform for urban audiences, where he recorded for various labels and influenced a generation of blues and folk singers.

Another important Lomax discovery was a white folksinger named Woody Guthrie (1912–1967). Born in Oklahoma, Guthrie was an itinerant sign painter and guitarist who gained fame as a member of the New York folk community in the 1930s. Guthrie was a prolific songwriter with an ear for the plight of the common man. His songs "This Land is Your Land" (1940), "Pastures of Plenty" (1941), and "Roll On, Columbia" (1941) have become American classics.

> **Note**
>
> Woody Guthrie's son Arlo (b. 1947) is a popular folksinger in his own right, most famous for the 1967 recording of his song "Alice's Restaurant Massacree."

Guthrie performed and recorded across the country until the early 1950s, when an inherited disease, Huntington's Chorea, began to affect his motor skills. He was eventually hospitalized and became unable to perform. He died in 1967 at age 55.

One of Guthrie's closest friends was a young banjo player named Pete Seeger (b. 1919); the two often performed together at union rallies and labor meetings. Seeger later achieved fame as a member of the folksinging group the Weavers. In the late 1940s and early 1950s, the Weavers enjoyed mainstream pop success with upbeat arrangements of folk songs like Lead Belly's "Goodnight Irene" (1934) the traditional African tune "Wimoweh," and the native Israeli "Tzena, Tzena, Tzena." Their concerts and recordings helped to popularize many traditional songs now considered standards in the folk repertoire, including

"On Top of Old Smokey," "Kisses Sweeter Than Wine," "Rock Island Line," and "The Midnight Special." While the group eventually came under political pressure because of their support of the labor union movement, they became the inspiration for many of the popular folk groups of the 1960s folk revival.

Folksinger Woody Guthrie.

After the breakup of the Weavers, Seeger continued with a long and successful solo career. He is the author of several well-known songs, including "If I Had a Hammer" (1949, with Lee Hays), "Where Have All the Flowers Gone" (1962, with Joe Hickerson), and "Turn! Turn! Turn! (To Everything There Is a Season)" (1962, based on Ecclesiastes 3, verses 1–8, from the New Testament Bible).

Note
The other members of the Weavers were Ronnie Gilbert (b. 1926), Lee Hays (1914–1981), and Fred Hellerman (b. 1927).

Peter, Paul, Mary, and Bob: The 1960s Folk Revival

After the Weavers disbanded in 1952, folk music got quiet for a while. However, a new generation of folksingers and folk fans was waiting in the wings for what became the 1960s folk revival.

The revival actually started in the late 1950s, when new groups of young, relatively clean-cut folksingers started appearing in the coffee houses of New York City and college towns around the country. These groups, such as the Kingston Trio, the Chad Mitchell Trio, and the Limeliters played a somewhat sanitized version of traditional folk, complete with three (or more) part harmonies inspired by the Weavers. These groups placed several songs on the pop charts of the day, including The Kingston Trio's "Tom Dooley" (1958) and "Greenback Dollar" (1963).

Perhaps the most popular of these 1960s folk groups was Peter, Paul and Mary. The trio, made up of Peter Yarrow (b. 1938), Noel "Paul" Stookey (b. 1937), and Mary Travers (b. 1937), had numerous hits during the decade, including the songs "Puff the Magic Dragon" (1962, written by Yarrow and Leonard Lipton), "Leaving on a Jet Plane" (1967, written by John Denver), and "Blowin' in the Wind" (1963).

That last tune was written by a young folksinger named Bob Dylan (Robert Allen Zimmerman, b. 1941). Dylan was a disciple of Woody Guthrie who traveled from his native Minnesota to visit the ailing Guthrie in his hospital room in New York City, and then stayed to partake of the city's bustling folk music scene.

Bob Dylan and Joan Baez performing at 1963's Civil Rights March on Washington, D.C.

> **Note**
> Of all the interpreters of Dylan's songs, perhaps the sweetest sounding is Joan Baez (b. 1941). Baez is a singer, not a songwriter, who has performed the works of Dylan and other folk and country writers of the era.

While his early tunes were of the social protest variety, Dylan later pioneered the stream-of-consciousness narrative style, filled with literary references, which inspired generations of songwriters to follow. Arguably the most influential songwriter of the 1960s, Dylan's tunes were performed by dozens (if not hundreds) of his contemporaries in both the folk and rock fields. It's fair to say that Dylan changed the face of American popular song more than any other composer since 1950.

Dylan's most notable compositions include "Don't Think Twice, It's All Right" (1962), "A Hard Rain's A-Gonna Fall" (1962), the aforementioned "Blowin' in the Wind" (1963), "The Times They Are A-Changin'" (1964), "Mr. Tambourine Man" (1964), "It Ain't Me Babe" (1964), "Like a Rolling Stone" (1965), "Positively 4th Street" (1965), "Just Like a Woman" (1966), "All Along the Watchtower" (1968), "Lay Lady Lay" (1969), "Forever Young" (1970), and

"Knockin' on Heaven's Door" (1973). His most important albums include *The Freewheelin' Bob Dylan* (1963), *Highway 61 Revisited* (1965), *Blonde on Blonde* (1966), *Nashville Skyline* (1969), and *Blood on the Tracks* (1975).

Dylan wasn't the only important folksinger of the 1960s, of course. Other notable folk composers and performers include Phil Ochs (1940–1976), Tom Paxton (b. 1937), Buffy Sainte-Marie (b. 1941), and Canadian Gordon Lightfoot (b. 1938).

Contemporary Folk

As most musical trends tend to do, the folk movement of the 1960s splintered into many smaller, more focused movements in the 1970s, 1980s, and 1990s. These contemporary folk genres include the bluegrass and old-time music revivals, the beginnings of interest in world music, New Age and "new acoustic" music, and so-called Americana. In addition, many folk performers crossed over into related genres, performing in the folk-rock and country-rock styles.

Several of these new singer/songwriters were promoted as "New Dylans," beginning with Loudon Wainwright III (b. 1946) and Chicago's Steve Goodman (1948–1984), who wrote the classic tune "The City of New Orleans" (1972). Female singer/songwriters also gained popularity, ranging from the introspective Joni Mitchell (b. 1943) to the more playful Canadian sisters Kate (b. 1946) and Anna McGarrigle (b. 1944) and New York's singing Roches—sisters Maggie (b. 1951), Terre (b. 1953), and Suzzy (b. 1956).

Of these contemporary folksingers, Joni Mitchell is perhaps the most famous and the most influential. One of the first popular female singer/songwriters, Mitchell started writing in the confessional folk vein and eventually moved into more sophisticated jazz-like stylings. Her albums *Blue* (1971) and *For the Roses* (1972) influenced several generations of female folksingers, while the later *Court and Spark* (1974) and *Heijira* (1976) were more jazz-oriented. Notable songs include "Both Sides Now" (1968), "Big Yellow Taxi" (1970), "Carey" (1971), "River" (1971), "Help Me" (1974), and "Free Man in Paris" (1974).

Mitchell inspired the generation of female folksingers that bloomed in the 1980s and 1990s. These singers, including Shawn Colvin (b. 1956), Dar Williams (Dorothy Williams, b. 1967), Lucy Kaplansky (b. 1960), and Jewel (Jewel Kilcher, b. 1974), extended the traditional folk approach to include more rock- and pop-oriented harmonies and instrumentation.

Note

In the "it's a small world" department, know that Loudon Wainwright was once married to Kate McGarrigle (a union that produced son Rufus Wainwright and daughter Martha Wainwright, both musicians) and had a long-standing relationship with Suzzy Roche (resulting in daughter Lucy Roche, herself a budding singer/songwriter).

Country Goes Mainstream

Folk and country both evolved from the same Appalachian folk tradition, but in significantly different ways. In the case of country music, it blended folk music with the rural blues to create a unique musical form.

Country music is, like the blues, a deceptively simple musical form that lends itself to numerous variations. Even though many country songs are built around three chords and a plain melody, these songs can be interpreted in a variety of styles, from the gritty sounds of honky-tonk to the rock-tinged stylings of modern country.

Traditional Country

Country music developed in the American south, melding Appalachian folk melodies with the scales and vocal stylings of the rural blues. Old-time country music was simple and folky, often performed with just guitars and fiddles—and a distinct vocal twang.

The first popular country recordings were made in the 1920s, primarily "old-timey" tunes played on fiddle and acoustic guitar. These first recordings, on local labels, inspired Victor Records to send a crew to record country acts in Bristol, Tennessee. These "Bristol Sessions," recorded in 1927, yielded the first recorded performances of both Jimmie Rodgers (1897–1933) and the Carter Family.

Rodgers, known as the Father of Country Music and the Singing Brakeman, achieved national popularity by honing the rough edges off the traditionally rural country sound. A former railroad worker, Rodgers turned to performing when he was in his teens; he had a bluesy vocal style and a trademark high-pitched yodel that translated well on record. Rodgers cut 110 songs in just six years, including "Blue Yodel No. 1 (T for Texas)" (1927), "In the Jailhouse Now" (1928), and "Blue Yodel No. 9" (1930), recorded with jazz great Louis Armstrong.

The Carter Family was the royal family of traditional country music. Led by patriarch A. P. Carter (1891–1960), the family sang traditional country tunes with the tight harmonies of mountain gospel music; their signature songs include the traditional tunes "Wildwood Flower" and "Keep on the Sunny Side." The Carter Family included Maybelle Carter (1909–1978), sister-in-law of A. P. and the mother of June Carter (1929–2003)—who later became the wife of country legend Johnny Cash.

Western Swing

One interesting variant of traditional country music is the genre known as *Western Swing*. This unique combination of traditional country music with jazz styles was born in the late 1920s in the Texas-Oklahoma region, where local country musicians were influenced by blues and jazz recordings. The result blended the two styles, creating country music with a swinging accompaniment.

The Western Swing sound was created by a band called the Lightcrust Dough-boys, which, like most of the Western Swing bands that followed, included fiddle(s), steel guitar, and a ragtime-influenced piano. The Doughboys, popular in 1931–1932, featured fiddler Bob Wills (1905–1975), who later formed his own band, the Texas Playboys, and further propagated the sound.

Note

From 1925 to the present day, the most popular country acts have performed on the Grand Ole Opry—a weekly radio broadcast live from Nashville, Tennessee. Not only did the Grand Ole Opry establish performers as legitimate stars (and national stars at that, thanks to the program's national audience), it also cemented Nashville as the capitol of country music.

Western Swing continued through the 1940s, through a slate of Southern California bands, but then entered a state of dormancy. The sound was revived in the 1970s, when new bands such as Asleep at the Wheel introduced a new generation to Western Swing.

Honky-Tonk

Another new country style emerged after the second world war, when the local honky-tonk—often a small bar located on the outskirts of town—became a favored place to listen to and dance to music.

The typical honky-tonk employed small-time local musicians, some of whom later became big-time stars, and gave birth to a new style of music that would define mainstream country music in the late 1940s and 1950s. Honky-tonks were noisy places; it was difficult to hear musicians over the raucous crowd. The music, then, benefited from the introduction of electric instruments and amplification, in the form of electric guitars and basses. In addition, the traditional gospel-tinged country lyrics seemed out of place in these sin-filled dives, which led to new lyrics about loose women, drifting husbands, and strong whisky.

Note _____

Hank Williams Sr. was the honky-tonk performer. His son, Hank Williams Jr. (b. 1949), became a top country performer in his own right, from the 1970s to today.

The preeminent honky-tonk musician of the post-WWII period was Hank Williams (1923–1953). In songs like "Honky Tonkin'" (1948), "Cold, Cold Heart" (1951), "Hey Good Lookin'" (1951), and "Your Cheatin' Heart" (1953), Williams defined the honky-tonk sound.

Bluegrass

At the end of World War II, Western Swing blended with traditional country and honky-tonk to create a new form of music called bluegrass. This is high-energy music, typically played at a fast tempo, using a unique combination of instruments—mandolin, banjo, guitar, fiddle, and bass, along with one or more singers.

The acknowledged "father of bluegrass music" was Bill Monroe (1911–1996). He formed his group the Blue Grass Boys (named for his home state of Kentucky) in 1946. Band members included vocalist/guitarist Lester Flatt (1914–1979) and banjo player Earl Scruggs (b. 1924), who would later become bluegrass stars in their own right.

Bluegrass's popularity spread in the 1950s, moving from rural America to select urban centers. Bluegrass also benefited from the 1960s folk revival, with new bands such as the Greenbriar Boys and the Charles River Valley Boys springing up in New York and Boston, respectively.

The bluegrass style remains popular today, thanks to the modern bluegrass sounds of mandolinist David Grisman (b. 1945), vocalist/fiddle player Alison Krauss (b. 1971) and her group Union Station, singers Patty Loveless (Patty Lee Ramey, b. 1957) and Ricky Skaggs (b. 1954), and the groups New Grass Revival and Nickel Creek.

Country-Pop

With the rise of rock and roll in the 1950s, country music was forced to adapt to the new sound that was sweeping the nation—even in country's home base in the south. This led to country labels using more pop-oriented production techniques to create a smoother sound than was typical with older country music.

In the 1950s, RCA Records producer/guitarist Chet Atkins (1924–2001) combined elements of country and pop music in what became known as the *Nashville sound*. Atkins abandoned traditional country instruments such as fiddles and banjos, instead surrounding the songs' simple melodies with polished pop-oriented orchestral arrangements. The result, a lush sound that blended rural sensibility with urban sophistication, increased popularity for the country genre and created a number of pop crossover hits for artists such as Eddy Arnold (b. 1918), Jim Reeves (1923–1964), and Patsy Cline (1932–1963). These hits included Reeves's "Four Walls" (1957), Cline's "Crazy" (1961), and Arnold's "Make the World Go Away" (1965).

By the late 1960s the Nashville Sound had metamorphosed into *countrypolitan*, with an even heavier emphasis on pop production flourishes; most countrypolitan recordings featured multiple layers of keyboards, guitars, strings, and vocals. The sound was typified by the recordings of producer Billy Sherrill (b. 1936), who created crossover hits for George Jones (b. 1931), Charlie Rich (1932–1995), Conway Twitty (1933–1993), Tammy Wynette (1942–1998), Lynn Anderson (b. 1947), and other artists. Typical countrypolitan songs include Wynette's "Stand By Your Man" (1969), Anderson's "I Never Promised You a Rose Garden" (1971), and Rich's "Behind Closed Doors" (1973).

Progressive and Alternative Country

Not all country fans and musicians appreciated the often bland sounds of mainstream Nashville country-pop. By the late 1960s, a faction of young singer/songwriters embraced a music that was equal parts traditional country, classic honky-tonk, hard-driving rock and roll, and introspective Dylan-influenced folk. This new progressive country sound was a direct reaction to countrypolitan and the Nashville sound, both rootsier and more intellectual than the top-40 country music of the time.

The top progressive country artists include Willie Nelson (b. 1933), Kris Kristofferson (b. 1936), Waylon Jennings (1937–2002), Townes Van Zandt (1944–1997), and Jimmie Dale Gilmore (b. 1945). These artists created distinctive songs that pushed the boundaries of the country genre; many also found acceptance from the rock audience of the day. Representative songs include Kristofferson's "Help Me Make It Through the Night" (1970), Van Zandt's "Pancho and Lefty" (1972), Nelson's "Bloody Mary Morning" (1974), and Jennings's "Amanda" (1974, written by Bob McDill).

Another notable outlaw country performer was the legendary Man in Black, Johnny Cash (1932–2003). Cash's deep baritone voice perfectly complemented

Note

Progressive country is sometimes called *outlaw country*, since it doesn't conform to Nashville's standards. (To some fans, outlaw country is a slightly harder-edged version of progressive country.)

his earnest compositions, most of which combined the emotional honesty of folk music, the rebelliousness of rock and roll, and the world weariness of country. Cash's most memorable recordings include "Folsom Prison Blues" (1956/1968), "I Walk the Line" (1956), "Ring of Fire" (1963), "Jackson" (1967), and "A Boy Named Sue" (1969). He remained popular throughout his entire career, releasing a series of *American* albums in his final decade that won him legions of new fans.

In the 1980s and 1990s, progressive country evolved into *alternative country*, actually a collection of subgenres that describe artists working outside of the Nashville mainstream. Alt country artists blend traditional country sounds with a strong rock and roll aesthetic, and include Ryan Adams (b. 1974), Steve Earle (b. 1955), Emmylou Harris (b. 1947), k. d. lang (Kathryn Dawn Lang, b. 1961), Lyle Lovett (b. 1957), Lucinda Williams (b. 1953), and the groups Uncle Tupelo and Old '97s.

Note

Johnny Cash wasn't the only musical talent in his family. He was married to June Carter Cash, younger member of the famous Carter Family; his daughter Rosanne Cash and stepdaughter Carlene Carter are also talented musicians in their own right.

Country-Folk and Americana

During the 1980s and 1990s, numerous artists blurred the lines between country and folk music, creating a subgenre alternately known as *country-folk* and *Americana*. Like traditional folk musicians, most country-folk artists write and perform the majority of their own material, and tend to find greater appreciation among the folk audience. That said, many of these artists have found success as songwriters, supplying tunes to mainstream Nashville artists.

The most popular country-folk and Americana artists include Mary Chapin Carpenter (b. 1958), Beth Nielsen Chapman (b. 1958), Iris DeMent (b. 1961), Nanci Griffith (b. 1953), John Hiatt (b. 1952), Shelby Lynne (Shelby Lynne Moorer, b. 1968), John Prine (b. 1946), and Gillian Welch (b. 1967). Representative tunes include Griffith's "Love at the Five and Dime" (1986), Prine's "Speed of the Sound of Loneliness" (1988), and Carpenter's "Down at the Twist and Shout" (1990).

Contemporary Country

A new breed of mainstream country music emerged in the late 1980s. This music was heavily influenced by pop/rock sensibilities, spawning crossover superstars like Garth Brooks (b. 1962), Vince Gill (b. 1957), and Toby Keith (b. 1961). A wave of male singers—dubbed "hat acts," after their ubiquitous cowboy headwear—dominated the country charts with songs that sounded more like rock than traditional country, often with a noticeable "good ol' boy" swagger.

By the 1990s, the emphasis had shifted to female vocalists, typically bathed in glossy pop productions. These vocalists—most notably Shania Twain (Eileen Regina Edwards, b. 1965), Faith Hill (b. 1967), LeAnn Rimes (Margaret LeAnn Rimes, b. 1982), and Martina McBride (Martina Mariea Schiff, b. 1966)—deemphasized traditional country twang and found massive success with a mainstream audience. This is the sound of country music today: frothy, pop-like tunes with a rock beat and traditional country instruments (steel guitar, fiddle) added for effect, sung with just a hint of old-school country twang.

Adding Rhythm to the Blues

Folk, country, now rhythm & blues—all musical forms that blossomed in the years immediately after the second world war. In the case of rhythm & blues, or R&B as it's often called, the music evolved from the blues and jazz music of the 1940s. In its original form and in later incarnations as soul, funk, and contemporary R&B, this music brought black culture to white audiences across America.

Jump Blues

Let's go back a bit, before World War II, all the way to the beginning of the twentieth century. This is when the first commercial records became available; these 78 RPM discs fed a market hungry for new recorded music, led to the creation of the music recording business, and fueled the careers of a large number of recording artists.

But unlike today's multiracial society, America at that time was still highly segregated. So from the early days of recording through the end of World War II, records by black artists were marketed separately from those by whites—typically labeled as "race records."

After the war, however, black music started to move onto the pop charts, under the new name of rhythm & blues. R&B has its roots in the jump blues ensembles of the late 1940s and early 1950s, notably the band led by saxophonist Louis Jordan (1908–1975). During the big band era, Jordan's band was arguably the third most popular African American band in the country, after Duke Ellington and Count Basie. When the big band era ended, Jordan formed a smaller ensemble (the Tympany Five) that played a new type of dance music for urban audiences. This music, dubbed jump blues or jump jazz, blended jazz, blues, a shuffle beat, and lighthearted lyrics. The music proved as popular among whites as it was among blacks, leading to the emergence of other black artists with similar crossover appeal.

Atlantic Records: The House That Ruth Built

Perhaps the most important R&B artist of the 1950s was Ruth Brown (Ruth Alston Weston, 1928–2006). Brown's first hit, "So Long" (1949), was quickly followed by dozens more during the following decade, including "I'll Wait for You" (1951) and "(Mama) He Treats Your Daughter Mean" (1953). Known as "Miss Rhythm," Ruth introduced the fledgling R&B style to a wide audience of both blacks and whites, and served as the inspiration for subsequent generations of female soul singers.

Brown recorded for the newly formed Atlantic Records, which became known, in a play on Yankee Stadium's slogan, as "The House That Ruth Built." Atlantic was founded in 1947 by Ahmet Ertegün (1923–2006) and Herb Abrahamson (1916–1999), who were later joined by famed producer Jerry Wexler (b. 1917). The label became home to the industry's top R&B and soul artists, including Solomon Burke (b. 1940), Ray Charles, Aretha Franklin, and the Drifters.

Ray and Sam

Of these later Atlantic artists, Ray Charles (1930–2004) was arguably the most influential. After signing with Atlantic Records, Charles transformed himself from a jazz-influenced pianist into a soul-stirring R&B performer with his first major hit, "I Got A Woman" (1954). His intense, gospel-influenced vocals, along with his pounding piano accompaniment, set the pattern for later hits, including "What'd I Say" (1959) and "Hit the Road, Jack" (1961). Charles was also instrumental in bridging the R&B, pop, and country genres with his land-mark 1962 crossover album, *Modern Sounds in Country and Western Music.*

Charles's main competition among male singers in the later 1950s was Sam Cooke (1931–1964), who came out of a gospel background. Cooke's first hit, 1956's "You Send Me," showed a similar mix of gospel-tinged pleading in the vocal to Charles's "I Got A Woman," but had a more pop-oriented accompaniment. Cooke continued to cut classic R&B songs like "Chain Gang" (1960) and "Bring It On Home to Me" (1961), but increasingly sought a middle-of-the-road audience with more commercial material and smoother arrangements.

Leiber and Stoller

Other influential R&B hitmakers during the 1950s were the vocal groups the Coasters and the Drifters. These two groups had the distinction of being pro-duced by the team of Jerry Leiber (b. 1933) and Mike Stoller (b. 1933), two early Brill Building songwriters and producers who brought "uptown" sophistication to "downtown" R&B.

Leiber and Stoller introduced numerous new techniques in pop music produc-tion. In particular, they added strings and more sophisticated production to a standard R&B beat—a sound that influenced both Phil Spector (who studied under the pair) and Berry Gordy's Motown sound.

As songwriters and producers, Leiber and Stoller's best-known R&B hits include "Searchin'" (1957), "Young Blood" (1957), "Yakety Yak" (1958), "Along Came Jones" (1959), "Charlie Brown" (1959), and "Poison Ivy" (1959), all for the Coasters; "Ruby Baby" (1956) and "There Goes My Baby" (1959), for the Drift-ers; "Stand By Me" (1961) and "Spanish Harlem" (1961), for former Drifter Ben E. King (b. 1938); "Love Potion No. 9" (1959), for the Clovers; and "Hound Dog" (1952, originally recorded by R&B singer Big Mama Thornton) and "Jail-house Rock" (1957), for Elvis Presley.

Note

The first R&B record with background strings was the Drifters' "There Goes My Baby." The sound was so unique—and so foreign to listeners in 1959—that Atlantic producer Jerry Wexler famously said, "It sounded like a radio caught between two sta-tions." But in a good way, of course.

The Motown Sound

By the 1960s, R&B as a genre began to break down into distinct streams. Motown picked up the teen-pop end of the spectrum, while soul took up the gospel intensity and high energy of the best R&B performers.

What we now call the Motown sound—and the resulting Motown and Tamla record labels—sprang from the creative efforts of two men: Berry Gordy (b. 1929), a one-time boxing promoter and would-be songwriter, and Smokey

Robinson (William Robinson, b. 1940), a songwriter, singer, and Gordy's right-hand man through most of the 1960s. Together, they helped create a legacy of music that appealed to both black and white audiences around the world.

Thanks to a talented staff of studio musicians (dubbed the Funk Brothers), Motown's recordings had a distinctive sound that set them apart from other 1960s productions. This sound, dubbed "The Sound of Young America," blended elements of Atlantic R&B, black gospel, and Phil Spector–styled pop into a pleasing concoction that sounded great coming from the tinny car radios of the time. The success of Motown on mainstream radio showed the potential for black music to cross over onto the traditionally white pop charts, which would have a profound impact on the development of all forms of popular music.

Motown depended on a strong stable of both songwriters and performers. The performers (including the Marvelettes, Martha and the Vandellas, the Supremes, the Miracles, the Four Tops, and the Temptations) are well known; the songwriters, less so. But these talented composers and lyricists—including Brian (b. 1941) and Eddie Holland (b. 1939), Lamont Dozier (b. 1941), Norman Whitfield (b. 1943), Barrett Strong (b. 1941), Smokey Robinson, and Gordy himself—created a catalog of pop classics that retain their appeal even today.

The classic Motown sound evolved over the years, adding rock and psychedelic elements in the late 1960s. In the early 1970s, several Motown artists rebelled against Gordy's formulaic approach and were able to achieve independence while still maintaining popular success. Most noteworthy among these were Marvin Gaye (1939–1984), whose landmark 1971 album, *What's Going On*, provided a black perspective on current events, and Stevie Wonder (Steveland Hardaway Judkins, b. 1950), who had a string of critically acclaimed early 1970s albums, culminating in the multi-disc set, *Songs in the Key of Life* (1976).

Soul and Funk

Motown represented the most commercial style of black music in the 1960s, but it wasn't the only black music on the radio. A less polished—but still commercial—type of soul music was being made in Memphis, by the artists of the local Stax record label. The Stax sound, as represented by artists Rufus Thomas (1917–2001), his daughter Carla (b. 1942), Otis Redding (1941–1967), Isaac Hayes (b. 1942), Sam and Dave, and Booker T. and the MGs, was raw and unornamented, typically just a singer accompanied by rhythm section and a small group of horn players.

Similar soulful sounds were coming from Muscle Shoals, Alabama, and New York City, via the venerated Atlantic label. The Queen of Soul was unarguably Aretha Franklin (b. 1942), who had begun her career singing gospel music in her father's church. Atlantic producer Jerry Wexler recognized her potential and sent her to Muscle Shoals to produce her greatest hits, including "Respect" (1967), "(You Make Me Feel Like) A Natural Woman" (1967), "Chain of Fools" (1967), "Think" (1968), and "Rock Steady" (1971).

If Aretha was the Queen of Soul, the Godfather of Soul was James Brown (1933–2006), who in the mid-1960s created a highly rhythmic style of R&B

called *funk*. Brown combined stripped-down harmonies, driving rhythms, and high-energy vocals to create a compelling musical mix. Some of Brown's best-known tunes include "Papa's Got a Brand New Bag" (1965), "I Got You (I Feel Good)" (1965), "Cold Sweat" (1967), and "Say It Loud—I'm Black and I'm Proud (Part 1)" (1968).

Funk went mainstream in the late 1960s, thanks to the efforts of Sly Stone (Sylvester Stewart, b. 1943) and his group Sly and the Family Stone. Hailing from the San Francisco Bay area, the Family Stone was a band that mixed races (black and white musicians playing together) and genres (a frothy blend of funk, soul, and rock). Sly influenced countless funk bands in the 1970s and beyond; the group's hits include "Dance to the Music" (1967), "Everyday People" (1969), "Hot Fun in the Summertime" (1969), and "Thank You (Falettinme Be Mice Elf Agin)" (1969).

Urban Contemporary and Dance

The softer side of R&B was represented by the style currently known as urban contemporary. This type of music features pop-oriented vocalists singing lush, commercial ballads.

The urban contemporary style has its roots in Sam Cooke's crooning in the late 1950s, and in the precise stylings of Dionne Warwick (Marie Dionne Warrick, b. 1940) in the 1960s. Working with legendary songwriters Burt Bacharach and Hal David, Warwick had a string of high-class hits that included "Walk On By" (1964), "I Say a Little Prayer" (1967), "Do You Know the Way to San Jose" (1968), and "I'll Never Fall in Love Again" (1970).

In the early to mid-1970s, the soul ballad style was given a funkier edge by Philadelphia-based songwriter/producers Kenneth Gamble (b. 1943) and Leon Huff (b. 1942), with artists such as Billy Paul (b. 1934), the O'Jays, the Intruders, and Harold Melvin and the Blue Notes. The so-called Philadelphia sound was viewed by many as the rightful inheritor of the Motown crown, as Gamble and Huff incorporated sophisticated orchestral "sweetening" over a tight rhythm section and group vocals.

In the 1980s and 1990s, this style of soft soul crooning became formally known as urban contemporary, and began to incorporate up-tempo dance tracks as well as soulful ballads. Many urban contemporary artists, such as Whitney Houston (b. 1963), Luther Vandross (1951–2005), and Kenneth "Babyface" Edmonds (b. 1958), were able to cross over into the pop charts, while other artists, such as Janet Jackson (b. 1966) and En Vogue, blended urban contemporary with elements of hip hop to create dance-oriented hits.

The biggest R&B artist of the 1980s was Janet's big brother Michael Jackson (b. 1958), who as a child was the lead singer in the successful Motown group the Jackson 5. Jackson's adult style combined elements of soul, rock, and dance music; his 1982 album *Thriller* became the biggest-selling album of all time, and he was the first black artist to find stardom on MTV. Jackson's most important solo recordings include "Rock with You" (1979), "Thriller" (1982), "Billie Jean" (1982), "Beat It" (1982), and "Bad" (1987).

Don't Knock the Rock

The term *rock* has become somewhat generic, referring to a wide range of popular music in the second half of the twentieth century. Everything from Chuck Berry's pounding three-chord rockers to the sweet harmonies of the Beatles to the angry white noise of Sonic Youth has been categorized as rock—and correctly so.

In all its forms, rock is defined by its energy, its driving beat, its simple melodies and catchy hooks, and, above all else, its attitude. From Brill Building pop to heavy metal, from punk to grunge, rock is about youth and rebellion. For all the music has changed and splintered over the years, this much has remained constant.

The Beginnings of Rock and Roll

The question of which was the very first rock and roll song is open to endless debate. Some claim the honor of first rock song goes to Fats Domino's "The Fat Man" (co-written with Dave Bartholomew), released way back in 1950. "The Fat Man" was a rewrite of an old blues tune called "Junker's Blues," with all the drug references removed. It wasn't a straight-ahead rocker; like most of Fats's tunes, "The Fat Man" had a rolling (but not rocking) boogie-woogie rhythm, and had more in common with his earlier blues numbers than it did with the later rock and roll movement. That said, it did sell a million copies.

Note

While its pedigree as the first-ever rock song is in doubt, "Rocket 88" can lay claim to at least one true first—it was the first recording to feature a fuzz guitar sound. This is thanks to Ike Turner, who dropped the guitar amp on the way to the studio. The result was a loosened speaker cone—and the rock guitar sound we've all grown to love.)

Other music historians claim that Jackie Brenston's (1930–1979) "Rocket 88" was the first rock song. Written by Ike Turner (1931–2007) and released in 1951, "Rocket 88" is the spiritual predecessor to hundreds of rock and roll car songs, extolling the praises of the writer's brand-new Oldsmobile Rocket 88. Like "The Fat Man," "Rocket 88" was an obvious and somewhat (although not completely) cleaned-up rewrite of an earlier R&B tune, Jimmy Liggins's "Cadillac Boogie," released in 1947. Also like "The Fat Man," "Rocket 88" has more of a rolling boogie-woogie feel than a true rock sound. When you listen to it, it has more in common with 1940s jump blues than it does with what we now call rock and roll.

To a more general audience, the title of first rock and roll tune would probably have to be "Rock Around the Clock," by Bill Haley (1925–1981) and the Comets, released in 1954. To experienced ears, however, this song is closer to a big band novelty tune than it is to a rock number, the title and the hoopla notwithstanding. Then there's the issue of Bill Haley himself, at the time a roly-poly 30-year-old with little in common with his teenaged listeners. For that matter, the song's co-writer, Max Freedman, had just celebrated his 63rd birthday when the tune was released; not really the typically rebellious rock and roll teenager.

Whichever of these tunes you pick for the first rock song, one thing is clear. The music we now call rock developed gradually after World War II, out of a convergence of a number of different styles, artists, and influences. Rock emerged from a musical stew that included traditional country, honky-tonk, electric blues, jump blues, and R&B. And, to no small degree, rock resulted from a collision between the black and white musical worlds.

> **Note**
>
> To demonstrate how slowly rock and roll infiltrated the general culture, just look at the top tunes of 1955—the year that "Rock Around the Clock" was the overall number-eight song. Joining Bill Haley on the charts that year was Mitch Miller's sing-along "The Yellow Rose of Texas" and Pat Boone's white-bread cover of Fats Domino's "Ain't That a Shame."

Enter the King

While radio formats and record releases were highly segregated in the 1950s, there was no controlling the free interchange of musical ideas once the music was available, on disc or over the air. The greatest 1950s rock stars brought together influences from both black and white musical styles.

That was certainly true of rock's first true superstar, Elvis Presley (1935–1977). Elvis was famously described by record producer Sam Phillips as a "white man who sounds black." And, indeed, Elvis' first commercial release, from 1954, paired an R&B hit ("That's Alright, Mama," originally recorded by Big Mama Thornton) with a country song ("Blue Moon of Kentucky," by Bill Monroe), both processed through Elvis's unique sensibility.

As the musician most responsible for popularizing rock and roll on an international level, Elvis was one of the most important figures in twentieth-century popular music. That was a big accomplishment for a country boy from Tupelo, Mississippi. Elvis got his first guitar at age nine, and his family moved to Memphis two years later. There Elvis started playing with other musicians, as well as singing gospel in his church choir. He grew up listening to a mix of "hillbilly" music on the radio and black blues music performed live in Memphis' many clubs.

Elvis made his first recording in 1953, at the age of 18, as a present for his mother. That recording was made at the now-famous studio of Memphis-based Sun Records, and it caught the ear of Sun's boss, Sam Phillips (1923–2003). Phillips, who was already in the business of recording artists such as Howlin' Wolf and B. B. King from Memphis's thriving blues scene, was on the lookout for a crossover artist to deliver black music to a white audience, and Elvis fit the bill.

Presley was the first performer to fuse country and blues music into the style known as rockabilly, and the first white vocalist to sing in a "black" style. He also was the first rock artist to inspire a mania among his fans, thanks to his sneering good looks and hip-swiveling style. His records sold millions of copies; he almost single-handedly established rock and roll as a viable musical form.

Elvis's most important early recordings include "Heartbreak Hotel" (1956), "Hound Dog" (1956), "Love Me Tender" (1956), "All Shook Up" (1957), and "Little Sister" (1961). After a stint in the Army and too much time spent acting in bad movies, Elvis had a late-1960s critical resurgence with the contemporary hits "Suspicious Minds" (1969), "In the Ghetto" (1969), "Kentucky Rain" (1970), and "Burning Love" (1972). He died in 1977 at the age of 42, of a drug overdose.

> **Note**
>
> Elvis's record label, Sun Records, became the home for that variant of the rock and roll style known as rockabilly. A more country-flavored music than mainstream rock, rockabilly was a major element of Presley's early style. Sun's rockabilly artists included Johnny Cash, guitarist/singer Carl Perkins (1932–1998), and piano-playing rocker Jerry Lee Lewis (b. 1935).

Black Artists in a White Man's World

Despite the segregation practiced by the music industry, many black artists were also successful in the early years of rock and roll. We mentioned Fats Domino (Antoine Dominique Domino, b. 1928) earlier; he combined a lazy, New Orleans backbeat with pop-flavored material on hits like "Ain't That a Shame" (1955) and "Blueberry Hill" (1956). Also from New Orleans was Little Richard (Richard Wayne Penniman, b. 1932), a manic performer who combined a gospel fervor with piano-pounding theatrics on his songs "Tutti Frutti" (1955), "Long Tall Sally" (1956), and "Good Golly Miss Molly" (1956).

Arguably the most influential black musician on the rock and roll style, however, was one Chuck Berry (Charles Edward Anderson Berry, b. 1926). Berry defined the instrumental voice of rock and roll, in particular its guitar sound and the straight-ahead $\frac{4}{4}$ rock beat. He was also a key shaper of the rock and roll song form, and a surprisingly intelligent lyricist; Berry was able to craft songs that addressed classic teenage topics from a teenaged perspective in the teenage vernacular. His key recordings include: "Maybellene" (1955), "Roll Over Beethoven" (1956), "Rock and Roll Music" (1957), "School Day" (1957), "Sweet Little Sixteen" (1958), "Johnny B. Goode" (1958), "Memphis, Tennessee" (1964), and "No Particular Place to Go" (1965).

Teen Pop

The first classic era of rock and roll is generally defined as lasting from about 1954 through 1959. At the turn of the decade, Elvis Presley was inducted into the Army, Texas rocker Buddy Holly (1936–1959) died in a tragic plane crash, Jerry Lee Lewis fell from grace when he married his 13-year-old cousin, and Chuck Berry was imprisoned for violating the Mann Act by transporting an underage woman across state lines for "illicit purposes." Rock's early giants were all missing in action.

The final blow for this first-generation rock, however, was the established music industry's ability to co-opt the surface appeal of the music by offering up stars who combined teenage good looks, snappy songs, and just enough rebelliousness to please the growing teen audience—without scaring away their parents. This type of faux rock was typified by singer Pat Boone (Charles Eugene Patrick Boone, b. 1934), who offered a string of heavily watered-down covers of R&B hits, going so far as to bowdlerize the lyrics. For example, in Boone's hands Fats Domino's "Ain't That a Shame" became the more grammatically correct—but far less satisfying—"Isn't That a Shame." It was a shame.

The most successful purveyor of the new teen pop was businessman/promoter/ TV host Dick Clark (b. 1929). Clark's enormously popular *American Bandstand* television program became a launching pad for numerous teen singers, including several native to the program's hometown of Philadelphia. It was surely coincidental that Clark had ties with several local record labels, who in turn released the recordings of his latest TV "discoveries." This led to the brief careers of a number of white-bread teen idols, such as Paul Anka (b. 1941), Frankie Avalon (b. 1939), and Bobby Vee (b. 1943).

Brill Building Pop

Just because the singers were white bread, however, didn't mean that the songs they sang were insipid. While some were, a greater number were professionally crafted pop songs that came from a veritable songwriting factory.

By the 1950s, Tin Pan Alley and the New York music business had moved uptown to that stretch of Broadway between Forty-Ninth and Fifty-Third streets. The hub of this activity was the Brill Building, located at 1619 Broadway, along with a neighboring building at 1650 Broadway. From the start, the Brill Building had a number of music publishers as tenants, including Famous Music, Mills Music, and Southern Music. By 1962 the building was home to more than 150 music publishing companies, and this concentration of companies made the Brill Building (and its across-the-street companion) a kind of "one stop shop" for aspiring musicians.

From the mid-1950s to the mid-1960s, Brill Building songwriters sent one song after another to the top of the pop charts. Brill Building songs fueled the careers of many a teen idol, and helped to create the Girl Group craze of the early 1960s. They were also influential in inspiring the compositions of John Lennon and Paul McCartney, as well as the sound and the songs of the Motown label.

And just who were these celebrated Brill Building songwriters? Here's a short list of the most successful songwriting teams that called the Brill Building their home:

◆ Doc Pomus (Jerome Solon Felder, 1925–1991) and Mort Shuman (1936–1991) were responsible for writing more than 500 songs between 1958 and 1965. Doc wrote the words, Mort wrote the music; together, these two white guys from Brooklyn created an early type of "blue-eyed soul" for the Drifters and the Coasters and other top black acts—as well as for Elvis and various teen idols. Their best-known songs include "A Teenager in Love" (1959), "Hushabye" (1959), "Save the Last Dance for Me" (1960), "This Magic Moment" (1960), "I Count the Tears" (1960), "Little Sister" (1961), "(Marie's the Name of) His Latest Flame" (1961), "Suspicion" (1962), "Can't Get Used to Losing You" (1963), and "Viva Las Vegas" (1964).

> **Note**
>
> Don't tell me pop music can't be heartfelt. Doc Pomus wrote the words to "Save the Last Dance for Me" at his wedding reception. Doc, a victim of polio and confined to crutches, had just married gorgeous blonde Broadway actress Wilma Burke, and spent the reception on the sidelines, watching his new wife dance with a bevy of eligible partners. That inspired the heart-wrenching lyrics that remind the subject of the song not to forget who's taking her home—and to "save the last dance for me." This reminds me of what Atlantic frontman Jerry Wexler once said about Doc: "If the music industry had a heart, it would be Doc Pomus."

- Neil Sedaka (b. 1939) and Howard Greenfield (1936–1986) wrote catchy tunes both for Sedaka as a solo performer and for Connie Francis and other pop singers of the day. Their songs include "Stupid Cupid" (1958), "Oh! Carol" (1959), "Stairway to Heaven" (1960), "Calendar Girl" (1961), "Happy Birthday, Sweet Sixteen" (1961), "Where the Boys Are" (1961), "Next Door to an Angel" (1962), and "Breaking Up Is Hard to Do" (1962). Sedaka enjoyed a brief comeback as a writer and performer after he broke with Greenfield in the early 1970s, with songs such as "Laughter in the Rain" (1974), "The Immigrant" (1974), and "Bad Blood" (1975), all written with lyricist Phil Cody.

- Gerry Goffin (b. 1939) and Carole King (b. 1942) were young, married songwriters who wrote for artists as diverse as the Drifters, the Shirelles, the Monkees, Aretha Franklin, Dusty Springfield, and Blood, Sweat & Tears. Goffin wrote the words and King the music; their best efforts melded keen observations on the human condition with sophisticated harmonies, creating a body of work that shaped the sound of early 1960s pop music. Their songs include "Will You Love Me Tomorrow?" (1960), "Take Good Care of My Baby" (1961), "Chains" (1962), "The Loco-Motion" (1962), "Hey Girl" (1963), "One Fine Day" (1963), "Up on the Roof" (1963), "I'm Into Something Good" (1964), "Oh No Not My Baby" (1964), "Pleasant Valley Sunday" (1967), and "(You Make Me Feel Like A) Natural Woman" (1967). After divorcing Goffin in 1968, King had unparalleled success as the progenitor of the 1970's singer/songwriter movement; her 1971 album, *Tapestry*, sold more than 20 million copies and won a Grammy for Record of the Year.

- Barry Mann (b. 1939) and Cynthia Weil (b. 1941), another married songwriting team, had dozens of hit songs to their names. Mann and Weil ably navigated the changing pop music trends of the 1960s; their compositions run the gamut from light pop to Girl Group classics to straight-ahead rock, with the common thread being Weil's socially-conscious lyrics. Their best-known song is also the most-played pop tune in the twentieth century; according to performing rights organization BMI, "You've Lost That Lovin' Feelin'," (co-written with Phil Spector in 1965), has been performed more than eight million times. Their other notable Brill-era songs include "Kicks" (1966), "On Broadway" (1963), "Only in America" (1963), "Walking in the Rain" (1964), "We Gotta Get Out of This Place" (1965), and "(You're My) Soul and Inspiration" (1966). At the dawn of the twenty-first century Mann and Weil are still married and still writing together, most notably the song "Somewhere Out There" (1986), the theme to the movie *An American Tail*.

◆ Ellie Greenwich (b. 1940) and Jeff Barry (b. 1939), yet another married songwriting team (now divorced), provided the fuel to the musical fire known as the Girl Group sound, and were also favored songwriters for Phil Spector's Wall of Sound productions. They wrote dozens of top-ten hits in the early 1960s, including "Be My Baby" (1963), "Da Doo Ron Ron" (1963), "Do Wah Diddy Diddy" (1963), "Baby I Love You" (1964), "Chapel of Love" (1964), and the classic rock and roll Christmas anthem, "Christmas (Baby Please Come Home)" (1963). After divorcing Greenwich in 1965, Barry went on to co-write songs for the cartoon group the Archies ("Sugar, Sugar," 1969, and "Jingle Jangle," 1970), as well as several well-known television show themes (*The Jeffersons*, *One Day at a Time*, and *Family Ties*).

◆ Burt Bacharach (b. 1928) and Hal David (b. 1921) were perhaps the least Brill-like of all the Brill Building artists. In reality, the duo's time at the Brill Building was only a brief part of their careers; they started writing well before the height of the Brill Building era, and quickly moved beyond typical Brill Building work for hire. Somewhat older than their Brill-era colleagues, Bacharach and David were arguably the most sophisticated and mature songwriting team of the 1960s; their songs (many performed by compatriot Dionne Warwick) incorporate complex harmonies, meters, and structure, along with unusually adult lyrics. Their string of classic hits include "Make It Easy on Yourself" (1962), "(They Long to Be) Close to You" (1963; a hit for the Carpenters in 1970), "I Just Don't Know What to Do With Myself" (1964), "Walk on By" (1964), "What the World Needs Now Is Love" (1965), "Alfie" (1966), "I Say a Little Prayer" (1967), "The Look of Love" (1967), "One Less Bell to Answer" (1967, a hit for the Fifth Dimension in 1970), "Do You Know the Way to San Jose" (1968), "This Guy's in Love with You" (1968), "I'll Never Fall in Love Again" (1969), and "Raindrops Keep Fallin' on My Head" (1969).

Note _____

In 1968, Bacharach and David teamed up for a Tony-nominated Broadway musical, *Promises, Promises*. Bacharach also composed the music for several films, including *What's New, Pussycat?* (1965), *Casino Royale* (1967), and *Butch Cassidy and the Sundance Kid* (1969).

The Girl Group Era

During the early 1960s, many of the Brill Building songwriters fed songs to a succession of female vocal groups—so-called *girl groups*. These were groups of teenage girls—both black and white—who sang songs about romantic love, problems in school, and other youthful topics. Many of these groups were formed spontaneously by the girls themselves, and then were discovered and promoted through an independent label owner or producer. Popular girl groups included the Shirelles, the Ronettes, the Crystals, and the Shangri-Las. While the singers themselves were often interchangeable, their material, from the best of the Brill Building songwriting teams, was always top-notch.

Phil Spector and the Wall of Sound

One of the leading teen-pop producers, for girl groups and others, was Phil Spector (b. 1939). He began his career as a member of the pop-harmony group the Teddy Bears, penning their sole hit, "To Know Him Is to Love Him." As a producer, Spector hoped to create what he called "teenaged symphonies." These were recordings that employed a large stable of professional Los Angeles studio musicians (known collectively as the "Wrecking Crew") to create a dense sonic style that became known as the Wall of Sound.

To create his Wall of Sound, Spector utilized multiple guitars, drums, strings, and vocalists, all packed together and playing live in a small, reverb-soaked recording studio. He used this production technique for recordings by many of the most popular girl groups of the time, including the Ronettes and the Crystals, and also by performers like the Righteous Brothers and Ike and Tina Turner.

Spector's finest work is perhaps his famous holiday album, 1963's *A Christmas Gift for You*, which features the Wrecking Crew and Spector's stable of vocalists—including Darlene Love and Ronnie Spector—at the top of their form. In fact, I count this as my personal favorite album of the rock era; it's a terrific, joyful piece of work from all concerned.

> **Note**
>
> One musician towers above all the others in this chapter in terms of number-one hits—and you've probably never heard of him. That musician is drummer Hal Blaine (Harold Simon Belsky, b. 1929), part of the Wrecking Crew of Los Angeles studio musicians in the 1960s and early 1970s. Hal played drums on more than 8,000 different tracks for hundreds of different artists. Hal's steady backbeat was the secret ingredient behind 40 number-one singles, 150 that made the top ten, and 6 consecutive Grammy Record of the Year winners: "A Taste of Honey" (Herb Albert & the Tijuana Brass, 1966), "Strangers in the Night" (Frank Sinatra, 1967), "Up, Up and Away" (Fifth Dimension, 1968), "Mrs. Robinson" (Simon & Garfunkel, 1969), "Aquarius/Let the Sunshine In" (Fifth Dimension, 1970), and "Bridge Over Troubled Water" (Simon & Garfunkel, 1971).

Surf Music and the Beach Boys

Another popular sound of the early 1960s was that of surf music—guitar-based rock songs about girls and cars and surfing and other California-based youth activities. The primary purveyors of the surf sound were the Beach Boys, led by composer/singer Brian Wilson (b. 1942). Wilson and his two brothers, Carl (1946–1998) and Dennis (1944–1983), along with cousin Mike Love (b. 1941) and friend Al Jardine (b. 1942), modeled their vocal harmonies on the Four Freshmen and other 1950s pop groups.

Wilson, an untrained but naturally brilliant composer and arranger, was a flawed genius who expanded rock's vocabulary to include complex harmonies, sophisticated chord progressions, and an overriding spirituality. While Wilson's early tunes were simple three-chord constructions extolling the joys of surfing and hot rods, his later compositions with lyricists Tony Asher and Van Dyke Parks explored more adult themes and were more musically complex.

Wilson's crowning achievement was the 1966 album *Pet Sounds*, considered among the greatest rock albums of all time. Wilson's innovative arrangements and production techniques (learned at the knee of Phil Spector), influenced and inspired John Lennon and Paul McCartney in their expanding body of work. His most memorable tunes from this period include "In My Room" (1963), "Surfer Girl" (1963), "Don't Worry Baby" (1964), "The Little Girl I Once Knew" (1965), "Caroline No" (1966), "God Only Knows" (1966), "Good Vibrations" (1966), "Heroes and Villains" (1966), and "Wouldn't It Be Nice" (1966).

Enter the Beatles

In spite of the genius of Phil Spector, the enthusiasm of the girl groups and surfer bands, and the skilled songwriting from the Brill Building teams, American popular music in the early 1960s was considered a bit tame. That all changed in 1964, when the British group the Beatles arrived on American shores. The Fab Four, as they were known, livened up the music scene with their perky blend of American country, R&B, and early rock and roll. It also didn't hurt that they were smart, funny, and terribly photogenic.

The Beatles had the good fortune to be fronted by two Brill Building–caliber songwriters, John Lennon (1940–1980) and Paul McCartney (b. 1942). These talented composer/performers were perhaps the most skilled, successful, and influential songwriters of the 1960s; they defined pop music for the second half of the century.

Lennon and McCartney's skill as songwriters and their ongoing performance of their own songs influenced generations of popular performers to eschew outside songwriting; this inadvertently led to the death of the professional songwriter, as exemplified by the Brill Building teams. To be "like the Beatles" meant to be both songwriters and performers, even if an artist had little or no formal musical training. In the case of Lennon and McCartney, their lack of musical training was overshadowed by their huge natural talent. Their compositions progressed over the course of the 1960s from simple melodic constructions to more harmonically complex experiments, all the while maintaining a keen sense of melody.

From the start, the Beatles had a unique sound, understanding that the recording of a song was at least as important as the composition itself in communicating with their audience. By the mid-1960s, the group began experimenting further in the studio, producing unique effects using backwards tape loops, double and triple tracking, experiments with vocal processing, and feedback. They also pioneered the "concept album" with 1967's *Sgt. Pepper's Lonely Hearts Club Band*; the creation of a "group within the group" was also a first, which would influence future artists to create musical alter egos.

Of course, the Beatles as a group were more than just Lennon and McCartney. Also integral to the group's chemistry were lead guitarist George Harrison (1942–2001), who himself became an able songwriter as he matured, and drummer Ringo Starr (Richard Starkey, b. 1940). Together, they created a sound that was unique from their first recording to their last.

The Beatles' body of work includes more than a hundred well-known songs, including "Can't Buy Me Love" (1964), "A Hard Day's Night" (1964), "If I Fell" (1964), "Help!" (1965), "In My Life" (1965), "Nowhere Man" (1965), "Norwegian Wood (This Bird Has Flown)" (1965), "Ticket to Ride" (1965), "Eleanor Rigby" (1966), "Here, There and Everywhere" (1966), "Yesterday" (1966), "All You Need is Love" (1967), "A Day in the Life" (1967), "The Fool on the Hill" (1967), "Hello Goodbye" (1967), "Penny Lane" (1967), "She's Leaving Home" (1967), "Strawberry Fields" (1967), "Hey Jude" (1968), "I Will" (1968), "Come Together" (1969), and "Let It Be" (1970).

Note

It may be difficult to grasp in this modern world where artists take three or four years to produce a single recording, but back in the 1960s the Beatles were expected to release two albums each year, along with two or more non-album singles. That type of forced productivity undoubtedly contributed to the group's—and the era's—unmatched creativity. Can you believe how much the Beatles accomplished—and how far they progressed—in a short, six-year recording career?

The British Invasion

With the success of the Beatles, suddenly all things British were the rage, and dozens of groups were marketed as "the next Beatles." While the Beatles quickly developed their sound in innovative ways, many of the British Invasion groups that enjoyed initial success—including Gerry and the Pacemakers, the Dave Clark Five, Herman's Hermits, and Peter and Gordon—quickly faded from the scene.

One group that did have lasting success was the Rolling Stones. In contrast to the teen-friendly Beatles, the Stones were cleverly marketed as the "bad boys" of rock and roll. Originally a blues band playing covers of American material, band members Mick Jagger (b. 1943) and Keith Richards (b. 1943) eventually started to write their own material. The Stones' more aggressive sound and lyrics, in songs such as "(I Can't Get No) Satisfaction" (1965), "Paint It Black" (1966), and "Let's Spend the Night Together" (1967) influenced other hard-rocking British bands, including the Animals, the Kinks, and the Who.

With a few exceptions, the British Invasion died out toward the end of the 1960s, and the Beatles themselves broke up in 1970. Post-Beatles, all four of the lads had continued success as solo songwriters and performers; McCartney and Starr continue to perform to this day. Tragically, John Lennon was killed by assassin Mark David Chapman in 1980; George Harrison died of cancer in 2001. Fortunately for all fans of popular music, their work lives on.

American Rock in the Late 1960s

The British Invasion immediately changed the pop music landscape in America. The earlier teen-pop stars like Frankie Avalon and Paul Anka were swept off the charts, replaced by self-contained rock combos. The idea of a group that played its own instruments, wrote its own material, and managed its own career was almost entirely new to the American pop scene, and very alluring to performers from various stylistic backgrounds.

In the mid-to-late 1960s, what was previously known as "rock and roll" matured into just "rock," which combined influences from many different musical styles—folk, country, jazz, pop, and the like. The world of rock music also splintered into many subgenres, each with its own distinct style.

One popular genre was so-called psychedelic rock, which came out of the San Francisco Bay area. This music was an attempt to capture the drug experience by performing music in a looser, more improvisational style.

The longest-lasting of the psychedelic bands was the Grateful Dead, which began its life as a communal group living together in a rented house in San Francisco's Haight-Ashbury neighborhood. The Dead combined elements of blues, jazz, bluegrass, avant-garde classical, and pop music into a musical stew that appealed to the burgeoning hippie culture—and inspired the jam band movement of the 1990s.

Another influential psychedelic artist was guitarist Jimi Hendrix (1942–1970). Perhaps the greatest live performer in this style, Hendrix created unique sounds on the electric guitar through different playing methods and creative use of amplification, distortion, feedback, and effects.

The 1960s came to a close with two major festivals, each emblematic of the era. The Woodstock festival, held August 15–18, 1969, in upstate New York, was the ultimate hippie dream—a three-day gathering of peace, love, and music. Dozens of rock artists gave memorable performances, from the folk-rock guitar of Richie Havens (b. 1941) and the ethereal harmonies of Crosby, Stills and Nash, to the electrified psychedelia of Jimi Hendrix and the boozy blues of Janis Joplin (1943–1970). It was a defining moment in the new culture.

The second festival represented the dark underbelly of the 1960s. The Altamont Speedway Free Festival on December 6, 1969, was the Satanic mirror image of Woodstock. Held at a desolate race track in Southern California, the festival's "security force" was the notorious Hell's Angels. When a scuffle broke out during a set by rock's bad boys, the Rolling Stones, one listener was savagely beaten to death by the Angels while a horrified crowd witnessed the event. It was a fitting end to a turbulent and often confusing decade.

Singing the Praises of Top-40 Radio

I grew up listening to the top-40 radio of the 1960s and early 1970s. It was a great time to listen to the radio; anything and everything could come out of that tinny little speaker, and I loved it all.

Today's youngsters have no conception of what a wide-ranging variety of music used to be available from your local radio station. Today's stations micro-cast to specific subgenres within subgenres; you never get a chance to hear anything outside a very narrow field of interest.

That wasn't the case in the 1960s. Back then, your local top-40 radio station played a little bit of everything. It wasn't unusual to hear a British invasion tune by the Beatles, followed by a surf tune by the Beach Boys, followed by a funky Motown number, followed by some sweet Brill Building pop, followed by a little bit of country (Roger Miller, anyone?), followed by some Frank Sinatra or Jack Jones. Yes, it was a bit of a hodge-podge, but it exposed you to *everything* that was happening at the time.

Because of this variety, it was possible for any song in any genre to gain widespread exposure. Today, most people don't know about most bands; back then, if an artist had a big hit, everybody knew it. There was no hiding from any of the great music of the day.

And that's why I mourn the loss of old-school top-40 radio. If a song is a good song, I want to hear it; I don't want my local station not to play it just because it doesn't fit the playlist format. But the golden days of top-40 radio are long gone, I'm afraid. If you want to hear a variety of new music today, you have to actively seek it out; it won't be delivered to you.

Rock in the 1970s, 1980s, and Beyond

Once the innocence of the 1960s was shattered, rock could no longer be a unifying force in the musical culture. As rock moved into the 1970s, the number of subgenres began to multiply; artists experimented with different combinations and permutations of available musical forms.

Among the various types of rock that gained some degree of popularity in the following decade were the following:

- **Country-rock,** blending traditional country and honky-tonk with a rock beat, as performed by the Byrds, the Band, Pure Prairie League, and the Eagles.

- **Singer/songwriter,** blending confessional folk with well-crafted pop melodies, as written and performed by Carole King (after her Brill Building career), James Taylor (b. 1948), Carly Simon (b. 1945), and Harry Chapin (1942–1981).

- **Glam rock,** a gender-bending, highly theatrical form of Rolling Stones–brand rock, influenced by the Velvet Underground and the Stooges and performed by Brits David Bowie (b. 1947), T. Rex, Roxy Music, and Queen.

- **Progressive rock,** also known as *art rock*, which blended the rock beat with classical music and literary-based subjects, as exemplified by King Crimson, Genesis, Pink Floyd, and Emerson, Lake and Palmer.

- **Disco,** which gave pop-rock a heavy dance beat in the mid-1970s, as performed by KC and the Sunshine Band, Chic, the Bee Gees, and the Village People.

- **Punk,** a glam-inspired reaction to the excesses of mid-1970s prog rock and disco that stripped the music down to its essentials, as performed by the New York Dolls, the Ramones, the Sex Pistols, and the Clash. (This style continued in the hardcore movement of the 1980s, led by the bands Black Flag and Minor Threat.)

- **New Wave,** a more melodic and commercial offshoot of punk music in the early 1980s, as played by the Talking Heads, Blondie, the Police, the Cars, and Elvis Costello (b. 1954).

- **Heavy metal,** which emphasized rock's raw, guitar-based power, as performed by Led Zeppelin, Black Sabbath, and Metallica.

- **Dance-pop,** which added a techno beat to its disco underpinnings, as performed by Michael Jackson, Janet Jackson, and Madonna (Madonna Louise Ciccone Ritchie, b. 1958), and a variety of manufactured dance "artists."

- **Hair metal,** or pop metal, a 1980s movement that combined heavy metal with glam rock, as performed by Def Leppard, Bon Jovi, Guns N' Roses, and Mötley Crüe.

- **Alternative rock,** a 1980s grab-bag of mostly underground, punk-inspired pop and rock, featuring bands like U2, R.E.M., Sonic Youth, the Red Hot Chili Peppers, and Jane's Addiction.

- **Grunge,** the popular early 1990s blend of punk, heavy metal, and alternative rock, performed primarily by Seattle-area groups like Nirvana, Pearl Jam, and Soundgarden, as well as Chicago's Smashing Pumpkins.

- **Teen-pop,** the late twentieth-century version of early 1960s teen idols, commercially constructed music performed by mostly manufactured girl and boy bands, such as the Spice Girls, Backstreet Boys, and N*SYNC, as well as solo performers like Britney Spears and Christina Aguilera.

Despite this fragmentation of form, there were always a few artists who continued to play straight-ahead rock music. The chief proponent of the basic rock form—and one of the best-selling artists of the late 1970s and 1980s—was Bruce Springsteen (b. 1949). Springsteen, known as "The Boss," was hailed by mid-1970s critics as "the savior of rock and roll." His music embodies all the best aspects of the rock genre, combining driving rhythms, majestic "wall of sound" production values, and thoughtful lyrics. His roots-oriented rock has enjoyed enormous popularity through three decades, with his concerts with the E Street Band approaching the fervor of religious revivals. Key albums include the classic *Born to Run* (1975), *Darkness on the Edge of Town* (1978), *The River* (1980), *Nebraska* (1982), *Born in the U.S.A.* (1984), *The Rising* (2002), and *Magic* (2007).

Getting Hip to Hip Hop

Now we come to the last major popular music movement of the twentieth century, that music that is variously known as rap or hip hop. This style of music is now over a quarter-century old, and has gone through many changes in its short history.

The Roots of Rap

Some critics mistakenly view rap music as an evolution of the R&B and soul styles. This could not be farther from the truth; other than the fact that both R&B and rap are performed primarily by black artists, the one has little to do with the other.

Note

Rap is the general term for the musical expression; it is a part of a broader movement, known as hip hop, that includes dance, graffiti art, fashion, and political expression. Nonetheless, the two terms are used somewhat interchangeably to refer to a variety of musical styles.

Rap did not evolve from soul music. In fact, rap isn't a native American form at all. The first generation of rappers came from Jamaica, where deejays would talk, often in rhyme, over reggae music being played on public sound systems or in record stores. This rapping found its way to the United States via the Jamaican immigrant population, coming first to urban neighborhoods in New York and Los Angeles. Mobile deejays outfitted trucks with powerful sound systems that they would set up in a local park or playground; they would spin their records, while improvising boasts over the music. Eventually, the role of rapper and deejay separated, with the rapper taking on the job of drawing the crowds, while the deejay focused on manipulating the turntables. Break-dancers would also congregate around the rappers and deejays to dance to the music, and often crews of rappers, dancers, deejays, and assorted other performers came together as semi-permanent performing troupes.

So, while the hip-hop beat is influenced by classic R&B and funk riffs, the concept and lyrics come indirectly from Jamaica.

The first commercially successful rap group was New York's Sugarhill Gang; their 1979 release "Rapper's Delight" is generally credited as the breakthrough rap recording. Other successful early rappers include Kurtis Blow ("The Breaks," 1981), Afrika Bambaataa ("Planet Rock," 1982), and Grandmaster Flash and the Furious Five ("The Message," 1982).

The Next Generation

Rap's second generation was represented by the group Run D.M.C., who began recording in 1983. The group featured two rappers, Run (Joseph Ward Simmons, b. 1964) and D.M.C. (Darryl McDaniels, b. 1964), along with dee-jay Jam Master Jay (Jason Mizell, 1965–2002). The group wed heavy-metal rhythms with a tough, urban sensibility, epitomized by their 1986 cover of Aerosmith's "Walk This Way," the first rap recording to cross over to popularity among traditional rock fans. Other popular second-generation rap artists include the Fat Boys and L. L. Cool J (James Todd Smith, b. 1968).

Gangsta Rap

The next innovation in rap came with the so-called *gangsta* style, originating in the cities of America's West Coast. Gangsta rap deals with pimping, hustling, and other facets of urban street life, often with violent and offensive lyrics. The 1986 single "6 'N the Mornin'" by Ice-T (Tracy Marrow, b. 1958) is considered among the first gangsta rap recordings, but it was N.W.A.'s 1988 album, *Straight Outta Compton*, that was the most influential and controversial work in the new style.

N.W.A.'s members included Dr. Dre (André Romell Young, b. 1965), Eazy-E (Eric Lynn Wright, 1963–1995), and Ice Cube (O'Shea Jackson, b. 1969), all of whom went on to have their own solo careers. Other gangsta rappers include 2Pac (Tupac Amaru Shakur, 1971–1996) and the Notorious B.I.G. (Christopher George Latore Wallace, 1972–1997).

The gangsta mentality continues in much of the hip-hop music of today. Artists such as Busta Rhymes (Trevor Tahiem Smith, b. 1972), 50 Cent (Curtis James Jackson III, b. 1975), Ja Rule (Jeffrey Atkins, b. 1976), and white rapper Eminem (Marshall Bruce Mathers III, b. 1972) all include violent imagery in their songs; some have had open feuds with other rappers and have even been arrested for various types of criminal behavior.

> **Note**
>
> A crucial link between Run D.M.C. and N.W.A. was the group Public Enemy. Their influential 1988 release, *It Takes a Nation of Millions to Hold Us Back,* featured rapper Chuck D's politically charged lyrics and is regarded as one of the top hip-hop albums of all time.

> **Note**
>
> While rap artists certainly exhibit a fair amount of male posturing, there are also a handful of female rappers who hold their own with the boys. These include Queen Latifah (Dana Elaine Owens, b. 1970), Lil' Kim (Kimberly Denise Jones, b. 1974), Missy "Misdemeanor" Elliott (b. 1971), Lauryn Hill (b. 1975), the mixed-media crossover artist MIA (Mathangi "Maya" Arulpragasam, b. 1977), and the 1980s female rap crew Salt-N-Pepa.

Hip Hop: The Future of Popular Music?

Like it or not, hip hop is here to stay—and is becoming more mainstream. While some bemoan its violent imagery or lack of melody, others accept it as the kind of rebellious music that rock has always been. Some alternative bands, such as Whole Wheat Bread, have combined rap elements with a more traditional rock or grunge style; some hip-hop artists, such as the Roots, are including samples of old school rock and soul melodies. The result is the kind of cross pollination that has informed American popular music from the 1900s to today.

Listening List

Here's a challenge for you—put together a short list of the must-have albums for all types of popular music since 1950. Well, I doubt if you'd call the following list short, but it does touch upon just about everything you should be listening to—from Woody Guthrie to Public Enemy.

20 of Hank Williams' Greatest Hits (Hank Williams Sr.)

30 #1 Hits (Elvis Presley)

30 Greatest Hits (Aretha Franklin)

A Christmas Gift for You (Phil Spector, various artists)

Abbey Road (The Beatles)

Back to Mono: 1958–1969 (Phil Spector, various artists)

The Best of Louis Jordan (Louis Jordan)

The Best of Ruth Brown (Ruth Brown)

Blonde on Blonde (Bob Dylan)

Blue (Joni Mitchell)

Born to Run (Bruce Springsteen)

Columbia Country Classics, Vol. 1: The Golden Age (Various artists)

Columbia Country Classics, Vol. 2: Honky Tonk Heroes (Various artists)

Columbia Country Classics, Vol. 3: Americana (Various artists)

Columbia Country Classics, Vol. 4: The Nashville Sound (Various artists)

Columbia Country Classic, Vol. 5: A New Tradition (Various artists)

The Definitive Collection (Chuck Berry)

The Drifters: All-Time Greatest Hits and More 1959–1965 (The Drifters)

Dusty in Memphis (Dusty Springfield)

The Essential Jimmie Rodgers (Jimmie Rodgers)

The Essential Johnny Cash (Johnny Cash)

The Freewheelin' Bob Dylan (Bob Dylan)

Gold: British Invasion (Various artists)

The Greatest Songs of Woody Guthrie (Woody Guthrie)

The Hip Hop Box (Various artists)

Hitsville USA: The Motown Singles Collection 1959–1971 (Various artists)

Hot Rocks 1964–1971 (The Rolling Stones)

It Takes a Nation of Millions to Hold Us Back (Public Enemy)

London Calling (The Clash)

One Kiss Can Lead to Another: Girl Group Sounds, Lost and Found (Various artists)

Pet Sounds (The Beach Boys)

Portrait of a Legend 1951–1964 (Sam Cooke)

Revolver (The Beatles)

Sgt. Pepper's Lonely Hearts Club Band (The Beatles)

Songs in the Key of Life (Stevie Wonder)

Stax 50th Anniversary Celebration (Various artists)

Thriller (Michael Jackson)

Ultimate Hits Collection (Ray Charles)

The Very Best of Burt Bacharach (Various artists)

The Very Best of Peter, Paul and Mary (Peter, Paul and Mary)

The Weavers Greatest Hits (The Weavers)

What's Going On (Marvin Gaye)

Woodstock: Music from the Original Soundtrack and More (Various artists)

Timeline: Post-1950 Popular Music

1950	The Weavers record "Goodnight Irene"; Fats Domino releases "The Fat Man"
1951	Jackie Brenston releases "Rocket 88"
1952	Dick Clark launches *American Bandstand*
1953	Ruth Brown releases "(Mama) He Treats Your Daughter Mean"
1954	Ray Charles releases "I Got a Woman"; Bill Haley records "Rock Around the Clock"; Elvis Presley releases "That's Alright, Mama"
1955	Little Richard releases "Tutti Frutti"; Chuck Berry releases "Maybellene"
1956	Johnny Cash records "I Walk the Line"; Sam Cooke releases "You Send Me"
1957	Chet Atkins develops the Nashville Sound
1958	The Kingston Trio records "Tom Dooley"
1959	The Drifters record "There Goes My Baby"; Berry Gordy founds Motown Records; Buddy Holly dies
1960	The Shirelles release "Will You Love Me Tomorrow?"
1962	Peter, Paul and Mary record "Puff the Magic Dragon"
1963	Bob Dylan releases *The Freewheelin' Bob Dylan*; Phil Spector releases *A Christmas Gift for You*
1964	Dionne Warwick records "Walk On By"; The Beatles arrive in America

1965	The Righteous Brothers release "You've Lost That Lovin' Feelin'"; the Rolling Stones release "Satisfaction"
1966	The Beatles release *Revolver;* The Beach Boys release *Pet Sounds*
1967	The Beatles release *Sgt. Pepper's Lonely Hearts Club Band;* Aretha Franklin releases "Respect"; Otis Redding killed in a plane crash
1969	Elvis Presley releases "Suspicious Minds" and "In the Ghetto"; Woodstock and Altamont music festivals
1970	Kris Kristofferson writes "Help Me Make It Through the Night"; Jimi Hendrix and Janis Joplin die
1971	Joni Mitchell releases *Blue;* Marvin Gaye releases *What's Going On*
1974	The New York Dolls launch the punk rock movement
1975	Bruce Springsteen releases *Born to Run*
1976	Stevie Wonder releases *Songs in the Key of Life*
1979	The Sugarhill Gang releases "Rapper's Delight"
1982	Michael Jackson releases *Thriller*
1986	Ice-T releases "6 'N the Mornin'"
1988	Public Enemy releases *It Takes a Nation of Millions to Hold Us Back*
1991	Nirvana releases *Nevermind*
1999	Britney Spears debuts with "... Baby One More Time"

Part 3

World Music

Western Europe and North America don't have a lock on important music. This part takes you on a quick tour of music history in the rest of the world— from Chinese opera and Indian *ragas* to Brazilian sambas and Jamaican reggae!

The Music of Asia and India

In This Chapter

◆ Discovering the music of China

◆ Learning about Korean music

◆ Discovering the roots of Japanese music

◆ Understanding the music of India

When early humans migrated out of Africa 50,000 or so years ago, they didn't just go north into Western Europe. Our prehistoric ancestors traveled everywhere their feet could take them, populating Asia and the Indian subcontinent, as well as the Americas and Australia (the landmasses were all connected back then). This means that the history of music is not limited to just Western Europe; there is music history in every region of the world.

In this first chapter in our section on world music, we examine the music of Asia and India. It's a rich history, and the music—while odd-sounding to Western ears—has its own undeniable beauty that reflects the rich cultures of these areas.

If you think Asian music is nothing more than the twanging strings you hear in Chinese restaurants, or that Indian music starts and ends with the sitar, there's a lot you have to learn about the music of this region. Read on to find out what you've been missing.

The Music of China

We'll start our musical history tour of the Far East with the largest and oldest country in the region. Chinese music has a style all its own—several different styles, actually, from traditional to folk to pop. And the history of Chinese music is as old and as interesting as the history of Western music, stretching back more than 3,000 years.

Understanding Chinese Tonality

Just as Western music is based on its 12-tone scale and system of notation, the music of China has its own unique system of tuning, pitch, and notation. It's that tuning system, or scale, that gives Chinese music its distinctive sound.

Most Chinese music uses a pentatonic scale—five notes that approximate the five similar pentatonic notes in the Western scale. The notes of this scale are called *gong, shang, jue, zhi,* and *yu;* in relation to the Western major scale, they represent the first, second, third, fifth, and sixth tones of the scale.

Interestingly, the Chinese scale does not employ even-tempered tuning, as the Western scale does. With even-tempered tuning, an A in one octave sounds the same as the A in another octave—just an octave higher or lower. In the Chinese scale, a note in one octave is not necessarily the same as the same-named note in a different octave. So, for example, a melody that starts on the *shang* of one octave might have a slightly different sound than one started on the *shang* of a higher or lower octave. The effect of changing the starting point of a melody is thus similar to shifting from a major to a minor key, sort of.

The History of Chinese Music

Music in China dates back to the dawn of Chinese civilization. Artifacts suggest a well-developed musical culture as early as the Zhou dynasty (1122–256 B.C.E.), which mirrors the musical development of ancient Egypt and Mesopotamia.

The oldest documented written music in China is a melody titled *Jieshi Diao Youlan,* or "Solitary Orchid." This is a piece of music for the *guqin,* a Chinese stringed instrument, written around the sixth century C.E. The Youlan manuscript appears to be a copy of an earlier piece of music, complete with corrections.

Note

Chinese mythology mentions Ling Lun as the first creator of music in China. Legend has it that in 2697 B.C.E., Emperor Huang-ti sent Ling to the mountains to create a flute that would emit the same call as the mythological phoenix. The result was a series of bamboo flutes that made the sounds of various birds.

The role of music in Chinese culture differed under different rulers. During the Qin dynasty (221–206 B.C.E.), music was denounced as a wasteful pastime; almost all musical books, instruments, and manuscripts were ordered destroyed. That changed during the Han dynasty (206 B.C.E.–220 C.E.), which formed the Imperial Music Bureau to supervise court and military music, as well as determine what folk music would be officially recognized by the state.

During the reign of Han Ming Di from 58 to 75 C.E., the Han palace had three official orchestras—one for religious ceremonies, one to play for royal archery contests, and a third for entertaining the royal banquets and harem. During the Tang dynasty (618–907 C.E.), emperor Taizong (599–649) had 10 different orchestras, as well as a huge outdoor band with nearly 1,400 performers.

Chinese opera first evolved in the period of the Three Kingdoms (220–280), in the form of *Canjun* opera—although the most organized form of Chinese opera appeared in the Tang dynasty (614–907), with the "Pear Garden" opera troupe.

During the Song dynasty (960–1279), and further into the Ming (1368–1644) and Qin (1644–1912) dynasties, a second form of opera called *nanxi* (southern drama) came to the forefront. These earlier styles led to development of *jingju*, or Beijing opera, during the nineteenth century; this happened at about the same time as the Romantic period in Western music.

During the rise of the Republic of China, starting in 1912, the New Culture Movement evoked a great interest in Western music. This led to a large number of Chinese musicians studying Western classical music, as well as the adoption of the Western system of music notation. Symphony orchestras were formed in most major cities, and American jazz and popular music were introduced to the culture.

With the revolution that established the People's Republic of China in 1949, the state denounced both Western and Chinese popular music, instead embracing traditional Chinese folk music and revolutionary music over Western. The subsequent Cultural Revolution promoted revolutionary songs almost to the exclusion of other genres.

Isolationism didn't last forever, however; after the Tiananmen Square protests of 1989, Western music again began to filter into the Chinese mainland. This led to the emergence of Chinese rock and pop music (dubbed *C-pop*), which remains popular to this day.

Traditional Chinese Music

China's musical heritage continues in the modern performance of traditional music—those musical forms that originated in the dynastic periods before the establishment of the Republic of China.

Traditional instrumental music in China is typically played on solo instruments or in small ensembles. Instruments include flutes, bamboo pipes, plucked and bowed stringed instruments, and various drums, gongs, and cymbals.

Traditional Chinese vocal music has a distinct sound, especially to Western ears. The vocals are typically solo, with little group choral work. Singing is traditionally in a thin, non-resonant voice, often in falsetto.

Chinese Opera

Probably the best-known type of traditional music is the Chinese opera. There are more than 350 distinct forms of Chinese opera, from the various dynastic periods to the present.

Of these, the best known is the Beijing opera, which emerged in the mid-nineteenth century. This type of opera features distinctive, high-pitched vocals, usually accompanied by string instruments and percussion. There are more than 1,000 extant works in the Beijing opera style, with texts typically taken from historical novels about political and military struggles.

A scene from a typical nineteenth-century Chinese opera.

Chinese Folk Music

The dominant ethnic group in China is the Han, and Han folk music remains popular to this day. It is often played at weddings and funerals, as well as other public events. This style of music is typically played on the *suona*, which is a type of oboe, or the *sheng*, a type of pipe; it is often accompanied by percussion instruments. The music itself is diverse, sometimes happy, sometimes sad, depending on the occasion.

Other types of folk music are common in other areas of the country. For example, in southern Fujian and Taiwan, the *nanyin* is a ballad sung by a female vocalist, accompanied by pipes and other traditional instruments; the music is sorrowful and full of mourning for lost loves. In Nanjin and Hangzhou, *sizhu* ensembles use flutes and string instruments to produce the type of melodious music that is recognizable to Western ears. And in Guangzhou, *guangdong* is a form of instrumental music based on Cantonese opera, together with jazz and other Western influences.

National Music

In addition to these traditional music forms, the Chinese communist government uses music to promote national pride. This government-promoted symphonic music is called *guoyue*, or "national music." Lighter forms of *guoyue* are termed "patriotic music," the equivalent of other countries' national anthems. "Revolutionary music" is a more political type of *guoyue*, often propagandistic in nature.

The Music of Korea

Western ears tend to lump all Asian music together into a single "oriental-sounding" bag. But not all Asian music is the same; different countries have developed significantly different musical traditions.

To that end, Korean music is distinct from that of Chinese music. Although they use similar instruments, Korean musical forms are original and in some ways more elaborate than Chinese musical forms. In fact, Korean music shows a bit of influence from Indian music, due to a medieval trading and religious relationship between the two countries.

History of Korean Music

The history of music on the Korean peninsula dates back to the Age of the Three Kingdoms of Korea (57 B.C.E.–676 C.E.). It was during this period that two of the most important native Korean instruments were developed, the *geomungo* and the *gayageum*, both zither-like stringed instruments. This era also saw an influx of musical culture from China, as part of a cultural exchange taking place at the time.

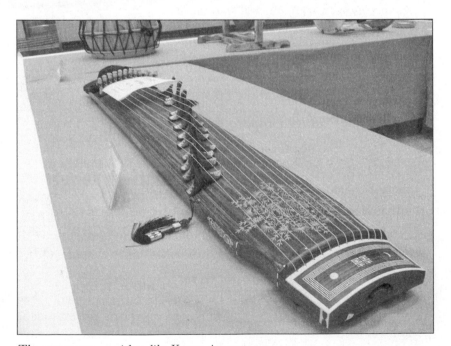

The gayageum, *a zither-like Korean instrument.*

During the Goryeo dynasty (918–1392), a ceremonial court music called *aak* emerged; this is an elegant music that evolved from imported Chinese ritual music. This period also saw the development of *hyangak* ("village music"), another court music typically accompanied by traditional folk dances.

This type of music remained important through the early and middle years of the Joseon dynasty (1392–1910). In the later years of this dynasty, folk music gained prominence as music disseminated downward to the lower levels of society. This period also saw the rise of *pansori*, a type of Korean opera performed by a single vocalist and accompanying drummer.

Traditional Korean Music

Traditional Korean music can be roughly divided into two major categories—*chong-ak*, or music for the ruling class, and *sog-ak*, or music for the common people.

Much *chong-ak* is court music, including ritual, banquet, and military music. Ritual music includes Confucian music and royal shrine music; banquet music is played during the different courses of courtly buffets; and military music is played for the nation's many military processions. Other types of *chong-ak* include *p'ungnyu*, a type of sophisticated ensemble music; *gagok*, a vocal music for mixed male and female voices; and *sijo*, indigenous Korean popular song.

The commoner's *sog-ak* includes shaman music, Buddhist music, and folk songs. Also popular is *nong-ak*, a type of farmer's music; *pansori*, a form of dramatic song; and *sanjo*, an instrumental solo music.

The Music of Japan

There are many styles of music native to the islands of Japan. Over the years, Japanese music has evolved into a unique blend of ancient and modern musical forms.

The History of Japanese Music

Japan's musical history is one of importation and assimilation. While native folk music existed, it was primarily designed to accompany Buddhist rituals. This native music remained somewhat primitive until the Nara period (710–794), when more complex court music arrived from China, Korea, and India. At the time, this music was played primarily by foreign musicians.

Chinese influence continued into the Heian period (794–1185), when Japanese musicians took over the performance chores. Although the musicians of this period still tended to play Chinese instruments, the music gradually developed Japanese characteristics.

The next era, the Kamakura period (1185–1336), was the era of the Shogun. During this period music lost most of its international characteristics; the emphasis was on Buddhist chants and dramatic music.

Dramatic and theatrical music continued to thrive during the Muromachi period (1336–1573), eventually giving form to *noh* opera. At about the same time, wandering priests began to play the *shakuhachi*, a bamboo flute.

Noh continued to flourish during the Azuchi-Momyama period (1568–1603), as well as the following Edo period (1603–1868). The Meiji period (1868–1912) saw an influx of Western culture to the previously closed country; brass bands and military music eventually drowned out traditional Japanese music, in the form of nationalistic songs and marches.

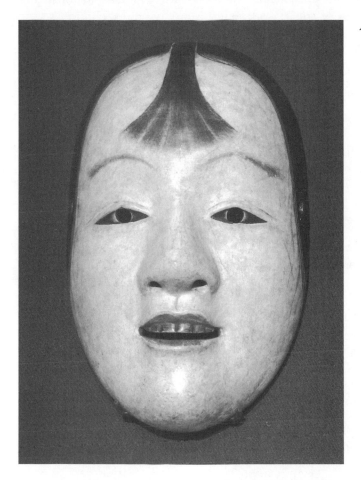

A Japanese noh *mask.*

During the ensuing years this sense of national pride led to a resurgence of traditional Japanese music. Modern culture eventually blended the traditional music with more modern forms, to create the various types of Japanese music that remain popular today.

Traditional Japanese Music

One of the oldest forms of traditional Japanese music is *shomyo*, a type of Buddhist chant that dates back to the eighth century. *Shomyo* became an important source of all forms of Japanese music that developed in later years.

Orchestral court music, or *gagaku*, has been performed for nobility and the upper classes since the Heian period. There are three types of *gagaku*. *Kokufu kabu*, or Japanese Song Dance, is a pure Japanese vocal music with instrumental accompaniment. *To-gaku* is a similar music, but of Chinese origin. And *Komagaku* is *gagaku* of Korean origin. Instruments used in *gagaku* include flutes, mouth organs, zithers, and drums.

Almost as old are Japanese folk songs, or *minyō*, in which singers are accompanied by the *shamisen* (lute), *shakuhachi* (bamboo flute), and *taiko* (drums). There are four primary types of *minyō*: work songs, religious songs, children's songs, and songs for gatherings such as weddings and funerals.

Japan's musical theater tradition originated in the fourteenth century with *noh*, a type of folk opera. *Noh* is a drama with music (*nohgaku*) and dancing (*shimai*). It's a highly stylized and symbolic drama, usually performed by a handful of male actors and musicians; the main character often wears a mask that fits the role. The vocal part (called *utai*) is derived from *shomyo* chants, and includes both singing and stylized speech; the singing is not always accompanied by instruments. When instruments are used, they typically include a *nohkan* (bamboo flute) and three types of drums.

Popular Music in Japan

Let's be honest; few people in Japan today listen to that country's traditional music—just as few Americans listen to Appalachian folk songs or Stephen Foster tunes. The music of modern-day Japan is the same type of popular music that we hear on American radio, but with a distinctly Japanese flavor.

Unlike many other countries where American pop music has totally or mostly supplanted local music, Japan has a thriving local musical culture. Although American music is heard in Japan and has informed local music trends, local music remains tops with local audiences.

From the 1960's Group Sounds trend, where Japanese bands tried to emulate British Invasion groups like the Beatles and the Rolling Stones, to the cute *aidoru* (idol) girl-pop singers of the 1970s and 1980s (including the popular duo Pink Lady) to the manufactured J-pop of the 1990s and today, Japanese pop music has had a unique local flavor. Japanese artists tend to be well-marketed; they often host their own TV shows, and appear in multiple media (anime, movies, radio shows, video games, and so on) to promote their latest releases. A lot of Japanese pop is marketed directly to high school girls, who emulate their clothing styles. Unlike ultra-sexual American pop princesses, these Japanese artists tend to be more cute than threatening.

Unfortunately, few of these Japanese artists have gained international success. Perhaps it's the language barrier, perhaps it's the cultural differences that make Hello Kitty such a phenomenon over there, but Japanese pop has yet to translate well in America and elsewhere. In fact, about the only places you're apt to hear Japanese pop music in America today are in imported Japanese cartoons (anime) and on video game soundtracks. That's a shame; some of the music is quite good, and worth searching out.

The Music of India

India has one of the world's oldest musical traditions; the country's classical music (*marga*) dates back to the Indus Valley civilization (3300–1700 B.C.E.). Scriptures from that era depict several different types of musical instruments, such as the seven-holed flute, and excavations from that period have found various types of stringed instruments and drums. In addition, the oldest of Hindu scriptures, the Vedas (c. 1000 B.C.E.), include a number of hymns. So this is music with a long history—at least as old as that of the Middle East.

The Sound of Indian Music

Classic Indian music is monophonic, based around a single melody line (*raga*) played over a fixed drone. Indian music uses a 12-note scale, like Western music, but it's a just tuning, not a tempered one, so it sounds a little "off" to Western ears.

Note

The most common *tala* is the *tintal*, which has a cycle of 16 beats divided into 4 bars. Bars 1, 2, and 4 are accented while bar 3 is light.

The rhythmic pattern of a composition is called the *tala* (literally, "clap"). The *tala* is similar to the meter or time signature in Western music, but structurally more sophisticated. In essence, the *tala* is a long and complex rhythmic pattern that is repeated over and over throughout the composition. This pattern is typically played by various percussion instruments, such as the *tabla*.

The other common Indian instrument is the *sitar*, a plucked string instrument with a hollow neck and a gourd resonating chamber. The *sitar* produces a very rich sound with complex harmonics.

An Indian sitar (left), and a set of Indian tablas (right).

Northern and Southern Music

Indian music flows from two regional traditions, the *Hindustani* music of the north and the *Carnatic* music of the south. Both styles use similar *raga* and *tala*.

Hindustani music took form in northern India during the thirteenth century. It developed from existing folk, religious, and theatrical practices. Unlike the southern music, *Hindustani* music was influenced both by Hindu musical traditions and by Persian performance practices.

The musical style found in the south of India is called *Carnatic*. This music can be traced back at least to the fifteenth century. It's a melodic music with improvised variations. Unlike the music of the north, the emphasis here is on vocal works, complete with lyrics; most *Carnatic* compositions are written to be sung.

Indian Folk Music

There are also various forms of folk music found in Indian culture. These include *Bhavageete*, a form of expressionist poetry set to light music; *Bhangra* and *Dandiya*, two forms of dance-oriented folk music; *Lavani*, folk songs sung by female singers; *Rajasthani*, a symphonic type of music played on string, wind, and percussion instruments; and *Qawwali*, a form of Sufi devotional music.

Indian Popular Music

Most Westerners know modern Indian music from the works of Ravi Shankar (b. 1920). A master sitar player and composer, Shankar came to the attention of Western audiences through his work with George Harrison of the Beatles. He was the opening act for Harrison's 1971 Concert for Bangladesh, and has played on numerous Western pop albums. He is also, not surprisingly, a superstar in his own country; in 1999 he was awarded the Bharat Ratna award, India's highest civilian honor.

The biggest form of Indian pop music today is *filmi*, or songs from Indian film musicals. These musicals are tremendously popular within India, bolstering the native "Bollywood" film industry. *Filmi* adds Western orchestration to traditional Indian classical melodies, for a crossover sound that appeals to listeners of all ages. Also popular are *Bhangra* and *Dandiya*, traditional folk songs turned into modern dance music.

Listening List

For this chapter's listening list, we have a sampling of classical Chinese, Korean, Japanese, and Indian recordings—as well as some more popular music from Ravi Shankar and a nice "best of" album of Bollywood film music.

The Best of Bollywood (Various artists)

Classical Chinese Folk Songs and Opera (Wei Li)

Eleven Centuries of Traditional Music of China (Various artists)

Note

One of the first instances of sitar in Western pop music was on the Beatles' 1965 recording of "Norwegian Wood (This Bird Has Flown)." George Harrison himself played the sitar on that recording.

Note

Ravi Shankar is the father of American pop vocalist Norah Jones (b. 1979).

The Essential Ravi Shankar (Ravi Shankar)

Gagaku: The Imperial Court Music of Japan (The Kyoto Imperial Court Music Orchestra)

An Introduction to the Chinese Opera, Vol. 1 (Shanghai Kun Opera Group; Sichuan Yibin Opera Company)

Japan: Traditional Vocal and Instrumental Music (Soloists of the Ensemble Nipponia)

Japanese Noh Music (The Kyoto Nohgaku Kai)

Korean Court Music (Various artists)

Korean Traditional Music (National Center for Korean Traditional Performing Arts)

Masters of Indian Classical Music (Various artists)

Traditional Music of India (Ali Akbar Khan)

Timeline: Asian and Indian Music

2500 B.C.E.	First Indian instruments
1000 B.C.E.	Indian hymns in the Vedas
550 B.C.E.	First written Chinese music
206 B.C.E.	Han dynasty forms Imperial Music Bureau
25 C.E.	Buddhism introduced to China
500	Korean *geomungo* and *gayageum* instruments developed
600	Height of Chinese court orchestras
700	Emergence of Japanese *shomyo* chant
750	Foreign court music imported into Japan
1000	Emergence of Japanese *gagaku* court music
1167	Genghis Khan born
1185	Japanese Shogun era begins
1200	Korean *aak* court music emerges
1250	Emergence of Indian *Hindustani* music
1274	Mongols under Kublai Khan attempt to invade Japan
1300	First Chinese opera
1350	Japanese *noh* opera emerges
1368	Beginning of Chinese Ming dynasty
1400	Emergence of Indian *Carnatic* music
1700	Chinese *xiwen* opera emerges
1750	Korean *pansori* opera emerges
1850	Emergence of Beijing opera
1862	Beginning of Japanese Meiji restoration
1868	Japan establishes new imperial government
1903	Mao Zedong born

1894	Beginning of Sino-Japanese War
1904	Beginning of Russo-Japanese War
1912	Republic of China established
1921	Chinese Communist Party formed
1937	Japan invades China
1941	Japan attacks Pearl Harbor
1945	Japan surrenders to America, ending WWII
1949	People's Republic of China established
1952	U.S. post-war occupation of Japan ends
1965	Beatles release "Norwegian Wood"
1971	Ravi Shankar headlines Concert for Bangladesh
1976	Pink Lady begins string of Japanese #1 hits
1989	Chinese Tiananmen Square riots

The Music of the Middle East

In This Chapter

◆ Understanding the sound of Middle Eastern music

◆ Examining the history of Middle Eastern music

◆ Learning about the music of each of the three major Middle Eastern regions—Arabia, Persia, and Turkey

As you recall from Chapter 1, the Middle East was home to some of the first documented music, including early instruments and the first written song. While the Middle East gave birth to the music that eventually evolved into what we know as Western music, it also has a rich musical tradition of its own. And say what you will, Middle Eastern music sounds a whole lot different from the Western music we listen to today.

What we call Middle Eastern music includes the music of three separate cultures: Arabic, Turkish, and Persian. This covers the region from Iran to Egypt to Northern Africa. While the music of all three regions is similar, differences can be found in the types of scales and microtones used in each region.

The Sound of Middle Eastern Music

While Middle Eastern and Western music evolved from the same roots, they took distinctly different directions. This is particularly noticeable in the tonal structure of the music, which is what makes Middle Eastern music sound so much different from traditional Western music.

Middle Eastern Tonality

What's different about Middle Eastern music is that it has more than 12 tones in a scale. Instead, Middle Eastern music is build on microtones—intervals smaller than the Western half tone or half step. A microtone can be exactly half the size of a Western half tone, in which case it's technically a quarter-tone. But

Middle Eastern microtones aren't always that neat and clean; microtones can be any interval smaller than a half step.

For example, Safi al-Din (1252–1333), a thirteenth-century music theorist and poet, introduced a system of tuning that divides the octave into 17 microtones. In this system, there are two different sizes of microtones, the larger *Limma* and the smaller *Comma*. Using the *Limma* (L) and *Comma* (C) intervals, Safi's scale looked something like this:

LLC LLCL;   LLC;   LLC LLCL

You might try to play this on your instrument of choice, but you'd have some difficulty doing so. That's because microtones are not easily reproducible on Western musical instruments. The piano, for instance, is built on a series of 88 half tones. A Middle Eastern microtone would fall somewhere in the cracks between the black and white keys on the piano keyboard.

It isn't easy to play microtones on a Western brass or woodwind instrument, either, as the tuning is built on the 12-tone scale. It's a little easier with string instruments, especially those without frets, like the violin; just slide your finger a little higher or lower than normal to play a microtone.

This is probably why the most common Middle Eastern instruments are string instruments, such as the Persian lute known as the *oud*. The *oud* doesn't have frets on the neck as a Western guitar does, enabling the player to play any combination of microtones on the instrument.

Middle Eastern Rhythm

It's not just the scales and tonality that are different in Middle Eastern music. Like Indian music, Middle Eastern music is more rhythmically complex than the common ¼ meter of Western music.

Middle Eastern music is based on a series of rhythmic modes, much like the Indian *tala*. These are complex patterns that are repeated over and over again in the course of a performance, typically on a drum or percussion instrument of some sort.

For example, our old pal Safi al-Din outlined eight of these rhythmic modes, as follows:

Oo. Oo. Ooo. O. Ooo.   (3+3+4+2+4)

Oo. Oo. O. Oo. Oo. O.   (3+3+2+3+3+2)

O. Ox O. Ox O. Ox O. Ox   (2+2+2+2+2+2+2+2)

Ooo. Ooo. O. O. O. O. O. O. Ooo.   (4+4+2+2+2+2+2+2+4)

O. O. O. O. O. O   (2+2+2+2+2+2)

O. Oo. O. Oo.   (2+3+2+3)

Ooo. Oo. Oo. O. (4+3+3+2)

O... O. O... O... O. O... (4+2+4+4+2+4)

In this system the uppercase O indicates the initial or accented beat; the lower-case o represents an unaccented note, optionally sounded; the x represents the final note, always sounded; and the period or dot indicates the final note, not sounded—kind of a silent separator.

For example, that first rhythmic mode would sound something like this:

BOOM bam <rest>   BOOM bam <rest>   BOOM bam bam <rest>
BOOM <rest>   BOOM bam bam <rest>

And repeat—over and over again.

These rhythmic modes are played over a traditional Western time signature, which creates some very sophisticated polyrhythms. The most widely used time signature in Middle Eastern music is 6/8, with 3/4 and 2/4 heard on occasion.

The History of Middle Eastern Music

While each region of the Middle East has its own distinct musical history, there are four general periods of musical development that encompass the entire area. These periods do not directly correspond to the Western musical eras (Baroque, Classical, Romantic, and so on).

As with Western music, little is known of Middle Eastern musical trends and styles before the advent of written language. This prehistoric period lasted until approximately 622 C.E.

The period from 622 to the 1300s is called the Development period. This period consists primarily of Arabic and Persian music, with Turkish music emerging toward the end of the period.

As with Western music of the time, the early Middle Eastern music was influenced by Greek musical forms. This was particularly true as to tonality, which means that the music of this period was more Western sounding than it is today. That said, the latter years of this period saw the establishment of microtonal systems and rhythmic modes.

The Conservation period lasted from the mid-1300s to about 1800, or about to the dawn of the Romantic period in the West. There was a lot happening during these years, geopolitically (the migration from Spain, the rise of the Ottoman Empire, and so on), which ironically led to a period of musical stagnation in the Middle East. In other words, the music that existed at the end of the 1300s pretty much remained as-is into the 1800s.

The Modern period dates from 1800 to today. During this era Western and other non-Arab influences led to a decline in traditional instruments and musical forms, and Middle Eastern music became somewhat Westernized.

Regional Music of the Middle East

While all Middle Eastern music shares a similar tonal and rhythmic tradition, there are important differences between each of the three major regions. We'll examine these regional music traditions next.

Arab Music

The music of the Arabian Peninsula is a mix of native music from local tribes and the music of all the other peoples of the Arabic world. It has also been influenced by the peoples with which the Arabs have traded and interacted—the ancient Greeks, Persians, Kurds, Turks, Indians, Somalis, and the like. There is even, in later Arabic music, a European influence. As I said, it's a mix.

The earliest Arabic music has its roots in Arabic poetry, dating back to the fifth century C.E. Jahiliyyah poets of that era were said to recite poems with a notable musical rhythm and intonation. True singing was entrusted to women with beautiful voices, who accompanied themselves on various stringed instruments. This type of singing continues to this day.

Note

Much Arabic music is characterized by virtuoso female singers who perform highly ornamented melodies. They use the technique of *melisma* to sing up, down, and all around the main pitch without changing syllables.

During the eleventh century, the Arabs invented the *Ghazal*, or love song, which remains popular in the music of the region. This was also when the *oud* was developed; it remained a popular instrument throughout the sixteenth century, when it fell into disuse until a revival in the 1800s.

After the sixteenth century, musical forms from other countries insinuated themselves into Arabic culture. It remained this way until 1922, when Egypt was granted its independence after 2,000 years of foreign rule. This led to a wave of nationalism, with foreign musical styles replaced by more traditional Arabic forms. During this period Cairo became a center for musical innovation; not only were traditional forms revived, but new Arabic popular music emerged. Note that even the modern popular music of the region retains much of the traditional flavor, in terms of scales, tonality, and rhythm.

Persian Music

What we call Persian music is the traditional music of Iran and other Persian-speaking countries. Music in this region can be traced back to the days of the Elamite Empire (2700–539 B.C.E.), with excavated statues and artwork depicting various types of ancient musical instruments, such as lutes, guitars, and flutes.

Note

Gusheh and *dastgah* are pitches only, without rhythm. These melodies and modes are applied to traditional rhythmic modes and cycles.

Classical Persian music is heavily improvised. Composition is based on a series of modal scales and tunes, much as with Arab and Turkish music. Musicians learn a repertoire of more than 200 series of musical phrases called *radif*, each of which are further divided into short melodies called *gusheh*, which are then divided into 12 modes called *dastgah*. Each *gusheh* and *dastgah* has a distinct name.

Persian classical music is vocal music. In fact, since the music is heavily improvised, the vocalist has great latitude as to what notes are sung and what mood is expressed. In some instances, the vocalist is responsible for choosing the *dastgahs* and *gushehs* to be performed. Vocalists are typically accompanied by at least one string or wind instrument, along with one or more percussionists.

Turkish Music

Of all the Middle Eastern regions, Turkey is closest in culture to Western European nations. As such, Turkish music has strong European influences, and in fact incorporates elements from Western Europe, Central Asia, Greece, the Arabic peninsula, Persia, and throughout the Ottoman Empire. In turn, this music has influenced those cultures' musics, as well.

Turkish classical music emerged as music played for the royal Ottoman courts. As was common in Europe during the Renaissance and Baroque eras, musicians were employed by wealthy families in a type of patronage system. This music is termed *saray*, or palace, music.

In rural areas, Turkish folk music held sway, often performed by wandering minstrels. Much of this music is religious in nature, often of the Islamic Sufi sect. The music itself is as tonally and rhythmically complex as Turkish classical music, with odd time signatures ($5/4$, $7/8$, and the like) relatively common. Like other Turkish music, this folk music exhibited influences from surrounding countries and cultures.

> **Note**
> The Ottoman royal courts also gave birth to *Mehter takimi*, an Ottoman military band. This is the oldest type of marching band in the world, the forerunner of modern Western brass bands.

The Music of Israel

Any discussion of the music of the region needs to include the music of Israel. While Israeli music doesn't have the same roots as other Middle Eastern music, its own tradition is long and fascinating.

Remember, of course, that the modern nation of Israel didn't exist prior to 1947. That means that all Israeli music is, by definition, immigrant music, derived from the many cultures from which the Jewish state was founded.

Much Israeli music is traditional Hebrew religious music. Other influences include Russian folk music, Eastern European klezmer music, and Arabic music—in other words, music from all the different areas from which the Israeli settlers came from. The result is a musical stew with its own particular musical characteristics.

What does the Israeli music of today sound like? There is frequent use of minor keys, which belies the Russian and Eastern European influences. Dance rhythms, such as the *hora* and *debka*, come from Turkey and other areas of the Middle East. Middle Eastern instruments, such as the tambourine and *darbuka* (a type of hand drum), are also common. But the lyrical content is distinctly national, focusing on ancient Jewish texts and the more modern Israeli experience.

Israeli music continues to evolve, much as the nation of Israel itself continues to establish its national identity. Like the nation of Israel, Israeli music attempts to meld its unique national identity with its place in the Middle Eastern region; the result is a music as unique as the country.

Listening List

We have a short but sweet listening list this chapter, with a few choice recordings of each regional style—as well as a little Israeli music thrown in, for good measure. Listen and enjoy!

Arabic Groove (Various artists)

Authentic Israeli Folk Songs and Dances (Various artists)

Faryad (Masters of Persian Music)

Iran: Persian Classical Music (Various artists)

The Rough Guide to the Music of Israel (Various artists)

The Rough Guide to the Music of Turkey (Various artists)

Traditional Arabic Music (Arabesque)

Turath: Masterworks of the Middle East (Simon Shaheen)

Turkish Sufi Music (Ali Ekber Cicek)

Timeline: Middle Eastern Music

1000 B.C.E.	Ancient musical instruments of the Persian Elamite Empire
800 B.C.E.	Five- and seven-tone scales appear in Babylonia
8 B.C.E.	Jesus of Nazareth born
400 C.E.	Jahili poets create earliest Arabic music
476	Fall of the Roman Empire
622	Beginning of Development period
1000	Development of the *Ghazal* Arabic love song
1050	Invention of the *oud*
1099	Crusaders capture Jerusalem
1299	Beginning of the Ottoman Empire
1300	Safi al Din introduces 17-note tonal system
1350	Beginning of Conservation period
1800	Beginning of Modern period
1922	Egyptian independence; end of the Ottoman Empire
1935	Modern-day country of Iran established
1947	State of Israel established

Chapter 15

The Music of Africa

In This Chapter

◆ Discovering the sound of African music

◆ Learning about African musical instruments

◆ Understanding the role of music in African society

◆ Uncovering Africa's regional music

◆ Discovering African popular music

All of mankind sprang from those early humans of the African continent. Some went north, to the Middle East and then on to Western Europe; others went east, to Asia and India. But the home of humanity—and the home of humanity's music—is in Africa.

That's not to say that Africa, in either culture or music, is homogeneous. Far from it. In fact, the music of Africa is as varied as the continent's many nations, regions, and ethnic groups. But while there is no single pan-African music, there are characteristics that are shared in the musics of different regions.

The Sound of African Music

What does African music sound like? Well, like the music of Asia, India, and the Middle East, it's a highly rhythmic music. In fact, the only music in the world that isn't rhythmically complex is Western music; the reason for this is subject to much debate. Personally, I blame the monks and the Mass—both of which took the rhythm out of the music to focus on the modes. But that's just conjecture.

The reality is, all the other music in the world evolved from the highly rhythmic music of the African continent. It is this rhythmic aspect that unites the music of various groups and regions.

African music is comprised of complex rhythmic patterns, often involving one rhythm played against another to create a *polyrhythm*. The most common polyrhythm plays three beats on top of two, like a triplet played against straight notes, as shown in the following example.

A three-against-two polyrhythm,
common in African music.

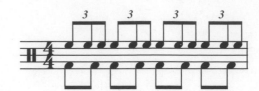

To hear how this sounds, start by beating the bottom line of eighth notes with your right hand on your right knee. Then superimpose the top line of triplets by beating your left hand on your left knee. It feels awkward at first, especially to us Westerners, but once you get the hang of it, it's kind of cool. Just imagine; this kind of rhythm comes as naturally as breathing to the natives of Africa. Little kids in Africa can play these rhythms that take Westerners years to master.

Beyond the rhythmic nature of the music, African music differs from Western music in that the various parts of the music do not necessarily combine in a harmonious fashion. African musicians, unlike Western musicians, do not seek to combine different sounds in a way that is pleasing to the ear. Instead, their aim is to express life, in all its aspects, through the medium of sound. Each instrument or part may represent a particular aspect of life, or a different character; the through-line of each instrument/part matters more than how the different instruments and parts fit together.

Understanding African music gets even more difficult when you consider that it does not have a written tradition; there is little or no written music to study or analyze. This makes it almost impossible to notate the music—especially the melodies and harmonies—using the Western staff. There are subtle differences in pitch and intonation that do not easily translate to Western notation.

That said, African music most closely adheres to Western tetratonic (three-note), pentatonic (five-note), hexatonic (six-note), and heptatonic (seven-note) scales. Harmonization of the melody is accomplished by singing in parallel thirds, fourths, or fifths.

Another distinguishing form of African music is its call-and-response nature: one voice or instrument plays a short melodic phrase, and that phrase is echoed by another voice or instrument. The call-and-response nature extends to the rhythm, where one drum will play a rhythmic pattern, echoed by another drum playing the same pattern.

African music is also highly improvised. (This speaks to the lack of a written tradition.) A core rhythmic pattern is typically played, with drummers then improvising new patterns over the static original pattern.

> **Note**
>
> What we call African music refers to music of sub-Saharan Africa. Music north of the Sahara is Middle Eastern music.

> **Note**
>
> Polyphony is also common in African music, especially among the southern African cultures. For example, traditional Zulu choral music has different voices entering at different points in a continuous cycle, overlapping in a complex pattern.

Musical Instruments of Africa

The rhythmic nature of African music explains the large number and types of drums and percussion instruments used. While a drum is a drum is a drum, to some extent, the flora and culture of each region influences the construction of instruments in that region. For example, wooden drums are more popular in the forest regions of West Africa than in the treeless savanna areas of Southern Africa.

Percussion instruments used throughout Africa include all-wood drums, drums with calf heads, rattles, clappers, cymbals, slit gongs, and bells. Melodic instruments include harps, fiddles, musical bows, flutes and trumpets, and xylophones and similar tuned mallet instruments. Wind instruments are often made out of animal tusks and horns, conch shells, gourds, or just plain wood.

Note

It is said that a complete talking drum language exists with which messages can be transmitted.

Particularly interesting are the talking drums of West Africa. These drums are made to "talk" by varying the pitch of the drum; the drum is held under the arm, with pressure on the cords adjusting the pitch. The drum head is struck with a curved stick.

An African talking drum.

Also popular is the *djembe* (pronounced "jen-bay"). Unlike the talking drum, the *djembe* is played with bare hands. The pitch is fixed, which makes the *djembe* similar to the Caribbean conga drum—but with a deeper bass note.

The fixed-pitch djembe *drum.*

Note _____

That's not to say that all African music is played by amateurs. Professional musicians have been present in African society from at least the tenth century. Kings and ruling families have long employed court musicians, and "talking drummers" have been used to transmit important messages.

The Role of Music in African Society

Music is more important to African society than it is to Western society. In the West, music is a luxury or entertainment; in Africa, it is an integral part of everyday life.

Africans embrace music into their lives at an early age, often making their own musical instruments by the age of three or four. Children play musical games, and are capable of dancing to and playing very complex rhythms. (In the West, in contrast, almost all traditional and popular music is based on equally divisible four beats per measure—often grouped in four-measure phrases. How boring.)

Music has ceremonial, ritual, and social functions in the African culture. Important stages of a person's life are often marked by and celebrated with music. There are lullabies for babies; game songs for children; and music for adolescent initiation rites, weddings, funerals, and the like. And, not surprisingly, this ritualistic music is often accompanied by equally ritualistic dance.

African Popular Music

The African popular music of today blends traditional African rhythms with Western rock and pop influences. The result is a lively world music that both influences and has been influenced by the music of the West.

Just as there are many different types of Western pop music, there are also many different types of African popular music. For example, so-called *highlife* music originated in Ghana during the late nineteenth century, then spread to Sierra Leone and Nigeria during the 1920s. Highlife can be played by ballroom-style dance bands or rock-type electric guitar bands; it is an up-tempo music characterized by jazzy horns and multiple guitars.

Afrobeat combines highlife, jazz, funk, and native *Yoruba* music from Nigeria, fused with African percussion and vocal styles. It was popularized in the 1970s by bandleader Fela Kuti (1938–1997) and drummer Tony Allen (b. 1940). Afrobeat is an up-tempo, highly energetic music, complete with complex polyrhythms and copious amounts of improvisation.

During the 1960s, *Yoruba* also inspired a variant of highlife called *juju*. This type of music features the talking drum, along with shimmering steel guitar melodies.

Another popular type of African popular music today is *soukous*, a style of Congolese guitar band music. *Soukous* developed in the towns of central Africa and features a blend of Afro-Cuban rhythms with bell-like electric guitar parts.

Some of the best-known types of African popular music come from South Africa. The first South African genre to attract international attention was *kwela*, or "pennywhistle jive" music, which was popularized in the 1950s. *Mbaganga* is a popular form of dance music that uses a combo composed of lead singer and chorus, saxophone, accordion, organ, electric guitar, bass, and drums. The Zulu *isacathamiya* male choral style came to America in 1951, via the recording "Wimoweh" by the Weavers; this style was resurrected in the 1980s by the South African group Ladysmith Black Mambazo. And South African jazz gained prominence in the 1960s, thanks to trumpeter Hugh Masekela's (b. 1939) 1968 hit "Grazin' in the Grass" and his wife Miriam "Mama Afrika" Makeba's (b. 1932) 1967 song, "Pata Pata."

African Music in the Americas

African music has been a dominant influence on the music of North, Central, and South America—as well as Cuba and other Caribbean cultures. The influence on North American music has been mainly tonal, shaping the development of the blues scale and call-and-response singing; the influence on other cultures has been strongly rhythmic.

In all cases, African music migrated to the New World via the slave trade that existed from the 1600s through the mid-1800s. While slave owners tried to eliminate the slave's native musical culture, enough survived to influence the popular music of today.

Think of it. Native African music informed the slaves' work songs and spirituals, which in turn informed the blues, which in turn inspired everything from jazz to soul to rock and roll. Whenever you listen to the Rolling Stones or Motown or Miles Davis, you're hearing echoes of music born on the African continent.

In some instances, the influence has been more direct. Witness the rise of African jazz of the 1960s, as well as the world-beat music of the 1980s, popularized by musicians such as Peter Gabriel and Paul Simon. Simon's 1986 album *Graceland* was particularly effective in exposing Western audiences to African music and musicians.

Today, audiences in America and beyond are discovering African music— particularly African popular music—as part of the world music trend. That's a good thing; it's about time we got in touch with the music that has so informed our own popular culture.

Listening List

This chapter's listening list includes a sampling of traditional music from across Africa's various regions, as well as some of the more important forms of today's African popular music.

African Jazz n Jive (Various artists)

African Tribal Music and Dances (Various artists)

African Voices (Various artists)

Afrobeat (Various artists)

The Best of Ladysmith Black Mambazo (Ladysmith Black Mambazo)

Graceland (Paul Simon)

Grazing in the Grass: The Best of Hugh Masekela (Hugh Masekela)

Putomayo Presents: African Groove (Various artists)

The Rough Guide to Congolese Soukous (Various artists)

The Rough Guide to Highlife (Various artists)

The Rough Guide to the Music of Nigeria and Ghana (Various artists)

The Rough Guide to South African Jazz (Various artists)

Timeline: African Music

750	Islam sweeps into North Africa
1562	England begins African slave trade
1652	Dutch establish colony at Cape of Good Hope, later to become country of South Africa
1832	England abolishes slavery
1863	The Emancipation Proclamation frees American slaves
1879	Zulu war with Great Britain
1880	Highlife music develops
1890	Virginia Jubilee Singers minstrel troupe visits South Africa
1925	Highlife music spreads to Sierra Leone and Nigeria
1939	*Isacathamiya* vocal style develops
1951	The Weavers release *Isacathamiya*-influenced single, "Wimoweh"
1952	Mau Mau uprising in Kenya
1955	*Kwela* music becomes popular in South Africa
1968	*Juju* music develops
1970	Birth of Afrobeat
1967	Miriam Makeba releases "Pata Pata"
1968	Hugh Masekela releases "Grazin' in the Grass"
1986	Paul Simon records *Graceland* with African musicians

Chapter 16

The Music of Latin America and the Caribbean

In This Chapter

◆ Understanding the music of the Caribbean islands

◆ Learning various Caribbean musical styles, including *reggae*, *calypso*, and *rumba*

◆ Understanding Latin American music

◆ Learning various Latin musical styles, including *samba*, *bossa nova*, and *Tejano*

Our tour of world music ends just a little south of the United States border. While you might think that the music of Latin America and the Caribbean would have more in common with North American music than anywhere else, you'd be wrong; the music of this region is a mix of native styles and styles that crossed over from Africa. This blend makes Latin and Caribbean music some of the most interesting music anywhere in the world—more rhythmic than other Western music, with a great deal of variety from country to country.

The Sounds of the Caribbean

The music of the Caribbean is really the music of individual islands. Each island in the area has its own native flavor and history, with the entire region informed by European and (primarily) African influences.

The regional differences reflect the native cultures of each island. The commonalities reflect the Caribbean's common history of European colonization and African slave trade.

The History of Caribbean Music

The history of Caribbean music is tied up in the history of the Caribbean itself. That history is one of a native land invaded by outsiders; violence, slavery, and even genocide factor in. It's surprising that the music itself is so gentle, with this type of formative background.

Blame it all on Christopher Columbus, the first European to land in this region in 1492. Based on Columbus's voyage, Spain claimed the entire region as its own. That didn't sit well with either the natives or Spain's European neighbors; within a few years, bloody battles raged across the islands of the Caribbean, fought by Spain, France, England, Denmark, and the Netherlands. All this fighting (and the diseases brought from Europe) decimated the native tribes, with entire cultures wiped out.

Thus the Caribbean was colonized as part of the various European empires. The native culture was further eroded when the Europeans imported African slaves to work the sugar and coffee plantations on their island colonies. In many cases, the native cultures—and the native musics—were replaced with those brought over from Africa.

At this point, whatever common Caribbean culture existed was splintered. Each of the European powers carved out their own cultures on their respective islands. Even with the ending of the colonial period, this is the Caribbean we have today—a series of subtly different cultures from island to island.

This island-specific culture also informs the music of the Caribbean. Every island has its distinct musical styles, all inspired, to one degree or another, by the music brought over from the African slaves. As such, most Caribbean music, however unique to its own island culture, includes elements of African music—heavy use of percussion instruments, complex rhythmic patterns, and call and response vocals.

That said, it's important to recognize the musical styles unique to each island. In many cases, the difference between one style and another comes down to the rhythms utilized in each music; there is almost a different rhythm for every island. Let's look at some of the most popular styles.

Calypso

Calypso is the music of the island of Trinidad. It's a sweet and joyful music, generally sung to a guitar and maracas accompaniment, often with steel drums providing harmony.

Calypso music dates back to the arrival of the first African slaves brought over to work Trinidad's many sugar plantations. Calypso evolved from the work songs sung by the slaves in the sugar fields.

The first calypso recording was made in 1914. The music continued to gain popularity, especially during the island's Carnival season. Calypso began to be noticed by the outside world in 1944, when the American Andrews Sisters did a cover version of Lord Invader's native hit "Rum and Coca Cola."

Further notice came in 1956, when Harry Belafonte (b. 1927) recorded his album *Calypso*, which featured the hit "Banana Boat Song ('Day-O')." This album was the first to sell over a million copies, and brought calypso to the attention of mainstream American audiences.

Popular native calypso artists include Lord Invader (Rupert Grant, 1915–1962), Lord Kitchener (Aldwin Roberts, 1922–2000), and Mighty Sparrow (Slinger Francisco, b. 1935).

Soca

Soca is kind of an offspring of calypso music. Also born on the islands of Trinidad and Tobago, soca has a more up-tempo beat that sounds kind of like a fusion of American soul music with traditional calypso.

The father of soca was Lord Shorty (Garfield Blackman, 1941–2000). He started out as a calypso singer, but in the early 1970s he started experimenting with Indian rhythm instruments in a calypso setting. The result was the new soca music, in the form of the hit 1973 song "Indrani." The album that followed, *Endless Vibrations*, attracted other musicians to the soca style.

Note

In the early 1980s, Lord Shorty abandoned the soca style, converted to Rastafarianism, and changed his name to Ras Shorty I.

Rapso

Trinidad and Tobago are host to yet another interesting musical style called *rapso*. This is a unique form of street poetry that originated in the 1970s, emerging from that era's Black Power Movement.

The father of rapso is Lancelot Layne (d. 1990). His 1970 hit "Blow Away" established the style, which has since evolved to include heavy dance rhythms that accompany the politically charged lyrics. Other popular rapso artists include Cheryl Byron (d. 2003) and Brother Resistance (Lutalo Massimba, 1956).

Ska

Let's travel from Trinidad over to Jamaica, which has its own rich musical tradition. One of the earliest forms of Jamaican popular music was *ska*, which originated in the 1950s. It's similar to calypso in feel, but has a snappy and insistent accent on the "and" of every beat in a measure, for a very jumpy, upbeat feel.

The first ska recording was "Easy Snapping" by Theophilus Beckford (1935–2001) in 1959. In 1964, Millie Small (b. 1946) had an international hit with the ska-flavored tune, "My Boy Lollipop." Other popular ska artists include Prince Buster (Cecil Bustamente Campbell, b. 1938), Laurel Aitken (1927–2005), and Don Drummond (1932–1969) and the Skatalites. Many well-known reggae artists, including Bob Marley and Jimmy Cliff, started out playing ska.

Rocksteady

Slow down ska to a mid-tempo and you get the Jamaican music called *rocksteady*, which evolved in the mid-1960s. With rocksteady's slower beat, musicians could experiment with more complicated melodies and a bit of soul and gospel influence. Popular rocksteady artists include Prince Buster, Anton Ellis (b. 1949), Desmond Dekker (1941–2006) and the Aces, and the Tennors.

Reggae

Note

Reggae is often associated with the Rastafarians, a religious movement that accepts Haillie Selassie, former emperor of Ethiopia, as God incarnate. Rastafarians often wear their hair in dreadlocks and view smoking marijuana (*ganja*) as a spiritual act.

Rocksteady was a transitory music between ska and reggae, which came on the scene around 1968. Jamaica's most popular musical style, reggae is typically played at a slow tempo with heavy accents on the off-beats—beats two and four in a measure. Reggae song lyrics often deal with poverty, injustice, politics, and other social issues.

The first international reggae hit was 1969's "The Israelites," by Desmond Dekker and the Aces. The one person responsible for establishing reggae as an essential musical form, however, was Bob Marley (1945–1981). Marley was a singer, guitarist, and songwriter; his group the Wailers helped to popularize reggae internationally, starting with their 1972 album *Catch a Fire*. Other popular reggae artists include Toots and the Maytals, Peter Tosh (1944–1987), and Jimmy Cliff (b. 1948).

Dub

Note

That's right—Jamaican dub music was the forerunner of American rap.

Over the years, reggae has given birth to several newer, Jamaica-based musical styles. One such style is known as *dub*—a form of remixing an instrumental version of a song with added electronic special effects, such as echo and reverberation. Deejays then talk or sing over the instrumental track. Dub was pioneered in the late 1960s by King Tubby (Osbourne Ruccock, 1941–1986), along with Daddy U-Roy (Ewart Beckford, b. 1942).

Dancehall

In the 1980s, a new form of reggae called *dancehall* exploded on the Jamaican scene. Dancehall is distinguished by sexually explicit and violent lyrics; later dancehall artists have been as criminally complicit as their American hip-hop cousins. These artists include King Yellowman (Winston Foster, b. 1959), Shabba Ranks (Rexton Rawlston Fernando Gordon, b. 1966), and the band T.O.K.

Reggaeton

The latest offshoot of reggae is reggaeton. Not strictly a Jamaican music, it originated in Panama in the early 1990s, and is now popular across Latin America and the Caribbean. Reggaeton is an urban dance music that blends reggae and dancehall with hip hop and various Latin American genres; the music is typically combined with rapping in Spanish.

Salsa

A more traditional Caribbean music is *salsa*. While it's now kind of a pan-Latin style, it originated on the island of Cuba, specifically from Cuban immigrants in the New York City area. Salsa came to the fore in the 1960s and is now entrenched throughout Latin America and the Caribbean.

Salsa is a hybrid of Cuban, Puerto Rican, and other Latin styles mixed with American jazz, pop, and R&B influences. It's a dance-oriented genre, closely associated with the style of salsa dancing, backed with plenty of Latin percussion instruments—claves, cowbells, timbales, and congas, especially. These percussion instruments play a common rhythm called the *clave*, which incorporates a 3-2 beat over a two-measure phrase, as shown in this example.

Salsa music's clave *rhythm.*

Mambo

Another famous Cuban music is the *mambo*. Like salsa, mambo is both a music and a dance style. Mambo dates back to 1938, when a song called "Mambo" was written by brothers Orestes (1908–1991) and Cachao López (Israel López, b. 1918). This song used syncopated rhythms derived from African folk music, and inspired the mambo dance that emerged in the late 1940s in Havana.

The style was later adopted both by native musicians and by jazz artists in the United States, fueling the 1950s Latin jazz trend exemplified by the music of Tito Puente, Dizzy Gillespie, and others.

Rumba

Cuba is also home to the *rumba*, another African-inspired musical style. As with other forms of Cuban music, the rumba is both a musical and a dance style.

Rumba developed in the late nineteenth century as a sexually charged dance. It was introduced to the United States during World War I, and was later popularized by various Latin dance bands. It's characterized by heavy use of the conga drum; lower-pitched drums are used to establish the base rhythm, while a single higher-pitched drum plays an improvised rhythm.

There are actually three different types of rumbas. *Rumba Yambú* is slower than the other rumbas; *Rumba Guaguancó* is a medium-tempo rumba with complex rhythms; and *Rumba Colombia* is the fastest rumba, in a ⁶/₈ meter. (The other rumbas are all in ²/₄.)

Habanera

Here's another unique musical style from Cuba, the *habanera*. Like the *salsa*, it has a characteristic rhythm, as shown in the following example.

The habanera *rhythm.*

Habanera is one of Cuba's oldest musical styles. It developed in the nineteenth century from the *contradanza* dance rhythm, which itself came from France via Haiti. (Yes, it's all a bit intermingled.) In fact, the earliest identified instance of *habanera* was in 1836, when a song collection included "La Pimienta," a song identified as in the *"contradanza habanera"* style.

The Sounds of Latin America

Central and South America—the areas from Mexico on south that we collectively call Latin America—are just as diverse, musically, as the islands of the Caribbean.

The History of Latin Music

As in the Caribbean, the music of native Latin Americans has been all but obliterated by the influx of European culture. As such, today's Latin music is a synthesis of European, African, and the few indigenous elements that remain.

Note

Accounts by Spanish colonizers in the sixteenth century report that Aztec music was religious in nature, performed by professional musicians; instruments were considered holy and mistakes made by performers were seen as being offensive to the gods. (Holy wrong note!)

We do know a little about the music of the native Latin American peoples. Ancient Mayan and Aztec civilizations played a number of different instruments, including the *tlapitzalli* (flute), *teponatzli* (log drum), conch-shell trumpets, drums, rattles, and the like. The Incas of South America played ocarinas and panpipes. The Indian music of Ecuador, Peru, and Bolivia used flutes and other wind instruments made from wood and animal bones, as well as drums and rattles.

The native music was superseded by European music when Spain and Portugal colonized the region. This led to the infusion of European string and wind instruments to the native culture. In addition, some African rhythms and vocal styles became native, thanks to the African slave trade.

As you can see, every region in Latin America has its own unique musical heritage—far too many to mention all here. We will, however, look at some of the most well-known Latin musical styles.

That said, there are some commonalities between the various regions, thanks to the shared European colonial heritage. Specifically, almost all Latin music shares the common Spanish *décima* song form, African syncopated rhythms and call-and-response vocal techniques, and European harmony. Look for these characteristics in all the regional music styles discussed next.

Samba

We'll start in the largest country in South America, Brazil. This country's national musical style is called the *samba*. The samba dates back to Angola and the Congo in Africa, with the native samba dance. The rhythms of the samba were melded to European harmonies common in Portugal; the result is the distinctive musical form known today.

Samba first came to prominence early in the twentieth century, emerging from the culture of the immigrant blacks in the city of Rio de Janeiro. The first samba recording, "Pelo Telefone," was made in 1917 by Donga and Mauro Almeida. The music got a boost from the establishment of "samba schools" in the late 1920s, as well as the broadcast of the music over the new media of Brazilian radio.

The samba beat is a syncopated rhythm in ²⁄₄ time, usually played by a *surdo* (bass drum). It's a pulsating rhythm consisting of a dotted eighth note followed by a sixteenth note, repeated, as shown in this example.

The Brazilian samba *rhythm.*

Bossa Nova

Over the next few decades samba music developed in several directions. One of the most notable offshoots was *bossa nova* (literally "new beat") music, which gained popularity in the United States during the 1960s thanks to João Gilberto, Antonio Carlos Jobim, and jazz saxophonist Stan Getz, who collaborated on the 1964 top-40 hit, "Girl from Ipanema," from the album *Getz/Gilberto*.

Note _____
Learn more about the American bossa nova trend in Chapter 10.

Bossa nova is a lighter, whiter kind of samba; it's less percussive but more complex, harmonically. As such, it gained a large following among American college students and the hipster set.

Merengue

The Dominican Republic is the host of our next Latin musical style, *merengue*. This is a lively type of music (with accompanying dance) that arose in the 1920s and 1930s.

Note _____
The island nation of Haiti has its own version of the *méringue,* which is much slower in tempo.

Merengue is a very fast music, almost to the point of being frantic. Traditional merengue is played by various percussion instruments and an accordion; modern merengue loses the squeezebox and adds rock, pop, and hip-hop elements.

Tango

As I'm sure you've already noted, much Latin music is wedded to accompanying dance styles. Such is the case in Argentina and its native music/dance style the *tango*.

You probably have seen someone somewhere dancing the tango; it's a very sensual type of dance. The music for the tango is equally sensual, whether it's adapted for a big band or played by the traditional Argentinean sextet—two violins, piano, bass, and double *bandoneóns* (a type of squeezebox or accordion).

The tango originated in Buenos Aires's immigrant population in the late nineteenth century. It gained widespread popularity in the 1920s, and experienced a "golden age" during the American big band era (roughly 1935–1952). It has waxed and waned in popularity since, always present in one form or another—*tango nuevo*, *neo-tango*, and other variations.

Música Criolla

In the mountain nation of Peru, Spanish, African, and native Andean influences are combined in *música criolla*. This general style encompasses several substyles, including *marinera* (a graceful native dance music), *festijo* (a lively dance music), *landó* (a slow blues), and *vals criolla* (a guitar-based music in ¾ time).

Música criolla was created by African slaves during Peru's colonial period. It is typically played with a mix of Spanish and native Indian instruments, with lyrics in Spanish.

Mariachi

Now we move to Mexico, and its native *mariachi* music. This music gets its sound by mixing African-influenced rhythms from southern Mexico with folk dances from the north. Traditional mariachi music is played by acoustic guitar ensembles, often accompanied by violins and trumpets; these groups often dress in highly ornamented jackets, large bow ties, and sombreros.

Ranchera

Another traditional Mexican music, often played by mariachi groups, is *ranchera*. The traditional ranchera is a song about love, nature, or patriotism, typically in a major key. The basic rhythm varies as to the subject of the song; ²⁄₄, ⁴⁄₄, and even ¾ meters are common.

Tejano

Another form of Mexican folk music is *Tejano* or *Tex-Mex* music. This music actually originated among the Hispanic population of central and southern Texas. It's Mexican music influenced by American rock, blues, and country music.

Note

The term "Tex-Mex" is also used to describe *Tejano*-influenced American rock and roll performers, including the Sir Douglas Quintet, Sam the Sham and the Pharaohs, and Los Lonely Boys.

Tejano emerged in the 1940s, with more of a polka or waltz sound. In the 1950s, Isidro Lopez (1929–2004) revolutionized the Tejano sound by fusing the earlier accordion-based sound with big band orchestration. The style has continued to evolve, incorporating more and newer American musical forms.

There are three main styles of Tejano music today. *Conjunto* employs a band comprised of *bajo sexton* (12-string guitar), accordion, bass, and drums. *Orchestra* employs a larger band with electric guitar, synthesizer, bass, drums, and a brass section. *Modern Tejano* is more pop oriented, using electric guitars, synthesizers, bass, and drums.

World Music _____

It's appropriate that our study of music history ends just south of the U.S. border. This reminds us that even our closest neighbors have a much different musical history than we do in America and Western Europe—and that the history of music involves more than just Bach and Beethoven.

I think the recent popular interest in world music is a good thing. The best and most interesting music intermingles various musical styles; music without new influences eventually stagnates and dies. We'll always have "pure" musical forms in the music of the past; thanks to music notation and modern recording technology, that will never be lost to us. But by combining the best of our musical tradition with other musical cultures, we'll create new and exciting musical forms. That's how music has always evolved, and will continue to do so.

So as you continue your study of music history, don't limit yourself to a particular era, style, or region. Move beyond Bach and Beethoven to examine Bacharach and the Beatles; study Gershwin and Berlin, yes, but also Indian *ragas*, Chinese opera, and Mexican *Tejano* music. You'll better understand your favorite music when you compare and contrast it to the music of other eras and other regions; all music is and should be world music—yesterday, today, and tomorrow.

Listening List

Our final listening list is a grab bag of different Caribbean and Latin American styles. Much of this Latin music is dance music—so be prepared to get on your feet and groove to the rhythm!

16 Carnival Hits (Mighty Sparrow and Lord Kitchener)

Best of Ska (Various artists)

The Best Tango Album in the World, Ever! (Various artists)

Calypso (Harry Belafonte)

Catch a Fire (Bob Marley and the Wailers)

Cugat's Favorite Rumbas/Mambo at the Waldorf (Xavier Cugat)

D Rapso Nation: Anthology of the Best of Rapso (Various artists)

Dancehall Classics (Various artists)

Getz/Gilberto (Stan Getz and João Gilberto)

The Greatest Salsa Ever, Vol. 1 (Various artists)

Let's Do Rocksteady (Various artists)

Mambo Mania! The Kings and Queens of Mambo (Various artists)

Mariachi: Folklore de Mexico (Various artists)

Peru: A Musical Journey (Various artists)

Putomayo Presents Cuba (Various artists)

Putomayo Presents Mexico (Various artists)

Putomayo Presents Samba Bossa Nova (Various artists)

Reggae Pulse: The Heartbeat of Jamaica (Various artists)

Reggaeton Hits (Various artists)

The Rough Guide to Merengue (Various artists)

Soca 101, Vol. 1 (Various artists)

Totally Tejano Vol. 1: Old School (Various artists)

Trojan Dub Box Set (Various artists)

Timeline: Latin American and Caribbean Music

1914	First *calypso* recording
1917	First *samba* recording
1920	*Tango* gains popularity
1928	First *samba* school
1930	Rise of *merengue*
1935	Start of the *tango's* golden age
1938	López Brothers write "Mambo"
1944	Andrews Sisters cover "Rum and Coca Cola"
1946	First *Tejano* music
1948	*Mambo* dance emerges in Havana
1953	U.S. Latin jazz trend
1956	Harry Belafonte releases "Banana Boat Song"; Isidro Lopez revolutionizes *Tejano* sound
1959	First *ska* recording, "Easy Snapping"
1964	Millie Small releases "My Boy Lollipop"; release of *Getz/Gilberto*
1965	Rise of *salsa*
1966	Birth of *rocksteady*
1968	Birth of *reggae*
1969	Desmond Dekker releases "The Israelites"; birth of *dub*
1970	Lancelot Layne launches *rapso* with "Blow Away"
1972	Bob Marley releases *Catch a Fire*
1973	Lord Shorty releases "Indrani," first *soca* recording
1979	Sugarhill Gang releases first rap recording, "Rapper's Delight"
1981	Bob Marley dies
1988	Rise of *dancehall* music
1994	Rise of *reggaeton*

Glossary

a cappella Vocal music without instrumental accompaniment.

Afrobeat Up-tempo mixture of jazz, funk, and native styles from Nigeria.

air (1) A *melody*. (2) Melodious composition.

alternative country A contemporary evolution of *progressive country* that operates outside the traditional Nashville country music scene.

alternative rock Catch-all term for post-*punk* bands from the mid-1980s to the mid-1990s.

Americana See *country-folk*.

ancient music Music from the end of the prehistoric era (4000 B.C.E.) to the end of the Roman Empire (476 C.E.).

anthem (1) The Protestant church's version of the Latin *motet*. (2) A religious choral composition in English.

antiphon A phrase sung by one choir in response to another.

antiphonal A singing style characterized by two or more parts of a choir singing alternately, one answering another.

Appalachian folk music *Folk music* native to the American Appalachian region. Derived from Irish and Scottish folk music.

aria A solo vocal piece performed in an opera or oratorio, typically in A-B-A form.

arietta A shorter and simpler *aria*.

ars antiqua The primary *Medieval* Western European musical style, based on *plainsong* and *organum*. From the Latin, "old art."

ars nova The new style of musical composition in fourteenth-century France and Italy, characterized by a greater variety of rhythm and meter, as well as greater independence in part writing. From the Latin, "new art."

art rock See *progressive rock*.

atonal   Having no tonal center, and no underlying key. In pure atonal music, the notes of the *chromatic scale* are used impartially and independently, with no home degree or *tonic*.

avant-garde   See *free jazz*.

backbeat   In ⁴⁄₄ time, beats two and four; in popular music, the backbeat is typically played by the drummer on the snare drum.

ballad   (1) A song to be danced to. (2) Self-contained narrative song, such as Schubert's *Erlkönig*.

ballade   A type of piano *miniature*, typically dramatic or heroic in nature.

ballata   A poetic form of secular song in fourteenth- and early fifteenth-century Italy.

ballet   An entertainment in which dancers perform to music to tell a story or express a mood.

ballet d'action   Late eighteenth-century dramatic *ballet*.

ballet de cour   A *ballet* of the seventeenth-century French court.

band   A body of instrumental players. Sometimes defined by the primary instrumental grouping or function, as in "brass band" or "dance band."

bar   See *measure*.

Baroque era   Music associated with that period from 1600–1750, characterized by flamboyant, heavily ornamented melodies. Notable Baroque composers include Claudio Monteverdi, George Frideric Handel, Johann Sebastian Bach, and Antonio Vivaldi.

basse danse   Graceful court dance of the early Renaissance.

basso continuo   Continuous bass; a bass line in music of the seventeenth and eighteenth centuries, played by the organist.

beat   Any pulsing unit of musical time.

bebop   A style of *jazz* music, developed in the late 1940s, that utilizes sophisticated chords played at a very fast tempo. Chief proponents of the style include saxophonist Charlie Parker and trumpeter Dizzy Gillespie. Also known as *bop*.

Beijing opera   The most popular form of Chinese opera, characterized by high-pitched vocals accompanied by string instruments and percussion.

bel canto   (1) Literally "beautiful singing"; Italian vocal style characterized by flowing melodic lines delivered by voices of great agility, smoothness and purity of tone. (2) A form of Italian opera characterized by singing in this style.

bent pitch   See *blue note*.

Big Band jazz   A particular form of *swing* music as played by big bands from the late 1920s through the end of World War II.

blue note   The flatted third, fifth, or seventh tone of the scale, common in *blues* and *jazz*.

bluegrass   A form of popular music that blends aspects of *Western swing* and *honky-tonk*; typically played by banjo, mandolin, fiddle, and similar instruments. Bill Monroe is known as the "father of bluegrass music."

blues   A uniquely American style of music that uses a set series of chords (called the *blues progression*) and a defined 7-note scale (called the *blues scale*). In the 12-bar blues form, the singer sings and plays three melodic phrases, each four bars long.

blues progression   A 12-bar sequence of chords common in blues and jazz music, as follows: I-I-I-I-IV-IV-I-I-V7-IV-I-I.

blues scale   A seven-note scale (counting the octave) used when playing blues progressions, containing the tonic, flatted third, fourth, flatted fifth, natural fifth, and flatted seventh degrees of the scale.

bolero   A Spanish dance in triple time.

boogie-woogie   A jazz piano style that reached its greatest popularity during the 1930s, characterized by an unchanging left-hand pattern.

book musical   A type of American musical theater in which the songs are tied with the plot to tell a coherent story.

bop   See *bebop*.

bossa nova   (1) Brazilian dance, similar to the samba. (2) *Brazilian jazz*.

bourrée   Lively French dance in duple meter, popular in the Baroque period.

brass   The family of instruments, typically made of brass, that produce sound by blowing through a mouthpiece. The brass family includes the trumpet, trombone, tuba, and French horn.

brass band   A type of concert band, comprised of brass, woodwind, and percussion instruments, popular in the second half of the nineteenth century. Repertoire consists primarily of *marches*.

Brazilian jazz   A 1960s mixture of *cool jazz* and Brazilian *samba* rhythms, pioneered by Brazilians João Gilberto and Antonio Carlos Jobim, and popularized in the United States by saxophonist Stan Getz and guitarist Charlie Byrd.

Brill Building   Literally, the building located at 1619 Broadway in New York City. Loosely, refers both to this building and a neighboring building at 1650 Broadway, both of which housed songwriters and music publishing companies from the 1950s through the 1970s. The Brill Building complex was the nexus of the East Coast popular music establishment and home to numerous hit songwriting teams, such as Carole King and Gerry Goffin, Barry Mann and Cynthia Weil, and Ellie Greenwich and Jeff Barry.

British Invasion   Refers to that period in the mid-1960s (starting in 1964) when a wave of British rock groups, led by the Beatles, crossed over to and began to dominate the American market.

BMV *Bach Werke-Verzeichnis* ("Index to Bach's Works"), the initials preceding numbers that catalog the works of J. S. Bach.

cadenza In opera, a flourish of difficult, fast, high notes sung at the end of an aria, designed to demonstrate the vocal ability of the singer.

cakewalk Syncopated, strutting dance, originating in the American South of the nineteenth century.

call and response Performance style with a singing leader who is imitated by a chorus of followers; also called *responsorial singing*, and commonly heard in spiritual or gospel music.

calypso The national music of Trinidad, characterized by joyful steel drum playing.

Canjun The very first form of Chinese opera, popularized in the period of the Three Kingdoms (220–280 C.E.).

canon Strictest form of contrapuntal imitation.

cantata Vocal genre for solo singers, chorus, and instrumentalists based on a lyric or dramatic poetic narrative. It generally consists of several movements including recitatives, arias, and ensemble numbers.

cantata da camera Secular *cantata*; literally, "chamber cantata."

cantata da chiesa Non-secular *cantata*; literally, "church cantata."

canticle (1) A Bible hymn as used in the liturgy of a Christian church. (2) Concert work, usually with religious text.

cantus firmus The foundation voice in multiple-voice compositions of the *Medieval* period.

canzona Song form, similar to the *madrigal*, originally practiced by troubadours of the sixteenth century.

Carnatic The music of southern India.

carol A song for two to three voices, usually with text related to the birth of Christ.

chaconne A dance in triple time with a repeating bass line. Also known as a *passacaglia*.

chamber music Music for a small group of solo instruments.

chamber opera An *opera* with a comparatively small number of singers and instrumentalists.

chamber sonata See *sonata de camera*.

chanson Song form for solo voice or small group of voices, originating in France in Northern Italy in the fourteenth century.

Chicago blues A style of *blues* that developed in the late 1940s and early 1950s in the Chicago area. Chicago blues took *Delta blues*, amplified it, and put it into a small-band context.

choir   A group of singers who perform together, usually in parts, with several singers on each part.

chong-ak   Traditional music of the Korean ruling class.

choral prelude   See *chorale prelude*.

choral symphony   A *symphony* that incorporates a choir.

chorale   (1) Baroque congregational hymn of the German Lutheran church. (2) Singing group.

chorale prelude   A solo keyboard piece that grew out of the custom of playing organ preludes and interludes in the services of the Protestant church. Also known as *choral prelude*.

chorale variations   Baroque organ piece in which a *chorale* is used as the basis for a set of *variations*.

chord   Three or more notes played simultaneously.

chord progression   A series of chords over a number of measures.

chorus   (1) Fairly large group of singers who perform together, usually with several on each part. (2) A choral movement of a large-scale work. (3) In *jazz*, a single statement of the melodic-harmonic pattern. (4) In popular music, the part of the song (typically following the verse) that recurs at intervals; also known as the B section of a song.

chromatic   Pitches outside the underlying key or scale. The opposite of *diatonic*.

chromatic scale   A scale containing 12 equal divisions of the octave—all the white keys and black keys within an octave.

chromaticism   (1) The use of chromatic intervals, chords, and scales. (2) A style of composing that employs chromatic harmony.

church sonata   See *sonata da chiesa*.

Classical era   Music associated with that period from 1750–1820, characterized by simple lyrical melodies, often expressed in majestic orchestral and choral works. Notable Classical-era composers include Ludwig van Beethoven, Franz Joseph Haydn, and Wolfgang Amadeus Mozart (collectively known as the *Viennese school*).

classical music   Generic term for "serious" Western music.

classic jazz   The earliest known form of jazz, developed in New Orleans in the early 1900s. Also known as *Dixieland* or *New Orleans jazz*. Important classic jazz artists include trumpeters Louis Armstrong and Bix Beiderbecke.

clave   (1) A Latin percussion instrument consisting of two wooden cylinders struck together. (2) The most basic Latin rhythm, consisting of a 3-2 two-bar pattern.

clavier   Generic term for keyboard instruments.

comédie-ballet   A late seventeenth-century French combination of *opera* and *ballet*.

common time   The ¼ or C time signature.

concert aria   A virtuoso solo song, with accompaniment, based on the Italian operatic *aria*.

concert overture   See *overture*.

concertino   (1) A short *concerto* for orchestra and one or more soloists. (2) A small instrumental ensemble within a larger orchestra.

concerto   An instrumental work in which one or more solo instruments are contrasted with a larger orchestra.

concerto da camera   *Concerto* designed for performance in a secular venue; literally, "chamber concerto."

concerto da chiesa   *Concerto* designed for performance in a church; literally, "church concerto."

concerto grosso   *Concerto* with a small group of soloists in addition to the traditional orchestra or string ensemble; literally, "great concerto."

conductus   Metrical Latin song for two or three voices.

consonance   Harmonious combination of tones. The opposite of *dissonance*.

contemporary jazz   See *post bop*.

continuo   The small group of instruments that the recitatives in Baroque music.

contrapuntal   See *counterpoint*.

cool jazz   A smoother, more melodic type of 1950s jazz, mixing aspects of *bebop* and *swing*, with less dissonance and more complex group arrangements. Proponents of this style include trumpeter Miles Davis and pianists Dave Brubeck and Bill Evans. Also known as *West Coast jazz*.

counterpoint   Two or more simultaneous, independent lines or voices in a piece of music. The art of counterpoint developed in the ninth century, and reached its zenith in the late sixteenth and early seventeenth centuries; some music theorists apply strict rules to the creation of contrapuntal lines.

country   A form of American popular music that grew out of rural Southern *folk music* to encompass *honky-tonk music*, *Western swing*, *bluegrass*, and other indigenous forms. Also known as *country-western*.

country blues   Early guitar-driven *blues* form, performed primarily on acoustic instruments, complete with elaborate finger picking and slide playing.

country-folk   A modern blend of country and folk music. Also known as *Americana*.

country-rock   A mixture of the *rock* and *country* idioms, first popularized in the 1960s.

country-western   See *country*.

countrypolitan   Country music blended with pop production values; popularized in the 1960s.

courante   A French dance in rapid ¾ time.

courtly love   The Medieval concept of noble, often illicit love. Also known as *fin amours*.

crooning   A style of singing popular during the big band era (1920s–1940s) characterized by a smooth tone that is light in intensity. A crooner sometimes scoops or slides into pitches when singing.

crossover   A recording or artist that appeals primarily to one audience but also becomes popular with another.

da capo aria   Lyric song in *ternary* (A-B-A) form.

dance-pop   A modern, techno-flavored version of traditional *disco* and dance music.

dancehall   A type of Jamaican music with violent and sexually explicit lyrics.

dastgah   One of 12 musical modes in Persian music.

Delta blues   A form of *blues* music developed on the Mississippi Delta, characterized by an intense, highly charged style of performance.

diatonic   Notes or chords that are contained in the underlying key or scale. For example, in the key of C Major, the diatonic notes are C, D, E, F, G, A, and B; all other notes are *chromatic*.

disco   Mid-'70s dance style emphasizing a heavy, repeated beat, melodic riffs, and simple lyrics.

dissonance   A combination of tones that sounds discordant and unstable, in need of resolution to a more pleasing and stable harmony. The opposite of *consonance*.

divertimento   An eighteenth-century Italian suite of light, entertaining music.

Dixieland   See *classic jazz*.

downbeat   The major beats in a measure; in ⁴⁄₄ time, the downbeats are 1, 2, 3, and 4.

drame lyrique   Lyrical French opera of the late nineteenth century.

dub   A Jamaican musical form that was the precursor to American *rap*; it involves a deejay talking or chanting over existing instrumental music.

duet   A musical composition for two performers.

dynamics   Varying degrees of loud and soft. For example, *forte* signifies a loud dynamic, while *piano* signifies a soft dynamic.

electric blues A form of *blues* music, developed shortly after World War II, that incorporated the newly popular electric guitar.

electronic music Music that employs computers, synthesizers, and other electronic equipment to generate, modify, and combine all manner of sounds.

embellishment Melodic decoration, either improvised or indicated through ornamentation signs in the music.

entr'acte A musical composition played between acts or scenes of an opera.

equal temperament Adjustment in tuning of musical intervals away from "natural" scale so that *diatonic* notes (for example, C-sharp and D-flat) are played at the same frequency, rather than being treated as separate pitches.

étude A type of piano *miniature* intended for the improvement of the performer's technique; typically restricted to the exploitation of one kind of passage.

fancy English equivalent of *fantasia*.

fantaisie French equivalent of *fantasia*.

fantasia An instrumental composition that avoids conventional forms and structures.

fantasie German equivalent of *fantasia*.

figured bass See *basso continuo*.

film music Music written to accompany the action in motion pictures.

fin amours See *courtly love*.

finale The last song of an act, or the last movement of a multiple-movement work.

folk music (1) Traditional songs, generally local or regional in origin. (2) Traditional American music, typically consisting of vocals accompanied by guitars and other acoustic instruments.

forte Loud. (Abbreviated as *f*.)

free jazz A type of jazz that eschews traditional arrangements and tonalities; employs complex tonalities and chord structures, typically played at very fast tempo.

fughetta A shortened type of *fugue*.

fugue A contrapuntal form that is built from a single subject.

funk An offshoot of 1960s soul music with more of an emphasis on rhythm than melody or harmony.

fusion A blending of *hard bop* harmonies and *jazz* improvisation with a driving *rock* beat. Also known as *jazz-rock*.

gagaku Traditional court music of Japan.

galliard   Lively French court dance in triple meter.

gangsta rap   A style of *rap* music that deals with pimping, hustling, and other forms of street life, often with violent and obscene lyrics.

gavotte   A French dance in common time.

Gesamtkunstwerk   "Total artwork," a term coined by Richard Wagner to describe the synthesis of all the arts in his later operas.

gigue   (1) English *Baroque* dance type in lively compound meter. (2) A standard movement of the Baroque *suite*.

Girl Group sound   Popular music from the early 1960s, performed by groups of teenage girls. Girl-group songs were often written by *Brill Building* songwriters.

glam-rock   Gender-bending, highly theatrical form of rock that developed in Britain in the early 1970s. Also known as *glitter rock*.

glitter rock   See *glam-rock*.

gospel   Twentieth-century sacred music style associated with the Protestant African American church.

grand motet   A *motet* for large ensembles of voices and instruments.

grand opera   A large-scale French dramatic opera.

Gregorian chant   A type of *plainsong* common in the sixth century, named for Pope Gregory I.

groove   (1) A specific beat. (2) A dance-oriented type of jazz, derived from *soul jazz* in the late 1970s, with a deep bass line and blues-oriented chord progressions.

ground bass   A repeating bass line, typically a short motif over which other parts play changing harmonies.

grunge   A form of raw *rock* that blends aspects of *punk* and *heavy metal*, popularized in Seattle in the early 1990s.

guoyue   Chinese national or patriotic music.

gusheh   A short melody in Persian music; part of a *radif*.

gypsy jazz   A type of small group European jazz, popular in the 1930s, that blended American *swing*, French dance hall music, and Eastern European folk music. Also known as *jazz manouche*.

habanera   Cuban dance music in moderate duple meter.

hair metal   A combination of *heavy metal* and *glam rock*.

half step   The smallest distance between notes in the Western chromatic scale.

hard bop   An offshoot of *bebop*, first developed in the mid-1950s, that features soulful melodies and rhythms, often borrowed from R&B and gospel music.

harmonization   The choice of chords to accompany a melodic line.

harmony   (1) The sound of tones in combination. (2) Accompanying parts behind the main melody.

heavy metal   Loudly aggressive guitar-dominated rock appealing primarily to a male, adolescent audience.

heptatonic scale   Seven-note *scale* used in non-Western music, fashioned from a different combination of intervals than Western major and minor scales.

highlife   Up-tempo popular music from Ghana.

Hindustani   The music of northern India.

hip hop   See *rap*.

homophony   Music comprised of melody and accompanying harmony, as distinct from *polyphony* or *monophony*.

honky-tonk music   A form of electrified *country* music, originally played in bars and "honky-tonks." From 1948 to 1955, this music became the predominant country form.

hot jazz   An extension of *classic jazz*, augmented with extended group improvisations, popularized by trumpeter Louis Armstrong.

humoresque   A lively and capricious instrumental composition.

hymn   Song in praise of God.

idée fixe   "Fixed idea," a recurring musical idea that links different movements of a work.

Impressionism   Early twentieth-century musical style, popularized by Claude Debussy, where solo and instrumental music is created from subtle blends of sound intended to suggest a mood or subject.

impromptu   A type of piano *miniature* in songlike form.

improvisation   Spontaneous creation of a musical composition while it is being performed; a musical performance without a written score.

interdeterminancy   A twentieth-century musical approach that leaves to chance various aspects of the musical performance. Some composers who employ interdeterminancy use colors and symbols in place of standard musical notation.

intermedio   Music performed between the acts of a play.

intermezzo   A short musical entertainment between acts of a play or opera.

interval   The distance between two pitches. Typically measured in half steps or whole steps, or expressed numerically (second, third, fourth, and so on).

invention   Name given by J. S. Bach to short, highly contrapuntal keyboard compositions.

isacathamiya   Zulu male choral singing, popularized in South African popular music.

isorhythmic   The art of repeating a rhythmic idea over and over, typically in multiple voices.

jazz   A style of music that incorporates and encourages *improvisation*. Originally derived from American *blues*, *gospel*, and *ragtime* music, infused with European harmony.

jazz manouche   See *gypsy jazz*.

jazz-rock   See *fusion*.

jig   Vigorous dance in compound meter, developed in the British Isles.

jingju   See *Beijing opera*.

jota   Spanish dance song in a quick triple meter, typically with guitar and castanet accompaniment.

jump blues   A mid-to-late 1940s *blues* style that was a precursor to early *rock and roll*. An up-tempo, jazz-tinged style, usually featuring a vocalist in front of a horn-driven combo or orchestra. Typified by a driving rhythm, shouted vocals, and honking saxophone solos. Also known as *jump jazz*.

jump jazz   See *jump blues*.

K. number   See *Köchel catalogue*.

key   (1) The relationship of tones with a common center or tonic; the central pitch within a key is called the *tonic*. (2) A lever on a keyboard or woodwind instrument.

key signature   The sharps or flats that are placed at the beginning of a staff to indicate the *key* of the music.

Köchel catalogue   The listing of Mozart's compositions, in chronological and thematic order, as originally devised by Ludwig von Köchel in 1862. Also known as the *K. number* system.

Latin jazz   A mixture of traditional jazz harmonies with Afro-Cuban and Latin rhythms.

leitmotif   A short musical passage associated with a character or situation in a musical drama.

libretto   The text of an opera or oratorio. (Literally, "little book.")

lied   German for "song;" most commonly associated with the solo art song of the nineteenth century, usually accompanied by piano.

lieder   Plural of *lied*.

lyric opera   Hybrid form combining elements of *grand opera* and *opéra comique*.

madrigal Secular work for voices, originating in Renaissance Italy (but also popular in England), set to a short, lyric love poem. A madrigal can be either with or without instruments.

major scale The most common scale, consisting of the following intervals: whole-whole-half-whole-whole-whole-half.

mambo Cuban dance music with a characteristic quadruple-meter rhythmic pattern.

march A musical style incorporating characteristics of military music, including strongly accented duple meter in simple, repetitive rhythmic patterns.

marga The classical music of India.

mariachi Traditional Mexican music, played by an ensemble of trumpets, violins, acoustic guitar, and bass guitar.

masque A staged performance that combines music, poetry, song, and dance; typically an aristocratic ceremonial entertainment, as popular in the seventeenth century.

Mass A choral composition set to the text of the central service of the Roman Catholic church. Consists of five passages set for choir or choir with vocal soloists: *Kyrie*, *Gloria in excelsis Deo*, *Credo*, *Sanctus*, and *Agnus Dei*.

mazurka Polish folk dance in triple meter.

measure A group of beats, indicated by the placement of bar lines on the staff.

Medieval era Music associated with that period from 476 C.E. to approximately 1400 C.E., characterized by chants and other simple non-secular forms of monophonic music. Notable Medieval composers include John Dunstable, Lionel Power, and Guillaume de Machaut.

melisma A group of notes sung to a single syllable, typically including both a primary note and *ornamentation*.

merengue A fast and frantic musical style from the Dominican Republic.

meter The organization of beats and their divisions.

microtonal music A twentieth-century musical form that uses the same serial approach as *twelve-tone music*, but divides the octave into more and smaller harmonic intervals.

microtone An interval smaller than a semitone, prevalent in some non-Western music and twentieth-century art music.

Middle Ages See *Medieval era*.

miniature A short piano piece based on a single musical idea. See also *ballade*, *étude*, *impromptu*, and *nocturne*.

minimalism   A twentieth-century musical style characterized by repeated simple melodies and rhythms employed with diatonic harmony and long pedal points; the effect of these repeated phrases is often hypnotic.

minor scale   One of three scales, each with a flatted third of the scale.

minstrel music   Music sung for the American minstrel shows of the mid- to late 1800s. Typically bowdlerized versions of black music performed by white musicians in blackface.

minuet   A dance in triple time.

miny   Traditional Japanese folk songs.

modal music   A type of composition based on one or more modes; an important style of jazz music, popularized by trumpeter Miles Davis and pianist Bill Evans.

mode   A set of scales, based on centuries-old church music, that preceded today's major and minor scales. The modes are based on and named for the note of the major scale on which they start and stop; these include the *Dorian, Phrygian, Lydian, Mixolydian, Ionian, Locrian,* and *Aeolian* modes.

modern mainstream   See *post bop*.

monody   A type of accompanied solo song popular in the seventeenth century, distinguished by a *recitative*-like vocal part and *figured bass* accompaniment.

monophony   Literally, "one sound"; music that contains a single melodic line without harmonies or counterpoint. The opposite of *polyphony*.

monothematic   Work or movement based on a single theme.

motet   Short unaccompanied choral work, derived from the *conductus*.

motif   A brief melodic or rhythmic idea within a piece of music.

motive   See *motif*.

movement   Self-contained part within a larger musical work.

music drama   German form of dramatic opera, used by Richard Wagner to describe his operas.

music theater   A type of composition, typically a concert piece, performed in a semi-staged presentation. Not to be confused with the more developed *musical theater*.

música criolla   The traditional music of Peru, combining Spanish, African, and native Andean influences.

musical   See *musical theater*.

musical comedy   See *musical theater*.

musical theater   A type of light musical entertainment, derived from the earlier *operetta*, that combines popular song with dancing and dramatic action in service to the plot. Also known as *musical comedy* or *musical*.

musique concréte   A twentieth-century musical form that employs recordings of everyday sounds, combined in various ways.

nanxi   Southern drama, a form of Chinese opera.

Nashville sound   A 1950s and early 1960s blend of country and pop music, created by producer Chet Atkins.

nationalism   Serious musical forms that embrace elements of *folk music* native to specific countries.

neoclassicism   A twentieth-century musical form that blends formal themes from the *Classical* era with a modified sense of tonality that embraces *chromaticism* and other elements of the modern era.

neoromanticism   A twentieth-century musical form that blends formal compositional techniques from the *Romantic* era with a modified sense of tonality that embraces *chromaticism* and other elements of the modern eras.

New Orleans jazz   See *classic jazz*.

New Wave   Popular music style derived from *punk* in the late 1970s, employing more sophisticated harmonies, instrumentation, and arrangements.

nocturne   A type of piano *miniature*, of romantic character.

noh   Japanese opera with music and dancing.

non-secular music   Music that is sacred in nature.

notation   The art of writing musical notes on paper.

nuove musiche   See *new music*.

ode   A ceremonial vocal work, typically with orchestral accompaniment.

opera   Drama set to music; a musical drama that is generally sung throughout, combining vocal and instrumental music with dramatic acting, scenery, and costumes.

opéra bouffe   See *opera buffa*.

opera buffa   A type of comic opera popular in the eighteenth century. In France, known as *opéra bouffe*.

opéra comique   A lighthearted French opera with spoken dialogue.

opera seria   The serious operatic form that dominated the seventeenth and eighteenth centuries.

opéra-ballet   French form that combines music and dance.

opera-oratorio   An opera that is presented on stage in the static manner of a concert performance or oratorio.

operetta   Literally, a "little opera"; a play with overture, songs, entr'actes, and dances, a type of light opera or musical comedy.

opus   (1) A single work or composition. (2) When followed by a number, e.g., Opus 12, used for the numbering of a composer's works.

oratorio   Large-scale dramatic choral work originating in the *Baroque* period, based on a text of religious or serious character, performed by solo voices, chorus, and orchestra; similar to opera but without scenery, costumes, or action.

orchestra   A group of instrumentalists organized for the performance of symphonies and other instrumental works, or to accompany an opera or other staged presentation.

organum   An early form of melodic harmonization (c. 900–1200), characterized by several parallel voices.

ornamentation   Notes that embellish and decorate a melody.

outlaw country   See *progressive country*.

overture   (1) The instrumental introduction to an opera or other musical drama. (2) An independent single-movement instrumental work, typically used to open a concert. Some overtures are written in *sonata* form, while others are more like *symphonic poems*.

passacaglia   See *chaconne*.

pentatonic scale   One of two five-note scales commonly used in folk and Asian music. The major pentatonic scale contains the major scale degrees 1-2-3-5-6.

percussion   The family of instruments that produce sound when you hit, beat, crash, shake, roll, scratch, rub, twist, or rattle them. Included in this family are various types of drums and cymbals, as well as mallet instruments (marimba, xylophone, and so forth) and timpani.

phrase   Within a piece of music, a segment that is unified by rhythms, melodies, or harmonies and that comes to some sort of closure.

piano   (1) Soft. (Abbreviate as *p*.) (2) Short for *pianoforte*.

piano quartet   Standard chamber ensemble of piano with violin, viola, and cello.

piano trio   Standard chamber ensemble of piano with violin and cello.

pianoforte   Popular acoustic keyboard instrument, commonly known as the *piano*. Literally, "soft-loud."

pitch   The highness or lowness of a tone.

plainchant   See *plainsong*.

plainsong   The large body of traditional ritual melody of the Western Christian church; a change composed of a single line of vocal melody, typically unaccompanied and performed in a free rhythm. Also known as *plainchant*.

polka   Lively Bohemian dance.

polonaise   A national Polish dance, in triple time and of moderate tempo.

polyphony   The mixing together of several simultaneous melodic lines.

polyrhythm   Two or more rhythms played simultaneously, or against each other.

polytonality   Employing more than one tonality simultaneously.

pop   Abbreviation for popular; typically used to describe popular music of various types.

post bop   The 1980s/1990s version of traditional jazz, incorporating *hard bop* harmonies with a variety of *swing*, *rock*, and *funk* beats. Also known as *modern mainstream*.

prehistoric music   Music of the prehistoric era. Also called *primitive music*.

prehistory   That era before written history, up to approximately 4000 B.C.E.

prelude   The instrumental introduction to an individual act within an opera or suite.

primitive music   See *prehistoric music*.

programme music   Instrumental music that tells a story, illustrates a literary idea, or evolves a pictorial scene.

progressive country   A mix of traditional country with elements of honky-tonk, rock and roll, and folk music. Also called *outlaw country*.

progressive rock   A style of *rock* music popular from the late 1960s through the mid-1970s that featured ambitious instrumentation, extended compositions, and lyrics influenced by myth, science fiction, and other literary sources. Also known as *art rock*.

psychedelic rock   Popular in the late 1960s, an attempt to capture the drug experience with a loose, loud, improvisational style of music. Also known as *acid rock*.

punk   A "back to basics" movement in rock that occurred in the mid-1970s, in reaction to the increasing commercialism and aging of the previous generation of rock stars.

quadrille   A type of square dance popular at the court of Napoleon in the early nineteenth century.

quarter tone   An interval half the distance of a Western half-step; difficult to notate, and impossible to play on a traditional keyboard instrument.

quartet   (1) A composition for four voices or instruments. (2) A group of four vocalists or instrumentalists.

quintet   (1) A composition for five voices or instruments. (2) A group of five vocalists or instrumentalists.

radif   One of a series of 200 or so musical phrases or short songs in Persian music.

raga   Indian melodic pattern. There are various raga "systems" that describe different series of pitches, patterns, and ornamentation.

ragtime   African American piano style that developed sometime in the 1880s–1890s, which became briefly popular around the turn of the century, and helped introduce syncopation into American popular music.

ragtime-blues   A lighthearted form of *blues* music from the middle South, known for its syncopated *ragtime*-like melodies.

ranchera   A traditional Mexican music played by *mariachi* ensembles.

rap   A late twentieth-century form of popular music characterized by a heavy beat and spontaneously composed lyrics, often without a discernable melody. Also known as *hip hop*.

rapso   A musical style from Trinidad that incorporates elements of political street poetry.

recitative   (1) A solo vocal declamation that follows the inflections of the text rather than the melody. (2) A vocal passage that is more recited than sung; found in opera, cantata, and oratorio.

reel   Dance in rapid quadruple time for two or more couples; popular in Scotland, Ireland, and parts of England.

reggae   Rhythmic music originating in Jamaica in the mid-1960s; characterized by offbeat rhythms and chanted vocals over a strong bass line.

reggaeton   An urban dance music popular across all of Latin America and the Caribbean.

religious blues   A form of *blues* music that combines lyrics about religious experiences with blues guitar accompaniment. This form is closely related to African-American *spirituals*, with the singer often shouting the lyrics to express a deep religious conviction.

Renaissance era   That period of music from approximately 1400 to 1600, characterized by a rise in polyphony, primarily within vocal forms. Notable Renaissance composers include Josquin des Préz, Guillaume Dufay, and Giovanni Pierluigi da Palestrina.

requiem   The Roman Catholic Mass for the dead.

responsorial singing   See *call and response*.

rhapsody   A composition, in a single continuous movement, based on popular, national, or folk melodies.

rhythm   The organization of sound in time; the arrangement of beats and accents in music.

rhythm and blues (R&B)   Popular African American music style of the 1940s through the 1960s featuring a solo singer accompanied by a small instrumental ensemble (piano, guitar, bass, drums, tenor saxophone), driving rhythms, and *blues* and *pop* song forms. R&B has its roots in the jump jazz ensembles of the late 1940s and early 1950s. See also *soul*.

ricercare   A transcription of a vocal work for keyboard or instrumental ensemble.

ritornello   The instrumental prelude to an individual song within a cantata, concerto, or aria.

rock   An American popular music, originating in the 1950s as *rock and roll*, that combines elements of *blues*, *country*, *R&B*, and traditional *Tin Pan Alley* styles. Typically, although not exclusively, electric guitar-driven, and often performed by small groups.

rock and roll   See *rock*.

rocksteady   A Jamaican music that sounds like slowed-down *ska*, with more involved melodic lines.

Romantic era   Music associated with the period from 1820 to 1900, characterized by emotional musical expression and sophisticated harmonies, often employing chromaticism and a moving away from traditional tonality. Notable Romantic composers include Johannes Brahms, Antonín Dvořák, Franz Liszt, Felix Mendelssohn, Richard Strauss, Pyotr Tchaikovsky, and Richard Wagner.

ronde   Lively Renaissance "round dance," in which participants dance in a circle or line.

rondeau   Medieval and Renaissance fixed poetic form; type of *chanson*.

rondo   A type of instrumental composition in which one section intermittently recurs; the usual form for the last movement of a *concerto* or *sonata*.

round   A short unaccompanied vocal *canon* in which subsequent voices enter in turn at the unison or octave.

rumba   Cuban dance music characterized by heavy use of the conga drum.

sacred music   Religious or spiritual music, for church or devotional use. Also called *non-secular music*.

salsa   Originally from Cuba, a pan-Latin dance music characterized by the use of the *clave* rhythm.

samba   Brazil's national musical style, a syncopated rhythm in $2/4$ time characterized by a dotted eighth note followed by a sixteenth note, repeated.

scale   A sequence of related pitches, arranged in ascending or descending order.

scat singing   A jazz vocal style that sets nonsense syllables to an improvised vocal line.

secular music   Music than is non-religious in nature.

semitone   The interval of a half-step.

serialism   The ordering of pitches, rhythms, and dynamics in a pre-determined fashion. See also *twelve-tone music*.

sextet   (1) A composition for six voices or instruments. (2) A group of six vocalists or instrumentalists.

shomyo   Japanese Buddhist chant.

sinfonia   Short instrumental work, found in Baroque opera, used to facilitate scene changes.

singer-songwriter   *Soft rock* songwriters who performed their own songs, often on acoustic instruments. An evolution of the 1960s-era folk and country rock movements, common in the early 1970s.

singspiel   Literally "song-play," a type of German comic opera with spoken dialogue.

ska   The precursor to *reggae*, a Jamaican musical style with an insistent accent on the "and" of every beat.

smooth jazz   A type of commercially popular jazz that blends clear melodies and slick arrangements with melodic improvisation.

soca   An offspring of Trinidadian *calypso* music, adding elements of American *soul* music.

soft rock   A toned-down style of rock, often performed by *singer-songwriters*, typically performed with acoustic guitar or piano accompaniment, usually backed by a low-key rhythm section.

sog-ak   Traditional music of the Korean common people.

solo   A vocal or instrumental piece or passage performed by one performer, with or without accompaniment.

sonata   (1) Composition for solo piano or another instrument with piano accompaniment. (2) Specific musical form based on the sonata; see *sonata form*.

sonata da camera   *Sonata* designed for performance in secular venues; literally, "chamber sonata."

sonata da chiesa   *Sonata* designed for performance in non-secular venues; literally, "church sonata."

sonata form   Specific musical form, established during the *Classical* period, consisting of three movements, allegro-andante-allegro.

sonatina   A short *sonata*, typically lighter and easier to perform than a regular sonata.

song   Short vocal composition.

song cycle   Group of songs, usually *lieder*, that are unified musically or through their texts.

soukous   Congolese guitar-band music.

soul   The 1960s/1970s evolution of *rhythm and blues*, which added the intensity of *gospel* music to a high-energy rhythmic beat.

soul jazz   An *R&B*-flavored type of jazz, first popularized in the 1960s, that incorporates a contemporary rock/soul beat, complete with a funky bass line, under *hard bop* and *bebop*-type chord progressions.

spiritual   American folk-hymn, typically of the African-American church tradition.

string   The family of instruments that produces sound by moving a bow across a string. The string family includes the violin, viola, cello, and double bass.

string quartet   A form of *chamber music* for two violins, viola, and cello.

string trio   A form of *chamber music* for two violins and cello, or violin, viola, and cello.

strophic song   A type of *lieder*, similar to a hymn, where each stanza receives the same melody. See also *through-composed song*.

subject   (1) A *motif*, phrase, or melody that is a basic element in a musical composition. (2) The initial melody or phrase in a *fugue*.

suite   (1) A piece of instrumental music in several movements, usually in dance style. (2) An assemblage of movements from ballet or opera scores. (3) Any original multi-movement composition.

swing   (1) A type of rhythm, associated with *jazz*, where eighth notes are played in a triplet rhythm. (2) A style of jazz, evolved from *hot jazz*, popular in the 1930s, typically practiced by big bands.

symphonic poem   A single-movement orchestral work on a symphonic scale; a type of *programme music*. Also known as *tone poem*.

symphony   A large-scale instrumental composition, usually in four movements.

syncopation   An accent on an unexpected beat, or the lack of an accent on an expected beat.

synthesizer   Electronic instrument, typically activated via a keyboard, that reproduces a wide variety of sounds via the use of sound generators and modifiers.

tala   Indian rhythmic system, similar to but more complex than the meter or time signature in Western music.

tango   Sensual Argentinean dance music, typically played at a slow walking pace in duple time.

teen-pop Manufactured, commercial pop music of the late twentieth century.

Tejano Mexican music that blends American rock and country influences. Also known as *Tex-Mex*.

tempo The rate of speed at which beats are played in a song. For example, a tempo of *presto* is very fast; a tempo of *largo* is slow. Sometimes expressed in precise beats per minute. Plural is *tempi*.

Texas blues A regional *blues* style typified by a relaxed, swinging feel. Early (c. 1920s) performances featured acoustic guitars; later (post–World War II) evolutions incorporated electric guitars over a horn-driven accompaniment.

Tex-Mex See *Tejano*.

theme A recurring melodic or rhythmic pattern.

third stream As coined by composer Gunther Schuller, music that combines elements of *jazz* and classical music.

through-composed song A type of *lieder* with different music for each stanza. See also *strophic song*.

time Fundamental rhythmical patterns of music.

time signature A symbol with two numbers, one on top of the other (like a fraction), that indicates the basic meter of a song. The upper number indicates how many beats are in a measure; the bottom number indicates the type of note that receives one beat. For example, the ¾ time signature specifies three quarter-note beats per measure.

Tin Pan Alley Colloquial name for New York City's music publishing area, centered on 28th Street, between Broadway and Sixth Avenue. Coined by writer Monroe Rosenfeld, who likened the cacophony of so many songwriters pounding on so many pianos to the sound of beating on tin pans.

toccata A short keyboard piece.

tonal center The key in which a piece of music is written.

tonality The organization of musical notes around a tonic, or home pitch, based on a major or minor scale or mode.

tone (1) A sound played or sung at a specific pitch. (2) Sound quality, or *timbre*.

tone poem See *symphonic poem*.

tragédie lyrique French tragic or epic opera.

trio (1) The second (B) section of a *minuet*, typically written in three-part harmony. (2) Any group of three performers. (3) Music written for three voices or instruments.

trio sonata Baroque-era *sonata* for voice, violin, and cello.

triple meter Metrical pattern with three beats to a measure.

triplet   A group of three notes performed in the space of two.

troubadour   Roving poet-minstrel, originating in southern France in the late tenth century.

twelve-tone music   A type of twentieth-century atonal music developed by Arnold Schoenberg, in which the twelve tones of the octave are played in a pre-determined order indifferent to their traditional tonal structure.

twentieth-century music   Serious or classical music of the twentieth century, in a variety of disparate styles.

upbeat   The eighth-note "and" after the downbeat.

urban contemporary   The current appellation for *soul* music.

verismo   Style of opera in which melodramatic situations are realistically portrayed in contemporary settings.

verse   (1) A short division of a musical composition. (2) In popular music, the first or A section of a song, preceding the chorus.

Viennese school   The name given to the style of music advanced by the key composers of the *Classical* period: Haydn, Mozart, and Beethoven.

virtuoso   Performer of extraordinary technical ability.

voice   Melodic or harmonic line.

voluntary   (1) An organ piece played before or after the service of the Anglican church. (2) An extemporaneous instrumental composition of the sixteenth century.

waltz   (1) Ballroom dance music in triple meter. (2) In the Romantic era, a short, stylized piano piece.

West Coast jazz   See *cool jazz*.

Western swing   A unique combination of traditional country music with jazz styles.

whole step   An *interval* equal to two half steps.

whole tone scale   A seven-note scale (including the octave) with each degree a whole step part. For example, the C whole tone scale includes the notes C, D, E, F-sharp, G-sharp, A-sharp, C.

woodwind   The family of instruments that produce sound by vibrating a wooden reed. The woodwind family includes the clarinet, saxophone, oboe, and bassoon. Also included are the flute and the piccolo, which do not use reeds.

work song   A cappella songs sung by African slaves while toiling at their labors in the field.

Key Composers

Adams, John (b. 1947)   Twentieth-century American composer

Arlen, Harold (1905–1986)   Twentieth-century American popular songwriter

Babbitt, Milton (b. 1916)   Twentieth-century American composer

Bach, Carl Philipp Emanuel (C. P. E.) (1714–1788)   German composer of the Classical era; son of J. S. Bach

Bach, Johann Sebastian (1685–1750)   prolific German composer of the Baroque era; perhaps the greatest composer of all time

Bacharach, Burt (b. 1928)   Twentieth-century American popular songwriter, often with lyricist Hal David

Barron, Bebe (b. 1927)   Twentieth-century American composer; wife of Louis

Barron, Louis (1920–1989)   Twentieth-century American composer; husband of Bebe

Barry, Jeff (b. 1939)   Twentieth-century American popular songwriter, often with partner Ellie Greenwich

Bartók, Béla (1881–1945)   Twentieth-century Hungarian composer

Beethoven, Ludwig van (1770–1827)   German-born composer who bridged the Classical and Romantic eras; member of the First Viennese School

Berg, Alban (1885–1935)   Twentieth-century Austrian composer; member of the Second Viennese School.

Berlin, Irving (Israel Isidore Baline, 1888–1989)   Twentieth-century American popular songwriter

Berlioz, Hector (1803–1869)   French composer of the Romantic era

Bernstein, Elmer (1922–2004)   Twentieth-century American film composer

Bernstein, Leonard (1918–1990)   Twentieth-century American composer

Berry, Chuck (Charles Edward Anderson Berry, b. 1926)   Twentieth-century American popular songwriter and performer

Binchois, Gilles de Bins dit (1400–1460)   Belgian chanson composer of the Renaissance

Bizet, Georges (1838–1875)   French composer of the Romantic era

Blackwood, Easley, Jr. (b. 1933)   Twentieth-century American composer

Blow, John (1649–1708)   English composer of the Baroque era

Boulez, Pierre (b. 1925)   Twentieth-century French composer and conductor

Boyce, William (1711–1779)   English composer of the Classical era

Brahms, Johannes (1833–1897)   German composer of the Romantic era

Britten, Benjamin (1913–1976)   Twentieth-century English composer

Brown, Earle (b. 1926)   Twentieth-century American composer

Bruckner, Anton (1824–1896)   Austrian composer of the Romantic era

Buttigieg, Ray (b. 1955)   Twentieth-century Maltese composer

Byrd, William (1542–1623)   English composer of the Renaissance period

Caccini, Giulio (1545–1618)   Italian opera composer who bridged the Renaissance and Baroque eras

Cage, John (1912–1992)   Twentieth-century American minimalist composer

Carissimi, Giacomo (1605–1674)   Italian composer of the Baroque era

Carmichael, Hoagy (Hoagland Howard Carmichael, 1899–1981)   Twentieth-century American popular songwriter

Carrillo, Julián (1875–1965)   Twentieth-century Mexican composer

Carter, Elliott (b. 1908)   Twentieth-century American composer

Chopin, Frédéric (1810–1849)   Polish composer of the Romantic era

Cohan, George M. (1878–1942)   Twentieth-century American popular songwriter

Copland, Aaron (1900–1990)   Twentieth-century American composer

Crüger, Johann (1598–1662)   German hymn writer of the Renaissance

de' Cavalieri, Emilio (1550–1602)   Italian opera composer who bridged the Renaissance and Baroque eras

Debussy, Achille-Claude (1862–1918)   French Impressionistic composer who bridged the Romantic era and the twentieth century

des Préz, Josquin (1450–1521)   Franco-Flemish composer of the Renaissance

Dufay, Guillaume (1397–1474)   Brussels-born composer of the Renaissance

Dunstable, John (1390–1453)   English composer of the Medieval period

Dvořák, Antonín Leopold (1841–1904)   Czechoslovakian composer of the late Romantic era

Dylan, Bob (Robert Allen Zimmerman, b. 1941)   Twentieth-century American popular songwriter and folksinger

Eimert, Herbert (1897–1972)   Twentieth-century German composer

Ellington, Duke (Edward Kennedy Ellington, 1899–1974)   Twentieth-century American jazz composer and bandleader

Emmett, Daniel Decatur (1815–1904)   Nineteenth-century American popular songwriter

Evans, Gil (1912–1988)   Twentieth-century American composer and arranger

Foster, Stephen (1826–1864)   Nineteenth-century American popular songwriter

Gershwin, George (Jacob Gershwin, 1898–1937)   Twentieth-century American composer, often with lyricist brother Ira

Gilbert, W. S. (1836–1911)   English composer of the late Romantic era; wrote light operettas with partner Arthur Sullivan

Glass, Philip (b. 1937)   Twentieth-century American composer

Gluck, Christoph Willibald von (1714–1787)   Bavarian-born composer of the Classical era

Gossec, François (1734–1829)   Belgian composer of the Classical era

Gounod, Charles-François (1818–1893)   French composer of the Romantic era

Greenwich, Ellie (b. 1940)   Twentieth-century American popular songwriter, often with partner Jeff Barry

Grieg, Edvard Hagerup (1843–1907)   Norwegian composer of the late Romantic era

Guthrie, Woody (1912–1967)   Twentieth-century American popular songwriter and folksinger

Handel, George Frideric (1685–1759)   German-born composer of the Baroque era

Handy, W. C. (1873–1958)   Twentieth-century American popular songwriter

Harris, Charles K. (1867–1930)   Nineteenth- and twentieth-century American popular songwriter

Haydn, Franz Joseph (1732–1809)   Austrian composer of the Classical era, member of the First Viennese School

Henze, Hans Werner (b. 1926)   Twentieth-century German composer

Herrmann, Bernard (1911–1975)   Twentieth-century American film composer

Hindemith, Paul (1895–1963)   Twentieth-century German composer

Ives, Charles (1874–1954)   Twentieth-century American composer

Jánaček, Leoš (1854–1928)   Twentieth-century Czechoslovakian composer

Janequin, Clément (1485–1558)   French chanson composer of the Renaissance

Joplin, Scott (1867–1917)   nineteenth- and twentieth-century American popular songwriter

Keiser, Reinhard (1674–1739)   German opera composer of the Baroque era

Kern, Jerome (1885–1945)   Twentieth-century American popular songwriter

King, Carole (b. 1942)   Twentieth-century American popular songwriter, often with lyricist Gerry Goffin

Korngold, Erich Wolfgang (1886–1957)   Twentieth-century Austrian American film composer

Lassus, Orlande de (1532–1594)   Franco-Flemish composer of the Renaissance

Leiber, Jerry (b. 1933)   Twentieth-century American popular songwriter and producer, with partner Mike Stoller

Lennon, John (1940–1980)   Twentieth-century English popular songwriter and performer, often with partner Paul McCartney

Liszt, Franz (1811–1886)   Hungarian composer of the Romantic era

Loesser, Frank (1910–1969)   Twentieth-century American popular songwriter

Lully, Jean-Baptiste (1632–1687)   French opera composer of the Baroque era

Machaut, Guillaume de (1300–1377)   French composer of the Medieval period

Mahler, Gustav (1860–1911)   Austrian composer who bridged the Romantic era and the twentieth century

Mann, Barry (b. 1939)   Twentieth-century American popular songwriter, often with lyricist/wife Cynthia Weil

McCartney, Paul (b. 1942)   Twentieth-century English popular songwriter and performer, often with partner John Lennon

Mendelssohn, Felix (1809–1847)   German composer of the Romantic era

Milhaud, Darius (1892–1974)   Twentieth-century French composer

Monteverdi, Claudio (1567–1643)   Italian composer who bridged the Renaissance and Baroque eras

Moore, Douglas (1893–1969)   Twentieth-century American composer

Morley, Thomas (1557–1602)   English madrigal composer of the Renaissance

Morricone, Ennio (b. 1928)   Twentieth-century Italian film composer

Mozart, Wolfgang Amadeus (1756–1791)   Austrian composer of the Classical era, member of the Viennese School

Mussorgsky, Modest (1839–1881)   Russian composer of the Romantic era

Offenbach, Jacques (1819–1880)   French composer of the Romantic era

Pachelbel, Johann (1653–1706)   German composer of the Baroque era

Palestrina, Giovanni Pierluigi da (1525–1594)   Italian composer of the Renaissance

Penderecki, Krzysztof (b. 1933)   Twentieth-century Polish composer

Peri, Jacopo (1561–1633)   Italian opera composer who bridged the Renaissance and Baroque eras

Pomus, Doc (Jerome Solon Felder, 1925–1991)   Twentieth-century American popular songwriter, with partner Mort Shuman

Porter, Cole (1891–1964)   Twentieth-century American popular songwriter

Power, Lionel (1375–1445)   English composer of the Medieval period

Prokofiev, Sergei (1891–1953)   Twentieth-century Russian composer

Puccini, Giacomo (1858–1924)   Italian opera composer who bridged the Romantic era and the twentieth century

Purcell, Henry (1659–1695)   English composer of the Baroque era

Rachmaninoff, Sergei (1873–1943)   Twentieth-century Russian composer

Rameau, Jean-Philippe (1683–1764)   French composer of the Baroque era

Ravel, Joseph-Maurice (1875–1937)   French Impressionistic composer who bridged the Romantic era and the twentieth century

Reich, Steve (b. 1936)   Twentieth-century American composer

Rimsky-Korsakov, Nikolai (1844–1908)   Russian composer of the late Romantic era

Robinson, Smokey (William Robinson, b. 1940)   Twentieth-century American popular songwriter and performer

Rodgers, Richard (1902–1979)   Twentieth-century American musical theater composer, often with lyricists Lorenz Hart and Oscar Hammerstein II

Rossini, Gioachino Antonio (1792–1868)   Italian opera composer who bridged the Classical and Romantic eras

Saint-Saëns, Camille (1835–1921)   French composer who bridged the Romantic era and the twentieth century

Sammartini, Giovanni-Battista (1700–1775)   Italian composer of the Classical era

Scarlatti, Alessandro (1660–1725)   Italian composer of the Baroque era; brother of D. Scarlatti

Scarlatti, Domenico (1685–1757)   Italian composer of the Baroque era; brother of A. Scarlatti

Schaeffer, Pierre (1910–1995)   Twentieth-century French composer

Schoenberg, Arnold (1874–1951)   Twentieth-century Austrian American composer

Schubert, Franz (1797–1828)   Austrian composer of the Romantic era

Schütz, Heinrich (1585–1672)   German opera composer of the Baroque era

Schuller, Gunther (b. 1925)   Twentieth-century American composer

Schumann, Clara Wieck (1819–1896)   German composer and pianist of the Romantic era; wife of Robert Schumann

Schumann, Robert (1810–1856)   German composer of the Romantic era; husband of Clara Wieck Schumann

Sedaka, Neil (b. 1939)   Twentieth-century American popular songwriter, often with lyricist Howard Greenfield

Sermisy, Claude de (1490–1562)   French chanson composer of the Renaissance

Shostakovich, Dmitri (1906–1975)   Twentieth-century Russian composer

Shuman, Mort (1936–1991)   Twentieth-century American popular songwriter, with partner Doc Pomus

Sibelius, Jean (1865–1957)   Twentieth-century French composer

Smetana, Bedřich (1824–1884)   Czechoslovakian composer of the Romantic era

Sondheim, Stephen (b. 1930s)   Twentieth-century musical theater composer

Sousa, John Philip (1854–1932)   Nineteenth-century American composer of marches

Springsteen, Bruce (b. 1949)   Twentieth-century American popular songwriter and performer

Stamitz, Johann Wenzel (1717–1757)   Czechoslovakian composer of the Classical era

Steiner, Max (1888–1971)   Twentieth-century Austrian American film composer

Stockhausen, Karlheinz (b. 1928)   Twentieth-century German composer

Stoller, Mike (b. 1933)   Twentieth-century American popular songwriter and producer, with partner Jerry Leiber

Strauss, Johann (I) (1804–1849)   Austrian composer of the early Romantic era; father of J. Strauss (II)

Strauss, Johann (II) (1825–1899)   Austrian composer of the late Romantic era; son of J. Strauss (I)

Strauss, Richard (1864–1949)   German composer who bridged the Romantic era and the twentieth century

Stravinsky, Igor (1882–1971)   Twentieth-century Russian composer

Sullivan, Arthur (1842–1900)   English composer of the late Romantic era; wrote light operettas with partner W. S. Gilbert

Szymanowski, Karol (1882–1937)   Polish Impressionistic composer of the twentieth century

Tchaikovsky, Pyotr Illyich (1840–1893)   Russian composer of the Romantic era

Telemann, Georg Philipp (1681–1767)   German composer of the Baroque era

Thomson, Virgil (1896–1989)   Twentieth-century American composer

Tiomkin, Dmitri (1894–1979)   Twentieth-century Ukrainian American film composer

Varèse, Edgard (1883–1965)   Twentieth-century Franco American composer

Verdi, Giuseppe (1813–1909)   Italian opera composer of the Romantic era

Vivaldi, Antonio (1678–1741)   Italian composer of the Baroque era

Wagner, Richard (1813–1883)   German composer of the Romantic era

Walter, Johann (1496–1570)   German hymn writer of the Renaissance

Weber, Carl Maria von (1786–1826)   German composer of the Classical era

Webern, Anton (1883–1945)   Twentieth-century Austrian composer

Weelkes, Thomas (1576–1623)   English madrigal composer of the Renaissance

Williams, John (b. 1932)   Twentieth-century American film composer

Williams, Ralph Vaughan (1872–1958)   Twentieth-century English composer

Wilson, Brian (b. 1942)   Twentieth-century American popular songwriter and performer

Wolf, Hugo (1860–1903)   Austrian composer of the Romantic era

Wonder, Stevie (Steveland Hardaway Judkins, b. 1950)   Twentieth-century American popular songwriter and performer

Xenakis, Iannis (1922–2001)   Twentieth-century Greek composer

Zappa, Frank (1940–1993)   Twentieth-century American composer and musician

Index

M

S

X-Y

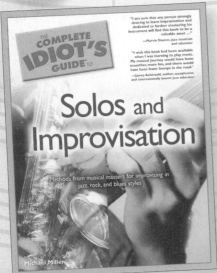
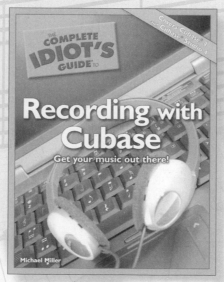
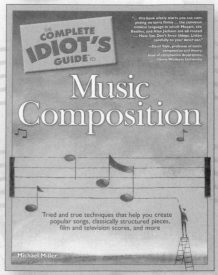

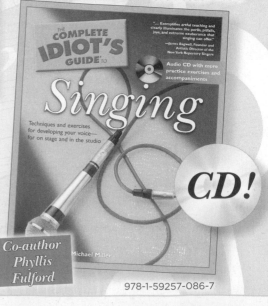